THE COBRA INDIAN LAGER GOOD CURRY RESTAURANT GUIDE

EDITED BY
PAT CHAPMAN

PIATKUS

Advertisements

Advertisements appear in this guide *only* by invitation of the editor. They are to the best of his knowledge reputable and good quality establishments, which have already been selected to appear in the guide. The inclusion of an advertisement does not therefore either buy entry to this guide, nor does it guarantee an uncritical entry. Revenues earned from advertising enables the guide price to be as low as possible, thus benefiting the buyers of the guide.

The contents of this book are as up to date and accurate as possible, but we cannot be held responsible for changes regarding quality, price, menu details, decor, ownership, even closure, since our report details were processed.

The publishers of this guide and the proprietors of The Curry Club wish to make it quite clear that they have absolutely no connections with any of the restaurants and establishments mentioned in this guide.

Restaurant reports are welcomed from members of The Curry Club and others. We do not pay for reports-they are sent in spontaneously and voluntarily. Our own research and Restaurant testing is normally done anonymously, the bill is paid and often no disclosure is made to our presence. On some occasions we accept invitations to visit restaurants as the guest of the house. We point out that in no circumstances do we tout for free hospitality and anyone doing so in the name of The Curry Club is an imposter.

First published in 1991 by
The Curry Club in association with
Judy Piatkus (publishers) Limited,
5, Windmill Street, London W1P 1HS

A catalogue recommendation for this book
is available from the British Library.

ISBN 0 86188 789 4

Typeset, printed and bound by
Lookers, 50 Willis Way,
Poole, Dorset. BH15 3TA

55 High Road
Bushey Heath
Herts
Tel: 01-950 4156
950 0475

Open 7 days a week including Sunday
and bank holidays 12.00 – 3.00
6.00 – 12.00

Other Curry Club publications by Pat Chapman and published by Piatkus Books

The Curry Club Vegetarian Cookbook
150 totally new recipes, all vegetarian, all authentic to the Curry Lands, plus helpful background information.

The Curry Club Indian Restaurant Cookbook
Hints, tips and methods and approximately 150 recipes, incorporating all your restaurant favourites.

The Curry Club Favourite Restaurant Curries
The Club's favourite restaurants give their favourite curry recipes plus many new tips and secrets

The Curry Club Middle Eastern Cookbook
150 spicy, tasty and delicious recipes from the 25 countries of the Middle East plus plentiful background information.

The Little Curry Book
A perfect small gift, this book contains anecdotes, fables and historical facts about curry, plus 16 popular recipes.

Pat Chapman is a Londoner and a curryholic. Born in 1940 he went to Bedales and Cambridge and did a short stint in the RAF, flying jets. Following that he specialised in industrial marketing then started his own business in 1970. He founded The Curry Club in 1982 and is now the country's foremost expert in the subject. (see page 23)

Contents

Acknowledgements

ASSISTANT EDITOR
Dominique Davis

RESEARCHERS
Linda Cook, Cheryl Benford, Libby Stuart, Pradeep Nair

This guide is possible thanks to many Curry Club members and others who have sent in reports on restaurants.

Especial thanks to the following regular, prolific and reliable reporters. (Apologies for any omissions).

Robin Arnot, Staffs; Steve Broadfoot, Liverpool; P & J Lovell, Brighton; Rachel Greaves, Devon; W Wood, Hornsea; A Perry, Bristol; J Capps, Romford; Linda Foye, Barry; Penny Hunter, Sussex; Peter Cash, Swinton; TG Webb, Cambs; J Longman, Bodmin; Alan Brown, Sussex; M Griffiths, N'ton; A Conroy, Durham; Jeff Neal, Bolton; P Williams, St Austell; Keith Paine, Tilbury; V Heywood, Burton; P Copeland, Oxon; D Gregory, Notts; Duncan Renn, Glos; JB Owen, SW6; Roger Hunt, Sidmouth; G Innocent, Dawlish; Deb McCarthy, E6; J George, SE22; N Parfit, Cambs; Stephen Morgan, Poole; A Frankham, Essex; J Tyler, Romford; Mrs Flashman, Tonbridge; Chris Dearman, Bucks; Dave Morris, London; Mike King, Sussex; Dr Greaves, Otley; D Balera, USA; H Davies, Woodley Berks; D Peel, Adlestone; S Parking, Essex; Brian George, Milton Keynes; M Tyler, Essex; Paul Chester, Cuffley; DM Weiss, London; Frank Taylor, Bromley; Dr Flemming, London; Mr and Mrs Lentz, Enfeild; T and G Travers, Wembley; Bob Rutter, Blackpool; Tim Softley, Essex; Mark Spedding, Northolt; Vince Tidswell, Clwyd; M Giles, Croydon; Mrs Wicks, Fleet; DR Chapchal, Fetcham; Ramesh Thakran, Cochin; Guy Renn, Lancs; Ken Lee, K Ingram, and Peter Holmes, Cross Hills; Patrick Harrison, Cambs; Elizabeth Defty, Durham; John Loosemore, Orpington; Nigel Green, Maidstone, Nigel Cornwell, Orpington; Tony Davis, Harrow; Reg Parrish, G Man; Ian Barle, Barking; Stephen Yarrow, NW6; Stephen Cowie, SW16; Bruce Edwards, Norwich; Michael Lloyd Jones, Cardiff; J Bonnick, Halisham; MM Cruickshank of Auchreoch; E Lewis, Swansea; Chris Barry, Cardiff; Richard Spiers, Wombourne; Ruth Burnett, Wilts; Marie Carlton, Stainton; Tim Baxter, Leeds; Peter Roberts, Warks; G Roy, M'head; G Smith, Royston; David Highton, Royston; Nigel Holt, Hitchen; S Johnson, Scunthorpe; Graham Smith, Beckenham; Paul Abolins, Didcot; Terry Dickinson, Doncaster; Paul Connor, Coventry; N Steele, Carlisle; J O'Daud, USA; Mrs Swan, Glasgow; GA Sinclair, Fife; Judith Williams, Llanelli; P Snelgrove, Conway; Don Turnbull, Wisconsin; Gareth Owen, Cardiff; Pamela Goodwin, Flint; RS Smith, Aylesbury; RG Adams, Slough; Ian Mackenzie, Edinburgh; Robin and Marion Cowie, Bristol; Gordon Loughlin, Formby; George Coleman, Eastbourne.

Introduction

Since we last published The Good Curry Guide, four a half years ago, a great deal has happened in the world of Indian food. Its popularity continues to soar, and a further 2,000 curry restaurants have opened up and down the UK. That means that somewhere in the land more than one new restaurant has opened every day. And despite the deepest of recessions, new Indian restaurants continue to open. Over the last eighteen months new openings have slowed down a little, whilst closures have increased. Times have undoubtedly been hard for the catering trade in general and we have many reports from restaurant owners of slack business, including the former prime-time weekends.

The better restaurants will, hopefully, weather this inclement period, making adjustments as necessary. One trend we have spotted, is that more and more restaurants are not opening at lunch time reflecting, perhaps, that no matter how good a bargain the lunch buffet might be, curry is not perceived by British public to be a lunch time activity.

Never-the-less, curry continues to be Britain's most popular dining-out food, and since we last published the Guide, its popularity in the super markets has grown rapidly placing curry at the top of the 'ethnic' foods market. We draw our information from numerous surveys, including one which The Curry Club carried out amongst its own members last year, and for those who enjoy facts and figures and statistics, we have published some of this information on page 18.

Keeping abreast of changes has kept us on our toes. Nearly every telephone number in the country has changed, with the alteration of codes and the enlargement of numbers. Not even London escaped.

Restaurant name changes have us baffled, but hopefully up to date. A single name change it quite common, but two in a short period is not unknown. For example quite why the New Delhi restaurant in Bournemouth changed its name to the Taj Tandoori and then changed yet again to the Bay of Bengal remains a mystery. But change it did.

Another mystery surrounds town council planning committees. How do they make their decisions? Why, for example do they turn down one scheme in a town then weeks later allow another one? How do they explain Didcot? Didcot is a small town (population 15,000) south of Oxford which until 1990 had no curry houses. Suddenly it was swamped with no less than four different applications. The Council granted permission to three of them to go ahead, and they opened within weeks of each other.

Restaurateurs desperate to get in on the act, are going for sites in smaller and smaller villages. There's the Madras in Coupar Angus, Tayside, Scotland, population 2,200 and near here the Pipasha in Churt, Surrey population 500. And I recently saw an application come up for a curry house in Hoo in Kent population 1,000. Where will it end? Hoo knows!

An innovation to this publication is the introduction of a sponsor. In common with other food guides, we strive to pack in as much information as we can, yet we endeavour to make the retail price as

reasonable as possible. We use two methods to achieve this: sponsorship and by taking advertisements.

We welcome as our sole sponsor COBRA INDIAN LAGER. Cobra is brewed and bottled in India and has been especially formulated to drink with curry. It was launched in Britain a year ago, since when it is rapidly gaining a reputation and a foothold in the better British curry restaurants, more and more of whom are stocking it. It is also establishing itself in off licences and supermarkets all over the UK. The story of Cobra appears on page 14.

Advertisements appear throughout the Guide and as we say on page 2, advertisers are invited by us to take space in our pages. They cannot buy their way in, and an ad does not guarantee an uncritical review. Restaurants are not obliged to advertise, and they are not pressurised. Our TOP 1000 do not have to pay for their reviews which go into the guide even if they decline to advertise.

Over the last few years a number of food guides have appeared which can only be described as bogus. They charge every restaurant anything between £70 and £200 for the entry which is written by a fraudster without any kind of knowledge of the subject, the quality of the restaurant or its food let alone any supporting back up material.

The Good Food Guide prosecuted a company which perported to be the genuine article, and we note the arrival and passing of more than one attempt to copy our guide.

We stress that this Guide is the original publication in its field. It is now in its eighth year (and third edition) and the information it contains is based on thousands of genuine reports sent to us each year by our thousands of Curry Club members.

These views, good and bad, appear in the celebrated Restaurant Roundup section of our quarterly Curry Club magazine (see page 23). Reviews there usually generate further correspondence about particular restaurants. And so a picture emerges.

Not all of our 15,000 members send in reports (though we'd welcome them if they did) and reports are also received and welcomed from non members too.

We have a 'hardcore' of reporters, who visit curry restaurants regularly and all over the country. One is a tax inspector's inspector another repairs church organs. Both travel all over the UK and they both dine out on curry several times a week. Between them they have visited several hundred such establishments in the last four years. Other regulars, men and women, also use their business travels to visit Indian restaurants and some of our correspondents are Asians.

We welcome the views of all these 'experienced' reporters. Many are as qualified as any professional restaurant inspectors. As they specialise in curry they may even be better attuned to this particular style of food. We also welcome 'first timers' and 'occasional' reporters. Everyone's view is important to us. Everyone is an expert on food (we all eat it) and we all know good standards or bad when we see them. And the bad is as important to us as the good.

We occasionally get phoney reports - written by pranksters or by someone with a chip on the shoulder. Sometimes we are 99.9% sure that a restautateur is praising his own establishment or condeming his rival's.

Most reports follow a pattern. A particular good restaurant should get good reports. But every now and then a bad report will arrive. We note it and put it aside. But if the balance should start to tip to more bad reports than good for that restaurant it may indicate a change in standards which we cannot ignore. The important thing is that we continue to get reports from you. Without them there is no Guide.

As an innovation for this Guide we asked all of our members simply to name their favourite restaurant(s), rather than to write a full report. The response to this was nothing short of phenomenal. We were swamped with sackfuls of mail for days. It was a great help and we always welcome just a 'one-liner' from you at any time.

We do not pay for reports, nor do we solicit them, but we welcome and need them, so whether you are an old hand or a first time curry diner, please do let us have your views.

We also continually update our information on curry restaurants. We comb other guides, and directories, newspapers and phone books and we sent a questionnaire to every relevant establishment in the UK (all 7,000). Many replied.

We then make the selection from 7,000 to 1,000 restaurants. It's an awsome task. 6,000 restaurants are omitted. But those we select are those we believe to be the best. We then send them a detailed questionnaire and finally telephone them to verify facts.

With this our third edition, we hope we have improved upon the last one. We have a new colour section and 96 more pages than last time, and we have 300 more entries, reflecting the growth in the market.

We hope we have not missed out your favourite. Or if we have put in a 'bad one' forgive us please. It is unlikely to cause you harm.

It may not be our fault, of course. These days, there is a lot of change afoot. Restaurants are being bought and sold, and owners are changing. Cooks and waiters are lured from one place to another. So standards can change almost overnight. Restaurants close or change cuisine equally rapidly, and we can get caught out. So do keep us informed. But on the whole it is unlikely that a top restaurant will change that much.

In the last four and a half years since our last edition, we have seen standards continue to rise as curry diners become more knowledgeable and demanding. It gives me great pleasure to witness this, indeed to be a small cog in the wheel.

We feel that the production of this guide should be helpful not only to readers and potential customers, it should also be of use to the restaurants themselves. We feel they have a right to be proud of their entry into this Guide.

It is, after all, prestigious to a restaurant to be singled out with a one in seven accolade of excellence from the dining public. All restaurants nominated in this guide will be awarded a certificate and a window sticker to display if they wish to.

A good number of our 1,000 have elected to join in our discount scheme, whereby they will give a discount of their choice to Curry Club members in return for a voucher. See page 288 for details.

Finally, I hope this guide will amuse and entertain you, as well as inform you and guide you to a good curry somewhere in the 1,000 best curry houses across the length and breadth of Great Britain and beyond.

I hope reading its contents will make your mouth water as much as it did mine when I wrote it. I trust that it will take you to places that you may otherwise not have tried where you will enjoy the cuisine of the sub-continent of India at the highest standards.

If this Guide achieves that, it will have done its job.

Bon apetit, and here's to good curries.

Pat Chapman
The Curry Club
Haslemere
August, 1991

What to Drink with Indian Food

The other day I was invited for lunch in London SW, to what was to me a new phenomenon - a beer bar. Infact I did not find out that it was a beer bar until I arrived outside. What is so different about a beer bar? Great Britain after all may have strange licensing laws, but it has had its public inns for over 1000 years. Today we have 68,000 pubs. We spend £5 billion on lager and the same on beer. In the 1960's the wine bar trend hit the UK, and suddenly every town seemed to have one. Wine consumption rapidly rose to today's £4 billion p.a.

We have no shortage of outlets. Yet the beer bar I visited is an innovation. It specialises in bottled beers. It has on display behind the large bar, some 50 or 60 types mostly imported from all over the world, including Cobra lager from India. There is a brasserie-style restaurant and a simple all purpose menu. I happened to choose that ever-so-English delight, Cottage pie, which went ever-so-well with Indian Cobra lager.

I enjoyed that lunch but I was struck by two things. Firstly, the rather comical 'coals-to-Newcastle' situation about drinking Indian brewed and bottled beer in London - Isn't India meant to have prohibition? Doesn't it have religious proscriptions on drinking? And don't we have the market cornered here anyway?

And secondly, how astonishing it is to see beer imported from so many counties all together in one location. We really take it all for granted. And yet each of these imported lagers has travelled hundreds, perhaps thousands of miles to get here with its own distinctive flavour, allowing a niche market to develop.

I am frequently asked what one should drink with curry. Champagne goes particularly well, of course (or sparking wine).

I am a firm believer that good table wine does too. I must qualify that a little, however. Fine wines are wasted. Their subtlety is overpowered even by mild spicing. But a good medium priced bottle of Shiraz red or Sauvignon white wine complements well cooked Indian food. Wine does not go well with curry house ultra-hot Vindaloos and Phals.

Lager remains the most popular drink with curry, but is equally inappropriate, being to gassy.

As with wine, a good, carefully brewed beer, complements spicy tastes. Cobra lager is one such beer. Indeed Cobra is unique having been specially formulated for this purpose.

At 5% alcohol volume and 1050 OG it packs a more concentrated punch than standard lagers, yet it is mellow and not excessively gassy. It is a gorgeous golden brown colour and when poured it develops a thick creamy head. It combines bitter and sweet tastes to refreshing perfection.

At Chinese restaurants you may well be offered Chinese

EXTRA
SMOOTH
IMPORTED
PREMIUM
INDIAN
LAGER
COBRA
5% Alc./Vol.
O.G. 1046 - 1052
650 ml.

brewed beer, or Thai beer in Thai restaurants and Singapori beer in Singaporean restaurants. So why not genuine Indian lager at Indian restaurants?

Unlike other lagers claiming to be Indian but brewed in Essex or somewhere, on London tapwater, Cobra is brewed and bottled in Southern India. It is infact a special brew for the UK only, manufactured by Mysore Breweries Ltd, in Bangalore.

Created in 1970, MBL now has a significant and increasing market share in the Indian domestic lager market. Contrary to popular belief the great majority of India's population are permitted to drink alcohol (the minority Moslem community are the principal abstainers) and the country has mature wine, spirits and beer industries.

It was, of course, the British who introduced breweries to India some 150 years ago. Today there are around 40 breweries all over India. MBL was set up with Danish (Carlsberg) collaboration. Its brewmaster is an Indian PhD who learned his trade in Europe with Pilsner Urquell and Heineken.

The factory is in the outskirts of Bangalore - India's fifth largest city, and its most modern and industrialised. It is here that India's computer, electronics, aeronautics and space industries are based. Bangalore is a garden city with an ideal climate and water which is naturally very pure, making it perfect for brewing. Award winning MBL is one of four major breweries in the city and Bangalore beer is acknowledged as world class. Furthermore, Bangalore enjoys its own products. It is the only city in India to have a pub culture with at least 100 pubs to choose from. I have been in some of these, and you would not know your are not in a London pub.

I have also visited Mysore Breweries to be shown around by enthusiastic management. It is spacious and it is equipped with the latest German and European plant. Huge stainless steel brewing vats and purification chambers stand immaculate and silent, contrasting with the gigantic bustling bottling rooms with metres of rattling conveyors, endlessly moving hundreds of tinkling bottles towards the electronic boxing machines. Constant streams of colourful Indian lorries back up to the loading bays to transport the next consignment of lager to any part of India. The brewery operates six days a week an can turn out 100,000 bottles a day. Unlike many Indian factories, MBL is highly automated involving a small skilled workforce of 500. The brands for home consumption include PALS and MBL (both 4% volume) and the extra strong aptly named KNOCKOUT (8% volume). Cobra is matured for 5 to 6 weeks and is double filtered.

Cobra lager is quite rightly establishing itself a satisfactory and expanding niche in the UK market.

Its large bottle (modelled on the original pint beer bottle) is typical in India but now unique to the UK. Like wine, you are encouraged to share your cold refreshing extra smooth 650ml of Cobra lager with your fellow diners. A conventional 'half pint' 330ml bottle is now also available. I predict a great future for the beer bar. I also predict a great future for the once-tasted-never-forgotten Cobra lager.

THE VEERASWAMY

London's Oldest Indian Restaurant

Established 1927

Truly Authentic Indian Cuisine

Open for lunch and dinner

99-101 Regent Street,
entrance Swallow Street,
London W1.
071 734 1401

Curry Statistics

A couple of years ago a Finish businessman made an appointment with The Curry Club to discuss the feasibility of establishing an Indian restaurant in Helsinki. We were able to point out that, whilst we did not have at our finger tips the curry eating habits and market statistics of Finland, at least he would be secure in the knowledge that his would be the only Indian restaurant in that Country. Whether the Finns would use it was another matter.

How different it all is in the UK. Here with 7,000 restaurants and a market still expanding, there is a need to understand these figures. For nearly 10 years The Curry Club has devoted considerable time to collecting and interpreting curry market information. We probably have the world's most comprehensive collection of data on the subject of curry and curry restaurants.

Without it, of course, we would not be confident in producing this Guide. We are also able to make our information available to others. From time to time major manufacturers in the food and beverage businesses approach us for help.

Equally rewarding are queries from potential restaurateurs. One recent enquirer was a delightful Bangladeshi, the owner of a clothing factory, who wanted advice about which city or town to open up in, what size his restaurant should be and any other information we could think of.

We were able to provide him with copious statistics, which would help him do his market research and to make his decision.

We have on our files 6980 curry restaurants in the United Kingdom today. They extended from Thurso (19 miles from John O'Groats) to Penzance (10 miles from Land's End), 850 miles (1360km) apart. Add in the Islands and we have curry houses as far north as the Shetland Islands and as far south as Jersey, 1,000 miles, 1600km apart.

Nowhere else on earth has more curry restaurants than Great Britain, not even India. London has the greatest concentration of them in the world with over 1,500 in the London postcode area of which 120 are in W1 alone.

London has the achievement of having more curry restaurants than India's capital city, Delhi.

The English counties have 4,700 Scotland 500, Wales 250, and Ireland just 35. This explains why London gets proportionally more space in this Guide than elsewhere.

The city with the second largest number of curry houses is Birmingham with 270, next is Manchester, 165, then Glasgow. Bradford comes fifth with 140.

These last two are interesting and controversial, because both Glasgow and Bradford vie with each other to be the curry capital of Britain. Infact exclusing London, Bradford wins by a long head (see entry under Bradford, West Yorkshire).

16 British cities have more than 30 curry restaurants each, and nearly every town all over the UK now has at least one. The growth of the Indian restaurant is nothing short of spectacular. There were six in 1950, 300 in 1960, 1200 in 1970, 3000 in 1980 and 6600 in 1990. Our prediction is that this growth will continue at a slower pace

and by the year 2,000 there will be around 10,000.

Although we describe our curry houses as 'Indian' we are not technically correct. 85% are run by Bangladeshis. Names like Ali, Uddin, Miah, Mohammed and Choudhury give the clue. The first two Indian restaurants in Britain were infact Indian (founded in 1911 and 1926). Probably less than 800 are Indian owned in the country today. There are even less owned by Pakistanis. There are rather more Nepalese establishments, although those actually offering true Nepalese food are few and far between.

We know of only a handful of Sri Lankan restaurants, and there are two Afghan curry houses (in London SW and W) and one Burmese in outer London (SE10).

There are no chains of restaurants larger than a dozen or so. Most curry houses are individually owned by a sole proprietor or a consortium of working partners (often previous cooks and waiters).

90% of all UK curry eaters make their first aquaintance of the food by visiting an Indian restaurant. More first-timer 'Indian' restaurant users are under 20 than any other age category and the average age of diners at curry restaurants is 24, reflecting it to be a favourite weekend night out activity of the younger age group, with their relatively high disposable income.

In 1991 it is projected that 2 million adults will visit the 'Indian' restaurant or takeaway per week. 52% visit once or twice a month whilst 6% visit six or more times a month. 28% of the UK population eat curry regularly, 8% never do and never will. At the curry restaurant, 49.3% spend £10-15, 28.8% £5-10, 2.5% £20-25 and 0.6% over £25. The total spend will approach £1,000 million in 1991.

Most 'Indian' restaurants do a negligible lunch time trade. Their busiest nights are, in descending order, Friday, Saturday, Thursday, Wednesday, Tuesday, Sunday and Monday.

Favourite drinks are, predictably, lager 45%, wine 21%, Beer 20%, Non-alcoholic 14%. Chicken dishes are favourite, 52.5%, with vegetarian next 16.6%, then lamb, meat and seafood.

57.5% of regular curry eaters prefer medium heat, 43.7% say they like it hot, whilst only 5.6% prefer it mild.

Between the ages of 24 and 40 attendance at the restaurant declines. Pressures of marriage, mortgage, house improvements and children occupy the mind and available finances. It is then that cooking curry at home comes into its own.

2.53 million households now cook curry at home more than once a fortnight (a rise of 80% since 1983). The Indian food ingredient market including frozen meals is worth £200 million in 1991, and is growing at the rate of 15% pa. Indian food accounts for 50% of the ethnic food market with Chinese at 33%.

The above statistics exclude the resident UK population of Indian, Bangladeshi and Pakistanis (1.5 million).

The conclusions we can draw from the above statistics are that once the curry eating habit is acquired it is permanent and mildly addictive. Unlike certain other food trends it is therefore not subject to the vagaries of fad and fashion. As the market matures curry restaurants can look forward to a higher average age, a larger percentage of users, much wider acceptance and a much higher percentage of spending in this market sector.

Our Bangladeshi friend has plenty to consider when making his decision. We wish him well.

Sources: Mintel, The Caterer, Nielsen, Taylor Nelson, Sharwoods, Keynote, Food File, NOP, OPCS, BBC, Curry Club User Survey.

THE CURRY CLUB

Pat Chapman always had a deep-rooted interest in spicy food, curry in particular, and over the years he built up a huge pool of information which he felt would be usefully passed on to others. He conceived the idea of forming an organisation for this purpose.

Since it was founded in January 1982, The Curry Club has built up a membership of several thousands. We have a marchioness, some lords and ladies, knights a-plenty, a captain of industry or two, generals, admirals and air marshals (not to mention a sprinkling of ex-colonels), and we have celebrity names - actresses, politicians, rock stars and sportsmen. We have an airline (Air India), a former R.N. Warship (HMS *Hermes*) and a hotel chain (the Taj group). We have members on every continent and a good number of Asian members too. But by and large our membership is a typical cross-section of the Great British public, ranging in age from teenage to dotage, in occupation from the refuse collectors to receivers. In fact thousands of people who have just one thing in common - a love of curry and spicy foods.

Members receive a bright and colourful magazine four times a year which has regular features on curry, the curry lands and other exotic and spicy cuisines. It includes news items, recipes, reports on restaurants, picture features and contributions from members and professionals alike.

The Club has produced a wide selection of publications, including this book and others listed on page 4, all published by Piatkus. There is also a cookery video.

On the social side, the Club organises regular activities all over the UK. These include monthly 'nights' in London and specific 'nights' elsewhere, enabling members to meet the Club organisers, discuss specific queries, buy supplies and enjoy spicy snacks or meals. The Club also holds day and residential weekend cookery courses, gourmet nights to selected restaurants and similar enjoyable outings.

Top of the list are our regular Curry Club Gourmet Trips to India and other spicy countries. We take a small group of curry enthusiasts to the chosen country and tour the incredible sights, in between sampling the delicious foods of each region.

If you'd like to know more, write to; **THE CURRY CLUB, STAFFORDSHIRE STREET, LONDON SE15 5TL.**

Our Top 100 Restaurants

We are asked repeatedly which are the best curry restaurants based in the U.K. It is a hard question to answer in the light of the astonishing number of good restaurants around the country. But it is an interesting question. Bowing, therefore to popular demand, we publish below our list of the restaurants we believe to be the U.K.'s top 100. Some are plush and expensive, others are simple and inexpensive. All have for several years served consistently well above average food, and they are unlikely to decline in standard. All are, of course, highly recommended, and your views on them and any you think are obvious omissions from this list are welcomed. They are listed in county order

Avon	Bath	Rajpoot
	Bristol	Rajdoot
Bucks	Milton Keynes	Jaipur
Devon	Plymouth	Khyber
Dorset	Poole	Rajpoot
Essex	Ilford	Jalalabad
	Maldon	Tandoori Garden
H & W	Evesham	Husseins
Hants	Portsmouth	Palash
	Southampton	Kuti's
Herts	Royston	British Raj
Kent	Folkeston	The India
	Orpington	Bombay Brasserie
Lancs	Chorley	Shaju's
Leics	Leicester	Curry Fever
Lincs	Boston	Star of India
G Man	Manchester	Ashoka
		Deansgate
		Gaylord
		Kathmandu
		Kohinoor
		Rajdoot
Middlesex	Southall	Brilliant
		Madhus Brilliant
		Omy's
		Sagoo and Takar (2)
	Wembley	Chetna's Bhel Puri House
Notts	Nottingham	Saagar
Oxon	Oxford	Polash
Staffs	Stafford	Eastern Eye
Suffolk	Woodbridge	Royal Bengal
Surrey	Purley	Araliya
Sussex	Brighton	Black Chapatti
	Steyning	Maharaja
Tyne and Wear	Newcastle	Rupali
		Sachins
		Vujon
Warks	Leamington	Ashoka
	Stratford	Husseins
West Midlands	Birmingham	Adil's
		Days of the Raj

Continued overleaf

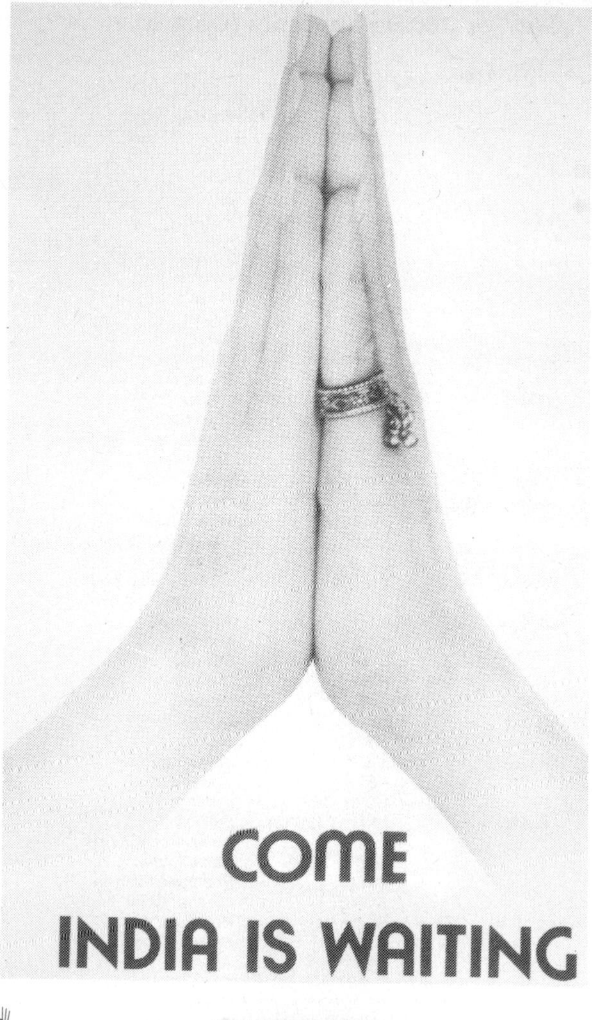

Our Top 100 Restaurants (Cont'd)

West Midlands	Birmingham	Maharaja
		Rajdoot
		Royal Al Faisal
	Coventry	William IV Pub
Wilts	Swindon	Biplob
S Yorks	Doncaster	Indus
	Sheffield	Nirmals
N Yorks	Skipton	Aagrah
W Yorks	Bradford	Aagrah
		Karachi
		Kashmir
		Hansa's
	Leeds	Aagrah
		Hansa's
Scotland Fife	St Andrews	Mandalay
		The New Balaka
Lothian	Edinburgh	Kalpna
		Lancers
		Shamiana
		Verandah
Strathclyde	Glasgow	Balbirs
Wales Glam	Cardif	Everest
	Swansea	Indian Ocean
S Ireland	Dublin	Eastern Tandoori
		Rajdoot
London	E1	Lahore Kebab House
		Namaste
London	N1	Sonargaon
	N14	Romna gate
	N16	Spices
	NW1	Diwana
		Viceroy
London	NW5	Bengal lancer
	NW10	Sabras
London	SE10	Mandalay
	SE23	Dewaniam
	SE26	Jehangir
London	SW1	Salloos
		Tandoori of Chelsea
	SW5	Star of India
	SW7	Bombay Brasserie
	SW10	Chutney Mary
	SW15	Buzkash
	SW17	Sree Krishna
London	W1	Anwar's
		Copper Chimney
		Gaylord
		Gopal's of Soho
		Jamdani
		Lal Qila
		Mandeer
		Ragam
		Shikara
	W2	Veeraswamy
	W2	Diwana Bhel Puri
	W2	Khan's
		Bombay Palace
	W2	Spice Merchant
	W5	Monty's
	W6	Tandoori Nights
		Malabar
London	WC2	India Club
		Taste of India

THE
WORLD'S FAVOURITE
BASMATI
Tilda
RICE

Those Restaurant Names

For a very long time it seemed that the standard name of the local curry house on nearly every High Street was the Taj Mahal. Restaurateurs felt that the average British diner would identify that name with 'Indian' food. Since then many Hindi and Urdu words have been used to christen the neighbourhood curry venue. Some use place names such as Agra, Asia, Bombay, Ganges, Indua, Khyber, and Rawalpindi, names which are recognisable to most diners as exotic and Indian. Safer bets are Gate of India, Light of India, Star of India and Golden Curry. Names such as these still abound up and down the country although in recent years many restaurants have been renamed to the town name tandoori (e.g. The Glasgow Tandoori). Restaurateurs shrewdly realised that by using their own town name they appeared to add respectability and authority, as if it operated on behalf of the town involved. No other cuisine has adopted this method (there are, as far as we know, no Peterborough Pastas nor Hull Hamburgers, no Chatham Chinese nor Durham Doners). Indian restaurants also traditionally use historic people and objects to name their premises- raj, rajpoot, rajdoot, rajrooj etc. are king warriors, and there are numerous Mumtaz's (the wife of the emperor Shah Jahan for whom the Taj Mahal was built) and one often sees such names as Shish Mahal (palace of mirrors) and Hawa Mahal (palace of winds). Gurka symbolises Nepalese food, and if you see Sylhet or Surma, it is a safe bet these are Bangladeshi - the former is a town and the latter a river in that country. The Koh-i-noor is the largest diamond in the world, now in the crown jewels, it used to be in the possession of the Moghul emperors. Recently there has been a move to name restaurants after films or television series. We know of 14 Gandhis in various parts of the country, all of which opened after the success of the film, plus a succession of Far Pavilions, Jewel in the Crowns and Eastern Eyes.

If you want to know what your favourite restaurant's name means you may have to ask the waiter but whatever the name it is the food which counts.

Index of National Cuisines

Most curry houses, whether up-market or the standard multi-menu venue, do not really mind being called Indian. It is a legacy of history, when the sub-continent was united under several empires, the last of which included British India. However, since 1947 countries have gone their own ways, notably Pakistan, Bangladesh and Sri Lanka. India's other neighbours - Afghanistan, Burma and Nepal
We list here an index of national cuisines, but we point out that the standard curry house curry transcends international boundaries and has developed a distinctive and particular style in the UK.

AFGHAN

Afghanistan's location had always held the strategic key to India until this century, for it was through the solitary mountain passes that the invaders came and possessed India from as early as 3000 BC. Located between Iran (formerly Persia) and Pakistan (formerly N.W. India) it brought the cuisine of the Middle East to India - and that of India to the Middle East. Kebabs and Birianis, and skewered spiced lamb over charcoal.

BANGLADESHI/BENGALI

Most of the standard curry houses in the UK are owned by Bangladeshis and nearly all of those serve curries ranging from mild to very hot, as explained in the Introduction. Bangladesh, formerly East Pakistan, is located at the northeast portion of India, and is to the east of the mouth of the river Ganges. Before Partition the area either side of the Ganges was Bengal. Today Bengal is the Indian state which shares its border with Bangladesh. In terms of food, the area enjoys prolific fresh- and sea-water fish - pomfret, hilsa, rue and enormous prawns and shrimps, and they specialise in vegetable dishes such as Niramish. True Bangladeshi/Bengali cuisine is nigh impossible to find in the UK.

BURMESE

Burma shares its boundaries with Bangladesh India, China, Laos and Thailand. Its food is a combination of the styles of its neighbours. Rice is the staple and noodles are popular too. Curries are very hot and there are no religious objections to eating pork or beef or other meats. Duck and seafood are commonly used.

GOAN

Goa is on the West coast of India, about 400 miles south of Bombay. It was established, in 1492, by the Portuguese who occupied it until 1962. It is now a state of India where Christianity prevails and there are no objections to eating pork or beef. The

food of Goa is unique. Their most famous dish is Vindaloo - but it is not the dish from the standard curry house - it is traditionally pork marinated in vinegar (the longer the bettter) then simmered in a chilli hot red curry gravy. Goa also has delicious seaford and fish dishes.

MOGHUL

The curry from the standard curry house is based on rich creamy dishes developed by the Moghul emperors. Authentically, this style of food should be subtly spiced. It can be found in an increasing number of 'haute cuisine' restaurants around the country.

NEPALESE

Nepal, located to the North of India, in the Himalayas, is famous for Sherpas and Ghurkas. The Nepalese enjoy curry and rice, of course, their own specialties are, perhaps, less well known. Momos, for example, are dumplings with a mince curry filling; Aloo Achar are potatoes in pickle sauce. There is an increasing, though still small, number of restaurants with Nepalese specials on the menu.

PAKISTANI

Pakistan was, until independence in 1947, the North West group of India states. Located between Afghanistan and India it contains the famous Khyber Pass. They are pre-dominantly

meat eaters, favouring lamb and chicken (being Moslem, they avoid pork). Charcoal cooking is the norm, and this area is the original home of the tandoor. Breads such as Chupatti, Nan and Paratha are the staple.

SOUTH INDIAN

Over 80% of the population of India are vegetarians; and the Southern half of India is almost exclusively so. Until recently the extraordinary range of vegetarian specialities were virtually unknown in the UK. The introduction of more and more restaurants offering South Indian fare coincides with the increasing awareness of vegetarianism. Specialities include many types of vegetable curry including Avial with exotic vegetables in a yoghurt base, and Sambar - a lentil base curry. Other delights include huge thin crisp rice-flour pancakes called Dosas, with a curry filling and Idlis - steamed rice or lentil flour dumplings. Restaurants serving this type of food are springing up all around the UK.

SRI-LANKAN

Sri Lanka is the small pearl-shaped island, formerly Ceylon, at the southernmost tip of India. Its cuisine is distinctive and generally very chilli hot. They eat similar fare to that of South India: i.e. vegetarian dishes, but they also enjoy meat, chicken and duck. Their curries are very pungent.

Curry Menu Glossary

Echoing what has been written on our earlier pages, the Indian restaurant menu can be a complex document: This glossary sets out to explain many of the standard dishes and items you will encounter in nearly every Indian-style restaurant. Spellings will vary vastly from restaurant to restaurant, reflecting the many languages and dialects in the subcontinent. (See *masala* and rhogan *josh gosht* for some examples.) Our spelling is as near as possible to the standard accepted way of spelling, translating phonetically from 'Delhi Hindi' to 'Queen's English'. A good many techniques and dishes have been created by restaurateurs over here - for example, Madras curry, Pullao Rice and Phal. They will not be found in traditional India. On the other hand, we have not attempted to include the many thousands of traditional Indian dishes you will find all over the subcontinent and in many cookbooks. The newer, more 'up-market' restaurants are tending to offer more selective menus with some traditional and unusual dishes . . . and our advice is to try them when you can.

A

AAM - or AM: Mango.

ALOO - Potato.

B

BALTI - Balti dishes seem to be found mainly in the West Midlands. Cubes of meat or chicken are marinated, then charcoal grilled, then simmered in a sauce and usually served in a KARAHI (sic.) See BOTI KABAB from which the word Balti derived.

BHAJEE - Dryish mild vegetable curry.

BHAJIA - Deep fried fritter- usually onion.

BHARE - Stuffed.

BHOONA - (or BHUNA). Cooking process - dry roasted or well fried. Usually mild and cooked with coconut.

BINDI - A pulpy vegetable also known as Okra or Ladies' Fingers.

BIRIANI - Traditionally rice baked with meat or vegetable filling with saffron, served with edible silver foil. The restaurant interpretation is a fried rice artificially coloured, with filling added (see PULLAO).

BOMBAY DUCK - A smallish fish native to the Bombay area known locally as Bommaloe Macchi. This was too hard for the British to pronounce so it became Bombay Duck. It is dried and appears on the table as a crispy deep fried starter or accompaniment to a curry.

BOMBAY POTATOE - Small whole potatoes in curry and tomato sauce.

BOTI KABAB - Marinated cubes of lamb cooked in a Tandoor oven.

BURFI - (or BARFI). An Indian fudge-like sweetmeat made from reduced condensed milk and in various flavours - plain, pistachio (green), etc.

C

CEYLON CURRY - These are usually cooked with coconut, lemon and chilli.

CHANA - Chick peas (a large lentil). Can be curried or fried.

CHILLI - The hottest of peppers. If your dish is not hot enough ask for chilli pepper (or cayenne) or pickle.

CHAPATTI - (The spelling can vary.) A dry 6in. disc of unleavened bread. It should be served piping hot.

CHUTNEYS - The common ones are onion chutney, mango chutney and tandoori chutney. There are dozens of others which rarely appear on the standard menu. (See SAMBALS).

CURRY - The only word in this glossary to have no direct translation into any of the sub-continent's 15 or so languages. The word was coined by the British in India centuries ago. Possible contenders for the origin of the word are: Karahi or Karai (Hindi) - wok-like frying pan used all over India to prepare masalas (spice mixtures), Karhi - a soup-like dish made with spices, chick pea flour dumplings and buttermilk; or Kari - a spicy Tamil sauce; Turkuri - a seasoned sauce or stew, or Kari Phulia- Neem leaves, small leaves, a bit like bay leaves used for flavouring.

D

DAHI - Yoghurt.

DAHI WALA - A meat dish cooked in a savoury yoghurt sauce. Lentils. There are over 60 types of lentil in the sub-continent. The common restaurant types are masoor (red which cooks yellow), chana and urid.

DHANSAK - Traditional Parsee chicken dish cooked in a puree of lentils, aubergine, tomato and spinach. Meat can be used alternatively. Some restaurants also add pineapple pieces.

DO-PIAZA - Traditional meat dish. Do means two; piaza onion. Onions appear twice in the cooking; first fried and second batch raw. The onions give it a sweetish taste.

DOSA - A South Indian pancake made from rice and lentil flour. Usually served with a filling.

DUM - Cooked by steaming, e.g. Aloo Dum - steamed potatoes.

E

EKURI - Spiced scrambled eggs.

F

FOOGATH - Lightly cooked vegetable dish.

G

GHEE - Clarified butter or margarine used in high quality North Indian cooking.

GOBI - Cauliflower.

GOSHT - Lamb.

GULAB JAMAN - An Indian dessert. Small 11/2in. diam. balls of flour and milk powder, deep fried to golden and served gold in syrup. Cake-like texture.

GURDA - Kidney. Gurda kebab is marinated kidney skewered, cooked in the Tandoor.

H

HALVA - Sweets made from syrup and vegetable fruit. Served cold in small squares. Is translucent and comes in bright colours depending on-subject used. Orange - carrot; green - pistachio; red mango, etc. Has texture thicker than Turkish delight. Sometimes garnished with edible silver foil.

HASINA KEBAB - Pieces of chicken breast, lamb or beef marinated in spices then skewered and barbecued with onion, capsicum and tomato. Turkish origin .

I

IDLI - Rice and lentil flour cake served with light curry sauce. South Indian.

IMLI - Tamarind. A date-like fruit used as a chutney and in cooking.

J

JALEBI - An Indian dessert. A flour, milk powder and yoghurt batter pushed through a narrow funnel into a deep fry to produce golden curly crisp rings. Served cold in syrup.

JAL FREZI - Sautéed or stir-fried meat or chicken dish, often with lightly cooked onion, garlic, ginger, green pepper and chilli.

K

KARAHI - A cooking dish. Some restaurants cook in small Karahis and serve them straight to the table with the food sizzling inside. (See also CURRY).

KASHMIR CHICKEN - Whole chicken stuffed with minced meat.

KASHMIR CURRY - Often, in the restaurant, a sweetish curry using lychees or similar.

KEBAB - Skewered food cooked over charcoal. A process over 4000 years old which probably originated in the Middle East. It was imported to India by the Moslems centuries ago. (See BOTI, HASINA, NARGIS, SHAMI and SHEEK KEBABS in glossary).

KEEMA - Minced meat curry.

KHURZI - Lamb or chicken, whole with spicy stuffings.

KOFTA - Minced meat or vegetable balls in batter, deep fried and then cooked in a curry sauce.

KORMA - To most restaurants this just means a mild curry. Traditionally it is very rich. Meat, chicken or vegetables are cooked in cream, yoghurt and nuts and are fragrantly spiced with saffron and aromatic spices.

KULCHA - Small leavened bread.

KULCHA STUFFED - Stuffed with mildly spiced mashed potato baked in the Tandoor.

KULFI - Indian ice cream. Traditionally it comes in vanilla or pistachio or mango flavours.

INDIAN BRASSERIE

Serving nouvelle Indian cuisine.

253 Kentish Town Road
London NW5

Telephone: 071 485 6688

L

LASSI - A refreshing drink from yoghurt and crushed ice. The savoury version is lassi namkeen and the sweet version is lassi meethi.

M

MACCHI - or (MACCHLI). Fish.

MADRAS - You will not find a traditional recipe for a Madras curry. It does not exist. But the people of south India eat hot curries. Some original chef must ingeniously have christened his hot curry 'Madras' and the name stuck.

MAKHANI - A traditional dish. Tandoori chicken is cooked in a ghee (see glossary) and tomato sauce.

MALAI - Cream.

MALAYA - The curries of Malaya are traditionally cooked with plenty of coconut, chilli and ginger. In the Indian restaurant, however, they are usually mild and contain pineapple, and other fruit.

MASALA - A mixture of spices which are cooked with a particular dish. It can be spelt a remarkable number of ways - Massala, Massalla, Musala, Mosola, Masalam etc.

MATTER - Green peas.

METHI - Fenugreek. A savoury spice in seed form. The leaves, fresh or dried, are also used in many northern dishes.

MOGLAI - Cooking in the style of the Moghul emperors, whose chefs took Indian cookery to the heights of gourmet cuisine three centuries ago. Few restaurateurs who offer Moglai dishes come anywhere near this excellence. True Moglai dishes are expensive and time consuming to prepare authentically. Can also be variously spelt Muglai, Mhogulai, Moghlai etc.

MULLIGATAWNY - A Tamil sauce (MOLEGOO - pepper, TUNNY water) which has become well known as a British soup.

MURGH - Chicken.

MURGH MASALA - (or Murgh Massalam). A speciality dish. Whole chicken, marinated in yoghurt and spices for 24 hours and stuffed and roasted.

N

NAN - Leavened bread baked in the Tandoor. It is teardrop-shaped and about 8 - 10in. long. It must be served fresh and hot.

NAN KEEMA - Nan bread stuffed with a thin layer of minced meat curry.

NAN PESHAWRI - Nan bread stuffed with almonds and/or cashews and/or raisins, baked in the Tandoor.

NARGIS KEBAB - Indian Scotch egg - spiced mince meat around a hard-boiled egg.

P

PAAN - Betel leaf folded around a stuffing - lime paste or various spices (SUPARI) and eaten after meal .

PAKORAS - To all intents and purposes, the same as the BHAJIA (see glossary).

PANEER - Cheese made from bottled milk which can be fried and curried (Matter Paneer).

PAPADOM - Thin lentil flour wafers. When cooked (deep fried or baked) they expand to about 8in. They must be crackling crisp and warm when served - if not, send them back to be reheated and deduct a lot of points from that restaurant. They come plain or spiced with lentils, pepper, garlic or chilli.

PASANDA - Meat, usually lamb, beaten and cooked in one piece.

PATIA - Restaurant seafood curry with thick dark brown sweet and sour sauce.

PHAL - A very hot curry (the hottest) invented by restaurateurs.

PICKLES - Pungent, hot pickled vegetables essential to an Indian meal. The most common are Lime, Mango and Chilli.

PRAWN BUTTERFLY - Jinga praj pati - marinated in spices and fried in butter.

PRAWN PURI - Prawns in a hot sauce served on a puri bread. Though sometimes described as Prawn Puree it is not a purée.

PULLAO - Rice and meat or vegetables cooked together in a pan until tender. In many restaurants the ingredients are mixed after cooking to save time. (See also BIRIANI).

PULLAO RICE - The restaurant name for rice fried with spices and coloured yellow.

PURI - A deep fried unleavened bread about 4in. diam., it puffs up when cooked and should be served at once.

Q

QUAS CHAWAL - (also KESAR CHAVAL). Rice fried in ghee, flavoured and coloured with saffron.

R

RAITA - A cooling chutney of yoghurt and vegetable, e.g. cucumber, which accompanies the main meal.

RASGULLA - Walnut size balls of semolina and cream cheese cooked in syrup (literal meaning: juicy balls). They are white or pale gold in colour and served cold or warm.

RASHMI KEBAB - Kebab minced meat inside an omelette mesh.

RASMALAI - Rasgullas cooked in cream. Served cold. Very rich, very sweet.

RHOGAN JOSH GOSHT - Literally it means red juice meat, or lamb in red gravy. It is a traditional northern Indian dish. Lamb is marinated in yoghurt, then cooked with ghee and spices and tomato. It should be creamy and spicy but not too hot. There are many ways of spelling it, as careful readers of the guide entries will spot - here are a few variations: Rogon, Roghan, Rugon, Rugin, Rowgan, Ragan etc.; Jush, Joosh, Jash etc.; Goosht, Goose, Gost etc.

S

SABZI - Vegetable.

SAG - Spinach.

SAMBALS - A Malayan term describing the side dishes accompanying a meal. Sometimes referred to on the Indian menu.

SAMBAR - A south Indian vegetable curry made largely from lentils.

SAMOSA - The celebrated triangular deep fried meat or vegetable patties, served as starters or snacks.

SHAMI KEBAB - Minced meat round rissoles.

SHASHLIK - Cubes of skewered lamb.

SHEEK KABAB - (or SEEKH). Spiced mince meat, skewered and grilled.

INDIA Ahh!

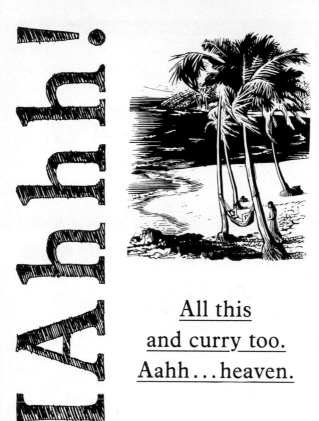

All this
and curry too.
Aahh . . . heaven.

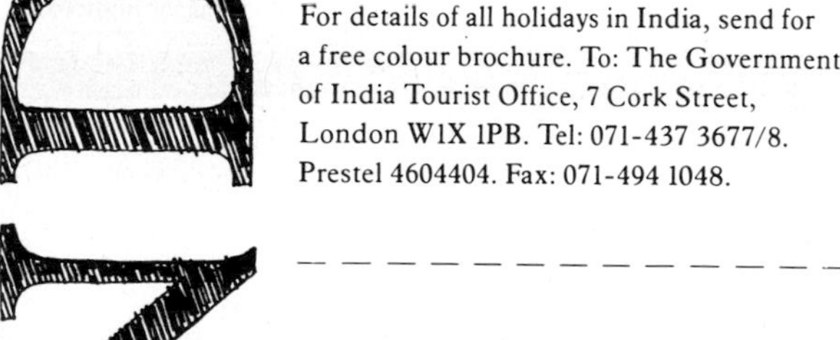

For details of all holidays in India, send for a free colour brochure. To: The Government of India Tourist Office, 7 Cork Street, London W1X 1PB. Tel: 071-437 3677/8. Prestel 4604404. Fax: 071-494 1048.

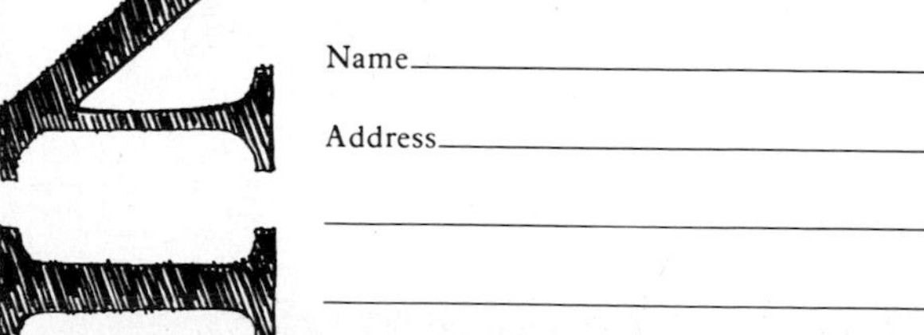

BHEL-POORI HOUSE

BHEL-POORI HOUSE

121-123 Drummond Street
London NW1
Telephone: 071-387 5556
071-380 0730
Fax: 071-383 0560
Open 12 noon-12 midnight
7 days a week

50 Westbourne Grove
London W2
Telephone: 071-221 0721
Open 12 noon-11pm
Closed Mondays
and 3pm-6pm each day
Open all day Saturday and Sunday

BHEL-POORI HOUSE

T

TANDOORI - A style of charcoal cooking originating in N.W. India (what is now Pakistan and the Punjab). Originally it was confined to chicken and lamb (see BOTI KEBAB) and nan bread. More recently it is applied to lobster etc. The meat is marinated in a reddened yoghurt sauce, then skewered and placed in a tandoor (clay oven). TARKA DHAL - Lentils fried and garnished with spices.

TAVA - A heavy steel shallow frying pan.

THALI - A set of serving bowls on a tray used by diners in south India.

TIKKA - Skewered meat, chicken or seafood, marinated and barbecued or tandooried.

TINDALOO - See VINDALOO.

U

URID - A type of lentil. Its husk is black and it comes whole, split or polished. Available as a dhal dish in some restaurants.

V

VINDALOO - A fiery hot dish from Goa. Traditionally it was pork marinated in vinegar with potato (ALOO). In the restaurant scene it now comes to mean just a very hot dish. Also sometimes called BINDALOO or TINDALOO (even hotter).

Y

YAKNI - Mutton.

Z

ZEERA - (or Jeera). Cummin or Cumin seed. Appears on the menu sometimes as ZEERA GOSHT. Lamb cooked with cummin.

What We need to know

We need to know everything there is to know about all the curry restaurants in the UK. And there is no one better able to tell us than those who use them. We do not mind how many times we receive a report about a particular place, so please don't feel inhibited or that someone else would be better qualified. They aren't. Your opinion is every bit as important as the next person's.

Ideally we'd like a report from you every time you dine out - even on a humble take-away. We realise this is hard work so we don't mind if your report is very short, and you are welcome to send in more than one report on the same place telling of different occasions. You can even use the back of an envelope or a postcard, or we can supply you with special forms if you write in.

If you can get hold of a menu (they usually have take-away menus to give away) or visiting cards, they are useful to us too, so please send them along with your report.

We acknowledge all reports received and most will appear, probably in the abbreviated form in the next edition of *The Curry Magazine* (the Curry Club members' quarterly publication.) They are also used towards the next edition of this guide.

We do not pay for reports but our ever increasing corps of regular correspondents receive the occasional perk from us. Why not join them? Send us your report after your next restaurant curry.

Thank You.

More information and report forms from:
The Curry Club,
Staffordshire St.
London,
SE15 5TL

County Index

ENGLAND

GREATER LONDON
(See also MIDDX)

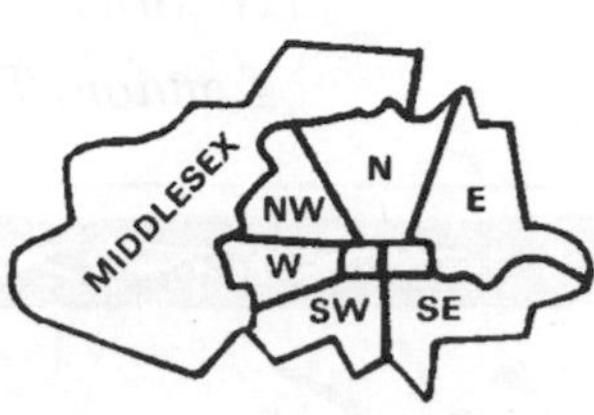

We have divided London into its well known post codes. We run alphabetically as follows: E, EC, N, NW, SE, SW, W and WC. Middlesex (the non London postcoded part of Greater London) appears later under 'M'

LONDON E

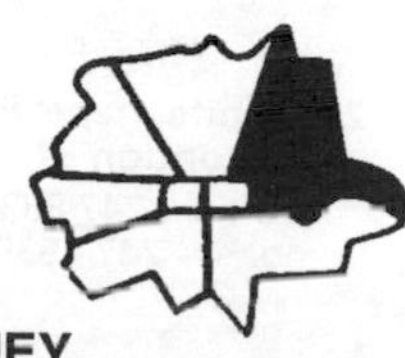

E1 : BRICK LANE AND STEPNEY

This area was once predominantly Jewish, containing tailors and cab drivers and salt-of-the-earth street markets. More recently it has become home to the country's largest Bangladeshi community. All around the area you will find small, very cheap curry restaurants and cafes. The most prolific street is the long and narrow Brick Lane, running between Shoreditch and Aldgate East tube stations. It has become a centre for cheap and cheerful curry cafes, snack bars and restaurants run by the thriving community. (To emphasise its roots you'll also find an all night fresh-baked bagel shop where cab drivers queue for sustenance). As for curry, most of the establishments are unlicensed and are fairly spartan (you can bring your own, obtaining it from the JR off-licence which sells chilled lager and white wine).
The number of curry houses has grown from nine in 1986 to twenty in 1991, reflecting exactly the growth of curry houses nationally. Here we single out six on Brick Lane.

ALADIN
132, Brick Lane, E1. Tel: 071 247 8210
Generally well reported but one party tells of excess oil and sameness of taste. It is very ethnic.

CLIFTON
126, Brick lane, E1. Tel: 071 247 3610
Very much an institute which, pleases some and deters others. Its regular trade consists of a 'very mixed bunch of all ages - workmen in overalls, businessman in suits.' MC. We hear that it has been re-decorated which we presume means exit the nubile wall paintings. 'The Lamb Roghan Josh the best I've tasted,' SP and 'Batara Masala Quail £3.50, in a tasty

sauce with plenty of tomato and Pullao Rice. Egg and mushroom Curry £2.30 was good though all portions a little small.' MT. 'All flavours were good and more spicy than average. Good value for money.' MC.

LALQUILA
176, Brick Lane, E1. Tel: 071 247 3700
New to our Guide, the Lalquila is another popular house in Brick Lane, about which we have received numerous votes from our readers. It serves formula curries with usual Bangladeshi Brick Lane panache at reasonable prices.

NAZRUL
128, Brick Lane, E1. Tel: 071 247 2505
Once again the Nazrul has come out top of the poll as your Brick Lane favourite. We hear of re-decoration here too - whether the 'loosely fitting toilet pedestal and leaky S-bends,' (DMW), are included, we await to hear, but the 'Methi Gosht £2.25 tasted fresh with the right bits of bark etc, with Sag Bhajia £1.30 and Special Rice £1.05, all reasonable quality with trouble clearing it all up.' DMW. 'It was extremely busy, we had to queue for 15 minutes for a table - it was worth it for excellent quantities and quality and cheap prices.' PC. 'Unlicensed, cafe type of place but they don't mind you bringing your own.' RP.

SHAMPAN
79, Brick Lane, E1. Tel: 071 375 0475
A licensed restaurant which is aiming to take Brick Lane up-market, evidenced by its cocktail lounge and 'rather more upmarket prices.' Reports please.

SWEET AND SPICY
40, Brick Lane, E1. Tel: 071 247 1081
A cheap and cheerful Bangladeshi cafe. Unlicensed, of course, and 'you take what is available from the limited menu.' My Indian students found the Aloo Ghobi and Chicken Curry far too hot! My group of 20 cost £50 to fill, can't be bad.' BG.

ELSEWHERE IN E1

DEEDAR
42, Hanbury Street, (off Brick Lane), E1. Tel: 071
Unlicensed cafe seating 28. 'The Chicken Jalfrezi and Madras curry were both very good with large chunks of meat. Banana Fritter and Pistachio Kulfi went down well.' JSK. The average spend here is £5 for a meal.

LAHORE KEBAB HOUSE **TOP 100**
2, Umberston Street, Stepney. E1. Tel: 071 488 2551
It has no license, and the decor and comfort is non-existant, but for £6 a head you take your fill from superb food.' RE. Cutlery (a spoon) is available on request as are raw chillies and onion. We have literally numerous reports all confirming superb food and excellent service. It is little used by Europeans and its food makes few compromises to them. In our TOP 100.

NAMASTE **TOP 100 & CC DISCOUNT**
30, Alie Street, E1. Tel: 071 488 9242
Namaste in Hindi means welcome. This well established restaurant has very recently welcomed a new master chef direct from India. Chef Cyrus was trained by India's foremost hotel group, TAJ Hotels. He worked for them for years culminating as executive chef at the Taj Holiday complex Goa. These qualifications puts him instantly amongst the UK's top 5 Indian chefs. His new menu at Namaste redas like an encyclopedia of good Indian food. It is innovative, varied and exciting. It includes Scallops in Chilli (piri-piri), Oysters in Semolina coated and deep-fried. Pomfret, Grey Mullet, Rabbit, Trout, Crab all in authentic preparations. I have known Chef Cyrus for years and he has already transformed the Namaste into a top restaurant. Despite it being early days, I am placing the Namaste into our TOP 100. They give discounts to Curry Club members at their quieter times, see page 288.

THE PACIFIC OCEAN
207, Mile End Road, Bethnal Green. E1. Tel: 071 790 2421
A standard, competent curry house.

PASSAGE TO INDIA
49, Mile End Road, E1. Tel: 071 790 7205
And another, where we hear the food is occasionally 'inspired'. TM.

SHALIQUES
32, Hanbury Street, Spitalfields, off Brickland. E1. Tel: 071 377 2137
'The list of curries was divided into more or less the 'Chapman Distinction: Mild, Hot, Bhuna and Masala': The Evening Standard quote is in the Shaliques menu. Well thankyou Fay for this new terminology! And, yes that is what the menu is about. You can add Medium, Tandoori and Biriani and you have the definitive, all purpose standard menu, the delight of all curryholics. But you won't find any red flock wall paper. This was the first 'up market' restaurant in the area. The staff are willing to please and seem to have an overwhelming desire to burst into song and dance. This takes place formally on Tuesdays and Saturdays when 'Ms Salique herself takes the stage to dance in her father's restaurant.' Clients are encouraged to join in on the spacious floor. The staff proudly tell of their national television appearances. Our reporters tell of a busy 'fun' place with above average food, Cobra Lager and lemon scented towels.

SITA **CC DISCOUNT**
222, Whitechapel Road, E1. Tel: 071 247 4936
and 114, Mile End Road, E1. Tel: 071 265 9040
Both restaurants are owned by S Das Gupta, both have the identical menu. Sita is the beautiful wife of Rama, both are major Indian Hindu Gods. The two Sita's are unusual, then for E1, being Indian rather than Bangladeshi. The menu (and the staff) are interchangeable between the two branches. The experienced curry diner will detect no difference, and 'most subtle spicing in diverse ingredients such as trout and lobster.' PT. Our check reveals that the Sita's prices are good for London. Popadoms are 30p, Pullao Rice £1.15, Chicken Bhuna £3.05. Both restaurants give discounts to Curry Club members at their quieter times, see page 288.

E2 : BETHNAL GREEN

AL AMIN **CC DISCOUNT**
483, Cambridge Heath Road, E2. Tel: 071 739 9619
A standard competent Bangladeshi curry house. Price check: Popadoms 30p each, Pullao Rice £1.10, Chicken Curry £2.70 and threy give discounts to Hospital staff and Curry Club members at their quieter times, see page 288.

E4 : CHINGFORD

PURBANI
34, The Avenue, Higham's Park, E4. Tel: 081 989 4174
Reports indicate good standards and plentiful helpings.

Four good restaurants in the East London suburbs.

E10 : LEYTON

SHISH MAHAL
815, High Road, Leyton, E10. Tel: 081 556 6717

E12 : MANOR PARK

SAGOR
538, High Road North, E12. Tel: 081 514 5825

E14 : DOCKLANDS

THE GAYLORD
14, Manchester Road, Isle of Dogs, E14. Tel: 081

E15 : STRATFORD

THE HEMELAYA
178, The Grove, Stratford, E15. Tel: 081 519 6887

LONDON EC

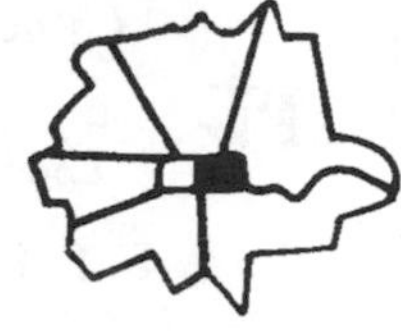

EC1

MOGHUL'S
4, Lindsey Street, Smithfield Market, EC1. Tel: 071 606 1652
Competent with one regular reporter going to the 'sensational' (MC) level (about Chicken Tikka Masala).

RAVI SHANKAR
442, St John Street, EC1. Tel: 071 833 5849
This is a branch of the Drummond Street, NW1, Ravi Shankar about which we exude later. See entry.

THE RAJ TANDOORI
52, Cowcross Street, EC1. Tel: 071 253 3847
Opposite Farringdon tube. Well reported.

EC4

HALAL
5, Ludgate Circus, EC4.
The oldest in the city, it has been serving 'authentic curry at very attractive prices since 1960. We always have Mutton and Chicken Tikka followed by Mutton Vindaloo with Potato and Onion Bhajia and Mushroom Bhajee. We eat Indian a lot. We find this place to be one of the best.' A and DB. It has a branch, The Halal, junction Aldgate and Leadenhall Street, EC3.

TEMPLE BAR TANDOORI
23, Fleet Street, EC4. Tel: 071 583 4673
'Shortish menu which covers basics. The Papadoms were free but not freshly fried.' DJT. 'Busy at lunch times with hoards of men outnumbering women 10:1. Good none-the-less.' (Mrs MC).

LONDON N

N1

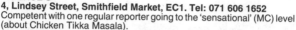

INDIAN VEGETARIAN BHEL POORI HOUSE
92/93, Chapel Market, N1. Tel: 071 837 4607
Bhelpoori was quite well established in London when Nurus Safa opened this one in 1987. Here you will find many crispy, chewy tasty vegetarian dishes, some hot and some cold. There are curries served with health conscious brown rice and thalis served with Whole Wheat Pooris. An entire and filling meal costs about £5. It is licensed, and there is a remarkable 'eat as much as you like', daily lunch at £2.95. And they offer discounts to Curry Club members at their quieter times, see page 288.

THE NORTHWEST FRONTIER
310/312, Caledonian Road, N1. Tel: 071 609 3989
A wave of designer restaurants evoking the 'good old days' of British rule started with the Last Days of the Raj. This is one of them. However, we

Jashan
The Indian Celebration

Tandoori-nights

should not complain of expensive surroundings in a restaurant, providing the food is up to it. The menu items are numbered from 1 to 98 Chicken Chat £1.75, to Lassi £1.25 yoghurt drink. Curry Sauce, incidentally, No: 68 is £1.00. You may therefore correctly deduce that this is a standard menu, with above average food.

PARVEEN TANDOORI **CC DISCOUNT**
6, Theberton Street, N1. Tel: 071 226 0504
Typical curries from a typical menu. No surprises. It's a popular place though some reports indicate a slight uneven-ness of standards. Discounts available for Curry Club members at their quieter times, see page 288.

THE SONARGAON **TOP 100 & CC DISCOUNT**
46, Upper Street, Islington, N1. Tel: 071 226 6499
Of course, we all make mistakes! In the last Guide, I made one here by getting confused about its name. It is a Bangladeshi restaurant owned by Al Haj Anar Ali, and a very good one. It has nothing to do with anything Goan. Of course this, little error was spotted by Jonathan Meades in a piece he wrote in the Times about the guide, and I thank Mr Meades for reminding me that Sonargaon was the former capital city of Bengal. And what of the restaurant itself? You continue to tell us that it is one of your favourite London restaurants. We sent out a questionnaire to all our 15,000 members. One question we asked was 'which is your favourite restaurant.' The response maintains the Sonargaon in our TOP 100. It is there not for culinary masterpieces nor for any aspiration to greatness. It is there as an example of the standard curry house operating at its best. The menu contains everything the conscientious curryholic enjoys in the everyday fix. In addition you'll find quail, duck and fish (Tandoori and Masala) at between £4.75 and £8, Raan £28 for four, roast leg of lamb, requiring a long marination, hence pre-booking and very slow roasting resulting in 'the most aromatic spicing and the tenderest meat just falling off the bone.' JTR. The curries, rices and breads are generally praised as being 'highly satisfying,' BP and 'worth the journey across the river.' CS. Top of the pile is the Kashi. This is a party piece in which the Sonargaon has always specialised. A whole baby Lamb (about 20lb/9kg) is marinated for at least 24 hours. It is stuffed with spiced Basmati Rice then slowly baked until tender. It is served with all the trimmings starters, side dishes and desserts etc. There is no price on the menu for this extravaganza. You are urged to consult with the staff. For those too shy to do so - firstly, it serves 25, and the price - £500. But for a major feast £20 a head is reasonable. Mr Ali tells us they do this dish two or three times a year. Discounts are available to Curry Club members at their quieter times, see page 288.

SURUCHI VEGETARIAN BHELPOORI RESTAURANT
18, Theberton Street, N1. Tel: 071 359 8033
Eminently popular vegetarian restaurant, owned by Khalil Miah (whose Suruchi Tandoori at 82, Mildmay Road, N1, serves regular Bangladeshi curries). This Suruchi has Gujarati and Bombay Poori dishes (around £1.60) and South Indian Dosas £2.65.

N2 : EAST FINCHLEY

MAJJO'S FOODS
1, Fortis Green, N2. Tel: 071
Takeaway only owned by Majoo Ashraf. It comes to our notice for its fresh cooking. Everything is cooked on the day and the menu changes accordingly. On Fridays there is fish curry and on Saturdays Beef Nahiri both £3.50. Majjo serves most food cold for reheating at home, 'it's much safer hygeine-wise, but I will microwave it if I know it is for immediate consumptiom.' Closed Sundays.

N3 : FINCHLEY

RANI
3/7, Long Lane, Finchley, N3. Tel: 081 349 4386
Ranu's has expanded since we last reported on it and now seats 90. It is a vegetarian restaurant run by Jyoti Pattni ably assisted by his wife

Shelia and mother Khundan. It is their home cooking which comes to our reporters' attention. 'We noticed a slight dip following the new building, but we're happy to say its back to normal.' RC. There is a published menu, but 'go for the special(s) of the day.' RL. Also specially mentioned are the home made chutneys - imli (tamarind), coconut, chilli and coriander, brown, white and green and some 'super-scrumptious breads.'

N4 : FINSBURY PARK

BEEWEES
97, Stroud Green Road, N4. Tel: 071 263 4004
We reported on Sam Ramgoolie's amazing home made rum punch last time. It has now become a by-word at Beewees. His 'West Indian Goat Curry mopped up with those soft and floppy rotis... all amazing.' GR.

CROUCH HILL TANDOORI
10, Crouch Hill, Finsbury Park, N4. Tel: 071 281 6871
'Because I like to try new things I went for the Sizzler Juliet for £6.30, which with slivers of lamb and ginger fried with spices and brandy with Niramish for £2.30, mixed dry fried vegetables. A memorable combination.' MA.

JAI KRISHNA RESTAURANT
161, Stroud Green Road, N4. Tel: 071 272 1680
It's the same unpretentious unlicensed (bring your own) popular cafQ serving first class vegetarian Indian food, for little more than a fiver a head.

SUNDERBAN
50, Blackstock Road, Finsbury Park, N4. Tel: 071
The Chicken Chat was really superb and the Chicken Chilli Masala was totally enjoyable with finely spiced Rice £1.10 was abundant and the Chapattis hot and soft and served in towels.' VT.

N7 : HOLLOWAY

TAJ MAHAL **CC DISCOUNT**
35, Holloway Road, N7. Tel: 071 607 2980
Jeera or butter whole baby chicken £6.50 are well rated here. A more than competent curry house where discounts are available to Curry Club members at their quieter times, see page 288.

N8 : HORNSEY

BAMBAYA
1, Park Road, Crouch End. N8. Tel: 081 348 5609
Caribbean vegetarian and seafood is on offer here. Spicy items including West Indian curries are available. They welcome children.

JALALIAH
163, Priory Road, N8. Tel: 0871 348 4756
A well liked standard curry house. 'The vindaloo was the hottest curry I've ever had. It reduced me to hiccups and gulping copious water much to the glee of the 'told you so' waiters.' AS. Inexpensive and very good.

JASHAN
19, Turnpike Lane, N8. Tel: 081 340 9880
The Jashan, formerly the Turnpike Tandoori, has rapidly become established as 'a purveyor of high quality food.' We choose our words with care here, because it is a well known secret that the Jashan is a supplier of curries to Harrods Food Hall. The chefs are Indian and the subtle differences on the menu and in the taste of the food show it. Hariyali Gosht £4.25 is literally meat with green herbs - or lamb with spinach and fresh coriander. More than one correspondent praises the breads - 'the stuffed parathas are flaky and supreme.'

N10 : MUSWELL HILL

CURRY AND TANDOORI GARDEN
291, Muswell Hill Broadway, N10. Tel: 071 883 0557
Recommended.

N12 : NORTH FINCHLEY

CURRY ROYAL
932, High Road, N12. Tel: 081 445 1650
A new entrant to our Guide, the Curry Royal has a number of loyal regulars who have reported on its virtues. It has a reliable house, offering the familiar favourites cooked well, served amiably at reasonable prices.

N13 : PALMERS GREEN

DIPALI
82, Alderman's Hill, N13. Tel: 081 886 2221
'Comprehensive menu with all the old favourites plus spcials. Mas Bhaji is a whole trout, marinated and fried. First class Kulfi. Hot towels between course. The first of many enjoyable evenings.' DS. 'Another long established safe house. The vegetarian Thali and the Korai Gosht (served in a sizzler) are superb and the Boti Puri - finely minced meat in a spicy sauce is divine.' PJ.

N14 : SOUTHGATE

ANARKALI MOGHUL BRASSERIE
193, Bramley Road, Oakwood, N14. Tel: 081 367 7331
A recommended local with a standard menu plus some unusual items (duck and salmon).

ROMNA GATE TANDOORI **TOP 100**
14, The Broadway, Southgate Tube Station, N14. Tel: 081 882 6700
The decor is outstanding and should win an award in its own right. The room is made spectacular and intimate by the skilful use of elegant coloured glass partitions, mini waterfalls and wrought iron work. The Romna Gate received a huge number of votes in our favourite restaurant poll plus strings of reviews prasing it. Only one out of many found some aspects disappointing. The service is perhaps a little uneven. Another of our regular correspondents visited at Sunday lunch time to find it nearly empty, but the food 'as usual demanding a return,' PC. The little service bell on each table is a good idea. We are pleased to retain this restaurant in our TOP 100.

N16 : STOKE NEWINGTON

SPICES RESTAURANT **TOP 100**
28/30, Stoke Newington Church Street, N16. Tel: 071 254 0528
This is very much a family business owned by Mrs Khaleda Choudhury, and managed by her very charming son Atique, who is often to be found in attendance. Spices is a vegetarian restaurant serving a wide selection of starters: Bombay Cold Chat countered by Hot Soup, Rissoles, Samosas and Pakoras, averaging £1.60. For main courses the choice takes the diner 'down south' for paper thin rice pancakes (Dosas) served with curry sauce (Sambar) and chutney, averaging £3.80. Chapsy £3.45 is the find of one of our scribes who tells us of 'two floating chupatties packed full of spicy spinach and sweetcorn curry.' ML. The Aloo Gobi (potato and cauliflower curry) with rice and salad and the Corn Korma with Lemon Rice and Raita both £3.50 are two recommended set meals. Spices is superior of Indian vegetarian food. We are pleased to place it in our TOP 100. It has a branch Spices Express, N19.

N18 : EDMONTON

ROSHAN TANDOORI
373, Fore Street, Lower Edmonton, N18. Tel: 081 807 5185
Recommended

N19 : EDMONTON

RAJ VOGUE **CC DISCOUNT**
34, Highgate Hill, N19. Tel: 071 272 9091
Opened by Abed Choudhury on a GLC redundancy grant, the menu is, we hear 'subtle and the food equally so. The Kebab Platter is an excellent mixture of Tandoori items and the curries admirable.' PJ. Recommended

ANARKALI
MOGHUL
BRASSERIE
193 BRAMLEY ROAD
OAKWOOD
LONDON
NI14
081 - 367 7331
081 - 367 7413
Noon til 2.30.
6 til Midnight.

by one of our sternest critics, the Raj frequently plays host to Spurs soccer stars and Ken Livingstone hhimself. It also offers discounts to Curry Club members at its quieter times, see page 288.

N20

HIMALAYA TANDOORI
1, Oakleigh Road, N20. Tel: 081 445 5213
One regular reporter in particular wrapped our knuckles for this restaurant's absence last time. 'Strength to strength. The Keema Naan was the best we've had. The Phall is completely different from anywhere else. It's hot but well balanced.' BE. Reports please.

N21

GANDHI
Avenue Pole, Ridge Avenue, N21. Tel: 081 360 4247
'We were invited into the kitchen and enjoyed watching the Tandoor at work. The meal and service were great. We had a copy of your Guide with us, maybe they spice it!' P and LG.

LONDON NW

DRUMMOND STREET, NW1

I often get asked where the best restaurants are. It's one reason for producing this Guide. As far as London is concerned, Drummond Street is one area which I recommend. Just behind Euston Station is easy to get to. It is short and will not win any awards for beauty. It lacks the ethnic glamour of Southall and Wembley or the intensity of purpose of Brick Lane, but it is a small concentrated sector of extremely good Indian food. There are green grocers and delis supplying Indian ingredients and a dozen or so takeaways and restaurants. Here is alphabetical order is our Drummond Street selection.

CHUTNEYS
134, Drummond Street, NW1. Tel: 071 388 0604
On the site of the Shah (London's third Indian - RIP) Chutneys is as far removed from the Shah as lasers are from elastic bands. It takes advantage of its long frontage of plate glass to produce a bright, light and airy look.
It is a vegetarian restaurant with 'an excellent value-for-money lunch buffet for £4.45 as-much-as-you-like. It is licensed and more formal in the a-la-carte evenings.

AMBALA SWEET CENTRE
112, Drummond Street, NW1. Tel: 071 387 3521
10am to 11pm. The Ambala started trading in 1965. It specialises in savoury snacks (Pakoras and Samosa etc), Indian sweets (Halva, Jalebi, Gulab Jamun, Barfi etc) and a few curries. All are to take out only. Established initially for the Asian trade it now has branches in Birmingham, Bradford, Luton, Leicester, Derby, Slough, Tooting, Wembley, Leyton, East Ham, Southall, Finchley, Glasgow and Manchester. Drummond Street is the flagship. All branches serve identical items at identical prices. The quality is first class and the prices are always reasonable. Be prepared to queue.

DIWANA BHEL PURI HOUSE **TOP 100**
114 and 121, Drummond Street, NW1. Tel: 071 387 5556
Midday to 11pm. It pioneered Bombay pavement kiosk snack food in the UK. Bhel Puri is a tantalising cold mixture of crispy chewy textures, sweet,

hot and sour tastes. Crunchy savoury squiggly biscuits share the bowl with diced potato, puffed rice and fresh coriander. Lace it together with yoghurt, and sauces brown, red and green and you have it. And have it you must. Once acquired, the habit is unbreakable. You might continue you meal with a dosa pancake filled with sambar curry boosted with coconut sauce. It's all vegetarian it's all fabulous, it's all authentic and for £5, I'm full for the day.' VC. Try the Diwana's legendary Kulfi.
They have a third branch at 50, Westbourne Grove, W2. Nearly always a queue, you can't book, its uncomfortable cafe style seating, it's brilliant. It's in our TOP 100.

GUPTA CONFECTIONERS
100, Drummond Street, NW1. Tel: 071 380 1590
10am to 9pm (Sunday 12pm to 7pm)
The lightness of touch remains at this snack and sweet takeaway. Freshly cooked samosas the ever superb pea kebab flow daily from the kitchens behind. There is another Gupta at Watford Way, Hendon.

RAVI SHANKAR
133, Drummond Street, NW1. Tel: 071 388 6458
Midday to 11pm. A vegetarian restaurant serving similar food to the nearby Diwana. The decor is somewhat smarter - the food Bombay and South Indian and very inexpensive. See branch entry EC1.

ELSEWHERE IN NW1

GREAT NEPALESE TANDOORI
48, Eversholt Street, NW1. Tel: 081 388 6737
Yes, you can get Nepalese food here. Haku Chulaya, potato pickle, £1.25, Masko Bara, urid dhal bread 95p, Kukhura-ko Masu (chicken curry) £3.75 are examples. Set lunch from £4.95 and set Nepalese dinner from £7. We've had mixed reports, telling us of inconsistencies in the quality of the food - this despite the Nepalese owner's wife being in charge of cooking.

THE KUNZAN **CC DISCOUNT**
112, Lisson Grove, Marylebone, NW1. Tel: 071 724 1450
Ceiling fans, chandeliers, pillars, arches and screens make the Kunzan an attractive venue. It's one of the Kensington Tandoori Group (see entry under W8) so its pedigree is assured. The menu offers no surprises, containing all the well known favourites. Our standard check reveals regular London prices. Popadoms are 40p each, Pullao Rice £1.65, Chicken Curry £3.20. There is a Sunday buffet where you can eat your fill returning as often as you wish for £5.95. The Kunzan offers discounts for Curry Club members at its quieter times, see page 288.

MUMTAZ
4/10, Park Road, Regents Park, NW1. Tel: 071 723 0549
It's had its good times and its not so good. The Mumtaz was one of Londons pioneer 'arty-smarty' restaurants. It still is very smart with slick uniformed waiters. It is not (and never has been) cheap. It attracts a regular following and booking is advisable. The Sunday buffet is popular. Reports welcomed.

TANDOORI NIGHTS
108, Parkway, Regents Park, NW1. Tel: 071 482 1902
This smart restaurant seats 60 and is split between the ground and lower ground floors. You'll find all your favourites on the menu. The cooking is under the direction of Pan Singh Rana. He trained at India's Oberoi hotel group then worked for the Kensington Tandoori Group (see earlier). Reports we get glow with praise for all the group's restaurants (branches are at Cockfosters, Herts and the Saheli Brasserie, 35, Great Queen Street, WC2). Prices are reasonable, Popadoms are 35p each, Pullao Rice £1.50 and Chicken Curry £3.50.

VICEROY OF INDIA **TOP 100**
3, Glentworth Street, off Baker Street, NW1. Tel: 071 486 3401
The Viceroy is quite huge (150 seats). It is not easy to locate - it doesn't rely on passing trade. It is, however, very well known having appeared in numerous guides including our own. It is even better known by the

Indian community whose upper echelons use the venue almost as a club. Many-a-function Indian wedding, Air India banquet, Government of India entertaining and so on takes place at the Viceroy. Its Indian owner, Mohindra Kaul, is well repected in these circles. The editor has eaten there on several occasions. We even put it in our TOP 30 last time. Why is it then that we receive a mixed bag of praise and criticism? One reporter (Mrs AR) told of hassle from the staff, extremely small portions and a rip off bill - £105 for four. This was just after we published our last edition in 1986 and she claimed it made the rest of the publication 'very suspect indeed'. She was not alone. More recently, we've had reports heaping praise on the place. 'The service was attentive, the quantities generous, and quality well above average.' PCC. 'I visited here with some Asian business acquaintances. We were all very impressed by everything. The food was excellent, the place immaculate and service unobtrusive.' IW. The decor is absolutely wonderful. Red brick contrasts with white marble in split level flooring. Open view kitchens allow the diner to watch the chefs at work. Each of the five chefs specialises in one area. There is even a sweets chef. Try the Gulab Jamun flambQed with brandy. Prices are higher than the norm, with 10% service expect to pay £15 a head plus drinks. Buffet lunch is £9.95. Despite my earlier proviso I am retaining this restaurant in our TOP 100.

NW2 : CRICKLEWOOD

KHANA
68, Cricklewood Broadway, NW2. Tel: 081 452 4789
Well reported curry house.

PINK RUPEE **CC DISCOUNT**
38, Cricklewood Broadway, NW2.081 452 7665
Unique name, but despite its owner being Nepalese the menu is standard curry house stuff. It's good though and reasonably priced for London. Papadoms are 30p each, Pullao Rice £1.25, Chicken Curry £2.95. Note the hours: 6pm to 2am daily. They give discounts to Curry Club members, see page 288.

NW3 : HAMPSTEAD and SWISS COTTAGE

BELSIZE TANDOORI **CC DISCOUNT**
58, Belsize lane, NW3. Tel: 071 794 8643
Well established (1968) Bangladeshl venue which, after a name change or two, continues to serve 'resoundingly successful curries,' GB. The prices are reasonable and they give discounts to Curry Club members at their quieter times, see page 288.

BULLOCK CART **CC DISCOUNT**
77, Heath Street, NW3. Tel: 071 435 3602
They've heard all the jokes about their name, but you're welcome to add yours if you wish. Name aside, it's an above average establishment serving 'good curries.' DR. Reasonable prices, and they give a discount to Curry Club members at their quieter times, see page 288.

CURRY MANJIL
34, England's Lane, NW3. Tel: 071 722 9101
We hear of 'well balanced spicing, freshness and excellence at this old Bengali establishment.' JG.

FLEET TANDOORI
104, Fleet Road, NW3. Tel: 071 485 6402
Continues to prosper although we did receive one report from one of our much travelled regulars who was 'underwhelmed by both food and service.' AD. It was lunchtime and empty. We hear it still buzzes at night. Reports please.

PADMA
72, Belsize Lane, NW3. Tel: 071 794 7952
Another long standing restaurants (1968) going about its business quietly and confidently. Prices outer London average.

NW4 : HENDON

PRINCE OF CEYLON
39, Watford Way, NW4. Tel: 081 202 5967
Worthy of its entry into this Guide not only because it cooks good food, but it cooks Sri Lankan (Ceylon) food. 'There are so few who do. Try the Hoppers (pancakes) or the Ambu Thiyal (fish curry) heaped with the many sambals (chutneys) which accompany it.' PTR. 'The main thing is to reap the rewards of being adventurous and try new things.' EC.

NW5 : KENTISH TOWN

BENGAL LANCER **TOP 100 & CC DISCOUNT**
253, Kentish Town Road, NW5. Tel: 071 485 6688
Call Kentish Town dowdy and you'll probably be thumped by the huge, personable owner of this restaurant, Stanley Krett. He describes himself as cockney with a Polish background. OK, so Kentish Town is not Hampstead, but as with many inner London suburbs it is on the way up, and Stan's Bengal Lancer not only reflects this, it leads it. It was established as far back as 1984, and it pioneered the nostalgic decor/ atmosphere now to be found from Dumfries to Devon. Clean lines, cane furniture, framed British Raj and Indian army prints, plants, airy bar and breezy staff are led by General Krett. He's often there and he's the first to tell you that he himself pioneered Indian cookery (he said that on national TV - but he'll probably still thump me!) despite the fact that it's been around for hundreds of years and his quieter partner, Akrim Ali, is to be found in the kitchen himself.
None-the-less and joking aside, the combination of flamboyant host and silent action man produces a super restaurant. The numbered menu (101 items) produces few surprises. It's all well known and much loved food. But the 101 items are, we are assured, generally cooked superbly. We have received a minor criticism or two, (this is not unusual, it seems) but we are happy to retain the Bengal Lancer in our TOP 100 list (see page 24). Prices are quite reasonable and they give a discount to Curry Club members at their quieter times, see page 288.

NW6 : WILLESDEN AND KILBURN

BENGAWAN SOLO INDONESIAN RESTAURANT
45, Kilburn High Road, NW6. Tel: 071 624 7477
Extremely popular with our correspondents who recommend Indonesian food, 'as a spicy alternative to standard curries' ST. Infact you can get curries here, 'The Gula Daging, a Sumatram Beef Curry £3.50, with Nasi Goreng, fried rice with all the trimmings £3.20 and an assortment of chutneys, left me wishing I'd not had the starter - but, oh my, it was memorable.' PT.

GEETA SOUTH INDIAN RESTAURANT
57, Willesden Lane, NW6. Tel: 071 624 1713
Geeta's is a very longstanding feature in Willesden. It was an early pioneer of South Indian vegetarian food in England. 'Everything is always so fresh and reflects a remarkable lightness of touch in the kitchens.' DTA. Sour green bananas, sweet yam potatoes, bitter gourds, all come lashed with savoury sauces. Dosas, Idlis, Upamas (variations on a theme involving rice and lentil flour). Samosa, soups (rasam), Coconut chutney, rice - it's all there, delicious and inexpensive.

NEW KILBURN SHAMA **CC DISCOUNT**
51, Kilburn High Road, NW6. Tel: 071 372 1148
When the owner is the chef it often means better cooking. Kaptan Singh's menu includes trout, and quail amongst a familiar cost list of curry goodies. It opened in mid 1990 to a flurry of reports but we'd like more please. They give discounts to Curry Club members at their quieter times, see page 288.

SURYA
59/61, Fortune Green Road, NW6. Tel: 071 435 7486
North and South Indian vegetarian dishes here. One correspondent raves about the Tali at £7.50, which he and his wife 'take regularly.' GP.

Another tells of the dish of the day, 'today it was Avial - a sour sauce, relieved with sweetish coconut, coated with some fresh exotic vegetables.' BP. Inexpensive and different.

VIJAY
49, Willesden Lane, NW6. Tel: 071 328 1087
A happy atmosphere is generated at Vijay's. Like nearby Geeta's, it's been around for a long time (1965) and helped to pioneer South Indian Vegetarian food to the UK. Unlike Geeta's it does serve meat and chicken dishes which 'are more than passable,' BT. The recent change of ownership has passed by unnoticed, and the vegetarian dishes are still 'the ones to go for, being light, tasty and GOOD FOR YOU!' CD. Masala Dosa, Uthapam, Sambar, Avial, Uppuma, Vadai Iddly and Rasam head the list. The staff will explain. Coconut chutneys and one popadom are free. Prices more than reasonable.

NW7 : MILL HILL

DAY OF THE RAJ **CC DISCOUNT**
123, The Broadway, NW7. Tel: 081 906 3363
'A very smart restaurant, which provides very good service. I recommend the Salmon Masala for £5.20, lightly spiced and with cream and almonds and the Kushboo, a curry with a thick herby/spicy sauce, £4.20 for chicken and £6.50 for King prawn.' CD. It was the LBC radio 'restaurant of the year' in 1989. They welcome Curry Club members and will give discounts on takeaways only (see page 288).

NW10 : WILLESDEN

BRENT TANDOORI **CC DISCOUNT**
24, High Road, NW10. Tel: 081 4590649
This takeaway-only is reported as being clean., generous, prompt and efficient. The food is evidently well liked and the prices reasonable. Owner MM Ali welcomes Curry Club members to whom a discount is available at quieter times, see page 288.

SABRAS VEGETARIAN **TOP 100**
263, High Road, NW10. Tel: 081 459 0340
Red, white and green - Indian national colours - are the theme here. The tiled floor, marble effect wall paper and good lighting give the place a bright, fresh and airy feel. It has only 32 seats and is nearly always full. Nalinee and Hemant Desai (the husband and wife team who own Sabras) are always present. She runs the kitchens, he front of house. They close on Monday's and for two weeks in Summer and two in winter, and last orders are at 9.45pm so it is advisable to phone to book.
The food is vegetarian only and brings together the choicest items from the Indian subcontinent. The menu is extensive and superbly explanatory. If you think vegetarian food is boiled cabbage and nuts, this menu will dispell that.
There is every combination of fritter and rissole, hot soup and cold bhel puri. Dhosas from South India vie for you to choose with Gujarati curries. There are five types of rice, four dals and seven breads. The best idea in the eyes of some of our correspondents is to go for set meals, £7.50 and £10 and in the winter months you might like the filling substantial Surati Undhui with four puris for £7.50, (vegetables from the town of Surat). Sweet offerings include five homemade items, plus three Kulfi, and Sabras is an agent for Royal Sweets.
You can eat your fill for £10 or less and they are licensed for wines and beers (no less than 24 from around the world). Indian Veena white wine and Omar Khayyan Indian Champagnoise are available at £6.50 and £12.50 respectively.
Connoisseurs tell us of authentic Indian spicy tea for £1.25. We called this restaurant outstanding in our 1984 Guide and we are delighted to retain it in our TOP 100. There is a service charge of 10%. They cannot do discounts for Curry Club members, but regulars might like to join their own Sabras Club to obtain a 10% discount.

NW11 : GOLDERS GREEN

GURKHA BRASSERIE
756, Finchley Road, NW11 Tel: 081 458 6163
'If it's Nepalese food you want, then this is your place.' RT. Its owner Hari KC was, we hear, a Gurkha himself and he is usually on hand to advise. New comers might choose the Nepalese Thali set meal which includes Momos (meat dumplings) and a selection of authentic tasty curries all for £9.

LONDON SE

SE1 : ELEPHANT AND CASTLE, WATERLOO AND SOUTHWARK

CASTLE TANDOORI
200, Elephant and Castle, SE1. Tel: 071 703 9103
Standard curries, 'mostly good but served apprehensively by a new lad.' VT. Useful late hours (London's latest?) 1am Sundays to Thursdays and 3am Fridays and Saturdays. More reports welcomed.

THAMES TANDOORI
79, Waterloo Road, SE1. Tel: 071 928 3856
Located under the railway bridge, it continues to trade adjacent to the fabulously named FISHCOTHEQUE (Fish and Chip Shop). I suggested last time they ought to change their name to TIKKATEQUE, but no takers. They still do 'superb tikkas', and according to one regular, 'I commute to Basingstoke. This place is my local - anything being better than BR food.' JT. 'The Murgh Makhani with fennel and tomato was creamy and excellent. The Chapattis were cold but the Kulfi good.' SB.

THAMILAN
182/84, Old Kent Road, SE1. Tel: 071 701 3353
It is one of London's few Sri Lankan restaurants. It opened in 1990 and brings 'a breath of fresh air to an area much in need of it.' RS. As is the custom the service is by graceful Sri Lankans: women in saris and courteous men.
The menu contains Sri Lankan favourites - Hoppers, Vadai, Hoppers and String Hoppers (a kind of noodle), Dosa Pancakes and many others. The staff are more than willing to help with your choice. The favourite introduction is the Royal Thali - a complete meal for £8. For a change try Palmyrah - a liquer toddy made from palm. More reports welcomed.

TOWER TANDOORI
74/76, Tower Bridge Road, SE1. Tel: 071 237 2247
Standard competent curries, we hear and a 'simply spendid Sunday buffet.'

SE3 : BLACKHEATH

SOPNA
39, Tranquil Vale, SE9. Tel: 081 852 7872
When we asked our Curry Club members to nominate their favourite restaurant(s) the Sopna received a good number of votes.

SE5 : CAMBERWELL

CAMBERWELL TANDOORI **CC DISCOUNT**
22, Camberwell Church Street, SE5. Tel: 071 708 4342
This establishment is also highly voted for by our regulars. The menu is fully comprehensive, the prices London suburb average (Papadoms 30p

each, Pullao Rice £1.25, Chicken Curry £3.25). The service is direct and confident. Discounts are available to Curry Club members on takeaway only, see page 288.

JOY BANGLA CURRY HOUSE
39, Denmark Hill, SE5. Tel: 071 703 3149
As a good reliable curry house, just as its name implies. 'Don't be put off by the plastic table mats and tatty menus. The food is excellent. The Butter Chicken was sumptuous, the Madras fragrant and the Korma aromatic - and the Kulfi - it was mouth watering.' DM.

SE7 : CHARLTON

TASTE OF THE RAJ
10, The Village, Charlton, SE7. Tel: 081 319 3439
'It's a good sized restaurant with good decor and lighting but the tables are unusually small. Meat Madras £3.25, had a lovely flavour with fresh coriander. They gave a brandy on the house, which they evidently do to all customers. Book at weekends - it's jam paked.' NC.

SE9 : ELTHAM

ELTHAM RAJ **CC DISCOUNT**
138, Wellhall Road, SE9. Tel: 081 859 8423
There are smoking and non-smoking areas in this attractive, seventy seat, pink and grey restaurant. The menu is standard Bangladeshi with all the old favourites. Prices are a little above average - Popadoms 40p each, Pullao Rice £1.40, Chicken Curry £3.20 and set meal £9., however they welcome Curry Club members and give discounts at their quieter times, see page 288.

LUNA TANDOORI
52, Eltham High Street, Eltham, SE9. Tel: 081 850 6578
We hear of springy cane chairs here, set admist mirrors and framed paintings. Mr IW couldn't resist a little joke: 'I hear a curry house has opened on the moon, the food is excellent, but the place has no atmosphere!' Fortunately Eltham's Luna has a great atmosphere provided by experienced, competent staff used to the odd wag.

MAHATMA TANDOORI
156, Bexley Road, Averyhill, SE9. Tel: 081 859 7954
DR says, 'It's worth an extra mile each way to go here for excellent food, generous helpings and reasonable prices.' What are your views?

SE10 : GREENWICH

MANDALAY **TOP 100**
10, Greenwich, South Street, SE10. Tel: 081 691 0443
Mandalay was once capital of Burma. It's greater claim to fame might lie with Bob Hope and Bing Crosby's 'Road.' Burma recently relaxed its restrictions on tourism and visitors are allowed in for up to 14 days. For those with neither time nor purse to make this fascinating trip, I must urge you to take to Road to Greenwich. There you will find Europe's one and only Burmese restaurant. The food combines the styles of its neighbours, Indian, Bangladesh, Laos, Thailand and China. Burmese cooking is quite distinctive in itself providing a 'missing link.' There are spicy curries and rice is a staple. Noodles and fish sauce are also indispensable. There are no religious proscriptions on eating so you will find recipes for Beef, Pork, Duck, Chicken, shellfish and fish in combination or solo.
The national dish is a soup called Mohinga. It's fish based and packed with noodles and is served with a string of accompaniments including pazoon (pakora-like fritters). The owner, Gerald Andrews is half Burmese and an excellent chef. He is always on hand to explain the menu, enthusiastically and comprehensively. Kaushwe Kyaw for example is noodles with chicken pieces spiced with garam masala and served as a cold starter. The 'meal-on-a-plate' dishes are substantial. Duck, pork or beef curries with coconut rice are fresh and sing with tantalising, 'what-is-it' combinations of fresh galangal tamarind, fish sauce, prawn paste,

coconut, coriander and chilli (they keep the heat well below authentic Burmese levels).
As with Indian food, sweets are a bit one paced. San win ma kin is a variation on halwa and is based on semolina fried with ghee and coconut milk, then baked. Burmese tea is served throughout the meal. The restaurant seats 58 and is now open on Tuesday to Saturday evenings only and for Sunday lunch. Booking is essential, but take the road to Mandalay and go there. Decidedly in our TOP 100.

MOGHUL TANDOORI
10, Greenwich Church Street, SE10. Tel: 081 858 6790
A lot of people have brought the Moghul to our attention. It seats 90 over two floors. It's largely the regular curry house menu but, for those who welcome a change, there are one or two Nepalese specials such as Aloo Tama for £1.95, potato, bamboo shoots, black-eyed beans and tomato cooked with green herbs and spices, and Kukhura-ko-Masu for £4, chicken curry on the bone Nepalese style.

SE11 : KENNINGTON

GANDHI'S
347A, Kennington Road, SE11. Tel: 071 735 9015
It continues to be commended.

SE13 : LEWISHAM

SPICE OF LIFE **CC DISCOUNT**
260, Lee High Road, SE13. Tel: 081 852 5414
Extremely popular forty seat Bangladeshi curry house offering 'just a little bit more... Kolijee Puri £1.95, for example is chicken liver spiced on puri bread and Lamb Tikka Badami for £5.25 involving almonds, cream and ghee. They pinched the chef from the Carioca and it shows' AT. 'The new carrot chutney which is supplied free with six others, is the talk of Lewisham.' MM. 'I've never tasted fish like the Tandoori mackerel - it makes my mouth water even to write about it.' MS. 'The standards of their dishes is equal to prestigious restaurants in the West End.' FT. They welcome Curry Club members and will give discounts at their quieter times, see page 288. Closed Tuesdays.

SE19 : NORWOOD

EASTERN PARADISE
36, Westow Hill, SE19. Tel: 081 761 1154
A popular place with an eye to good PR. 'We went for a takeaway and got a parking ticket. Next time we went (for a sit down meal) they gave us a free bottle of wine to make up for it.' LP

JALSHA GHAR **CC DISCOUNT**
138, Gipsey Hill, SE19. Tel: 081 761 6688
Many well known favourites are there on the menu along with some interesting specials. Chicken Zafrani £5.25, for example, involves saffron, egg, nuts and almonds and is very spicy. Tandoori Duck £4.75 is unusual. So is Karahi Jeera Tikka £4.35, where lamb is cooked with cummin. Nasi Goreng £4.45 is an Indonesian rice dish, spicy with shredded chicken, prawns egg and spring onions.
MA Hannan is the owner and he welcomes Curry Club members with discounts at their quieter times, see page 288.

SE22 : EAST DULWICH

GOLDEN TANDOORI
49, North Cross Road, SE22. Tel: 081 693 0402
Standard Bangladeshi cooking, popular in the area. It stays open late (1am weekdays, 2am Fridays and Saturdays).

SE23 : FOREST HILL

BABUR BRASSERIE
119, Brockley Rise, SE23. Tel: 081 291 2400
It's upmarket all the way. The forty seat room has plants and paintings and beige and pink table covers and maroon low-back chairs. The menu

is smart too with gold blocking and an explanation that Babur was the first Moghul Emperor. The cooking by M Khawaja (25 years a chef) is Moghul style. There are some nice touches. Aloo Choff £1.95, are mashed potatoes and vegetables rolled in cashew nuts and fried rissole - style. Mach Tikka £4.95, is tandoori cod, Patrani Machli £5.25 is halibut coated in a herby purQe, wrapped in banana leaf and steamed. There is a good vegetable selection - courgettes and red pumpkin appear amongst old favourites. Prices are higher than London suburb norm. They have a takeaway only branch, Babur Takeaway, 443, Brockley Road, Crofton Park, SE4.

DEWANIAM **TOP 100**
133, Stanstead Road, SE23. Tel: 081 291 4778
After all the years since we first wrote about the Dewaniam, we still know of no other Indian restaurant with such a wide range of ingredients. Quail, pheasant, partridge, goose, duck, venison, hare, lobster, trout etc. Cooking of these exotic ingredients is above average and to authentic Indian recipes. It would be as well to phone in advance to check whether an 'unusual' item is available. Given enough warning we're assured it will be. The cooking is very assured, and uses wine and brandy when necessary. Nawabi Pheasant £6.95, is marinated in yoghurt, red wine, fresh herbs and spices and barbecued in the tandoor. Brain Masallah £4.34, or Hare Biriani £7.50 are for thoise who seek the exotic and Shahi Jinga (Lobster) Massallah £18.95 is a gorgeous curry for those seeking luxury. Exceptionally good. In our TOP 100.

SE24 : HERNE HILL

HERNE HILL TANDOORI **CC DISCOUNT**
220, Railton Road, (opp BR), SE24. Tel: 071 274 4480
R Islam also owns the Harrogate Tandoori in N Yorkshire (see entry). Both are smartly appointed restaurants. Herne Hill seats 62 and it has been going since 1962 - nearly 30 years - a long time in curry house terms. Cooking is Banladeshi and it is 'formula curry'. Prices are outer London norm: Papadoms 35p, Pullao Rice £1.35, Chicken curry £3.25. Set dinner is £21.95 for two. Mr Islkam welcomes Curry Club members to whom discounts are available to Curry Club members at their quieter times, see page 288.

SE26 : SYDENHAM

JEHANGIR **TOP 100 & CC DISCOUNT**
67, Sydenham Road, SE26. Tel: 081 676 8641
'As soon as you step from an ordinary street scene into this restaurant you know it will be different. We were greeted by not one but two graceful waitresses in saris and were ushered to our reserved table to find Bombay mix to nibble.' GT.
The room is gorgeously decorated with vaulted archways, marble floors, hand painted ceiling complete with huge colonial fan, mahogany carvers and Wedgewood crockery. The menu is astounding. It runs to 10 pages and contains a massive 143 numbered items. It is a combination of Indian (North and South) and Sri Lankan with a touch of the Maldive Islands thrown in.
Everything is exceptionally well described. There are 23 starters, 'Hot Tempered Prawns for £3.75 are indeed hot and the Gothamba Roti for £1.25, a thin bread, is indeed silky. There are 8 types of Dosai (urid and rice flour panckaes), idlis and three hoppers.
Main courses include 13 chicken, 12 lamb and 10 seafood dishes, many of which use imported Sri Lankan fish. Breads, rice and biriyanis (their spelling) are followed by one of the most remarkable vegetarian selections we've seen. (over 23 dishes).
'Just reading the menu along took us a pair of G and T's. The choice is mind blowing.' BR. There are several thalis ranging from £9.95 to £17.50 per head.
Nice touches here include perfumed face towels and chocolate mints. They are extremely good with customer care. On the special occasion - cards, flowers or cake or champagne is given by the management. The Jehangir delivers to your home (3 mile radius over £10) which is useful. Jehingir was a great Moghul emperor, who described his luxurious palace

as paradise on earth. The Jehangir restaurant sub titles itself 'the taste of paradise'. The food service and decor is indeed way above average. Prices are a little above average, but you would expect that. We are pleased to put the Jehangir into our TOP 100. Mrs Kugan, the proprietor welcomes Curry Club members and will give discounts at their quieter times, see page 288. Note: it is closed on Mondays.

SE27 : WEST NORWOOD

PASSAGE TO INDIA
232, Gipsey Road, SE27. Tel: 081 670 7602
'In true Bangladeshi style, the food from the tandoori is its strength. Succulent, spicy chicken tikka that just melts in your mouth, excellent breads, particularly their Peshwari Naan. Rice dishes are a weakness, though. They fall short of mouthwatering spicing. Mr Ali cares for his regulars with a free snifter of brandy for the gentlemen and a Tia Maria for the lady'. JG.

LONDON SW

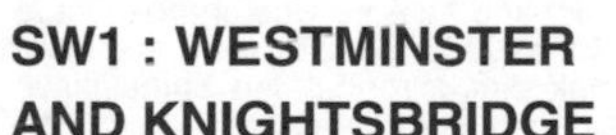

SW1 : WESTMINSTER AND KNIGHTSBRIDGE

JOMUNA
74, Wilton Road, SW1. Tel: 071 828 7509
We start London SW with a long established (1958) relatively inexpensive (rare for this area) standard curry house. 'The quantities are still on the small side, but the quality is all you'd hope for.' DC.

KUNDAN
3, Horseferry Road, Westminster. SW1. Tel: 071 834 3434
It's been called the 'third house' or 'the house of curry'. You'll seldom go in there and fail to see a politician or three who have skipped over the road from the other two Houses. (There are plenty of MP's and Lords who adore curry.) It's a tough life though and an hour in politics is a long time. Just as you are about to tuck in a loud bell rings. No, it's not the fire alarm, it's the division bell, and in a clattering flash the honourable members are off to the vote. You pay dearly for this excitement. The average price per head is £15, to which you add drink, cover charge and a service charge at a record breaking 15%. And the food: reports received tell us of inconsistencies in quality. On the whole it remains good for star gazing rather than star cuisine. More reports welcomed.

SALLOOS **TOP 100**
62/64, Kinnerton Street, Knightsbridge. SW1. Tel: 071 235 4444
When you do actually manage to locate Salloos in its maze of back streets which make Hampton Court look like Toys-R-Us, don't expect to walk in off the street and get a seat - it's eternally full. 'We're overbooked, actually,' said the rather superior hostess at her reception desk, when I made the mistake of popping in unannounced one Tuesday night. If you do take the trouble to book finding a parking place is the next drama. And be warned, Salloos is not cheap.
I get an enormous amount of reporting on this restaurant, written and by word of mouth, especially from the Asian community. Salloos is immensely popular with London's well healed Asians, both Indian and Pakistani, and they are probably more critical than the indigenous population.
So why is Salloos so special? Firstly, it is not an Indian restaurant. It is one of a rare breed - it is Pakistani. Secondly it is not a formula curry house. The emphasis here is on quality cooking. And it is here that the criticism is directed. At £3.50 for starters and £10 for main course dishes,

£4 for Pullao Rice and £1 for a chapatti, it is quite easy to spend £25 per head. With a cover charge, a hefty 15% service charge and a decent bottle of wine, you're up at £35 and more. This makes it expensive in the world of curry. And when you charge these sort of prices, your clientelle expects perfection in every department. Usually you get it ...' clearly there are chefs here who are comfortable with spicing. The cooking is so inviting and so sure.' TL. 'The waiter complemented us on our choice. The Bhajias were exceptional and the Basmati Rice beautifully spiced. Certainly an uplifting experience.' AD. 'It was the best Mulligatwany soup and Tandoori Chaamp Chop I've had.' CD. Not all the reporting is unanimous, 'Our breads were forgotten and were cold when , after three reminders, they came.' LSR. Despite these uneven reports we are in no doubt that it should be in our TOP 100, see page 24.

WOODLANDS **CC DISCOUNT**
37, Panton Street, SW1. Tel: 071 486 3862
'I thought it looked enticing. I was surprised how small it was.' JL. 'Having walked past on a dozen occasions, I eventually went in. The welcome, service and food amounted to a first class evening. Cashew nuts fried in crisp firm batter served with chutneys, vegetable Dosa served with hot sauce and coconut chutney was excellent.' DRC.
'Anthony and Cleopatra were having a rough time and so were Marion and I. By the interval we could stand it no longer and made tracks for the open air. Having become thoroughly miserable by this time what better to cheer us than a quick Indian indulgence and, but a moment's flight from the Haymarket Theatre, we found Woodlands. Having abandoned our (uncheap) theatre seats a little extra indulgence seemed tolerable. This was just as well otherwise the price list and 12% service charge would almost certainly have kept us out. But we decided to brave it and went into the long, narrow, white and pink dining room. An enthusiastic manager attempted happily to explain the incomprehensible vegetarian offers. Two Thalis were offered. I suppose we were fortunate in receiving a whole Popadom between us as we didn't know we'd ordered it but we thought it was setting the size of quantities for the rest when our Thalis arrived. The selections were presented with all the hoped for flourish but not the hoped for volumes. 'We won't get fat on that,' announced Marion. However, a few ecstatic nibbles of my lacey pancake later and I was converted. So was Marion who ate the rest of it. A couple of gastronomic orgasms later we were bursting. The food was so good I completely forgave the rocky table, nasty music and nearly forgave the 12%. It's only money after all.' RC. And things are improved for Curry Club members by ther discount available at their quieter times, see page 288.

SW2 : BRIXTON

DAWN OF THE RAJ
99, Brixton Hill, SW2. Tel: 081 671 4216
The usual selection of curries, 'A port in the storm,' for JD. No surprises but no shocks either.

SW3 : KNIGHTSBRIDGE AND CHELSEA

SHAHEEN OF KNIGHTSBRIDGE
225, Brompton Road, SW3. Tel: 071 581 5329
Standard curries served at a standard which never seems to vary. Prices are relatively cheap for Knightsbridge.

TANDOORI OF CHELSEA **TOP 100**
153, Fulham Road, SW3. Tel: 071 589 7617
The clue is in the name - it's decidedly up-market and its cooking reflects that, with greater subtlety, softer tones and an absense of hysterical food colouring. So no standard curry by number and heat grading menu. Certainly not! This carefully thought out selection of dishes, with some surprises. The Tandoori section includes Trout and main courses include Fish Masala and Jinga (Prawns) Chicken dishes include Murgh Moghlai - chicken cooked in yoghurt and garnished with whole almonds and edible silver leaf (said by the Moghul emperors to be an aphrodisiac - they ate copious quanitites of it and they bred prolifically!!). There are ample vegetarian dishes and a wine list as carefully thought out as the food. The

restaurant's owner, A Rajan, is a believer in good wine accompanying well cooked Indian food. 'It is not overpowered by subtle spicing,' he says. 'That is why we have Chateau Latour on the menu.' Asked if one should drink lager with his food he exploded 'Certainly not, spice and gas don't mix!' Expect to pay for the name and the location. £20-£30 per head is average). An exceedingly good restaurant in our TOP 100, see page 24.

SW4 : CLAPHAM

MAHARANI
117, Clapham High Street, SW4. Tel: 071 622 2530
SU Khan's Maharani is something of an institution. It was established in 1958, which, in curry house terms, is extremely long. It has therefore built up a couple of generations of regulars. After nearly 3 decades it knows what it is doing. Or it should do. However, about two years ago we detected an uneven patch. We hope it has recovered and is back to its normal self again. Its popularity with young trendies, of which Clapham now abounds is not in dispute. Booking is essential despite its large 102 seat capacity. The paintings on the wall, representing daily life in the sub-continent, are colourful, and contrast with a splendid mahogany ceiling and hanging plants. The menu is standard. Indeed the Maharani was one of the founder members of the formula. We hope that the Maharani remains at the top of its tree and welcome more reports please.

SHAH IN SHAH
126, Clapham High Street, SW4. Tel: 071 622 0452
Continues to be a popular standard curryhouse.

SW5 : EARLS COURT

BHARAT
275, Old Brompton Road, SW5. Tel: 071 373 8660
'A small restaurant with good service and food chosen from a standard menu. Onion Bhajia the best. The Vegetarian Thali consisted of Pea and Paneer, Mixed Vegetable Curry, Spinach Curry, Tarka Dhal, Raita, Pullao Rice and Naan Bread all for £12. Too much really but all good.' ED. Owner Abu Shahidullah at one time offered £100 if you could guess the exact geographical location of any of his recipes. The odds would be presumably with the house as SW5 is as good as any answer! Do they still do that?

STAR OF INDIA **TOP 100**
154, Old Brompton Road, SW5. Tel: 071 373 2901
The Star was founded in 1959 and was the sister to the now closed but well remembered Shah of Drummond Street (RIP). Now run by the sons of the founders, The Star has undergone a recent metamorphosis with a 'stunning and fabulous re-dec.' KB. The food remains as reliable as ever. In our top 100

SW6 : FULHAM

THE EAST INDIAN RESTAURANT
448, Fulham Road, Fulham Broadway, SW6. Tel: 071 381 2588
You'll get the perfect formula Bangladeshi curry from the long established (1964) East Indian. It will come as no surprise to find that Chicken Tikka Masala £5 and Chicken Korma £3.25 are their best sellers. For the record Pullao Rice is £1.25 and Popadoms 25p.

KABANA
541, King Road, Fulham, SW6. Tel: 071 731 0039
They tell us the most popular dish here is the Kabana Karahi Gosht £5. The Butter Chicken £5 is cooked in a ghee-based sauce and served with nuts and cream. Papadoms are 30p, Pullao Rice £1.50 and there is a service charge of 10%.

NAYAB **CC DISCOUNT**
309, New King's Road, SW6. Tel: 071 736 9596
Pakistani and Northern Indian cooking, 'from Delhi to Lahore is the style here', according to Praveen Rai, who says on his menu, 'there are dishes

EST. 1958

Maharani

INDIAN RESTAURANT

FULLY LICENSED

Highly recommended by the AA, RAC, Time Out, Capital Radio, What's On, Curry Club, City Limits, South London Press, and many well known celebrities including members of Parliament.

SUNDAY BUFFET UNTIL 4.30PM. £6.95 PER HEAD.

There is a wide variety of exotic delicacies on a buffet for you to select. You may help yourself as often and as much as you like. The buffet includes a portion of sweet.

TAKE AWAY SERVICE AVAILABLE

117 CLAPHAM HIGH STREET, LONDON SW4

TEL: 071-622 2530

Open: Monday to Friday	12 noon to 3 pm
	6 pm to Midnight
Saturday & Sunday	12 noon to Midnight

OPEN 7 DAYS A WEEK

NAYAB

INDIAN RESTAURANT

309 NEW KINGS ROAD
PARSONS GREEN
LONDON SW6
01-731-6993/01-736-9596

Monday to Saturday
Lunch: Noon – 2.45 p.m. Last Orders
Dinner: 7.00 p.m. – 11.45 p.m. Last Orders

Sundays
Lunch: 12.30 p.m. – 3 p.m. Last Orders
Dinner: 6.30 p.m. – 11 p.m. Last Orders

you won't recognise and some that you will. Some you won't find because they are not authentic Bangalore Phal, hottest of the hot, exist only in the mind of those 'curry house chef's' taking revenge on the indignities inflicted upon their establishments by those now known as 'lager louts'. The spelling of Bangalore Phal varies considerably, but is a derivation of the Hindi phrase 'Bhund Phar' which means, politely, bottom-ripping.' Well thank you Mr Rai - needless to say neither lager louts, Bangalore Phals, nor bottom ripping chefs inhabit the Nayab. Amidst an elegant menu nestle unique goodies such as 'Hot Legs' (Kalmi Kebab) barbecued drumsticks, £2.50. Tava Gosht Lahori £5.25, pan fried tandooried lamb. Haleem £4.95, pounded meat and wheat, and Meat Dhaba Wala £5.25 meat and mince curry. The Nayab first opened in SW10 and moved here in 1987, where it has settled happily. As you can see Mr Rai enjoys a joke and loves talking about food. He's often there and he welcomes Curry Club members who will obtain a discount at quieter times, see page 288.

UDDIN'S MANZIL
194, Wandsworth Bridge Road, SW6. Tel: 071 736 3584
Continues competently at reasonable prices.

SW7 : SOUTH KENSINGTON

BOMBAY BRASSERIE **TOP 100**
14, Courtfield Close, opp Gloucester Road Tube, SW7.
Tel: 071 370 4040
After an absence of some years I have been to the Bombay Brasserie on three occasions in the last year. One was an intimate meal for four, another was with a dinner group of twenty five and the third occasion was at a lunchtime formal function held by Indian businessmen. The turn out at the latter function was about sixty guests, Indian journalists included. The product they were launching, an Indian lager, placed them in the food and beverage trade, so you would expect, with such knowlegeable and distinguished company that the buffet lunch would be something outstanding. Astoundingly it was quite the reverse. It was frankly uninspired and boring and it left at least one Indian journalist apologising to me and offering to 'show you how good Indian restaurant food can be in the UK.' KM (see Omi's, Southall, Middlesex). The large dinner party was also held by a company in the UK food business, who were hosting a function for their clients attending a major exhibition. This was a set meal to a budget but there was ample choice cooked well and delivered with panache. The small dinner with friends was outstanding. The welcome, the service and the quality of the a la carte food and all that went with it could not have been bettered. On each occasion the action took place in the conservatory and the restaurant was, as usual, completely full. The point I am making is that I had all points of the compass, in the period of a few months. Poor, good and outstanding. Perhaps my own experiences help to understand the fluctuations we get in the many reports we receive. And in terms of numbers we receive, the Bombay Brasserie gets by far the most. Here are some comments: 'Over an eighteen month period I went there at least 15 times. I had no booking problems and superb service and food.' HD. 'My lunch visit gave me chicken pepperwalla (in a creamy sauce with black peppercorns), and Lamb Bohla Puri (meat on the bone for aded depth) both were superb as were the vegetables, bread and pudding. As much as you like for £10.' AD. 'A marvellous experience - tomato Pullao, Dhal - everything was superb.' JL. 'We agree the food and surroundings are exceptional - possibly the best. So too was the service.' P and LG. 'The Ragara Pattice and Sev Batata Puri both £3.50, were attractive and the Mutton Rasa with white rice excellent. Smallish rice portion but we couldn't have eaten any more anyway.' NS. 'A splendid welcome for a charming hostess. A good round table provided. The Maitre D appeared with menus instantly. Fresh Malala Popadoms appeared. The Bombay Tiffin was dreadful but Sev Batata Puri fantastic. The Achar Gosht was dreamy and Mirchi Chicken Kashmiri, both £8.50 excellent. Everyone was delighted with a very successful evening.' TD.
We had a wave of unfavourable reports three years ago but these have subsided into an occasion disgruntled protest.
I am still convinced that these come from diners expecting formula curries rather than the more authentic Indian cookery from this outpost of India's celebrated Taj Hotel Group. The five chefs (including the legendary

'Auntie' from Goa) each specialise in their own area. They produce supremely good food (usually) for the 180 seat restaurant from a tiny kitchen which says much for the discipline and training. If I have one criticism or recommendation it would be to stop serving the 'free' three vegetable curries. Firstly, they are unexpected, so it can play havoc with your ordering, secondly, they are generally cold and thirdly, they seem to be tired and jaded. It would be preferable to give larger rice portions. Despite the criticisms, The Bombay Brasserie is undoubtedly is world class, and at the top of its tree. It is expensive in formula curry house terms (to which it should not be compared), but placed alongside a top London French restaurant prices are favourable. With all the trimmings expect to pay £35 to £50. Booking (well in advance) is advisable. Despite our provisos, it decidedly remains very high in our TOP 100

MAJLIS
32, Gloucester Road, SW7. Tel: 071 589 3476

MEMORIES OF INDIA
18, Gloucester Road, SW7. Tel: 071 589 6450
Both in the same ownership. Both very popular. Tandooris are well reported as are Lamb Pasanda £4.90 and fresh vegetable dishes average £2.20.

SHEZAN
16, Cheval Place, off Montpelier Street, SW7.071 589 0314
Easy enough to find in a street opposite the world's most famous store. Ridiculous parking - take the tube. It'll probably be all you can afford when you get the bill so be warned. Despite the same warning last Guide, I still got a hefty complaint about its prices. The decor and presentation are top of the market. The food is, according to most reports, above average, but not outstanding.

SW9 : STOCKWELL

ROYAL TANDOORI **CC DISCOUNT**
66, Brixton Road, SW9. Tel: 071 735 6012
You tell us this is the best of the Brixton batch. It's formula Bangladeshi curry house stuff at reasonable prices. Popadoms 35p each, Pullao Rice £1.30, and Chicken Curry £3.20, made even more reasonable by a discounts for Curry Club members at their quieter times, see page 288.

SW10 : WEST BROMPTON

CHUTNEY MARY **OUR TOP RESTAURANT**
535, King's Road, SW10. Tel: 071 351 3113
This restaurant opened in August 1990 amidst a great deal of publicity and protest. Protest because of its conservatory from some rather narrow minded neighbours, but more of that later, and publicity because Chutney Marys proclaimed itself as being the world's first Anglo Indian restaurant. Great Britain's links with India go directly back nearly 400 years. The term 'Anglo-Indian' was in use before 1800 to describe a unique mixed culture, Indian words entered the English language - bungalow and verandah, boutique and mansoon, shampoo and shawl, polo and tattoo, juggernaut and dungerees, cummerband and cash - all were, and still are, Indian words.
'Chutney Mary' itself a somewhat derogatory term used by conservative Indians to describe a new breed of Indian woman who, at the latter days of the Raj, took the decision to forsake tradition and the sari for western ways. In the 1930's such freedom was frowned upon by both communities. It was unjustly regarded as being 'loose' and of dubious morality. The male version was called the 'Pickle John'.
Today we can smile at the notion, and be thankful that such pioneering has resulted in liberal thinking. We can enjoy its wit and the use of the name for a contemporary London restaurant.
The Chutney Mary name and concept is the brainchild of Namita Panjabi. Born in Bombay and educated at Cambridge University, her self declared mission in life to keep alive the culinary attributes of Anglo India. Though Namita is a modern Indian she is no Chutney Mary. She wears traditional Indian clothes and is an absolute stickler for detail. She is, in short a

perfectionist especially in culinary matters. She had been 'brought up on a hybrid blend of both strictly traditional Indian dishes and Anglo-Indian food'. Namita had a overwhelming desire to bring a collection of dishes to London.

To bring her concept into being, she researched for years to rediscover the 'forgotton foods' of India. But do not imagine that this will bring to your table a succession of wishy washy nondescript dishes. The great proportion of Chutney Mary's menu is truly authentic Indian cooking.

Chutney Mary does not escape criticism, of course. The decor has been described as tacky and excessive the food bland and the service absent. The editors of this Guide have been to Chutney Mary's on several occasions and they can vouch for excellence in all departments which can seldom be matched elsewhere.

The decor: The outside is an uninspiring modern London commercial property. Go through the mahogany and brass revolving door and step into the colonial fantasty world of the Verandah Bar. Bamboo chairs and tables, exotic palms, and coco plants, huge brass ceiling fans, brass cobra-snake lamp standards, and Roman blinds are set into place by a dramatic mahogany bar at the far end. An upright piano completes the scene.

You are invited to sit and relax in the splendour of days gone sipping your chota peg or your Cobra Imported Indian Lager in its authentic pint bottle. You can order pre-meal snacks (baskets of homemade samosas with chutneys for example) or you can have a complete three course lunch or supper for £9.95.

Those choosing to take a fully fledged meal descend to the lower level restaurant. First impressions are of uncluttered decor. Pale walls are enhanced by 19th century Raj prints, posters and murals. With mirrored alcoves with glass shelves are sprinkled with Indian nick nacks.

The square tables and their settings are very inviting. But there is more. Turn right and the scene is transformed into the Indian jungle. A vast conservatory extends the room into a courtyard. It was this which offended the neighbours. Without it Chutney Mary would be the poorer.

The toilets, incidently are, as you'd expect - immaculate. Floor to ceiling marble-effect tiles, large mirror, brass taps, tissues, hand cream - it's all there, spotless and inviting. The male toilet is called - wait for it - 'The Pickle John', and the female - well naturally - Chutney Mary!

The place is large, and its nonchalent 'no-expense spared' philosophy is captivating and enchanting.

The owners of Chutney Mary have gone to considerable trouble to create a 'Colonial Club' environment where their customers can relax into their own fantasty. If it requires a splash of show-biz designeritis to make take one out of the real world (not to mention the washing up) for an hour or three, then it has succeeded.

And so to the food. It is here that Miss Panjabi comes into her own. Everything that is on the menu is, 'home made.' Masalas (spice mixtures), some of which are especially mixed in India, (such as botle masala and special Dhansak Masala) and certain individual spices such as Kashmiri chillies (used for their deep red colour rather than for pure heat), edible silver leaf and fresh curry leaves.

In the kitchen, spotless and superbly equipped but relatively small, hence requiring tight discipline, is a small brigade of five chefs. They are all Indian and all have been brought to the UK by Namita for their particular skills. Each specialises in a different region of India.

The menu reveals Namita's strategy. There are ten starters, ranging from Curried Mango and Yoghurt Soup for £2.95, to Katori (Sheekh) Kebabs for £4.50 and Spicy Madras Prawns £5.25.

There are three categories of main course - Anglo-Indian which includes Bangalore Bangers and Mash £7.25, spicy masala pork sausages. Country Captain £8.95, is chicken breast braised with red chillies, raisins and spices served with lemon rice.

The second section brings to the fore 'unusual genuine dishes' from the Indian Christian communities.' Goan Green Chicken Curry £8.50 is fresh and perky enhanced with green chilli. Lamb Lonvas £8.95, by contrast is very mild but involving 21 aromatic spices.

The unabashedly Indian section includes Roghan Josh £8.95, Tandoori Salmon £9.25 and Chicken Purdah £9.50. It is a pilau encased in pastry.

The vegetarian has a sensible selection of main dishes, and these are supplemented with an ample choice of imginative side dishes and breads. Lachha paratha £1.25 is for example is a light layers flaky fried bread.

Recent additions to the menu includes Shah Jahan Korma - Chicken in a pure white very mild sauce and a tangy spicy fish dish, aromatic dal and the ever popular Chicken Tikka Bhoona Masala. All the food here is made for or by the restaurant. This includes the delightful chutneys and pickles which accompany the meals.
But if you are expecting standard curry house food, this is not the place to find it.
We have received an overwhelming postbag of praise about Chutney Mary. If there is criticism, it is about certain dishes being rather bland or sauces being boringly over-ground to a purée consistency. Regarding blandness, many dishes are spicy and hot (signified by a chilli sign on the menu) and you can always request extra spicing when you order.
Perhaps there is a slight reluctance, even timidity, on the part of the chefs to 'spice up', and it may be that for the concept of 'Anglo-Indian' this is correct and authentic. However, the restaurant is eager to please and it especially welcomes the views of its clients. In its first year it has achieved a great deal. Adjustments and fine tuning are being made in all areas, including the menu.
Chutney Mary is an outstanding and original restaurant, and if the owners continue to lavish the care and attention on it, which they have so far, particularly in the kitchen, it will mature into a pace setter for others to follow. We have decided to recognise its achievements so far and its potential by putting Chutney Mary at the top of our TOP 100.

SW11 : BATTERSEA

INDIA CUISINE **CC DISCOUNT**
286, Battersea Park Road, SW11. Tel: 071 228 8246
An old hand (1958) eastablished in the first wave of curry house expansion. The chef at BA Choudhury's restaurant is Indian and 'only cooks authentic dishes.' The food is well reported. There are unusual items, Hiran £5.50 is tandooried venison, Shakari Biriani £3.95 is, 'a delicious filling vegetable and rice combination.' PT. Evenings only. If you live in the SW11 area they'll free deliver to your home (ring the Indian diner 071 738 0404 for this service). Discounts are available to Curry Club members at their quieter times, see page 288.

KOH-I-NOOR **CC DISCOUNT**
159, Lavender Hill, SW11. Tel: 071 350 2110
A competent Bangladeshi curry house. Price check, Popadoms 35p each, Pullao Rice £1.40, Chicken Curry £3.20. There is a 10% service charge but this will be relieved by the discount available to Curry Club members at their quieter times, see page 288.

THE BATTERSEA VILLAGE RICKSHAW
27/29, Battersea High Street, Battersea Square, SW11.
Tel: 071 924 2450
Cute name which may lead you to believe it is something different and original. Our reporters tell us that it is actually formula curries, but that 'everything checked out fine.' CD.

SW12 : BALHAM AND CLAPHAM

BOMBAY BICYCLE CLUB
95, Nightingale Lane, SW12. Tel: 081 673 6217
Do they vie with each other for cute names (see previous entry)? It too does competent curry.

TABAQ **CC DISCOUNT**
47, Balham Hill, SW12. Tel: 081 673 7820
In 1988 the former Lahore was rebuilt to emerge as the Tabaq. Fifty-five seats were created in a bright and airy room with original Pakistani hand woven tapestries around the walls. The restaurant promises, 'to make your tastebuds stand to attention.' It also claims to be London's finest. Our reporters do not dispute that it is above average, so we'll settle for that. A Tabaq is a large serving dish decoratively laid up with food, put before the diners who help themselves from it.
The menu offers a sensible, not over large choice, which includes Sheek Kebab Machli £4.10 fish kebab, Gurda Kapura £4.75 lamb kidney and

sweetbread and Maghz-Ka-Masala £4.75 lamb brains. They cook to order so a 30-40 minutes wait is normal. Excellent stuff. Discounts are available to Curry Club members at its quieter times, see page 288.

SW14 : EAST SHEEN

TASTE OF RAJ **TOP 100**
130, Upper Richmond Road West, SW14. Tel: 081 876 8326
Nicely decorated establishment. 50 seats in two rooms. The cooking is Bangladeshi. The menu is quite selective but with many favourites. Chooza Zafrani £6.50, is a chicken cooked on-the-bone in a spicy sauce. Papadoms are 30p each, Pullao Rice £1.30, and plain Chicken Curry £3.70. There is a minimum charge of £8.50 and a service charge of 10%.

SW15 : PUTNEY

BUZKASH **TOP 100**
4, Chelverton Road, SW15. Tel: 081 788 0599
This is a rarity - an Afghan restaurant. It is one of a pair (they also run the Caravan Serai, W1). Afghanistan is the major land link between the Middle East and the subcontinent. It is extremely rugged and mainly Moslem. Many invaders came through Afghanistan (including the Moghuls) to bring submission and their culture to India. The Buzhash captures some of this atmosphere. The walls are covered with ethnic rugs, carvings and vicious-looking guns and knives. The food is a combination of Iranian and Indian. Meat (Lamb) predominates. A very nice touch is the free hot Pakora with chutney given at the beginning while you examine the menu. Try the Logery - a leg of lamb flavoured with spices and saffron or the Sekonja (skewered lamb cooked in the tandoor). Askaks are pastries filled with a spicy leek filling, mince and yoghurt. Lavash is the Afghan bread. Kohi is roast lamb spiced with char masala and blackcurrant. End with Carrot Kulfi or Coconut Halva.
The service is exemplary as is the presentation. The food is superb although portions are on the small side. Expect to pay £20 per head including drink. 12% service charge and 75p cover charge. In our TOP 100.

SW16 : STREATHAM

ANARKALI
229, Streatham High Road, SW16. Tel: 081 769 3012
Above average curry house. Chef specials appear on Sundays. reports welcomed.

BABAR
6, Leneagate Road, SW16. Tel: 081 769 7529
A good local.

MUGHOL **CC DISCOUNT**
154a, London Road, Norbury. SW16. Tel: 081 679 7700
Rumour has it that Steve Davis uses this place. It's popular with our reporters too, who, if they're members of the Curry Club will be pleased to know that they get a discount here, see page 288.

SHAHEE BHELPURI
1547, London Road, Norbury. SW16. Tel: 081 679 6275
It's good to see the bhelpuri vegetarian restaurant spreading to the outer suburbs. If it's new to you, it may take more than one visit to acquire the taste. Crispy cold and hot vegetarian snacks and main curries. They're light, healthy and very good, and they're relatively inexpensive.

TRIPTY **CC DISCOUNT**
109, Mitham Lane, West Streatham, SW16. Tel: 081 769 1081
'A restaurant which lives up to its name. Tripty means to satisfy in Bengali. It's not large (30 seats) but it's popular, so we always book. We love the

Maach Vajah £5.50 (Tandoori fish - real Bengali fish), and the Vegetarian Thali £6.50,' CP. Prices are very reasonable - Popadoms are 25p each, Pulao Rice £1.20, Chicken Curry £3 and MS Rahman welcomes Curry Club members to whom a discount will be given at their quieter times, see page 288.

SW17 : BALHAM AND TOOTING

CLIFTON CUISINE
242, Balham High Road, SW17. Tel: 081 673 0285
A fast food style place, where you can eat in (18 seats) or take out. Popadoms and Samosas are 35p each, Pullao Rice 75p, Chicken Curry £2.10, Meat Biriani £2.25. Cheap enough, even when 10% service charge is added.

KASTOORI
188, Upper Tooting Road, SW17. Tel: 081 767 7127
Vegetarian only dishes from North and South India and Gujarat. It's smart and rather expensive for Tooting. For example Popadoms are 50p each, Pullao Rice £2. Reporters tell of the curry of the day which changes daily and the Vegetable Kofta Kastoori. More reports welcomed.

KOLAM
58, Upper Tooting Road, SW17. Tel: 071 672 5328
Another all vegetarian establishment. Quite inexpensive. Reportedly very good.

PEACOCK TANDOORI **CC DISCOUNT**
242, Upper Tooting Road, SW17. Tel: 081 672 8770
Reports tell of a selective menu with some 'delightful specials'. I chose Channa Puri £1.95, chickpea on Indian bread for starter followed by Goa Fish £4.95 and Sag Kamal Kakri £3.75, lotus roots with spinach with no rice but Nan-e-Mugziat £1.50 bread with nuts, raisins and coconut. It was an absolute treat.' SV. Proprietor Yogi Anand will give Curry Club members a discount on takeaway meals only, see page 288.

RAJ OF INDIA
178, Mitcham Road, SW17. Tel: 081 672 3173
A good local serving formula curry.

SREE KRISHNA SOUTH INDIAN **TOP 100**
192/194, Tooting High Street, SW17. Tel: 081 672 4250
At first glance the SREE looks average. The decor isn't spectacular. The room is large (120 seats) and the menu seems to be a formula job. Look closer at the specials and it obviously specialises in South Indian vegetarian food. It also does meat dishes, but the chefs hail from Kerala, the southernmost state of India. The place is very highly rated. 'Masala Dosai £1.70, a pancake containing curry Sambar £1.60 lentil curry, and Avial £1.60, mixed exotic vegetable are just superb. And still nobody does it better.' FR. Regulars prefer to avoid the meat dishes saying they are not as good as the Keralan vegetable specials. The Ragam, W1 is in the same ownership, (see entry). In our TOP 100.

SW19: WIMBLEDON

AHMED
2 The Broadway, SW19. Tel: 081 946 6214
It's a good popular local, coomplete with fish tank, continuing to serve formula curries, which it has done under Athar Ahmed since 1967.

GODHULEE TANDOORI **CC DISCOUNT**
1, Kingston Road, SW19. Tel: 081 542 0243
Owner Abdul Kalan runs his Bangladeshi restaurant very competently, so we're told. It's a smart place with real leaves wallpaper, and the menu has all the favourites you'd expect of a good local. Prices are outer London average (Papadam 35p, Pullao Rice £1.30 and Chicken Curry 2.90) and Mr Kalan welcomes CC members to whom a discount is available at their quieter times, see Page 288.

LONDON W

W1

ANWARS **TOP 100**
64, Grafton Way, W1. Tel: 071 387 6664
Anwars is my kind of place. It's a cafe open from 10am to 10pm. It has a serving counter where you make your choice canteen style, and they ladle it out for you. Dishes vary from day to day, which adds to the fun, but there's a core line of regular favourites - kebabs, tandooris, curries, rice, breads and sweetmeats. After you've chosen, pay, then carry your tray to a formica table (or take out) and enjoy it. It's not licensed and it's inexpensive. The owners are Pakistani which ensures gutsy, spicy food. Unhesitatingly in our TOP 100.

THE CHAMBELLI
12, Great Castle Street, off Regent Street, W1. Tel: 071 636 0662
Since their Oberoi trained chef, departed for Pasandas new, we've not heard too much about the Kensington Tandoori Group's Chambelli. It used to be excellent. Any one agree?

COPPER CHIMNEY **TOP 100**
13, Heddon Street, off Regent Street, W1. Tel: 071 439 2004
This restaurant has branches in India, Bombay and Delhi, where it's pedigree is beyond dispute. London, however, has a big problem. I have numerous reports to hand and I've read some reviews by well known professionals. Many tell of indifferent, or down right rude service, an empty restaurant and a disappointing experience. This is truly a great shame, because there is no doubt about the food. It is absolutely first class. So what is the problem?
Firstly, I think the site is dreadful. The frontage is nondescript and its bright green neon sign does nothing except put you off. So no passing trade. Personally I have had superb service both times I have been there. The food was memorable and I remember the chef demonstrating the making of Romali Roti a thin bread, resembling a hankerchief The demo is spectacular requiring him to throw it in the air and catch it again. However, he did it behind a pillar, half out of sight rather typifying the laid back approach to life at this restaurant. Because of the excellence of the food, I've put it in our TOP 100, but reports from you will determine our next move.

DIWAN-E-KHAS
110, Whitefield Street, W1. Tel: 071 388 1321
and entrance on 45, Grafton Way
It's always busy, patronsied by Asians and local whites. It's been there since 1961 and so it knowns what it's doing.

GAYLORD **TOP 100 & CC DISCOUNT**
79/81, Martimer Street, W1. Tel: 071 636 0808
The Gaylord was founded in 1963, by Messrs Chai and Lamba, and it is a play on their names. They had established a restaurant called KWALITY in Delhi in 1950. Restaurants were extremely scarce in newly independent Indian. It became successful and before long a chain was established all over India. They next ventured into ice cream and are Asia's largest icecream producers. During the 50's, the enterprising pair opened a high-class restaurant in Delhi. It was their first Gaylord. Their 1963 London branch pioneered Indian 'Haute cuisine' in the UK. But I was taken to task for saying that they introduced Tandoori cooking to the UK. Veeraswamy's were doing it by 1960 (see entry). Today there are Gaylord branches all over the world. But they are no longer associated with others in the UK. The double shop front fascade is smartly picked out in white. Inside it's cool and calm, decorated in grey and browns with Indian pictures on the walls. The cool comes from the air conditioning, not the staff, who are relaxed and welcoming. It is often busy and is patronised by the Indian business community. The menu contains a full selection of favourites. Chicken Pakoras £3.95 and Bara Kebabs £4.25 (tandoori lamb chops) are two starters. 'They came with a fresh coriander

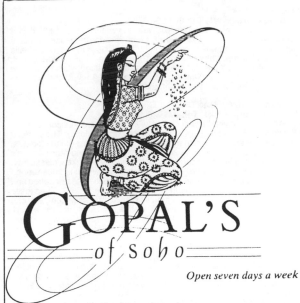

and chutney which acted as a fresh counterbalance.' JD. Main course specials include Batair Special £7.50, 2 quails in spices. Paneer Tikka £3.50 tandooried Indian cheese. Vegetable dish include Bhaigan Bharta, aubergine and Kamal Kakri, lotus roots both £2.95. With a massive service charge of 15% and a cover charge of 60p a meal with P la carte specials and drink will cost around £25 a head. This will be eased for Curry Club members who will be given a discount at their quieter times, see page 288. Gaylords is in our TOP 100.

GOPAL'S OF SOHO **TOP 100**
12, Bateman Street, W1. Tel: 071 434 0840
Accolades pour forth for Gopal's. It isn't often that a restaurant opens (1988) and is in the next Good Food Guide. Gopal's did it. The reason is because of the chef. NP Pittal (Gopal) was Amin Ali's secret weapon first at the Lal Quila and latterly at the Red Fort. We said of Gopal in our 1986 Guide that he is a master. He ranks in the top five Indian chefs in the UK. So it came as no surprise to find him getting itchy feet for his own place. Mr Pittal has clearly benefited greatly from his days with Amin Ali. He has decided that if you're going to do something you start at the top. No provincial or suburban outpost for Gopal's - No, he went straight into London W1, with an upmarket place, upmarket cocktail bar, wine list and menu, no takeaways ('no onion bhajias - too lowly.' DRC) and no second bests. Pricing is upmarket too, as you'd expect, but it is in line with any other establishment of its class. And you get what you pay for without hidden extra (service and cover) charges. Highly commendable. 'A browse through the menu really doesn't prepare you for the excellence to come. I had Patties £2.50, mashed potato rissole stuffed with lentil, and green chillies, my friend chose Karwar Kolmi £3.50, prawns dipped in semolina and crisp fried (Gopal says semolina gives crisper results than flour - Ed). To follow I had the celebrated Dum Ka Murg £5.50, chicken on the bone cooked in a sealed container with Hyderbadi spices and he had Shah Gustaba £5.50, lamb cooked Kashmiri style. We had all the trimmings, and ended with Kala Jamun £1.95, black curd-cake balls in syrup. The bill was £55 for two and worth every penny.' S and TD. In our TOP 100.

HARE KRISHNA
2, Hanway Street, W1. Tel: 071 636 5262
Recently under new management, 'and the better for it.' BR. It is a vegetarian only place. We said of it last time that 'despite constant rumours the management deny any connections with the white palid shaven shivering youths who jingle and chant up and down Oxford Street. This did not stop an American from writing from Portland, Maine to ask me whether he had to contribute to the movement. A useful inexpensive water hole, open noon to midnight and licensed.

THE INDIAN YMCA CANTEEN
41, Fitzroy Square, W1. Tel: 071 387 0411
This is one of my favourite water holes (which is decidedly inlicensed). It's in the downstairs canteen of a well marked modern building. The canteen is primarily for the residents upstairs, many of whom are Asian students, but I've been using it for years and nobody seem to mind outsiders. It's basic and unsophisticated curry - school dinner style. Take a plastic tray. Join the always busy queue. Point to your choice which is unceremoniously served from the warmer. Top up with chappaties, tea or coffee and pay at the till. It's absurdly cheap - it's hard to exceed £3.50. Then jostle for space at a formica table. The food's not brilliant but the company can be when you share your table with talkative students. Highly recommended. Note the hours: lunch 12.30 to 1.30, Dinner: 7 to 8pm. No variations.

JAMDANI **TOP 100**
34, Charlotte Street, W1. Tel: 071 636 1178
Amin Ali Is London's celebrity restaurateur. He started the co-operative venture backed by Camden Council which became the Last Days of the Raj, WC2. He has since had a hand in many very ventures including his own Red Fort, W1 (see entry), each of which had its own distinctive style, menu and success story.

In the Jamdani he has yet again created a unique style. The name 'Jamdani' refers to the very five muslin produced in Dhaka. Queen Victoria's wedding dress was made of it - and it is so fine that a metre of it will pass through a wedding ring. Samples of it hang on the walls vying

for attention with the display of antique pottery along the rear wall. The room itself is open and simple. The chairs are stainless steel and doubtless very expensive. The floor is quarry tiles, contrasting with the white stucco walls. Designed by Ffitch and Company and it shows. The cooking is under the control of expert chef Naresh Matta. 'One visit cannot do the menu justice. It was difficult to choose, so the four of us each had something diferent. Starters were Mini Dosa (Pancake filled with flaked fish), Mutter Kachori (pea in pastry), Sham e Gujarat (kind of Indian Hors d'ouvres) and Samosa. Our main courses included Tandoori King Prawns, lamb Lucknowi Koftas (soft mince meat balls in a creamy spice) Khargosh Achari (hare marinated in vinegar and cooked with shallots) and Kerala Fish masala (halibut in a coriander and coconut sauce). We shared Undhya Vegetables, coconut rice and bread. None of us could manage a sweet. We finished off with strong black coffee. We arrived at 12.30am to an empty restaurant and left a full restaurant with people still queueing for seats at 3pm. No doubt evenings are just as successful. About £85 for four.' FR.
At the invitation of the Russian Government, Amin Ali is to open a Jamdani Indian restaurant in Moscow. Praise indeed for the co-operative operator turned capitalist! In our TOP 100.

KANISHKA **CC DISCOUNT**
161, Whitfield Street, W1. Tel: 071 388 0862
The long standing Diwan-e-Am has been replaced in 1988 by the Kanishka. Owned by Jagdish Vitish, the cooking is Indian and very distinctive. On the menu are many goodies, from all parts of India. Sali Boti £4.95 is a dish served at Parsee wedings. Mutton is simmered with spices and dry apricots and garnished with potato straws. Scallops Masala £6.95, uses a Goan recipe with white wine, and the Goan Crab Curry for £6.95 uses only fresh crab.
There is a good value self-serve lunch £6.95, and there is a discount available to Curry Club members, see page 288.

LAL QILA **TOP 100**
117, Tottenham Court Road, W1. Tel: 071 387 4570
We get taken to task for omitting the Lal Qila from our TOP 30 list last time. One correspondent ran to pages of complaint. Even Jonathan Meades in a piece in the Times said, 'The Curry Club does not include it in its TOP 30 though it is patently in a class above an other they do name. All this despite our caveat last time. However, we'll make amends this time and put the Lal Qila into our TOP 100. However, we still carry a caveat. We've had many reports. Most are full of praise for partner chef Ayub Ali's food and the service. Some are highly critical. The food can be, and usually is, 'brilliant. We tried Lamb Brain Masala and Pasanda Nawabi both £6.95, sliced lamb with nuts in cream. The whole occasion in a full restaurant was flawless.' DM Nine reports like that come in and then a tenth, a blaster. This is not uncommon. We get such criticism for nearly every top restaurant. So in this case we observe it and report it and ask you to tell us our next move.

LAST DAYS OF THE EMPIRE
42, Dean Street, W1. Tel: 071 439 0972
Originally linked to the Last Days of the Raj (and originally sharing that name) this one went solo following an accrimonious legal disagreement. It has a smart bar area, mainly green and cream. It all looks expensive. 'I was made welcome on arrival. Shami Kebab was exceptionally good. Chicken Makhani was absolutely gorgeous. Awful onion Bhajia. It was surprisingly empty on a Saturday night but as we left a group of forty Dutch women arrived. I hope they enjoyed their meal as much as we did.' DRC.

MANDEER **TOP 100 & CC DISCOUNT**
21, Hanway Place, off Tottenham Court Road, W1. Tel: 071 323 0660
New decor and a new room - the Ravi Shankar hall at the Mandeer since our last guide, but old hands Chef Daudbhai and owners Mr and Mrs Ramesh Patel, have kept standards of food and service at their previous high. The Mandeer has been here since, 1960. It is Indian vegetarian food and it is absolutely authentic.
The menu is one of the most comprehensive for vegetarian food. To pick out but a few favourably reported items: 'Try the Puffed Lotus Savoury £4.25, lotus seeds in sauce, or the delightful vegetable samosas £1.60.'

RC. Set meals are excellent value from £6.50. Highly applauded is the Wednesday Special £8.50, served on Wednesdays only. 'It was a filling and satisfying meal and it remains a curry oasis,' GL. Follow with an authentic Indian sweet or a delicious Loseley Park ice cream. The Mandeer's wine list attracts comment with its organic wines, red and white. Also available is Veena £8.50, Indian white wine and Omar Khayyam £25, Indian champagnoise.

Closed Sundays and last orders at 10pm. In our TOP 100. Discounts are available to Curry Club members at their quieter times, see page 288 for details.

The Patels also own the lesser known but equally good Sharuna Vegetarian Takeaway, 107, Great Russell Street, WC1.

MAUYRA
343, Oxford Street, W1. Tel: 071 499 1975
A restaurant run by the Indian Tea Centre. At groundfloor level is the snack bar where you can get samosas with, of course, Indian tea. Downstairs in the Mauyra restaurant. It is competent but not outstanding. More reports welcomed.

NATRAJ
93, Charlotte Street, W1. Tel: 071 637 0050
A competent house of long standing still complete with red flock wall paper. TS describes it as 'a real little gem'.

NEEL AKASH
2, Hanway Street, W1. Tel: 071 580 9767
Good food dispensed with good service at inexpensive prices.

NEW DIWAN-I-AM
60, Blanford Street, W1. Tel: 071
'Since its move I frequent the place at least twice a week and find the staff pleasant, polite and helpful and the food consistently excellent. A special favourite is Masala Dhal.' JD. More reports welcomed.

PAPADAMS
125, Great Titchfield Street, W1. Tel: 071 323 2875
A catchy name (quite a good one, actually) which has been substantially promoted in London especially on LBC radio. When the dust settled on the bally-hoo we were left with a restaurant which, 'knows its business. We were given an effusive welcome and shown to a good table in a fairly busy room. All the food was well prepared and well cooked. We even ordered the house champagne.' DL. 'There aren't many Indian restaurants with tables and chairs on the street outside. We enjoyed our al fresco at Papadoms.' TDR. Expect to pay about £12-£15 per head with 10% service charge.

RAGAM **TOP 100**
57, Cleveland Street, W1. Tel: 071 636 9098
The southernmost state of India is Kerala. It is one of the most beautiful areas in India - lush and fertile, the growing area for pepper, turmeric, ginger and other spices, coconut, chillies, rice and lentils. Kerelan food is based on all of these ingredients. It is primarily vegetarian, but meat is eaten too. Ragam's is now in the same ownership as the Sree Krishna, SW17, (see entry). The menu is similar. Old hands swear by the South Indian vegetarian items such as Iddlis, dosias, uthappam, vadais etc. Exotic vegetables - gourds, several types, mangoes, bindi (okra) and yams make their appearance, in such dishes as Avial and Theeval Kuttu. Our advice is to copy the old hands and pass the meat dishes by. prices are reasonable. In our TOP 100.

RED FORT
77, Dean Street, W1. Tel: 071 437 2525
This is Amin Ali's flagship. A great site in the centre of Soho, guarantees a huge turnover of diners in this restaurant. It seats a substantial 160 on two floors.

Amin Ali's skill lies in encouraging the diner to spend, spend, spend. He was the inventor of the fancy named and fancy priced cocktail at the upmarket curry house. 'Between-the-sheets' and 'Peacock Throne', are cutely named but designed to lighten your purse by £3.95 a shot. Not a bad start (and Amin's a Moslem too!). The meal itself should set you back

a further £15-£20.
Recently we've had a string of poor reports. Since chef Pittal went (to Gopals) it really does seem to have gone down. Mr Ali himself seems to care more for the Jamdani. Whilst we still think it is good and worth trying, we'd like your reports to help us decide what happens next.

REGENT TANDOORI
16, Denman Street, W1. Tel: 071 434 1134
A standard curry house a samosa's thrown from Eros.

SHIKARA
3, Mill Street, W1. Tel: 071 491 8764
One of London's newer restaurants, conceived and financed by an Indian consortium. Shikara means hunter in Hindi, and the food here concentrates on the North West and Moghul areas of India. There are fine Tandooris and creamy Kormas and Pasandas. They also have food from Goa, Nariel Jhena £9.25 is coconut based King Prawn dish and there are South Indian vegetarian dishes as well. There is a minimum charge of £12, which is easy to achieve with a hefty £1.25 cover charge and 15% service charge. In our TOP 100.

THE VEERASWAMY **TOP 100**
99/101, Regent Street, W1. Tel: 071 734 1401
The Veeraswamy is London's oldest Indian restaurant. It was not the first - this accolate went to Mr Abdullah of the chutneys fame who opened London's first ever curry house in Holborn in 1911 (the Salut-e-Hind in Hand Court, Holborn). It had closed by 1924, but during its tenure it had attracted much attention, including that of King George V. The Veeraswamy opened in 1927, and it took advantage of the awakened interest in Indian food established by Abdullah. There followed a succession of owners and a massive decline of standards in the 1980's.
Avid readers of the Guide were quick to notice that we de-listed this restaurant in our previous (1986/7) guide.
Fortunately in 1988 it was rescued by a consortium of Indian businessmen who lavished a considerable amount of money on the place. Out, sadly, went the traditional and much loved furniture - the handcarved chairs, elephants and ornaments - who bought them incidently? - and in came 'the usual bland pink and greys, Truste House Forte style of hotel lounge decor. 'JR. The quality of the food took a quantum leap forward, as we shall see.
Its location - a chappati throw from Picaddilly-Circus is supreme, although it is on the first floor and the actual entrance is on the aptly named Swallow Street. Here one is pounced upon by a smart be-turbanned doorman who salutes, shows you to the lift and palms your proffered offering in one deft movement. (It's worth tipping on departure as well as arrival just for the slickness of it). Up one floor and you emerge into a spacious bar, where you chew on Bombay Mix and sup a Chota Peg whilst perusing the menu. Starters range from Rasam £2.25, spicy sour soup to Alu Tikka £3, a potato rissole with a spicy lentil core, all coated with chutney. Well reported is the Paneer Tikka £3, Indian cheese batter coated and fried. Main courses include such specialities as Goa Chicken £8.50, hot and spicy and Lobster Karwari £12.90, to a west coast recipe and Achar Gosht £8.50, lamb cooked in pickle based sauce. Raan of Lamb £8.50, whole leg marinated in mustard oil and grilled is popular and the vegetable list is well thought out. There is a lunch buffet at £12.50, service charge is a hefty 15% and with wine at £2.50 a glass and a bottle from £9 to £25 (Dom Perignon £79).
It continues to aim at visiting tourists and business men (which explains the phone at your table) who don't mind the bill exceeding £30 per head. In our TOP 100.

W2

Westbourne Grove is about 1/4 mile long and 1/4 mile from Paddington Station. Once it was a smart Georgian residential street. Today it plays host to no less than 14 curry houses, including two of the country's very best. The Postal boundary bisects the road between W2 and W11. You will find curry at numbers 3, 13, 23, 27, 50, 57, 107, 115, 116, 118, 157, 170 and 188, so this indisputably makes it UK, 'Curry Alley'.
These are the three we consider to be worthy of mention (in alphabetical order).

DIWANA BHEL POORI HOUSE **TOP 100**
50, Westbourne Grove, W2. Tel: 071 221 0721
An equally successful branch of the Drummond Street, NW1. flag ship serving crispy dlicious cold Bombay Kiosk food. (see NW1 entry for menu details). Inexpensive, very busy and in our TOP 100.

KHAN'S **TOP 100**
13/15, Westbourne Grove, W2. Tel: 071 727 5420
Khan's is unique and an institution. It's not all that old (1977) but owner Salman Khan is articulate and funny, and he knows how to run an enormous restaurant efficiently. Yes, it is enormous. It is London's largest and as far as we know the second largest in the UK with an astonishing 280 seats on the ground floors and a further room in the basement. Even with this astonishing capacity, you are advised to book at lunchtimes as well as evenings. It must be the envy of the UK's remaining 6,999 curry restaurants for the sheer volume of its trade. They reckon to do over 600 meals each and every day.
These they dispense with a unique take-it-or-leave-it blend of curtness, speed, efficiency and inefficiency. It's hardly surprising when you consider the scale of the operation - there is no time for reminiscing and joking with the patrons. Indeed this is all part of the Khan's ledgend. My files are littered with complaints about 'rudeness' and what one American correspondent called, 'an attitude problem', JO'D. We're used to all this now (but it was for these reasons that we mistakenly took Khan's out of our last Guide). Khan's customers are used to it too, it seems. 'I'm a regular here and if they don't make a mistake on my order and blame me for it, I'd think I was somewhere else!' As far as Salman Khan is concerned, 'it's all part of the fun!' As to the food there are 66 curry dishes to choose from. All the old favourites are there. Their claim that each dish is made with an appropiate blend of spices is bourne out, with 'subtle tastes, exquisite textures and mouthwatering eperience.' PD, RS and DA.
The Khan's experience should not be missed. You enter to a fairy land room whose high cloud painted ceiling is supported by a forest of gilt palm trees. There is a huge Hindi-arched mahogany bar, pink table cloths and black Bentwood chairs. Its atmosphere is quite different at night from daylight. Prices are really reasonable, with the average price for a dish £3. (Papadoms ate 25p each, Pullao Rice £1.20 and Chicken Curry £2.60.). There is a minimum charge of £4 50 and a service charge of 10%. Expect to pay £8-£10 per head. An absolutely top notch restaurant very high in our TOP 100.

KHYBER **CC DISCOUNT**
56, Westbourne Grove, W2. Tel: 071 727 4385
More than competent, ever busy curry house which regards itelf as more up market than most on curry alley. The place is smart and feels cool. Sunday buffet is a good value £5.95 (Children under 8 are halfprice) and you help yourself to what you wish. prices are more than reasonable - Papadoms 25p each, Pullao Rice £1.35, Chicken Curry £2.85. There is a service charge. They give discounts to Curry Club members at thier quieter times, see page 288. They have a branch in Ealing, W13, The Laguna.

ELSEWHERE IN W2

BABA'S BHELPURI HOUSE
29/31, Porchester Road, W2. Tel: 071 221 7502
Vegetarian South India and West Coast food is becoming more widely known in london, partly because simple cafe-style places like this do it so well and so inexpensively. Baba's is licensed (unusual for this style) and is closed on Mondays.

BOMBAY PALACE **TOP 100**
50, Connaught Street, Hyde Park Square, W2. Tel: 071 258 3507
Sant Singh Chatwal was a penniless ex-Indian-airforce pilot, expelled from Ethopia with nothing but a suitcase. He had to leave a thriving Indian restaurant behind.. it was the time of the overthrow of the Emperor Haili Selassi and the revolutionary climate made no allowance for foreigners running a capitalistic business. That was in 1976. Fortunately that suitcase contained half a million dollars. Chatwal opened a new restau-

rant in Montreal. Today he runs Bombay Palaces in New York, Houston, Chicago, Toronton, Vancouver, Washington, LA. and the newest in New Delhi. The London restaurant opened in September 1983. It is a beautifully appointed restaurant with cocktail bar and large dining roon. The menu is interesting because exactly the same menu appears in all the Bombay Palaces worldwide. Only the prices vary. The editor has dined on an identical meal in New York and London. The food is as good in both branches and it is good.
Starters include Alu Papri £3.25 thin potato crisps with yoghurt, tamarind and curry . Chooza Pakoras £3.50 are spicy chicken fritters, Shammi Kebabs £3.50 are succulent and superb.' RJ, and there are two soups at £1.95. Main courses include the Bombay Palace's unique Murgh Keema Masala £5.95, minced chicken breast, lightly sauteed in ginger, garlic, onion, tomato, green peas, yoghurt and spices.
Expect to pay around £25 for your meal with drink, service charge 15% and cover charge £1. Buffet lunch is £8.95. In our TOP 100.

GANGES
101, Praed Street, W2. Tel: 071 723 4096
Long established 1965, very competent curryhouse.

SPICE MERCHANT **TOP 100 & CC DISCOUNT**
Coburg Hotel, 130, Bayswater Road, Hyde Park, W2.
Tel: 071 221 2217
If you are looking for a unique sales proposition the Spice Merchant is it. The restaurant is part of the Coburg Hotel, a grand old Victorian 132 bed hotel, recently refurbished at great cost by its owner Akbar Vergee. Its second USP is the fact that it has a tube station entrance incorporated into its building. Queensway on the Central line is just two stops to Marble Arch. The Spice Merchant is the Coburg's only restaurant. In its basement location, it is decidedly smart. As you enter from the hotel or the street you are impressed by the staitcase down and the attractive wall mural. The restaurant itself is plain and simple but upmarket indeed. It reminds one very much in style of restaurants in top Indian hotels.
You are welcomed by a gracious dapper head waiter and shown to your place. Chef Rao is Taj Group trained and was sous chef at the Bombay Brasserie. He has had the once-in-a-life-time opportunity to design his own kitchen and it is superb. From it flow a regular procession of excellent dishes.
There are eleven non-vegetarian and seven vegetarian starters, of which Dhokri Chat £2.75, crisp lentil cakes topped with date and coriander chutneys and Dahi Pakodi £2.75 light lentil balls topped with yoghurt and herbs, stand out.
Of the seafood dishes, 'The Crab Karawi Curry £7.50 crab claws simmered in hot pepper, coocnut and cummin, is divine so is the Prawn Peri Peri - hot and succulent.' PT. Flavourings are subtle and 'uncompromisingly Indian. A dish such as Paya Curry £5.50, lamb marrow and trotters is like eating at home in Bombay and I finish my meal with Masala Tea and Supari Paan Mix.' SV.
They have a lunch buffet at £9.95, but Chef Rao's a la carte specialities are what you should go for. A decidedly excellent restaurant, deservedly building itself a good reputation. Very high in our TOP 100 and they are offering discounts to Curry Club members at their quieter times, see page 288.

W4 : CHISWICK

ANNAPURNA
101, Chiswick High Road, W4. Tel: 081 995 4432
You tell us that this remains Chiswick's favourite haunt.

W5 : EALING

CLAY OVEN
13, The Mall, Ealing Braodway, W5. Tel: 081 840 0313
A firm favourite with Ealing.

MONTY'S **TOP 100 & CC DISCOUNT**
1, The Mall, Ealing Broadway, W5. Tel: 081 567 8122
Highly acclaimed as Ealing's most popular venue. A standard menu with a couple of Nepalese specials. Price check: Popadoms 40p each, Pullao

Rice £1.60, chicken Curry £3.55. They give discounts to Curry Club members at their quieter times, see page 288. In our TOP 100.

YAK AND YETI
185, South Ealing Road, W5. Tel: 081 568 1952
The unusual name might lead you to believe you'll get Nepalese delights here. Infact, it is a standard curry house menu, competent, friendly and fairly priced.

W6 : HAMMERSMITH

LIGHT OF INDIA **CC DISCOUNT**
284, King Street, W6. Tel: 081 748 2579
An early arrival on King Street (1959), (which now has some ten curry houses). It is Nepalese owned, but their menu is standard Indian curry house. It is much loved and very popular. Price check, Popadoms 30p, Pullao Rice £1.00 and Chicken Curry £2.95, very reasonable for Lodnon and improved by the discount available to Curry Club members at their quieter times, see page 288.

MINAR
323, King Street, W6. Tel: 081
'A small upmarket restaurant with excellent food and attractive presentation.' MHB. Well reported buffet lunch.

RAJDOOT
291, King Street, W6. Tel: 081 748 7345
It's also been here for a long time and has established its clutch of regulars who tell us such things as 'can be chaotic.' Food generally good. The Bangalore Phal is sheer fire.' AD.

TANDOORI NIGHTS **TOP 100**
319/321, King Street, W6. Tel: 081 741 4328
This is part a group of highly successful restaurant scattered around London. It has a very smart gleaming white double frontage which stands out on 'Curry King Street'. The restaurant is under the command of Mohi Uddin and the Cheffing is headed by one of London's top Indian chefs - Pan Sing Rana, who was Oberoi trained and was formorly at the Kensington Tandoori. The combination ensures that this restaurant is a 'cut above' and it certainly makes it the best in the area. In our TOP 100

W8 : KENSINGTON

KENSINGTON TANDOORI
1, Abingdon Road, W8. Tel: 071 937 6182
A sound, careful restaurant although one of our regular reporters (AD) was 'unimpressed'. In general we believe the Kensington to be above average. Your views are welcomed.

MALABAR **TOP 100**
27, Uxbridge Road, W8. Tel: 071 727 8800
Every now and again a restaurant appears on the scene which immediately clamours for attention. The Malabar started in 1983 and is one of these. It is a partnership between the delightful ex dancer Jo Chalmers, her husband Tony and Chef Anil Best. In conversation with The Chalmers, you'll find an enthusiam verging on vocation.. and it shows. They have apeared virtually in every food guide (including ours since 1984), yet there is no sign of Guiditis (complacency from the resulting increase in trade). Prices are not the cheapest, it's true, but they're not the highest, Popadoms 50p, Pullao Rice £1.65, Chicken Curry £3.85, set lunch or dinner £26 for two. If that sounds like a standard curry house menu.. forget it.. it isn't.
Indeed the Malabar's menu is as for removed as it could be. A comforting fact is that it has changed little, if any since 1983. The starters include Devilled Kaleja £3.10, charcoal grilled chicken livers, Hiran £4.65 venison slivers in tamarind and Prawn Philouries £3.10, prawns in potato flour batter. Six lamb dishes and six chicken dishes include Lond Chicken £3.95, cooked with cloves and ginger. Vegetables include green banana and marrow. A throughly consolidated restaurant deservedly high in our TOP 100.

W12 : SHEPHERD'S BUSH

RAJPUT
144, Goldhawk Road, W12. Tel: 081 740 9036
In our 'favourite restaurant poll' (see intro) the Rajput shared the honours with the Shireen in W2.

SHIREEN
270, Uxbridge Road, W12. Tel: 081 749 5927
See comments above. More of your reports on both welcomed.

W13

WEST EALING
HAWELLI
129, Uxbridge Road, W13. Tel: 081 567 6211
One of Ealing's newer venues but highly rated by our reviewers.

LAGUNA
1/4, Culmington Parade, Uxbridge Road, W13. Tel: 081 579 9992
SK Lamba's Laguna is highly respected in Ealing (and they're spoilt for choice for restaurants of all types there). It's large (140 seats) but tastefully decorated and its well managed. The Khyber, W2 (see entry) is in the same ownership. prices are outer London average. A discount is available to Curry Club members at their quieter times, see page 288.

SIGIRI
161, Northfield Avenue, W13. Tel: 081 579 8000
Ealing has one of a rare bread - a Sri Lankan restaurant, and according to reports received they cherish it. Here you'll get Dosais, Uppaamas and Hoppers (appa) and light coconut based curries and chutneys. All this for under a tenner. More reports welcomed.

LONDON WC

WC1

CHAMBELLI
146, Southampton Row, WC1. Tel: 071 837 3925
Part of the Tandoori Nights Group, this restaurant benefits from good management and careful cooking.

GANPATH **CC DISCOUNT**
372, Gray's Inn Road, WC1. Tel: 071 278 1938
After a lot of literary composition I decided I can't improve upon our last Guide entry: It remains tatty, it remains in The Good Food Guide and it continues to serve darned good vegetarian food. Owner Chef R Sivananthan's Masala Dosa at £1.95, Idli £1.50, Sambar for £1.40, green Beans in Coconut at £1.60, Lemon Rice at £1.60 and 'exquisite onion bhajia' for £1.40.' LT, are consistently top of their tree and you can eat your fill for five or six pounds, doubling it with wine. A discount is available to Curry Club members at their quieter times, see page 288.

WC2: ALDWYCH:COVENT GARDEN

ALDWYCH TANDOORI **CC DISCOUNT**
149, The Strand, WC2. Tel: 071 240 2717
Traditional Indian decor and traditional Indian food here. It gets busy when London gets busy, but we hear of it as, 'a safe bet', DA. Syed Khan also owns the Temple Tandoori, EC4 and the Southbank Tandoori, SE1. Discounts are available to Curry Club members at their quieter times, see page 288.

AKASH
14/15, Irving Street, WC2. Tel: 071 930 0744
A standard curry house in the centre of the West End.

BHATTI
37, Great Queen Street, WC2. Tel: 071 831 0817
Great expectations in Great Queen Street were not forthcoming to one of our regular scribes, 'Service was cheeky and flippant. We didn't get what we ordered and the waiter blamed us. At £105 for six, it was an expensive mistake.' PH, but on the whole we hear that owner V Puri has maintained the high standards he set for himself he opened in 1985. It was LBC'S Indian restaurant of the year in 1986 and 1989, and we welcome more reports.

INDIA CLUB **TOP 100**
143, The Strand, WC2. Tel: 071 836 0650
One of our most reliable reporters works for the Inland Revenue and his job takes him to every tax office in the land. Consequently he visits seemingly every curry house in the land. His absolutely favourite he tells us, is the India Club. But, be warned , it may not be yours. It is out and out uncompromisingly Indian. But first a bit of background.
It opened in 1950 making it London's third or fourth Indian restaurant. It is located in the Strand Continental hotel (where rooms are still absurdly cheap). It is directly opposite the Indian High Commission (Embassy) in Bush House, and was and still is there to cater for their Indian staff. It is basic, redolant of many a Delhi Chaat House. The head waiter, Lawrence 'a charming elderly Indian gentlemen was serving.' DMW. 'Despite being painted recently, I'm glad to report it is as tatty as ever. The Masala Dosa is the best in the UK - nobody does it better.' JL.
The India Club (cafe might be more appropriate) does South Indian vegetarian food as well as meat and chicken. It is absurdly cheap. Expect to pay around £6 to £8. A service charge is (inexplicably) applied on groups of four or more. It is unlicensed but you can bring in your own with no corkage charge. Unhesitatingly high up in our TOP 100.

PUNJAB
80, Neal Street, WC2. Tel: 071 836 9787
Established in 1951 making it London's fourth or fifth is this venerable establishment. It was therefore one of the pioneers of the curry house formula. Punjabi food is spicy and tasty - not hot unless you want it so. Sag Gosht, Methi, Parathas and Keema, and Moghul dishes such as Pasanda, Korma and Roghan Gosht.. these are the foundation stones of the standard menu. The Punjab in all those years has had its ups and downs but we believe it to be competent and mature. Closed Sundays.

SAHELI BRASSERIE
35, Great Queen Street, WC2. Tel: 071 405 2238
Above average (normally) standard curry menu. Saheli means 'girl friend', so proprietor Mohammed Hanif told our correspoindent wishing to book for a 'romantic night out.' The Fleet Tandoori, NW3 and NW10 are branches.

SHAN
200, Shaftesbury Avenue, WC2. Tel: 071 240 3348
An Indian cafe now complete with carpets. Top end of Shaftesbury Avenue. Bottom end of market, ie: still cheap and cheerful. Noon to 9.30pm daily - closed Sundays.

STRAND TANDOORI
45, Bedford Street, WC2. Tel: 071 240 1333
A competent house, where 'everyone was more than satisfied.' DRC.

TASTE OF INDIA **TOP 100**
25, Catherine Street, WC2. Tel: 071 836 6591
Chic and stylish decor, the up-lighters giving it a very cosy feeling. Mahtab Chowdhury opened here in 1983. The chefs were trained in a major Indian Hotel Group (The Ashoka) and are therefore highly qualified. This shows in the subtlety of the cooking. The 140 seat restaurant is generally busy and booking is advisable. You don't need to book at its adjacent sister branch. Sited at no 27, The Jewel in the Crown opened in 1986, mainly to accommodate the 'Taste's' expansion. It cleverly occupies the basement (allowing the Taste to double in size above it) and it is a wine bar serving the some of the same Indian food. It is designed to catch the pre and post theatre crowds. In our TOP 100.

AVON

THE BENGAL BRASSERIE,
32 Milson Street, Bath. Tel: 0225 447906
12 - 2.30 6 - 11.30
This Restaurant opened in December 1987. It has come to our notice on a number of occasions. "Above average service by a couple of cheerful Iranians, both students and trying to make ends meet. Will make this our regular." P. & L.G. The Restaurant is pleasantly decorated in light pink with individual alcoves. Especially singled out is the Dhaka Lamb Bhadami (£5.50) which is thin fillets of lamb marinated in yoghurt and spices, the Afghan Chicken (£4.95) and Sabzi Jhal (£3.90) (mixed veg. cooked with chillies). Their "one plate" special lunches are designed for speedy service yet good tasty combinations of food. This Restaurant will give discounts for Curry Club members. See page 288.

THE EASTERN EYE,
11 Argyle Street, Bath 0225 22323
12 - 2.30 6 -11.30
Now well established, The Eastern Eye continues to please the residents of Bath. "I tried the Kid Josh which turned out to be lamb with cashews and coconut, my friend tried the Lamb Sula (lamb marinated in spices and yoghurt which is then tandooried and served in a delicious sauce). Both were subtle and delicious." K.T.".

THE MAHARAJA, **CC DISCOUNT**
26-27 Upper Borough Walls, Bath. Tel: 0225 28740
12 - 2.30 6 -11.30
"After a gap of nearly 12 months, a chance arose to revisit this Restaurant. It was a Monday and it was very quiet with only 2 American and 2 Australian tourists in the Restaurant, but the service was fast and efficient." T.S..
There are some nice specials on the Menu. If W. Chowdhry, the owner is present, which he often is, ask him to reminisce about his mothers authentic recipes, then try the Lobra Mawrapuri special £6.95, a combination of prawns, chicken and dhal with fresh chilli and herbs and sliced egg and tomato. Equally acceptable is Lamb-Ba-Dhania £6.95, cooked with butter beans and fresh coriander or the Xacutti £7.50, a very hot Goan recipe, Chuka Sobjee-Dhal £4.75, is a hot sour vegetable curry of pulses, vegetables and tomato. "The South Indian Rasam Soup is the perfect starter wetting the appetite for what is to come". D.S.S. "My work takes me all over the West Country. I look forward to Bath for the Keema Pullao at the Maharaja." W.C. This Restaurant is prepared to offer discounts to Curry Club members. See page 288. It has a branch, The Jaipur House, 23 High Street, Corsam, Wilts.

THE PRINCE OF INDIA,
2 Bladud Buildings, Bath. Tel: 0225 25765
12 - 2.30 6 - 11.30
The Prince of India may perhaps not be best known for its scenic attributes. "Scruffy decor but friendly atmosphere, don't know how Mr. Miah does it, food is always superb especially the Lamb Pasanda". B.T.

RAJPOOT, **TOP 100**
4 Argyle Street, Bath. Tel: 0225 668833
12.30 - 2.30 6 - 11.30
"NOT your average curry shop - totally exquisite. Really the best Indian food I have had anywhere (including India!). The quality of food and presentation and service is virtually perfect. Beautiful decor and waiters dressed in Indian costume. The food is mild but will cook to prefered strength. I cannot praise this Restaurant too much, the only one criticism is that it is so popular. I have introduced at least 30 people and all agree with me. Owner Mr. A. Chowdhury winces when he is asked whether his restaurant is part of a chain. It is independent, he insists, but he does own

Bath's Bengal Brasserie and the Raposhi and the Ghandi's Indian Food Centre, Bristol, all good enough to get into this Guide. The Raj Poot is celebrating it's first decade. "The experience begins as you enter. The decor is authentic and upmarket and the staff smartly uniformed, helpful and polite." K.A. The Restaurant is in 3 parts the Old India, The Indian Cottage and the Kamra. We settled into place and examined the Menu and revelled in the choice of unusual dishes". T.G. Specialities include Rezala, £5.95, a typical example of a ceremonial dish cooked with lamb. Sobji Dhansak, the traditional Parsi lentil based dish cooked in this case, with mixed vegetables, hot, sweet, sour and delicious, £4.50. Chicken Jhal Noorpuri, chicken breasts cooked with herbs and hot green chillies, £6.25. Kalia, £4.95, lamb cooked with potatoes in a thick tasty sauce, a traditional Bengali dish. Jaflang, £6.95. A curry using special herbs and spices, the recipes from the hills of Jaflang and Kacchi Akhni, a Biriani type of dish using a special blend of herbs and spices used with a small bowl of sauce, £7.95. The wine list is special too and it includes a very good selection of wines including the Indian White Wine, a pleasant wine which complements curry quite nicely, partly because it is made in India and partly because it is spiced with Indian herbs. The list also includes Indian Champagnois called Omar Khayyam bottled in India and very acceptable. The main 40 wines are carefully chosen from different areas of the world, each has a full description and it is clearly put together with some care proving that wine is perfectly acceptable with good curry. In our Top 100 (see page 288)

RUPOSHI,
3 Sussex Place, Widcombe Parade, Bath.
6 - Midnight
This is a take away only establishment which opened in 1988 but it has already caught the eye of a number of our correspondents. The Menu reads like the dictionary of the standard Curry House - there are no surprises. It leaves those to it's sister branch the Raj Poot, but what the Ruposhi does, it does well. Poppadums are 25p each, Pullao Rice £1.20, Chicken Curry £3.40 and Bombay Potatoes £1.60.

THE BRITISH RAJ,
1 Passage Road, Westbury on Trym, Bristol. Tel: 0272 500493
12.30 - 2.30 6 - 11.30
Apart from one report about poor service we have always had the thumbs up for this establishment. "I have eaten in all of Bristol's Indian Restaurants and this is my favourite" says B.T.H. who goes on, "their Chicken Tikka is superb as a starter. I usually have Vindaloo with loads of fresh coriander and Keema Naan packed with Keema Mince. My wife (who didn't like Indian food before she came here - poor woman) always has the Korma which she says is mild and superb".

THE GHANDI,
9 The Mall, Clifton Village, Bristol. Tel: 0272 744798
12.30 - 2.30 6 - 11.30
"This is a small establishment of about 20 seats with a cheerful Bohemian Bistro atmosphere. Good quality food is served, Rhogan Josh is average, Channa Masala above average. Prices are acceptable without being cheap. Best of all, I had the feeling of being able to sit down and relax in a happy atmosphere. I wasn't surprised that many of the other Restaurants in the City were virtually empty and this one was almost full". J.L.

THE GANGES,
368 Gloucester Road, Horfield, Bristol. Tel: 0272 45234
12.30 - 2.30 6 - 11.30
If the Menu gives you deja vu it is because it is in the same ownership as Bath's Raj Poot. "Excellent Menu of consistent quality, service first class and the place is spotlessly clean. The owner was on hand for a friendly greeting and help with the Menu. We like returning to this Restaurant, the one we know and trust". D.G. and J.M. "Absolutely our favourite. We have been there several times on our travels and it has always been first class. The service and the ambiance is good and the food always exquisite and they are very good indeed with children." A.D. Specials worth mentioning are Afghan Chicken, Prawn or Lamb, £4.95, cooked with coconut, bananas, pineapple and sultanas, Channa Gosht Pullao, Channa Dhal and lamb cooked with Pullao Rice gently fried and served with a special sauce, £6.45. Mutta Pullao Yakoti which is a Biriani of fresh peas and

lamb served with a special sauce and which is £6.45 and vegetarian thali which consists of potato, cauliflower, mushroom bhajia, dhal roshun, raita (yoghurt) chapatti and pullao rice served on the traditional thali plate at £6.25.

THE NATRAJ NEPALESE TANDOORI,
185 Gloucester Road, Bristol. 0272 248125
12.30 - 2.30   6 - 11
A new entrant to this Guide, the Natraj only started in 1988, but at once we began to receive good reports. "We have been in here at least once a fortnight since it opened and we have never had a bad experience." N.E. The decor reflects Indian culture, and the Menu has many good things on it. Unlike many Restaurants calling themselves Nepalese, this one does offer many specialities from Nepal. Specialities to note are the Gurkha Chick which is chick peas in a spicy sauce garnished with pullao rice, £6.25, Chicken Pokhara £5.50, mildly spiced chicken with thick sauce garnished with rice and fried mushroom. Momocha, £5.50, spiced minced lamb in a steam cooked pastry served with specially prepared Nepalese tomato pickle, gravy and pullao rice. Thukpa £5.50 Chicken, Lamb or Prawn served with noodles, tomato pickle and sauce. The Gurkha Curry, Chicken, Lamb or Prawn, £5.00, is a mildly spiced curry with a touch of ghee, bananas and sultanas, Nepal Chicken at £5.15 is mildly spiced with a thick sauce garnished with egg. Kasthamandapa is a medium spiced chicken or prawn or lamb curry in a Nepalese thick tasty sauce, £5.50. The Gurkha Naan, large enough for 2 at £2.00, is leavened bread with nuts baked in a clay oven and for those who want a taste of everything, ask the staff for the Gurkha Special which is a set meal enabling you to take many of these Gurkha Nepalese specials.

THE PUSHPANJI,
217A Gloucester Road, Bristol.   Tel: 0272 28034
This is a Vegetarian Restaurant, an unusual rarity in any City and we can do little better than quote in full this amusing quotation from one of our regular correspondents. "This is relatively new and is settled happily between some well established Indian Restaurants. We passed the place several times to gaze through the window but it's short opening hours usually prevented us indulging. My girlfriend was aghast when we arrived, having mistaken our destination and insisted on removing her ear-rings and makeup and donning my old sweatshirt before she would go in. Having dealt with her perceived state of over dressing we entered the shop front and chose our meal before being shown to a table in the "Bistro" style dining area. As usual I accidentally ordered too much. This was because the Thali was, of course, the complete meal in addition to the rice and starter I had already ordered. The first bit was chewed up "vine leaves" like compressed tea bags to look at (and similar taste), quite scrumptious in a weird way. Also little Dahi Wadas and Yoghurt Dip were very nice. The Thali had Tomato and Spaghetti Curry, Cauliflower Curry, Special Rice with vegetables, Raitha, Sambar, Soup, Naan (a bit of a let down that - very tough) and orange cake like stuff, (probably Halva). All good except the Naan and all good portions. My girlfriend had my extra rice (well some of it) and Courgette Curry. There was lots of fresh coriander leaf with everything and it all tasted pretty good. A truly superb café style (smart formica tables). Good Gujerati Vegetarian Restaurant, have been 6 times in the last 2 months and it has never failed to impress me. Friendly service, comfort and excellent quality food. Worth going just for the devine dosas, massive size and great flavour served with Raitha, a meal in its own. Lentil Fritters in Yoghurt delicious and a fabulous lemon milky dessert called Shrikant. Chocolate and Pistachio kulfi to finish. An excellent Restaurant." D.R.

RAJDOOT, **TOP 100 & CC DISCOUNT**
83 Park Street, Bristol.   Tel: 0272 28034
12 - 2.15   6.30 - 11.30
The Rajdoot is the creation of architect Des Sharda who also owns the Rajdoot in Bristol, Birmingham and Dublin. The Rajdoot is noticeable for its authentic elegant and exotic atmosphere, indeed it was one of the first to present itself in an upmarket and attractive way, and the architects training shows with the Indian arts and crafts colour styles and general layout. "The first thing that strikes you on entering is the large comfortable lounge where you can order from the Menu whilst you partake of a leisurely drink." J.M.

This Rajdoot like it's sister branches has regularly and consistently been noted in all the Good Food Guides including the previous editions of the Good Curry Guide. This branch has been open since 1970 and according to most of the reports we get the Restaurant is good enough to be in our top 100. Before we examine the Menu in more detail however it is worth pointing out that from time to time we do get some snortingly bad reports on occasions about this Restaurant, it's sister branches and other Restaurants which we consider to be top quality. Fortunately they are few and far between, but we believe that the reason for it might be that these Restaurants are not typical standard Curry Houses and the style of cooking which is subtle and expensive leaves peoples expectations wanting. The Rajdoot was one of the pioneers of new style authentic Indian cooking such as you would find in the sub-continent itself. Each dish is individually spiced, a claim made by many Restaurants, but actually fulfilled at the Rajdoot and the ingredients used are undoubtedly of top quality. The chef and the staff are Indian, also untypical, as most "Indian" Restaurants in the U.K. are run by Bangladeshi's and Pakistani's. To get down to the Menu the tandoori dishes are devoid of bright red and yellow and orange food colouring but are succulent and very tasty. Unusual subjects are the Tandoori Quail £4.45, the Fish Tikka £4.40 and the delicious Rashmi Kebab £4.40, chicken mince with onion, green chillies, fresh mint, coriander, herbs and spices. Also worth trying are the Gurda Kebabs, lamb kidneys, £4.15. Curries include Rogan Josh £4.65, aromatically spiced lamb with cashew nuts, Chicken Jalfrezi £4.75, diced chicken cooked in a spicy gravy and Lamb Loogli, a mildly spiced meat dish enhanced with yoghurt, eggs and nuts. "My favourite of all is the Chicken Tikka Masala £5.80, diced boneless chicken cooked over charcoal and finished in a red tandoori based sauce". D.C. Also highly spoken of is Jeera Chicken, £4.85, chicken fried in roasted cummin seed. Kidney Masala £4.40, lamb kidney cooked in spice with cream. Fish Masala £4.40, fish fillets cooked in a special sauce and two versions of lobster both £12.50; Lobster Masala cooked with fresh ginger and garlic and Lobster Bhoona, a dry mild curry cooked with spring onions and mushrooms. Set luncheon is available from £7.00, set dinner £11.50 to £14.50. Poppadums come free but there is a minimum charge of £8.50, a service charge of 12% and a cover charge of 50p. A nice touch is house coffee which is blended from coffee beans from East Africa. "Ordered Lamb Pasanda which to this day is the best Indian meal I have ever eaten". R.C. "Good decor, good food, good service. I remember the Pullao Rice being served from a big pot, exceptional." P. and L.G.
This Restaurant along with the other 3 Rajdoot's in this group offer Curry Club members a discount. See page 288. We are happy to keep this Restaurant in our top listing (our top 100) and we always welcome reports about it.

SITAR,
61 High Street, Westbury on Trym. Tel: 0272 507771
"This Restaurant has come to our notice on several occasions and we consider it worthy of entry into this edition of the Guide. We went there on its opening week and we have been back on several occasions and we are pleased to say that the high standards have been maintained." G.W. "There is clearly an effort made with the food and some of the choice on the Menu is different from other Restaurants we know. Fresh Trout £4.35. Murgh Makarni (chicken in a rich sauce) £4.95. King Prawn Suka £3.75. Very favourably impressed." D.G. and J.M.

TAJ MAHAL,
37a Cotham Hill, Cotham, Bristol 0272 745265
The Taj Mahal is an old favourite of our Guide readers and correspondents. Its Fan Club will tell you it's Bristol's oldest, established in 1959. It maintains its dedicated following, probably because it is carefully run by father and son Akrim and Amir Ali. "This Restaurant continues to improve. We can always be sure of our meal here." P.L.C. "A wide variety of choice. All dishes reasonably priced. Tandoori King Prawn and Chicken Tikka excellent. Main courses equally good. One of the better Indian establishments in this county." J.T. "Consistently impressed with the standard of food and service.
True to description prepared with the addition of fragrant warm and pungent spices from India delicately blended in meticulous proportions and free from that rancid ambiguity called curry powder. Our only criticism is that the bar and entrance is rather cramped." C.G.

MOGULS TANDOORI,
33 Old Church Road, Clevedon. Tel: 0272 873695
This Restaurant is probably typical of many up and down the country and we have received favourable reports about the standard Menu and efficient service. "I have had many meals here and found the food to be consistently good. Typical decor with subdued lighting and individually partitioned tables lead to a relaxed and intimate atmosphere." C.G. We have little more to add to this except to say that the prices are reasonable and that it is a safe bet.

THE CURRY GARDEN,
69 Orchard Street, Weston-Super-Mare. Tel: 0934 24660
The Curry Garden is in many respects the standard Archetypal Restaurant. It is run by Bangladeshi's as are 85% of all Britain's 'Indian' Restaurants. It has gaudy wall murals depicting the tiger, Indian Goddesses and river scenes and rather garish wallpaper (but not red flock). The Menu is equally standard stuff. It contains everything you would expect of a standard Curry House, nothing more, nothing less and no surprises. So go there for the expected and from the comments we have received you won't leave disappointed (including the flower for the lady!). Prices are very reasonable. Poppadums 35p. Chicken Curry £3.10. Chicken Tikka Starter £2.20. Pullao Rice £1.20. Minimum charge is £1.30. There is no service or cover charge.

BEDFORDSHIRE

THE ALMEEDA TANDOORI,
32 Woburn Street, Ampthill.
Tel: 0525 405570
The exterior of The Almeeda came as a surprise to S.H.D. "It is a former school. The interior is spacious and the food is ample and tasty." We received a number of comments in the same vain and we presume that it is the unusual surroundings which prompt the initial response. It appears the food is above average in quality and that on occasions the Restaurant is quite busy and it certainly is popular. The decor inside is described as a mirrored hall with cubicle candlelit tables. Prices are reasonable. Poppadums 35p. Chicken Curry £2.85. Pullao Rice £1.30 and there is a minimum charge of £8.50. Specials include the Tikka Special at £4.90. The King Prawn Delight at £7.50. The Almeeda Special at £5.90 and the Chicken Jalfrezi at £3.60.

THE AMRAM TANDOORI, **CC DISCOUNT**
53B Harper Street, Bedford. Tel: 0234 52359
Our correspondents are delighted to report that red flock is alive and well at the Amram Restaurant. Somebody should notify the Indian Restaurant Preservation Society and a Preservation Order should be slapped on this establishment. Red flock wallpaper is a rarity these days as are pictures of the Taj Mahal which adorn the walls. We are told of a friendly warm reception by correspondents who visit here. Indeed this Restaurant which was established in 1958 is one of the longest established in the Bedford area. Special dishes include the Begum Bejar, £6.45, chicken and minced lamb delicately blended and cooked with spices and nuts. Butter Chicken £6.45, chicken breast marinated in ginger, garlic, yoghurt and spices and cooked with fresh tomato cream and butter. Chicken Jalfrezi £6.65, chicken breast pieces marinated in fresh ground spices and cooked with tomato, onion and capsicum. Chicken Tikka Surma £8.75, boneless chicken marinated and served with salad, vegetable curry and rice and Chicken Tikka Sylheti £6.85, chicken cooked with lentils to a Bangladeshi recipe. Poppadums are 30p each. Set luncheon £5.70. Set dinner from £6.75 and there are no extra charges. This Restaurant offers a discount to Curry Club members. See page 288.

THE GRAND,
39 Tavistock Street, Bedford. Tel: 0234 59566
We begin our report by welcoming The Grand to this edition of the Good Curry Guide and apologising for your omission last time. This was unintentional and had more to do with the designers over-active scissors which led to your entry ending up on the cutting room floor and not in this Guide. Indeed this omission led to a string of complaints from the Guide's regulars (we don't think it was the owner or his wife). "Why oh why, did you miss out our favourite Bedford Restaurant". D.K. "We were quite surprised to find The Grand not in your guide". P.L. Actually The Grand is a consistently reliable standard Curry House with no surprises and a regular and loyal following who tell of friendly staff, competent service, ample portions and delicious food. And as that is the least that we look for when we go out for our curry night out, it is good reason indeed for The Grand to be in our present edition of the Guide.

THE JAMUNA TANDOORI, **CC DISCOUNT**
90 Tavistock Street, Bedford. Tel: 0234 48848
This Restaurant opened in 1986 above a well established takeaway which had been operating on the ground floor since 1982. Since it opened we had received good reports about the takeaway "We have used The Jamoona Takeaway since it opened and have always had good food from it". G.R. The Restaurant is now well established and its interior is attractively coloured with soft pink and white coloured walls and surroundings. "The staff are always very helpful and pleasant and we always enjoyed our meal here". B.W. The Menu has some nice touches herald of the naan culture 95p, leavened bread stuffed with vegetables and baked in the tandoor. The Bhoona Tikka Gusht is the favourite of K.R. and consists of tender pieces of lamb cooked in the tandoor and then simmered in a spicy gravy, £4.95. The Chicken Tikka Vindaloo, £4.95, chicken breasts tandooried and served in a very hot sauce will appeal to those who like it hot. The Maha Jahani Birianis averaging £5.00 are popular with many of our correspondents. Bombay duck is 30p. The place "indispensible" to A.R. There are no extras such as cover charge, service charge or minimum charges and the Restaurant offers face towels, coffee sweets and a flower for the lady. It also offers discount for Curry Club members. See page 288.

MAGNA TANDOORI,
50 Tavistock Street, Bedford. Tel: 0234 855735
The Magna makes its regular appearance in the pages of this Guide yet again, not because we hear of any culinary masterpieces but, as usual, we hear of careful consistent standard curries. "They continue to serve huge portions". N.B. and as before we have been advised by our regular correspondents that the Magna's Special Murgh Masala - whole chicken marinated in spicy yoghurt for 24 hours, then baked and served in a spicy sauce is well worth ordering. You must pay a deposit and the marination is why you must order 24 hours in advance but the results are "well worth waiting for". M.R. and we are told the rest of the Menu is very competent too. Prices are fair with Poppadums at 30p. Chicken Curry at £3.50. Pullao Rice £1.40.

THE SONALI TANDORI, **CC DISCOUNT**
51 Tavistock Street, Bedford. Tel: 0234 270771
Our Bedford correspondents have also pointed out that the Sonali is proving to be a competent performer. "Very impressed and have been back four times. Good food, good service and decor excellent. Had Lamb Pasanda and enjoyed it very much. An interesting and varied Menu with certainly no shortage of choice." P.A. Would like to hear more of your reports about this Restaurant so please send them in. It offers discounts to Curry Club members See page 288.

THE VICEROY OF INDIA, **CC DISCOUNT**
51 Sun Street, Biggleswade. Tel: 0767 312110
The Viceroy is sited in a small white detached house. It is unlikely to prepare you for the excellent presentation inside. "We chose the Restaurant to break our journey. We were very glad we did. We were made very welcome by the waiter dressed in Indian robes. The pink, blue and maroon decor was slightly on the garish side but it was spotlessly clean. I have never seen light fittings, fish tanks and even the studs on the upholstery gleam as those, as if they had been installed just that day. The

Owners of restaurants selected to appear in this guide are invited to advertise. We thank those who have done so – it helps keep the price of the guide as low as possible.

The editor of The Good Curry Guide welcomes your views on restaurants we list in this guide and on any curry restaurants or take-aways you visit. Please send them to: The Curry Club, PO Box 7, Haslemere, Surrey GU27 1EP.

The Curry Club's tri-annual glossy magazine – The Curry Magazine – carries in-depth information on Indian-style restaurants nationwide including update reports, new openings, and the bad ones – those with health or other problems. For more information write to: The Curry Club, PO Box 7, Haslemere, Surrey GU27 1EP.

Poppadums at 40p were really good and were served with the brightest red onion salad your have ever seen. Fine as long as you aren't allergic to artificial colours. The Onion Bhajia was really good, two large spheres of light crisp onions. The Murgh Tikka Do-Piaza at £5.70 was superb. Atta Paneer very good and slightly sweet, the Paneer in very small pieces. Mushroom Bhajia excellent. Niramis, a really first class mixture of long beans and other vegetables, very spicy. Vegan Brinjal Bhajia was marvellous. All the dishes were in reasonable quantities. I do like to have a dessert after an Indian meal but I do like Indian desserts. We were handed a scruffy Ice Cream Menu only. I know that Restaurateurs say most people don't know or like Indian desserts but they would never know if they are not offered them." N.C. This very detailed report echos many others in the same vane speaking of good value and excellent service. The Restaurant has two branches; The Viceroy, 2 Blackbird Street, Potton, Beds. and The Viceroy of India, 21 White Horse Street, Baldock, Herts. All 3 have a minimum charge of £10.00 but no service or cover charges and they offer discounts to Curry Club members. See page 288.

THE MOGUL,
39 New Bedford Road, Dunstable. Tel: 0582 429656
A perfectly standard Restaurant in an area where there are many perfectly standard Restaurants. The Mogul has achieved a number of good reports from our correspondents. Prices are reasonable. Poppadums are 35p. Chicken Curry £2.75. Pullao Rice £1.20.

THE RAJPUT,
31 High Street South, Eatenbray, Dunstable. Tel: 0582 661724
Again another competent Curry House in Dunstable which satisfies more than one of our correspondents. "I enjoyed my meal very much here." S.H. No surprises on the Menu. No surprises on the prices. A fair and square deal here and you will end up with a good curry.

THE AKASH TANDOORI,
60 North Street, Leyton Buzzard. Tel: 0525 372316
"This is a brightly lit Restaurant in a comfortable relaxed atmosphere. It is tastefully decorated. It is an average Menu with few specialities and no desserts on offer but it is excellent food, beautifully presented in adequate quantities. The selection of 6 chutneys on each table had us really pleased and the smiling waiter gave us the most pleasant service I can recall in years. Would love to return on a regular basis. My only regret is that distance prevents me from doing so." A.H. We also have regulars reporting warmly on The Akash where prices are fair and you should be assured of a competent curry.

INDIA PAVILLION
57, Lake Street, Leighton Buzzard.0525 378372
I was invited here by MR Rahman, the owner, for his fifth year celebration party. He had expected about 150 of his regulars to turn up for a Sunday evening free buffet. I got there late and there were people spilling out into the street and everywhere. The good humoured staff apologised about the food, 'we've actually had over 350 people turn up.' Obviously very popular. Reports welcomed.

THE BOMBAY BRASSERIE,
32 Wellington Street, Luton. Tel: 0582 22151
The Bombay Brasserie which was formerly The Gate of India, changed its name in the last few years. We have had a mixed bag of reports on this Restaurant; some raving over it and the occasional one not quite so hot. The same reporter (P.C. - not the editor) has himself varied between the best in Luton comment and complaints about poor service. On the whole however, we think that the Restaurant is worthy of its entry in the Good Curry Guide with food quality and quantity above average. Prices could be slightly high and this might be a result of its popularity, but clearly a watch needs to be kept by the Restaurant owners on the establishments standards, particularly on service.

SHALIMAR CURRY HOUSE, **CC DISCOUNT**
129 Dunstable Road, Luton. Tel: 0582 29753
This Restaurant commenced trading in 1973 and recently it changed ownership. Until that time we had received only average reports about its standards but since then we have received several reports which praise the establishment. One of the aspects of this Restaurant which catches our eye is its opening hours which are 4 p.m. to 4 a.m. 7 days a week, so if you happen to be travelling up or down the M1 in the middle of the night, or just a plain ordinary Luton curryholic insomniac we commend its extraordinary hours. As to the food, the prices are reasonable. Poppadums 25p. Chicken Curry £3.40. Pullao Rice £1.50. A set meal is available from £6.50. There is a minimum cover charge of £6.00 and no service charge or cover charge. The Restaurant will offer discounts to Curry Club members. See page 288.

BERKSHIRE

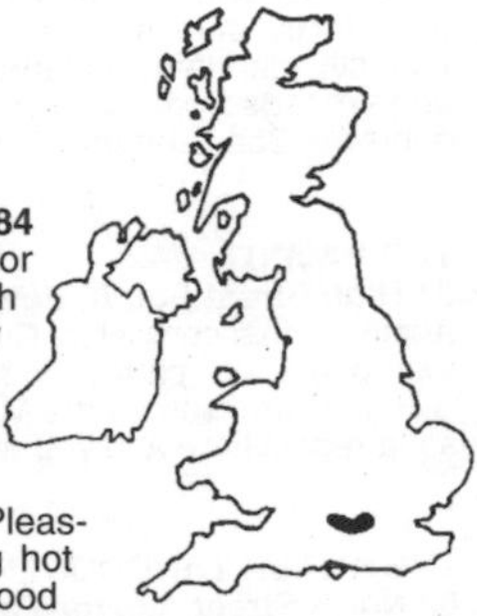

COOKHAM TANDOORI,
High Street, Cookham. Tel: 06285 22584
Reports here of a gorgeous mock tudor premises in a lovely village and a very plush Restaurant. "The service was very friendly and efficient. The Poppadums warm and crisp. The Onion Pakora was well cooked and well flavoured. The Chicken Jallal was excellent with good quality meat in a lightly spiced sauce, not unlike Korma. Pleasantly flavoured Bombay Aloo with piping hot Naan. It is not cheap but a fair price for good food and great ambiance." D.R. "I have recommended this place to dozens of my friends and it has become a confirmed firm favourite with all of us." A.S. Most of our correspondents agree that the Menu is good with some unusual dishes but the prices are a little high, however one recommends that the Meat Thali at £7.00 is more than you can eat, and that seems to us to be a very reasonable price.

SAQUI TANDOORI,
1 Dukes Ride, Crowthorne. Tel: 0344 77214
"There are advantages to going out to eat with 19 other people. I got to taste nearly everything on the Menu. Best were Sheek Kebab and Dhansak. There were no special features but it is an elegant Restaurant in its quiet way." J.L. Prices are a little high. Poppadums 40p. Chicken Curry £2.95. Pullao Rice £1.50.

THE GARDEN OF GULAB,
130-134 Wokingham Road, Reading. Tel: 0734 667979
"We went there fairly soon after it opened to find there was a good choice on the Menu with some nice specials. The quantities and quality were good and the food was tasty and hot in temperature. The waiters were really polite, the service was good, the surroundings very pleasant and we would definitely go back." S.B. Evidently that correspondent did go back because we have had other reports and other regulars in the area speak well of the Restaurant. We would welcome more reports.

PANGBOURNE TANDOORI,
26 Reading Road, Pangbourne, Reading. 0734 843731
The decor is mock tudor in this relatively new establishment and the welcome and the general ambiance is warm. "On the occasion of my visit the dishes varied in quality and quantity. The Prawn Puree was excellent. The Chicken Tikka Masala a little raw on spicing. The Special Pullao Rice was superb. The Mushroom Bhajia was great with the mushrooms hardly cooked (that is the best way - ed). The Poppadums were really crispy." T.D.

THE RAJ,
27 London Road, Reading. Tel: 0734 588754
We have received a number of reports about The Raj. Reading locals believe it to be one of the best, if not the best, in the city. We would like confirmation of this with more reports because we also hear about slow service. "The food tends to be hotter than average. Peshawari Naan the best I had anywhere. We had a large group and they made a few mistakes but overall it was excellent." G.P. More reports please.

STANDARD TANDOORI,
143 Caversham Road, Reading. Tel: 0734 590093
Standard curries at the Standard Restaurant at average prices, Favourable reports about this long established Reading Restaurant.

KHAN BRASSERIE,
78 Yorktown Road, Sandhurst. Tel: 0252 878795
Many warm reports from our correspondents. It is evident that the proprietor M.A. Khan is regularly on hand to ensure that the standards he has set are maintained. The specials include such niceties as Malai Chicken, £4.95, diced chicken cooked with butter, cream and a light spicy sauce. Chingri Bahar, £6.95, friend king prawn cooked with spinach. Gosht Lahjig, cooked lamb pieces cooked in fresh spices and herbs and decorated with mince, £4.95 and Muchly Veran Masala £3.95, fried fish cooked in onions. It is perhaps a little steep with Poppadums at 50p each and Pullao Rice at £1.50 plus a service charge of 10% but our reporters consistently tell us that it is good value for money. One reporter raves about the Murgi Massallum, for 2 people, requiring 24 hours notice, at £25.00. "Extremely good value when you consider all the trappings are there and we included our young son as the third person at the same price." C.R. Whilst another goes into ecstasy's over the Tandoori Garlic Chilli Chicken £3.95.

BARN TANDOORI,
Salt Hill Playing Fields, Bath Road, Slough. Tel: 0753 23183
We have heard of some Restaurants in some fairly strange places. We mentioned earlier a Restaurant in a former school. We know of Restaurants in churches and in portakabins. We recently heard of a curry Restaurant in a transport cafe, but one of the weirdest of all that we know of is the Barn Tandoori which is situated in a former cricket pavilion. That alone doesn't make it a contender for entry into the Good Curry Guide but it's ambiance, setting, service and food do. However it has not been an easy ride for owners Khorshed and Khondaker, to convert the former cricket pavilion into a fully licensed Restaurant. Being a former pavilion, the building is not surprisingly, sited at playing fields. The new owners, armed with Planning Consent, set about an expensive interior rebuild, putting in kitchens, a smart dining room and a bar. Then the Council struck. They discovered that there existed an old Covenant formulated ages ago when the playing fields were donated to Slough. It prohibits the sale of alcohol and also states that only meals of a simple nature could be sold at the pavilion, so having issued Planning Consent they then thereby refused a Drinks License knowing they could not revoke Restaurant use. At a great risk and expense the owners took the Council to Court and the Judge granted them their License stating that the Council had in effect, failed to bring up the subject of the Covenant at the right time. So back in 1987 the Restaurant opened, but the Council hadn't finished with them. Their next demand was that the owners should take down an illuminated sign put up, the Council said, without their permission. The Barn is located in a dark playing field and clearly the Restaurant needed to be illuminated. Having invested so hugely the proprietors felt they had enough on their hands building up their business without petty mindedness of the Council. The owners have apparently got over their initial teething troubles and we have many reports to hand talking of interesting location, good food and good service.

THE ROYAL INDIA,
72 Peach Street, Wokingham. Tel: 0734 789338
"This Restaurant is better than average but is quite expensive. For example a 10% service charge mysteriously appeared when I went there with a large group on one occasion. However the Chicken Tikka Masala and other dishes were very good indeed. Be warned though, Vindaloo is very hot." G.P.

GOLDEN CURRY, **CC DISCOUNT**
46 High Street, Eton, Windsor. Tel: 07535 863961
Windsor is one of those towns which always draws attention to itself and we regularly get reports from numerous visitors and tourists to the area. We even have on record reports as far afield as the United States of America and Australia. Of Windsor's 5 Indian Restaurants, one is in fact in Eton. One way to get to it is to walk across the footbridge from Windsor itself over the River Thames and you arrive in the pretty village of Eton and there, you find the Golden Curry Restaurant on the High Street. The Golden Curry has been there since the early 1960's and it does appear now to get the best reviews from our reporters. It is a very compact Restaurant and one is not aware that it seats as many as 65. The service is discreet, smart and friendly and the food is good. The Menu is a standard Menu offering no surprises, but everything that should be there, is there. Prices are as you would expect in a tourist town. Poppadums are 40p. Chicken Curry £3.50. Pullao Rice £1.40. Chicken Tikka Masala £5.10. Curry Club members will be allowed a discount. See page 288.

BUCKINGHAMSHIRE

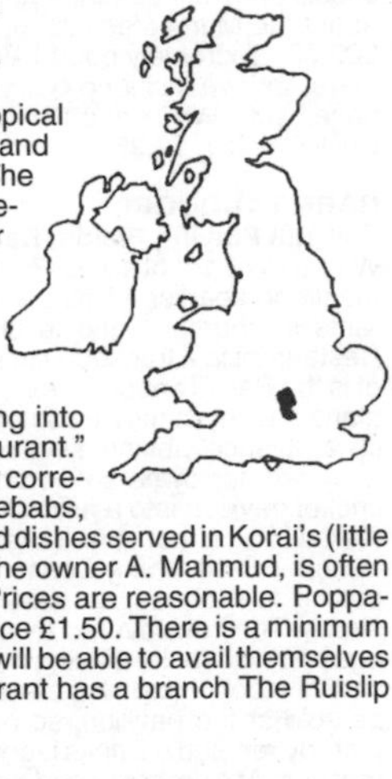

BUCKS TANDOORI, **CC DISCOUNT**
7 Broadway, Penn Road, Beaconsfield.
Tel: 04946 74582
This Restaurant was on the site of the Tropical Curry Tandoori which was gutted by fire, and was in our previous Good Curry Guide. The Bucks Tandoori opened in 1988 and immediately came to the notice of our regular correspondents. It is a large Restaurant seating about 100 and it is attractive in its decor with soft blues, flowers and candlelight. There is a fishpond near the door in the reception area. One correspondent has told us that "it is like slipping into exotica when you come into this Restaurant." K.W. Dishes particularly singled out by our correspondents include Shaslik and Hasina Kebabs, Chicken Jalfrezi, Chicken Tikka Masala and dishes served in Korai's (little handled chrome plated serving dishes). The owner A. Mahmud, is often to hand which ensures smooth running. Prices are reasonable. Poppadums 30p. Chicken Curry £3.95. Pullao Rice £1.50. There is a minimum charge of £8.50 and Curry Club members will be able to avail themselves of a discount. See page 288. The Restaurant has a branch The Ruislip Tandoori, Ruislip, Middlesex.

THE MOGHAL TANDOORI,
8 Warwick Road, Beaconsfield. Tel: 04946 4830
Although we have heard very little of The Moghal since it appeared in our last Good Curry Guide, what we have heard is favourable. The Menu is fairly standard and the prices are fairly average although there is still a 10% service charge we hear.

TROPICAL CURRY, **CC DISCOUNT**
33 London End, Beaconsfield. Tel: 04946 675474
Attractive white painted bow fronted windows lead you in to an equally attractive white walled Restaurant punctuated with black oak beams and nicely contrasted with pink table linen and green chairs. It is quite a large Restaurant of 90 seats and one that is very popular with its hard core of regulars, judging by the correspondence we receive. The Menu contains a good selection of starters including no less than 5 types of Kebab and Bombay Duck. It has the normal selection of curries and a representative selection of specials. Chicken Tikka Masala is £6.80. Murgi Masala £7.50, is a half chicken cooked in mind spices and herbs and Dhal Ferazhi is priced at £6.80. Poppadums are 25p and Pullao Rice £1.15. According to the Menu the minimum charge is £10.00 per head and 10% service

charge is levied but according to Mr. Rakib Ali the proprietor, the minimum charge is £9.25 per head and there is no service charge or cover charge included. We have heard one comment that the Lobster Dhansak was in fact King Prawn but other than that, all comments have been favourable. The Restaurant has a branch the Tropical Curry at Ickenham in Middlesex and a discount is available to Curry Club members. See page 288.

THE EMPIRE OF INDIA,
3A Straight Bit, Flackwell Heath, Bourne End. 06285 31383
Bourne End is fortunate to have 2 very good Restaurants in its precincts, the Empire of India is one of them. "Our second home. The service is friendly and efficient and because we are such regulars there is always a bottle of chilled white wine, poppadums, Bombay duck and chutneys waiting for us at the table. Portions are large and liberally garnished with fresh coriander." J.P. Booking is recommended, especially at weekends.

THE LAST VICEROY,
74 The Parade, Bourne End. Tel: 06285 31383
This Restaurant is part of the Kensington Tandoori Group of London. (See London entries). As with all their other Restaurants the cooking is overseen by their executive chef Pan Singh Rana (formerly of The Oberoy Hotel in Delhi). The food at The Last Viceroy has the same pedigree. However the service and the organisation at this far-flung out station leaves something to be desired. The problem seems to lie mostly in the booking system which is "a little chaotic with as many as 10 people waiting for a table, crammed in the small waiting area adjacent to the door. Tired of being pushed by others coming in, some people choose to wait outside. We have been twice and on each time similar bottlenecks occurred. No such problem with the meal however, being subtle and delicately flavoured. Lamb Pasanda and Chicken Tikka Masala exceptional." C. & D.P. and another quote says "Having booked a table there one hour ahead, when we arrived we were told to come back one hour later because our table was not ready, without an apology. We did go back, fortunately, because the food was superb. Jalfrezi was chilli based and very good. The Vindaloo was also favourable. The prices seemed high initially but the final bill was less than expected. "We would like more reports please.

THE DIPALEE, **CC DISCOUNT**
18 Castle Street, Buckingham. Tel: 0280 813151
Set in Buckinghamshire's county town, The Dipalee continues to earn its place in our Guide. "I not only found the Khurzi Feast because of your Guide, I found The Dipalee." S.S.T. We are pleased you did find the Guide useful and we understand the Khurzi Feast is still available. Give them 48 hours notice and they will give you a Khurzi Feast for 2 or 4, chicken or lamb is marinated in creamy spice and yoghurt mixture for at least 24 hours (hence the need to give them the warning). It is then slow roasted for about 6 hours and then served. It is a huge and filling meal. "It was so wonderful and we took home such an enormous doggy bag, we were able to keep eating this amazing feast for some days afterwards." S.S. Other specials include the Lamb and Chicken Pasanda, The Korai Chicken or Lamb, Chilli Masala Special (for the hotheads) and the Vegetarian Thali. Prices are acceptable. Poppadums at 35p. Chicken Bhoona £3.70. Pullao Rice £1.30. Minimum charge £6.50. No service or cover charges. A discount is available to Curry Club members at quieter times. See page 288. The Restaurant has a branch in Milton Keynes, The Jaipur.

THE AKASH TANDOORI,
21 High Street, Burnham. Tel: 06286 3507
Established in 1982 this Restaurant is sited in an historic building on the High Street and provides a standard Menu with one or two nice specials such as Murgi Massalam £6.25, Chicken Tikka Do-Piaza £5.25, Lobster Channa £7.25 and Akash Chicken Special, half a chicken cooked in herbs and mild spices £5.95. The Restaurant also does Khurzi Chicken or Lamb at a price of £52.00 serving 4 and this meal is served with starters, side dishes, special fried rice, house wine and coffee representing fairly good value. We have a regular correspondent who writes in about The Akash and has been for years. In our last Good Curry Guide we quoted him as saying he has been round the Menu twice. Since then he now claims to have eaten his way round the Menu no less than 5 times. Claiming it to be a kind of Culinary around the Menu in 80 weeks trip. We

have our faint suspicions that this is the owner writing in but full marks for originality. We also have sufficient reports from others to be sure that this is a good, safe bet. Prices are a tiny bit on the high side, Poppadums 40p, Chicken Curry £3.20, Pullao Rice £1.40, minimum charge £10.00. There is no service charge or cover charge. The Restaurant has a branch The Farnham Tandoori Restaurant at Farnham Common, Bucks.

PRINCE OF INDIA,
37 Elmshott Lane, Cippenham, 06286 663899
A medium sized 50 seat Restaurant. Opened in 1986, The Prince of India has established a satisfactory reputation for competence with its regular clientele. "The curry here is very acceptable". C.G. Specials include King Prawn Jalfrezi £7.50, Chicken Tikka Masala £5.00 and Kori, Chicken or Lamb £4.80, Poppadums are 40p, Pullao Rice £1.20. This Restaurant has other branches, The Prince of India, Egham, The Saagar Tandoori, Redbourne and The New Saagar, Harefield. (See next entry but one).

THE ASHIANA TANDOORI,
2-1 Broadway East, Denham. Tel: 0895
The walls and ceilings are in suede fabric and this is countered with lots of real mahogany. Tablecloths are brown and beige and the whole ambiance is one of space and elegance, yet with privacy built into it. The Ashiana, means the Dream House, was designed by Mr. Malick the sole owner who is often to be found in attendance. The Menu is fairly standard and it offers to prepare any Indian dish not included in the Menu. One correspondent writes of requesting Chilli Chicken "which turned out to be delightfully fresh, subtly spiced and freshly hot with green and red chillies combined. It wasn't on the Menu yet it only took them no more than 20 minutes to prepare." R.B. Specials include King Prawn Bhajee as a starter £2.65, King Prawn Delight - King Prawns cooked in creamed coconut £7.15 for a main course. Korai Lamb or Chicken - pieces of Lamb or chicken cooked in the Tandoor with herbs and spices and simmered in a special sauce £6.55. Lamb Peshwa, Lamb Tikka cooked in a dry sauce with capsicums and tomato. Typical prices are Poppadums 35p, Chicken Curry £3.75, Pullao Rice £1.25. Miniumum charge is £7.50. There is no service or cover charge.

THE PRINCE OF INDIA, **CC DISCOUNT**
22a Oakend Way, Gerrards Cross, 0753 884454
This Prince of India is part of a large Group which contains no less than 12 other Prince of India Restaurants. This Group has grown by some 8 Restaurants since the publication of the last Good Curry Guide and all the Restaurants in the group receive competent reports. Gerrards Cross branch is no exception with a 50 seat, air conditioned Restaurant. It is noted by our correspondents for the Korai Lobster at £9.95, the Chicken or Meat Tikka Masala at £5.90, Special Beef Curry at £8.75, the Tandoori Fish at £6.95, the Special Butter Chicken at £6.15, Special Lobster at £8.95. Other typical prices include Poppadums at 50p, Chicken Curry at £3.75 and Pullao Rice at £1.40 Set dinners run at £16.50 for one, £32.00 for two and £60.00 for four and this makes the Restaurant somewhat expensive. Minimum charge is £9.00 but there is no service or cover charge. The Restaurant will offer discounts for Curry Club members at quieter times. See page 288.

SHEESH MAHAL TANDOORI,
18 High Street, Iver. Tel: 0753 651123
"Set Menu for 4 was excellent value. The portions were very generous with a good varied Menu with average prices. We found the service extremely good. The Banana Fritters were absolutely delicious." P.D. & G.R.

THE JAIPUR,
502 Elder Gate, Milton Keynes. Tel: 0908 669796
Milton Keynes is one of those places you either love or hate. It was created out of nothing but countryside over the last 25 years and now has reached the stage where it has almost grown up. Built on a right angular grid system in the way that many American small towns are, it is centred around a large shopping centre. By the railway station is the hard to find Jaipur Restaurant, but find it you must because it is well worth a visit. Mr. A. Ahad the owner, has gone to a great deal of trouble and expense to create a very beautiful, very exclusive, upmarket Restaurant, in what was

before he started, a glass and concrete, rather plain dull shell in an office block. However you are not aware of these humble origins once you walk in to the Jaipur Restaurant. Jaipur is in Rajahstan. It is a very romantic city and it is the home of one of the world's richest ex-Maharajas, complete with fort, treasures, elephants, camels and picturesque scenery. One of the most notable things about Jaipur is that every building in this beautiful city is made from pink sandstone and even the paintwork is pink, so everywhere you look you get this wonderful splash of pink colour. Mr. Ahad has taken various shades of Jaipur pink and incorporated them into his decor. The walls, the curtains, the carpets, the chairs, the bar, the flowers, the tablecloths and the napkins, everything is in matching shades of pink. As you enter, you find yourself in a pretty little cocktail bar. There you can relax with a drink while you peruse the Menu and prepare your order. When you are ready you are shown into the main Restaurant. At 99 seats it is quite a large Restaurant yet it feels neither too large nor too small. It has an air of comfortable, spacious luxury and as you look around you will see that the centre of the Restaurant is dominated by a pink marbled circular fountain above which is an ornate chandelier and a circular ceiling centrepiece, around which pink and green flowers emerge. Whatever you choose from the Menu (pink of course) you can be sure it will be good. All the cooking is fresh and delicate and subtle. Starters include a delicious Aloo Chat, small pieces of potato cooked in a hot and spicy sour sauce £1.95 or Chicken Chat £2.25. The Chicken Kebabs £2.25, involve minced chicken with onions, herbs and spices which are skewered then tandoored. Tandoori specialities include Moghul Lamb Chops £5.25, Tandoori Duck, and Jaipur Tandoori Fish, a mildly spiced trout grilled over charcoal and served with salad. Other dishes of note include the Chicken Badami, tender pieces of chicken breast simmered in mild creamy sauce enhanced with almonds £4.95 and Chicken Jalpuri, a rich chicken curry cooked in a typical Rajastani style medium hot sauce at £4.50. The vegetable dishes are freshly cooked. The desserts include Rasmalai, cream cheese balls covered in a sweetened milk sauce flavoured with saffron at £1.95 and Kulfi, Indian ice cream at £1.50, Fresh Mangoes when available and a nice touch noted by more than one of our correspondents Lassi, sweet or salted yoghurt drink £1.50. We have had very many reports on this Restaurant since it opened in May 1988 and it has undoubtedly established itself as a top notch Restaurant. "This was not going to be the run of the mill place. No scrambling over old oil cans to find the smallest room. Provisions of nail brush and clothes brush to be found. The service has been known to be a bit slow but I use this Restaurant a lot. It is less than 50 yards from the office and I am sure they will do a good business from the 300 people who work in my office alone." T.S. Other reporters talk of the sitar player and pink champagne. On opening day the Restaurant achieved notoriety in Milton Keynes by obtaining a medium sized elephant who paraded around the town with Anneka Rice on her back. It certainly is not a cheap Restaurant, equally it is not exhorbitantly expensive and the management operates a strict door control requiring that smart dress is worn (no denim). One extremely good value way to experience this Restaurant is to eat the special Sunday Family Lunch at £7.95 where a 3 course vegetarian or non-vegetarianmeal is available on a self service basis where you can eat as much as you like from a wide variety of delicacies. Mr. Ahad has another branch The Dipalee Tandoori Restaurant in Buckingham (see earlier) and discounts are available to Curry Club members at quieter times (see page 288). It is essential to book at this Restaurant. See also inside front cover. We are pleased to place it in our top 100.

THE MILTON KEYNES TANDOORI,
Queensway, Bletchley, Milton Keynes, 0908 75209
This well established Restaurant (opened nearly 10 years) has also established itself a very good reputation in Milton Keynes. It obviously has its corps of regular supporters for whom it can do little wrong. Specialities include according to our reporters a rather excellent Pasanda, Rhogan Gosh Josh, Chicken Masala, Dhansak and Patia. This Restaurant appeared in the first edition of the Good Curry Guide but we have received a few discouraging reports, so it was omitted from the second edition. We are glad to see it back. We would welcome more reports.

THE NIGHT OF INDIA, CC DISCOUNT
The Agora Centre, Wolverton, Milton Keynes, 0908
Formerly known as The Agora, this Restaurant reopened as the Night of

India in May 1989. We are pleased to say that since its refurbishment we have received many good reports for this 70 seat Restaurant. This Restaurant does not operate a lunch trade, it has rather useful hours 6 p.m. to 2 a.m. every day. Its comprehensive Menu starts with Dhal or Muligatawny Soup at 90p and offers a wide range of starters from £1.30 for Samosas to £3.30 for King Prawn Butterfly. The Menu then covers tandooried dishes, chicken meat and seafood curries heat graded from very mild Korma at £3.40 to extra hot Phall at £3.60. There is a selection of Biriani dishes including, we are told, a very excellent Persian Chicken Biriani at £5.50. Poppadums are 25p each. Chicken Curry £3.30. Pullao Rice £1.25 and there is a minimum charge of £7.00. K. Kapoor, the owner, is often to be found on duty and the Restaurant offers a discount to Curry Club members at quieter times (see page 288).

THE BEKASH,
50 High Street, Stony Stratford, Milton Keynes. Tel: 0908 562249
The Bekash is another very competent Restaurant in an area where competence is the norm. We get consistently good reports from our correspondents as is witnessed by the fact that The Bekash is appearing for the third time in the Good Curry Guide. It is pleasantly decorated and has a 20 seater lounge with a fairly large 120 feet Restaurant. Prices are acceptable with Poppadums at 35p, Chicken Curry at £3.40, Pullao Rice at £1.40 and a set dinner for 2 at £19.50. "The Sunday buffet is superb value". D.T.

THE DHAKA DYNASTY,
2 Stanley Court, Weston Road, Olney. Tel: 0234 713179
This Restaurant started trading a few years ago to a fanfare of publicity and press. A lot of money was spent setting the Restaurant up and we are told that Amin Ali of Red Fort, London, W.1. fame was involved. Our reporters talk of attractively decored Restaurant and extremely good cooking. "Subtle spices abound in the cooking. We thoroughly enjoyed the Pakoras and the Chicken Makani and my husband had Tandoori Duck for the first time, it was outstanding." S.D.

THE PRINCE OF INDIA **CC DISCOUNT**
10-12 Aylesbury Road, Wendover. Tel: 0296 622761
This Restaurant is one of the chain of which we mentioned the Gerrards Cross branch earlier. Our local correspondents talk of good service, the prices a bit high but quality good. Meat Dhansak for example is £4.50, Tandoori Chicken Masala with Pullao Rice £6.25 and "Peshwari Naan the best." C.D. Discounts are available for Curry Club members at quieter times. See page 288.

CAMBRIDGE

KOHINOOR RESTAURANT
74 Mill Road, Cambridge. Tel: 0223 3236
We hear reports of new decor here with blue formica. Does that mean the peacock tapestry's have gone? Reports please about this and the Restaurant in general. The Menu is fairly standard with one or two interesting variations on the theme. Lamb or Chicken Kraya is chopped lamb or chicken with fresh chilli and onions in a thick curry sauce both £5.25. "Chicken Chawman (chopped cabbage), never seen that one before and Egg Naan very good. Tandoori Chicken Masala was first class and the Chicken Phall wasn't disappointing. Worth a trip from Romford." J.S.K. On the menu are curry gravy sauce and chilli gravy sauce at 50p and 60p respectively, a good idea. Typical prices are Poppadums 35p. Chicken Curry £2.40. Pullao Rice £1.10. Set luncheon £3.75. Set dinner £8.75. The minimum charge is £3.00 Service charge at 15% is rather steep. Hazir Miah, the owner, doesn't own any other branches and is offering discounts to Curry Club members at quieter times. See page 288.

THE MAHARAJAH
9-13 Castle Street, Cambridge. Tel: 0223 358399
"Stands on the corner of Castle Street and St. Peters Street. Approaching on foot a most unappetising smell of dustbins came from the back of the building. Pre prandial Poppadums were stale. The Bombay Duck however were beautifully dry, crisp and tasty. The Menu is standard and reasonably priced. The portions however were not over generous." J.N. That report very nearly took The Maharajah out of this Guide altogether but we have had so many good reports about the place that we left it in. This one is typical, "One of the more upmarket Restaurants so prices are slightly higher than other Restaurants in the city. Tables were nicely decorated and clean and portions of food good, service very attentive. Despite being the only person in the Restaurant the food took an eternity to arrive, although they do a brisk takeaway service. Rashmi Kebab at £1.75 was spicy and succulent with mint sauce. Lamb Pasanda £4.95 and Mushroom Pullao £1.25 were excellent. The Purees crisp and flaky." J.T.

RAJBELASH
36 Hills Road, Cambridge. Tel: 0223 354679
At the Curry Club we received several thousand restaurant reports every year. The Rajbelash has received quite a surprising amount. For those of you who read the Curry Club Magazine's Restaurant Round-Up you will see that there has been a battle between the Cambridge reporters as to which is the best Cambridge Restaurant. The Rajbelash wins. "They have friendly staff, an excellent Menu, a clean kitchen (containing a genuine clay oven) and, unusually, happy people. The Rajbelash has reliable food which is quite inexpensive, car parking, a distinct advantage locally, and a wide variety of specials which they vary from time to time." D.J. "Seats around 120 people. On every table were chutneys and a plate warmer. The Poppadums arrived within minutes but they had lost their crispness. The Onion Bhajia and Samosa (£1.65) for starter and the Chicken Korma for the main course were excellent. Must say too, that our Mushroom Pullao and the Purees were light and crisp. We give it full marks for service and value for money." J.T.

THE EMPRESS OF INDIA
74 Market Street, Ely. Tel: 0353 2281
This is a large Restaurant seating nearly 100 people. It is very clean and has quite plush decor. It is quite well patronised according to our reports and has a regular following. "The Meat Vindaloo with vegetables and rice registered a good average. Can't fault the food in any major way but to state, as the Menu does, that it is East Anglia's best Restaurant serving quality food is going too far." K.F. "The Menu is very varied, the quantities are good and the service is very pleasant. The decor gives a feeling of a classy atmosphere and the dishes are distinctively flavoured. The prices are a bit on the high side but it is very good value." P.W. Reports welcomed.

SURMA TANDOORI RESTAURANT **CC DISCOUNT**
78 Broad Street, Ely. Tel: 0353 2281
The Surma has been trading since June 1979 and has built up a strong corps of regular officionados. We said in our last Guide that the Surma's Menu is one of the best, most useful Glossary explaining literally what is what. We are pleased to tell you that the Menu hasn't changed, only the prices have gone up. Typical prices are now Poppadums 30p, Chicken Curry £2.95, Pullao Rice £1.20 and a large set dinner for one £10.95. This Restaurant gives discounts to Curry Club members at quieter times. See page 288.

TAJ MAHAL
4/5, Causeway Mews, High Causeway.
Very popular curry house about which we received many good reports offering all you Tandoori and curry favourites.

EASTERN GARDEN
39 Lincoln Road, Peterborough. 0733 48840
This Restaurant is rated by many of our regular correspondents as the best of Peterborough's 12 Indian Restaurants. It has a standard Menu but its quality, quantity and friendliness has it out as a very good establishment.

INDIA GATE **CC DISCOUNT**
9 Fitzwilliam Street, Peterborough. Tel: 0733 46160
The India Gate was established in 1984 and changed ownership as recently as 1989. It has come to our attention on a number of occasions as a competent standard Curry House. Prices are reasonable with Poppadums at 30p, Chicken Curry £3.20, Pullao Rice £1.20. The set luncheon is £5.99 and a set dinner for 2 is £21.95. This Restaurant offers discounts to Curry Club members at its quieter times. See page 288.

KUSHIARIA TANDOORI
21 Bridge Street, St. Ives. Tel: 0480 65737
This is a quote typical of those we receive: "I have visited this place frequently over the past 4 years and always found the service to be excellent and very friendly, courteous and very welcoming. The decor is quite understated but it's cosy. The premises are very small with as many tables as possible crammed in. Booking is essential. The Menu is varied and comprehensive. Portions are generous and the quantity is excellent. The best recommendation is consistent quality." M.M.

RAJ DOUTH **CC DISCOUNT**
112 High Street, St. Neots, Huntingdon. Tel: 0480 219626
This Restaurant opened in June 1983 and appeared in our first Guide. A few rather dodgy reports took it out of our second Guide but since then we are pleased to say that we have received consistently good reports about The Raj Douth. Prices are reasonable and this Restaurant offers discounts to Curry Club members in their quieter times. See page 288.

CHESHIRE

THE ASIA **CC DISCOUNT**
104 Foregate Street, Chester.
Tel: 0244 22595
"We got very good food here and the Tandoori Cocktails were a delight. The service was excellent, even before we told them we were members of the Curry Club. They couldn't do enough for us and apart from the carnation for the lady and a voucher for the wine, they gave us liqueurs and coffee on the house as well." B.T. "We think The Asia is probably the best Restaurant in Chester. The food is pretty good, King Prawn Tandoori Masala is £6.50 and that includes Pullao Rice." N.R. and P.J. This Restaurant offers a discount to Curry Club members in their quieter times. See page 288.

BOMBAY PALACE
11 Upper Northgate Street, Chester. Tel: 0244 371194
This is Chester's oldest Restaurant which recently underwent refurbishment, although you do not get an indication of this from the outside. It is quite small, it is simply decorated and it is very friendly. The Menu is standard, straight forward and reasonably priced. "I discovered this Restaurant by chance on a visit to Chester. The Vindaloo illustrated the perfect balance between heat and flavour. Especially noteworthy were the Mokonwala (their spelling, ed.) Meat Thali and Jal Thurzi (their spelling). I liked this place so much I did not bother to find another one in our weeks stay in the city." J.N. Reports welcome.

THE GATE OF INDIA,
25 City Road, Chester. Tel: 0244 27131
Chester's second oldest Restaurant opened in 1962 and it went into its present ownership in 1971. We get slightly mixed reports about this Restaurant. For example "The decor is clean but it is a bit tired. The service is pleasant. Our Mixed Kebab consisted of Shami Kebab, Onion Bhajia and Puree and was good value at £1.50. Rhogan Josh is brilliant." P.D. The prices in this establishment seem to be a bit high. The Rhogan

Josh for example is £4.75, Poppadums 50p, Chicken Curry £4.45, Pullao Rice £1.00. Minimum charge is £4.00 and there is no service or cover charge. It has remarkably late opening hours which are 6 p.m. to 2.30 a.m. week days and 6 p.m. to 3 a.m. at weekends.

THE BOMBAY,
31 High Street, Crewe. Tel: 0270 214861
This Restaurant appeared in our last Guide more by default than choice. We said about it then that it was a bit like sticking a needle into the preverbial haystack to select and recommend one as best in Crewe. We haven't received many reports on the Bombay in the intervening years but those that we have, point to the fact that our reasoning is correct and that you can expect a standard, reasonable, inexpensive and average meal at this Restaurant. Reports please

THE MONSOON TANDOORI, **CC DISCOUNT**
27 Welsh Row, Nantwich. Tel: 0270 629968
Nantwich is an attractive timbered Cheshire town and the Monsoon's exterior is in keeping with this atmosphere. Step in to the reception area and you at once see an attractive salmon covered velvet upholstery with high comfortable chairs and an intimate cosy atmosphere. On the walls are attractive paintings and the 40 seat Restaurant is set to give you a feeling of well being. "We go to this Restaurant regularly and find the service good." F.O. The Menu offers a well described selection of standard curry dishes on offer and vegetarian main courses, such as Aloo Mattar, peas with chick pea and herbs £3.90. Sag Aloo, spinach, potato and spices at £3.90. Mushroom Bhoona, mushrooms, herbs and tomato at £4.25. These same dishes are available as side dishes at about half the price. Poppadums are 25p, Chicken Curry £4.40, Pullao Rice £1.10. Set dinner goes from £6.95 to £9.40 and the minimum charge is a rather peculiar £1.10 but at least there is no service or cover charge. Weekend opening hours Friday and Saturday are 2 a.m. and the Restaurant offers a discount for Curry Club members at quieter times. See page 288.

THE SAPNA TANDOORI,
11 High Street, Sandbach. 0270 3823
One of our regular reporters finds the Phall Curry (extremely hot) to be to her delight. She also goes on to say that "the portions are very generous." They are well presented and they are of excellent quality. The service is both friendly and efficient. Don't be put off, she says, by the exterior decor, it does no justice to the interior." N.R. We welcome more reports.

CLEVELAND

THE DILSHAD,
49a Church Street, Hartlepool.
Tel: 0429 272727
"I have been visiting this Restaurant for the past 4 years and I can honestly say I have never had a bad meal. They are always excellent. The Chicken Sag Walla, fresh spinach, garlic and herbs is for example, delicious. The Naan Breads and the Chupattis are fresh, hot and soft. The most unusual thing is that you can't help noticing a very large artificial tree with coloured birds and green apples, also artificial. It is quite beautiful to see, I must try to take a photograph sometime. Some customers who come in after pub hours stand on chairs, sing loudly and shout Dilboy and Dilshad at the owner." D.D. On another occasion the

same reporter tells us "the waiters are quite pleasant which makes up for the owner who is always solemn." We are not surprised about that considering the previous comments. We can only suggest that you avoid this Restaurant after pub hours and we seriously considered taking it out of this Guide except that we had received many complimentary comments from other reports. We welcome more views on this Restaurant please.

KHAN TANDOORI, **CC DISCOUNT**
349 Linthorpe Road, Middlesborough. Tel: 0642 817457
417 Linthorpe Road, Middlesborough. Tel: 0642 813559
42 Brorough Road, Middlesborough. Tel: 0642 243024
Last time we commented that Mr. and Mrs. Durrani had built up a steady reputation for good food, friendly services and reasonable prices. Each of the Restaurants have their own chefs and waiters but the Menu in each of the 3 being identical. Prices are very reasonable with Poppadums at 20p, Chicken Curry £2.55. Pullao Rice 80p and set luncheon at just £2.60. There is no minimum charge, no service charge and no cover charge and every diner gets a free face towel, Bombay Mix to nibble at, After Eight mints and Pan Masala to nibble at with coffee. One of our reporters obviously knows these Restaurants very well and tells us that "Mr. and Mrs. Durrani's first Restaurant here was the Maharajah, a 10 pints and Vindaloo shop opened in the late 1950's. In 1972 the Durrani's became managers at the Lion of Asia in partnership with a Mr. Varook. Mr. Durrani, known to all as Khan opened Khans, Brorough Road in 1978 and the Khan Tandoori, Linthorpe Road in 1983. In late 1985 they bought the Lion and also called that Khan Tandoori. As to the food the standards are good, the quantities are frequently meagre. I often complain which does improve the situation for a bit." S.H. Here is another quote "My local and perhaps I am biased but from my first visit I have had no complaints. Portions are now of good size. Portions have increased in size and now are adequate and well presented. You are not rushed over or hovered over. Waiters are uniformed. The decor marbled pink and grey. I visit here quite often at lunchtime and everything is clean and tidy from the night before. Bombay Duck is also on the Menu but up to now I haven't found anyone who likes it - I do." L.M.D.
All three Restaurants offer discounts to Curry Club members at quieter times. See page 288.

THE KUSUMBAGH, **CC DISCOUNT**
294 Linthorpe Road, Middlesborough. Tel: 0642 218406
This Restaurant seats 72 people and is attractively fitted out with a suspended ceiling complete with brass light fittings over each individual table. The walls are half pined and half velour and each table has specially designed Indian chairs. We have good reports to hand about the food including the special Akbari Lamb at £45.00 which serves 4 people. We also hear well about the Chicken Tikka Masala at £4.95 and the Kusumbagh Special Curry at £5.95. Standard typical prices are Poppadums 25p, Chicken Curry £2.85, Pullao Rice £1.15 and set dinners go from £8.50 to the mentioned Akbari Lamb at £45.00. The Proprietor Mr. F.M. Abdullah is often on hand and this Restaurant offers a discount to Curry Club members at quieter times. See page 288.

THE NELSON TANDOORI,
23 Nelson Terrace, Stockton on Tees. 0642 616276
This is a standard Restaurant with a standard Menu with "a few novel starters and special main courses." C.G. Service is a bit slow so we hear, but the surroundings are pleasant. The food is reported to be excellent and good value for money. More reports please.

THE ROYAL BENGAL,
Prince Regent Street, Stockton on Tees. Tel: 0642 64331
The few reports we have in this area speak well of The Royal Bengal. For example "This is my favourite Restaurant in the area, it is especially good to take the family to - they let you use their family room." More reports welcome.

CORNWALL

THE HANNAN TANDOORI, CC DISCOUNT
47 Arwenack Street, Falmouth.
Tel: 0326 317391

"My business takes me to Falmouth in Cornwall quite regularly and being a curryholic I drop into The Hannan quite frequently. I like the gold framed, red velvet chairs, the mirrors and the Indian village painted scenes on the wall. The crystal glass on the table and the king patterned cutlery helped to set the scene. The Menu contains many old favourites and a few interesting specials including The Hannan Special Chicken Curry cooked with prawn which comes in a metal korai sizzling hot dish at £5.95. The Peswari Chicken or Meat, diced boneless chicken pieces or lamb grilled in a tandoori oven and then fried with chopped onion and green peppers and served in a special iron dish at £6.50 and the Moglai Chicken, mildly spiced and cooked with cream and yoghurt and egg and garnished with almonds at £6.95 and finally the Labra Pasanda, cooked with chicken, meat and prawn in cream and special spices at £6.95. Desserts claim to include Jalebi at £1.95 although this can be unavailable at times." F.R. Prices are a little high with Poppadums at 40p, Chicken Curry £3.95 and Pullao Rice at £1.65. There is the set dinner for 2 at £29.95 said to be "absolute enormous requiring doggy bags but very good." C.C. There is no minimum charge, no service charge and no cover charge. This Restaurant will offer discounts to Curry Club members at their quieter times. See page 288. The Restaurant by the way, gets it's name from the owner who is also the chef who is Abdul Hannan. Advice to all diners, if you want a good meal at this or any other Restaurant, if you ask for the owner particularly when he is the chef, by name, you will be sure to get a good meal.

THE NEW MAHARAJAH,
39 Cliff Road, Newquay. Tel: 063 73 77377

Since the publication of our last Guide this Restaurant has come to our notice in a number of ways. Firstly the owner Vasant Maru had to obtain work permits for 2 chefs that he brought in from India, one from Nepal the other from South India. He had to appeal to the House of Commons and had to prove that he had turned down nearly 500 applicants from Curry House cooks - not experts he said. Following that Mr. Maru moved the Restaurant from Number 34 to Number 39 Cliff Road to enable him to get a more spacious comfortable new place with a cocktail bar. "We are vegetarians and the dishes there are superb. I suspect the meat ones are too. My friends say they are." A.T. A report from Mr. and Mrs. K tell of the attractive cocktail bar and the vast and varied Menus. Kebabs and Madras Curry they say were excellent, although main portions they claim, tended to be rather small. The comment about quantities being on the small side do persist on the reports we receive although "quality and service has always been on the high side and much enjoyed. Decor is very good with a splendid view of the sea." A.D.B. We simply cannot understand Restaurateurs who clearly care very much about the food they serve, spoiling the ship for a hapeth of tar when it comes to serving small quantities. It is so relatively cheap to serve slightly more and get your diners leaving full and satisfied than it is to be mean, especially when prices are a little on the high side. We urge Mr. Maru to review his policy and look forward to receiving more reports on this Restaurant.

THE TAJ MAHAL,
63 Daniel Place, Penzance. Tel: 0736 66630

We have reported before that this Restaurant is situated in the delightful bowfronted premises that were previously 'The Officers Mess.' Proprietors Hannan and Amir have decorated the inside very tastefully but we hear that it is "slightly cramped and dimly lit. Portions we hear are adequate but sometimes they are barely warm. Psychedelic red kebabs were a little off putting although the Kulfi was excellent. Service was adequate." Mr. and Mrs. K. Prices are reasonable with Poppadums at 35p, Chicken Curry £2.90 and Pullao Rice £1.20.

THE VICEROY OF INDIA,
1 Alverton Terrace, Penzance. Tel: 0736 68413
The Viceroy is so to speak, the elder statesman of Restaurants in Penzance and the reports we receive on it are a little uneven but mostly gives the Restaurant the thumbs up. "The food was above average and when it was served the temperature was really hot. We had a very good Peshwari Naan and the prices for 2 at £12.00 were extremely reasonable." A.M. "The Restaurant was full on the Saturday night that we went in there in the height of the tourist season and the waiters, although obviously working to full capacity and a little bit harassed were always polite, even though they did muddle up our order a little bit. They made amends by supplying not one but two liqueurs later. Good effort." R.A. Saturday night is Saturday night of course and even in Penzance one must expect slight hiccups to take place. Prices are Poppadums 40p, Chicken Curry £3.10, Pullao Rice £1.30.

THE TAJ MAHAL,
57 Victoria Road, St. Austell. Tel: 0726
"My work took me to the depths of Cornwall and I found myself in St. Austell with the usual curryholic withdrawal symptoms. I badly needed a curry fix so I tried The Taj Mahal." S.W. The Restaurant is evidently a competent standard Curry House which satisfies the needs of our visiting and regular correspondents. "Good standard curry with generous portions." K.P.

THE SALTASH INDIAN,
23-25 Lower Fore Street, Saltash. Tel: 0752
"Competent if a little expensive. Prawn Vindaloo £3.60 was disappointing. It tasted just of raw chilli. The Chicken Biriani £5.15 was delicious and delicately flavoured as it should be. The Aloo Gobi at £1.65 and the Sag Bhajee at £1.65 both had too much powdered garlic for my taste but the portions are good and I would go. back." K.P.

THE GANGES,
St. Clements Street, Truro. Tel: 0872
This is a branch of The Ganges in Exeter and in Plymouth and judging by the number of reports we have received on this Restaurant it is probably the best in Cornwall. The Restaurant itself is "spacious, air conditioned and full of exotic plants. The Menu offers a very good selection of value for money specialities. The portions are very generous and they are attractively presented. Just one slight criticism, the Kulfri was very watery." K.A.

CUMBRIA

THE TAJ MAHAL,
252 Dalton Road, Barrow. Tel: 0229 28388
This is a useful place to know about in an area not highly endowed with Curry Houses. We understand that The Taj is a standard Curry House and that it has a following of locals who have come to rely on The Taj for their regular intake of the good stuff.

THE DHAKA TANDOORI, CC DISCOUNT
London Road, Carlisle. Tel: 0228 28355
The Dhaka attracts its fair share of comments, not all of it good. For example "Despite booking we had to wait for over an hour. It was very busy, as expected, on a Saturday night but we were at a loss to understand this popularity. The service was slow. The Chicken Biriani would have covered a beer mat." P.B. and "The meal was okay but everyone is packed in like sardines. The wine list is rather expensive for Carlisle. No Gewurtzraminer!." N.S. There is no doubt that judging by the reports we get that this 80 seat Restaurant does get very busy. It is rather a cute little place in a white painted cottage on the main road with ample parking behind and for all you curryholic travellers, it is on the A6 just half a mile from the M6 Junction 42 on the southern fringe of Carlisle City. This

Restaurant presumably suffers as many Indian Restaurants do, with Saturday night syndrome. That is to say it gets too busy on a Saturday but for the rest of the week it could do with more trade. Our advice then, is to go in the rest of the week when we hear such comments as "My partner and I enjoyed respectively the Dhaka Special at £4.70 and the Akni Chicken at £4.80. Prices are perhaps a little on the high side with Poppadums at 40p, Chicken Curry £3.40, Pullao Rice £1.25 and a set dinner for 2 £22.00. Mr. Fazrul Karim also owns the Arecha Eastern Cuisine Restaurant in Paddyham, Lancs. and the Far Pavilion Tandoori on the A6 bypass road Bolton Le Sands in Lancs. This Restaurant offers discounts to Curry Club members at its quieter times. See page 288.

THE SHAHA TANDOORI,
89 Botchergate, Carlisle. Tel: 0228 20050
This Restaurant attracts fair comment from our correspondents in the Carlisle area "I have never been disappointed here. We have never been disappointed here, we vote it's best value for money in the area but service can be poor when it gets busy." N.S.

THE STANWIX TANDOORI,
11a Scotland Road, Carlisle. 0228 31495
There is no doubt that curry is proving to be very popular in Carlisle. The city now has at least 4 Restaurants plus one takeaway but The Stanwix stands its ground and continues to receive good, reliable reports. For example "This is a good consistent Indian Curry House. It is nicely decorated and the staff are very friendly. It is expensive however and it is always popular but even when it is full we have always had good service." N.S. "We make regular visits here because of the high standard of the food and service." P.B.

THE TAJ MAHAL,
39 - 41 Botchergate, Carlisle. Tel: 0228
This is a newcomer to the Carlisle scene and it is, we understand, very luxurious. The lounge bar is very impressive and it is totally unlike the other 3 Restaurants in the city. This is reflected in the prices however which are a bit above the others but the food is evidently good. "I could not fault the meal even though I went prepared to be critical. Everything was excellent. I think it could now be the best in town." N.S. We would like more reports please.

CAGNEYS TANDOORI,
17 King Street, Penrith. Tel: 0768 67503
We have had a few reports about this Restaurant, this was one of them. "Upon recommendation we took a group of 20 people. The staff coped very well. They served a wide and varied selection of food. The Masalas were rich and tasty and we were very well looked after." G.P.M. Reports on this Restaurant are welcome.

THE ALI TAJ,
34 Tangier Street, Whitehaven. Tel: 0946 693085
Standard Curry House. Reports please.

DERBYSHIRE

THE RAJAH TANDOORI,
1 Dig Street, Ashbourne.
Tel: 0335 42537
"I dig the Rajah Tandoori" says one correspondent in a play on words on this Restaurant's address. Other reporters seem equally happy with the place telling us that we can expect to find standard curries efficiently and pleasantly served in nice surroundings.

THE MAHARAJAH TANDOORI,
19 Holywell Street, Chesterfield. Tel: 0246 278315
This Restaurant is run by a husband and wife team, Mr. and Mrs. Khan who "turn out a thoroughly decent meal." C.R. Chesterfield is not particularly well endowed with Curry Restaurants so it is good to hear that this one is well thought of, but we would like more reports of this Restaurant and the others in the area.

THE ABID,
7 Curzon Street, Derby. Tel: 0332 44786
Derby on the other hand is well bestowed with Curry Restaurants and we hear good reports about The Abid on Curzon Street. It is evidently capable of producing "a high standard of food cooked by the chef owner." R.D.

THE ADNAN RESTAURANT,
196 Normanton Road, Derby. Tel: 0332 360314
Normanton Road is curry alley in Derby with no less than 5 Indian Restaurants trading along its lengths. One of these is The Adnan.
"I adore the Special Garlic Chicken £8.25 served with garlic, plenty of it, and Curry Sauce, Pullao Rice and Naan. I work as a secretary at a local electrical firm and at first my boyfriend didn't like the idea of eating curries but fortunately I have converted him now and he too enjoys the Garlic Special." C.M. We also hear good things about the Special Persian Chicken Biriani cooked with almonds, sultanas, fried onions and garnished with an omlette £5.75. Also the Kashmiri Chicken, appropriation of Chicken in mild spices with cream, sultanas, almond, banana and pineapple £5.75. Another splendid special there is Murgh Masala, chicken cooked with mincemeat, onion and capsicum £6.60. Prices are Poppadums 35p, Chicken Curry £3.30, Pullao Rice £1.20 and a set dinner for 2 from £19.00. The minimum charge is £6.50. There is no service or cover charge. This Restaurant has a branch in Nottingham The Shahi Mahal Restaurant.

THE FULL MOON TANDOORI,
278 Normanton Road, Derby. Tel: 0332 368887
Squeals of protest went out from the Midlands after we published our last Guide "how could you have missed out The Full Moon Tandoori?" S.A. "This Restaurant really is the best one in the city, why wasn't it in your Guide?" N.M. Well to make amends, we welcome The Full Moon Tandoori to the pages of The Good Curry Guide. We have had literally dozens of testimonials from different correspondents, both in Derby and the Midlands and also people who travel up and down the country rating this Restaurant very highly and on the strength of that we are prepared to say that this Restaurant is the best in Derby. Detailed report to follow.

MOTI MAHAL DELUX,
77 Normanton Road, Derby. Tel: 0332 44254
Also very good we hear, on the prolific Normanton Road, is The Moti Mahal. "I sampled the buffet menu and you could tackle as many starters and main courses as you could eat. The place is spotless and everything looks good and new. It is all remarkably good value for money." G.K.M.

THE SHABAB TANDOORI, **CC DISCOUNT**
11 Curzon Street, Derby. Tel: 0332 41811
This Restaurant opened in 1989 so it is a relative newcomer to the Derby scene. However it has quickly established itself as a favourite in the city and it actively encourages trade by giving a free bottle of wine on takeaway orders over £15.00, which seems remarkably good value. It also offers a free delivery service for takeaways on orders over £10.00 within a 6 mile radius. Its opening hours are quite remarkable - 6 p.m. to 2.30 a.m. every day and 6 p.m. to 3 a.m. on Fridays and Saturdays. It has a standard Menu with such things as Korma, Medium Curry, Madras Curry, Vindaloo, Sri Lankan, Kashmir, Dhansak, Du-Piaza, Rhogan Josh, Patia, Bhoona and Malaya curries. Everything is clearly explained on the Menu and each section gives you the choice of chicken, beef,

prawn, king prawn, mushroom, kidney and vegetables. Prices are reasonable. Poppadums 25p, Chicken Curry £3.00, Pullao Rice £1.10. Set dinners go from £16.95. There is a minimum charge of £4.00 but no service or cover charges. Final incentive - discounts are offered to students, nurses and old age pensioners, also to Curry Club members who use the Restaurant at its quieter times. See page 288.

THE SHALIMAR
2 Midland Road, Derby. Tel: 0332 366745
"The Shalamir is noted for its extensive Menu. Good portions and late night opening hours. Sunday to Wednesday it opens till 2.30 a.m., Thursday to Saturday 6 p.m. to 3 a.m. It also offers a delivery service for orders over £10.00 within an 8 mile radius. Poppadums are served hot with chutneys, Mushroom Bhajee is delicate with light Purees. Main course portions are very generous. I come up from Romford on several occasions and make a point of visiting here." J.T.

THE ABID
129 Dale Road, Matlock, Derby. Tel: 0332 44786
We have good reports about this Restaurant which is said to be attractively decorated, spacious, yet comfortable. The waiters are "courteous and helpful. There is an extensive Menu with 3 varieties of Indian beer. Recommended dishes are Chicken Kashmiri, Mash Bhajee (a rather unusual but good potato mash curry), Naan Bread, Peshwari Naan, Special Rice which had plenty of prawns, egg and vegetables. It all looked and was appetising and wasn't at all greasy." M.T.

MEHRAN
2, Cromford Road, Langley Mill, Nr Heanor. Tel: 0773 531307
Near the Nottinghamshire border, the Mehran has established a good reputation with reporters as far afield as Nottingham, and Derby. We hear of competently cooked curries and friendly service, which is exactly what one hopes to find at any restaurant in this Guide.

DEVON

THE CURRY HOUSE
80 South Street, Exeter. Tel: 0392 76069
"I felt nostalgic here, it reminded me of the Sharma Valley, Wembley in the 1970's. It has got an unimaginative layout etc. but very good food. None of your clever names here, The Curry House is what it is - cheerful, a friendly atmosphere. As the evening wore on it became crowded with clearly devoted regulars." Prices are reasonable.

THE GANGES
156 Fore Street, Exeter. Tel: 0392 72630
This Restaurant is one of a small chain of four with branches in Paignton, Plymouth, Exeter and Truro. This Ganges was established in 1970 and for the most part it proves to be a reliable Restaurant. We have to hand reports about good standards although from time to time we get a slightly disturbing report which leaves the impression that the Restaurant "could do better." J.L. Reports welcome.

THE GANGES
33 Crossways Shopping Centre, Paignton. Tel: 0803 551007
Judging by the reports we receive, this Ganges is the best one of the four. We hear about consistently good service and good food. The decor is attractive and the staff very friendly. "We visit here every other Friday and have done for the past 3 years." Mr. & Mrs. W. The prices here appear to be quite reasonable with Poppadums at 30p, Chicken Curry at £3.10, Pullao Rice at £1.35.

THE KHYBER RESTAURANT **TOP 100 & CC DISCOUNT**
44 Mayflower Street, Plymouth. Tel: 0752 266036
Everything about this Restaurant spells stability. It opened in 1960 and was the first Restaurant of its kind in the West Country. Until quite recently some of the staff had been there since opening day and only retirement has removed them from the scene. Todays staff are a charming and very pleasant mixture of nationalities. All are loyal, regular members of staff including two young women, one from England, the other from Malaysia. The kitchen is headed by Serazul Islam who has been there 20 years and his assistant is a Scottish chef who knows more about Indian cooking than many Indians. The thing which is remarkable about this Restaurant is its owner Abdul Tarafdar makes a point of being on duty very nearly every one of the 7 days a week. He has no other branches and concentrates solely on making The Khyber especially excellent in quality. As part of the Restaurants 30 year celebrations, it was refurbished using blue and red as the strongest colour themes. Entering the Restaurant, patrons are greeted with a bold Turkish designed carpet. From then on, a journey into the exotic Indian world: shadowy pink walls ornamented with oriental stencil work and antique wood panelling, painting and objects of art surround the Restaurant with gold plated crystal wall and ceiling light fittings. Finally a candlelit table with white and peach tablecloths sets the scene before patrons finally decide to tuck into their favourite dishes. It is a very small Restaurant seating a total of 54 people on the upstairs and downstairs floors. In 1970 The Khyber was amongst the first in the country to use the, now common place tandoori oven - only then it had to be imported from India. With such a long history The Khyber has seen competitors come and go despite the obvious temptation he has resisted grandiose expansion schemes or plans to open other branches. He believes the only way to ensure the highest standards is to be present as many days of the year as he can, whenever the House is open. Mr Tarafdar and his staff care very deeply about the food they serve. The Menu is not over long but is does contain many old favourites such as Vindaloo, Madras, Aloo Gosht, Sag Gosht and Rhogan Gosht. It is the specials which make this Restaurant outstanding. All special dishes are served with Basmati Rice, Vegetable Bhajee, Poppadum and Pickles and this is reflected in the prices. Highly recommended are Trout Tal Curry £7.95, succulent slices of fresh local large fish, lightly spiced and cooked the Bengali way. Mint Gosht £7.95 is a lightly spiced lamb curry flavoured with mint. Goshtaba is a Kashmiri dish where lamb is stoneground, shaped into balls and cooked in a mild sauce. Equally good is the Lamb Kolhapuri at £7.95 which is a Southern Indian dish cooked with selected roasted spices. 3 newly introduced dishes include Jardaloo Sali £8.95 which is a parsi dish of delicately cooked lamb with ground almonds, pistachio nuts and garnished with dried apricots and fried potato sticks. Achar Gosht £8.95 is beef cooked with aubergine pickle, mango, mustard and fresh coriander leaves. It is a Ghurka dish and can be medium or hot and Murgh Badam Pasanda is breast of chicken cooked in a creamy sauce with a touch of turmeric, roast almonds and sultanas. This is a dish which would grace the tables of discerning Indians, £8.95. All of The Khyber's cooking is good and it sometimes is outstanding. "I happen to like Korma and I ask the Restaurant for their Lamb Korma. Far from being a standard pre-cooked curry in a standard pre-cooked sauce, this Korma was superb in its aromatic flavour and spicing. It is quite clear that this Restaurant knows everything there is to know about cooking with spices." C.N. The Khyber's wine list at the time of writing includes some extraordinary vintage bargain wines including clarets dating from 1972 and 1974 and vintage champagnes all at exceptionally good prices. We have received a particularly large amount of reports from this Restaurant, well above average and all but a few are very, very good. Of course we have had the odd grumble, but that can be said of every Restaurant in the land. We are unable to explain fully why a Restaurant doesn't satisfy a particular person on a particular date. It could be that the Restaurant is having an "off day" or it could be that the person themselves are having an "off day". However it is our duty to assess the merit of each report and indeed to pass on the information we receive to our readers. It is only fair to say that over the 25 years, the editor of this Guide has eaten at The Khyber Restaurant on many occasions. He has only recently got to know its owner where he has found a genuine interest in the exchange of information about Indian food. The Khyber's dedication to its job, interest in the food it cooks and general professionalism sets a standard which every other Restaurant in the land should follow. Its track record proves

it an entrant into many Guides, too many to mention. There are no hidden extras, no service charge, no cover charge and no chutney charge. It is an extremely good Restaurant, certainly the best in the West and unhesitatingly in our top 100. It is advisable to book into this Restaurant. The Khyber offers discounts to Curry Club members at its quieter times. See page 288.

THE KURBANI RESTAURANT **CC DISCOUNT**
1 Tavistock Place, Plymouth. Tel: 0752
This Restaurant opened in 1985 and it is elegantly decorated in beige, buffs, browns and magnolia. Stained glass peacocks and picture mirrors depict Indian village life and that of the Moghul courts. The walls are painted in magnolia, the tables have a darker shade of magnolia slips on white tablecloths. Gold coloured spoon backed mahogany chairs make the setting very attractive. We have received a number of good reports about this Restaurant. The Kuta Gosht £7.30 is pounded meat steaks cooked with fresh seasonal spices and served, as are all the specials, with Pullao Rice, Vegetable Curry and Poppadum. The Kata Masala Gosht is meat cooked with fresh spices and there are some rather good fish dishes including Muchli Ka Salan, fish cutlets in a spicy tandoori sauce £4.00 and Trout Masala, marinated trout cooked in a tandoor and served in a spicy masala sauce £5.00. The Restaurant prides itself that it serves home made pickles and it offers discounts to Curry Club members in its quieter times. See page 288. This Restaurant has a branch The Curry Centre in Horsham, West Sussex.

THE MAHARAJAH RESTAURANT **CC DISCOUNT**
114 Cornwall Street, Plymouth. Tel: 0752
This Restaurant opened in 1987 and is another up and coming Restaurant in Plymouth. Our correspondents talk of an attractive Restaurant decked out in burgundy silk with Indian line drawings on the walls set off with gleaming white tablecloths and silver ware. The Menu itself offers no surprises and includes such things as Chicken Tikka or Meat Tikka Korma, £6.25, Lamb or Chicken Pasanda £6.55 and Maharajah Chicken, Prawn or Meat Curry £6.25. Poppadums are 35p, Chicken Curry £4.25. Set dinner is £12.50 and there are no hidden extra charges. The Restaurant offers discounts to Curry Club members at its quieter times. See page 288.

VEENAS **CC DISCOUNT**
8 Beacon Terrace, Torquay. Tel: 0803 294902
Veenas opened in 1988 and is operated by Mr. R. P. Singh its owner. The menu is rather a strange mixture of curry and Italian food. It also concentrates quite largely on vegetarian food having brought itself to the attention of the vegetarian society and has an exceptionally good fish and seafood section. Monk Fish Kebab £7.95, is marinated monk fish pieces with peppers, mushrooms barbecued on skewers and served with Pullao Rice. King Prawn Piri Piri, prawns skewered in their shells with garlic and hot sauce served with hot bread £7.95. Salmon Steak £7.95, marinated in aromatic spices and garlic and served with wedges of tomatoes and lemon. Fresh Mackerel £5.50, Bengali style, simmered in delicate spices with mushroom and served with Pullao Rice, Crab Masalam, fresh Torbay crab £6.75, fresh Torbay crab sauted in an aromatic sauce served on Pullao Rice. All these fish dishes and others we haven't mentioned are, we are assured, absolutely fresh, as they should be. The vegetable curries include Spinach and Tofu £2.50, cooked with green peppers, tomatoes and flavoured with garlic. Chickpea £2.50, cooked in a homemade masala sauce. Proto Veg Chunks £2.50 sounds unappetising, but is according to our correspondents, quite delicious, soya vegetable chunks cooked with homemade garam masala flavoured with sweet curry leaves. Proto Veg Mince, Soya Mince £2.50, cooked in the same way. Sugar Beans Curry £2.50, and Cauliflower and peas home made. There are also a selection of Meat Curries including Shahi Chicken Italia, chicken pieces cooked in cream with prunes and almonds and Nawabi Kurma, chicken pieces marinated in yoghurt, ginger, garam masala and cooked in butter gee. What comes out in the reports we received is the unusual homemade nature of this Restaurant which manages successfully to break away from the norm. Typical prices are Poppadums 25p,

Chicken Curry £3.55, Pullao Rice £1.25. The Vegetarian Thali is £5.25 and a Non-Vegetarian Thali £6.95. There are no hidden extra charges and the Restaurant offers discount to Curry Club members at its quieter times. See page 288.

DORSET

THE BLANDFORD TANDOORI
39 East Street, Blandford. Tel: 0258 451189
This is quite a small Restaurant with about 34 seats. The reports we have to hand speak of "excellent and consistent curry." D.F. "and a friendly place at which it is good to be a regular." E.B. All reports welcomed.

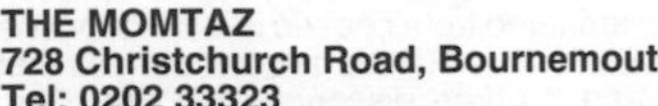

THE MOMTAZ
728 Christchurch Road, Bournemouth.
Tel: 0202 33323
207 Old Christchurch Road.
This Restaurant has 2 branches, the one at 207 taking over from the notorious Tandoori Oven where fun and games used to rule the roost. Our reporters talk of missing the discos, snake dancers, belly dancers and cabarets and all that used to take place at 207 but we now here of good quality food and excellent service at the 2 Momtaz'. One correspondent was amused to find the identical staff serving her a few days between visiting both branches. "I couldn't believe my eyes, the waiters at 728 were exactly the same as those at 207 and I had been to the one just a few days after going to the other." C.A. Obviously the staff swop quite freely between the branches and we understand that they are friendly and efficient. The food is competent and prices are reasonable.

THE KARACHI INDIAN
Old Christchurch Road, Bournemouth. Tel: 0202 21022
This Restaurant which opened in 1962 is one of the longest established Restaurants in the county. "The food remains consistently good." E.B. and we are told, whilst there is nothing spectacular here, everything is right - the Menu, the ambiance, the look, the service, the place - we love it all." A.C. "It's places like this that make curry worth eating." C.R.

THE BRIDPORT TANDOORI
68 South Street, Bridport. Tel: 0308 25266
Another good reliable place where a curry is a curry, there is nothing fancy, the service is straightforward and the prices are fair.

THE LAST VICEROY
Lymington Road, Highcliffe, Christchurch. Tel: 0202 272979
Consistent reports about good quality and good service at fair prices.

THE PARKSTONE TANDOORI
381 Ashley Road, Parkstone. Tel: 0202 721932
"We thoroughly enjoyed our visit to this small Restaurant. The bread products, Poppadums and Naan were amongst the best we have ever had. The service was well organised and the Rhogan Gosh was enlivened by green capsicums although it could have used a bit more spicing." J.L. More reports welcomed.

THE RAJ POOT **TOP 100**
69 High Street, Poole. Tel: 0202 676330
We believe The Raj Poot has blossomed considerably since its mention in the last Good Curry Guide. We have a collection of reports from reliable reporters which consistently speak of extremely good quality food, service and the expertise of the staff who guide you through the excellent Menu with knowledge, courtesy and genuine concern that the diners get everything they expect. The Restaurant itself has branches in Weymouth, Wareham and Dorchester but according to our reporters it is the

Poole branch which excels. "It is well worth going through the door and I still consider this to be amongst the best in the land. It is often jam packed but always makes customers feel unhurried. The food is excellent. Prices are perhaps a bit high but well worth every penny." J.L. "I keep returning here, the food is very authentic and individual flavours can be detected in all their dishes. I particularly like their Biriani and their Chicken Korma. Although a little expensive, it is superb, all the flavours coming out of a particular succulent, creamy sauce flavoured with coriander." N.W. On the strength of all these complimentary reports that we have received we are pleased to rate this as the best Restaurant in Dorset. In our TOP 100.

THE ROOPALI
Poole Road, Westbourne, Bournemouth. Tel: 0202
A Gujerati Vegetarian Restaurant, reported to prepare excellent food. Gujerati is a state of the western seaboard of India north of Bombay. It is notable for its gentle vegetarian cuisine. More reports welcomed.

THE RAJ OF INDIA
28 Salisbury Street Shaftesbury. Tel: 0425 52056
This is a small and friendly Restaurant where service seems to count above everything else. This report is a good example. "I called in there about booking on a Thursday night. It was over half full and the waiters were clearly doing a busy trade. Without consulting the Menu I asked could you please do me a Chilli Chicken with Pullao Rice, Mushroom Bhajee and Stuffed Paratha? Yes, said the waiter. 20 minutes later the most freshly cooked divine Chilli Chicken appeared along with all the trappings. It was only later when I consulted the Menu to look at desserts that I saw that Chilli Chicken wasn't on the Menu, they had cooked it specially for me. I thought that warranted a mention." W.B. Yes, it certainly did and that is the sort of thing we love to hear. We would welcome more reports please.

DURHAM

MILAN TANDOORI
18 Church Street, Bishop Auckland.
Tel: 0388 762606
"This is a newish Restaurant (it opened in 1988) with a downstairs takeaway. The upstairs is comfortable if unpretentious. The owner is welcoming and the staff friendly. Food is good and the prices average. We enjoyed Chicken Punjabi £3.95 and the Lamb Connoisseur £5.00 which we were told is the staffs favourite. We have never met that particular dish before but would certainly order it again. Poppadums were crisp and we will return." D.W. More reports please.

GARDEN OF INDIA
43 Bondgate, Darlington. Tel: 0325 467975
This is a small but tastefully decorated Restaurant. Here is a typical quote from a Durham correspondent. "I was very impressed with this Restaurant. The Menu had a really good range to suit everyone. The Bhoona Prawn on Puree Starter at £2.50 was delicious, soft in texture, tasty in taste. Vegetable Thali at £8.10 consisted of Mixed Vegetable Curry, Sag Bhajee, Cauliflower Bhajee, Onion Bhajee, Dhal, Pullao Rice, Cucumber Raita and Plain Naan. Every dish had its own flavour, the vegetables were crispy, they were quite delicious. When it came to coffee time they served a whole pot which was presented with Turkish Delight, Truffle and Mints. A thoroughly enjoyable meal." E.D. In this report the food, the service and the decor are of a high order "We have eaten here many times and we can't fault it. The extensive Menu offers house specials cooked in cream and wine. The spices taste fresh and they burst with flavour. The portions

are generous and the service - they lean over backwards. You must book at weekends, the word has got around. We think it is wonderful value for money. Flowers, chocolates and hot towels all add up to the welcome." J. & M.R.

THE RAJA
100 Main Street, Shildon. Tel: 0388 772451
This Restaurant is exactly what one is looking for when one is looking for a good curry. We are pleased to see that the prices haven't crept up very much in the intervening 4 years, in fact Poppadums are 25p as they were 4 years ago. Chicken Curry is £3.50. Pullao Rice is £1.20. The set dinner, Vegetarian is £7.00 and Non-Vegetarian £9.50. Correspondents particularly recommend the Thali trays which can be made to any heat strength as required. Here is a typical comment "We have been going there since it opened in 1977 and we think the reason for its success is that the Manager is invariably present. Personal service is the keynote of Abdus Subhan's success. The food is excellent and it is terrific value for money. People come back time and again, it's almost like a club itself. We highly recommend it." J. & M.J. and we are happy to pass your recommendation on via the pages of this Guide. The Raja has a branch in Bishop Auckland. It is Sabhan's Indian Takeaway on Newgate Street.

ESSEX

THE ABAHONI
31 Longbridge Road, Barking.
Tel: 081 591 5237
This quote is typical of those we receive "The surroundings are very pleasant and the standard of food is good. I personally don't like the green lighting in the Restaurant, can't see what you're eating. The Chicken Jalfrezi was VERY hot, nearer a Vindaloo. I ended up feeding my husband half of mine since he decided he liked it! The prices are reasonable." A.F.

THE MUMTAZ MAHAL **CC DISCOUNT**
10 Essex Way, Benfleet. Tel: 0268 751707
We hear of a warm and welcoming Restaurant although one correspondent called it a little dark, with plush burgundy velvet wall colouring (I think that is called red flock) with matching chairs. It has dimming gold spotlights over the table which gives a cosy image. The tablecloths are double covered with white under cloths and gold top cloths with burgundy napkins. There are arrays of flowers and hanging baskets and other displays in front of mirrored alcoves. The Restaurant has a reception area and is split between upstairs and downstairs with 90 seats. It opened in 1977 and the present owner Abdur Rashid took over in 1980. It is his only branch and he has established a well liked, well respected Restaurant. "The food and the service are excellent. The Vegetable Stuffed Paratha was out of this world. 4 of us had starters, main course with rice, breads, sweets and 2 coffees each, all for £45.00. We had Kansara After Curry Mints (not After Eight)." J.S.K. and "the house specials on the Menu were sumptuously produced. The starters and the side dishes were generous and the service good". I.D.B. The Menu produced no surprises. It is all standard stuff with every variation you can imagine on chicken, lamb, king prawn, prawn and meat. The Tandoori King Prawn Dhansak at £8.10 is "a little luxury I thoroughly enjoy on my regular visits to the Restaurant." R.A. Typical prices are Poppadums 40p. Chicken Curry £2.90. Pullao Rice £1.40. Set dinners for 4 people start at £11.00 and £12.00 per head. There is a minimum charge of £6.50 but no service or cover charge. "One of the blessings is the large car park at the side of the Restaurant but really it's the food that makes the day." W.E. The Restaurant offers a discount for Curry Club members on its quieter nights. See page 288.

THE CURRY PALACE
28 Fairfield Road, Braintree. Tel: 0376 20083
Although we don't hear a lot about this Restaurant from our reporters, that which we do hear satisfies us that it deserves its place in this Guide. Its prices are fair, its food is good, its clients are satisfied, what more can you ask.

THE VICEROY TANDOORI
110 High Street, Brentwood. Tel: 0277 212830
This Restaurant commenced trading in 1980 and is situated in a most beautiful 400 year old tudor listed building. The Viceroy's owner Hasnath Majumdar has no other branches and is often on hand to ensure that things run smoothly at his Restaurant. One of his regulars says "He is a chatty sort of a fellow and will tell you anything you want to know about Indian food or sociology (he has an Honours Degree in that subject)." Perhaps Mr. Majumdar should be aware that we have had 2 rather snorty complaints about his Restaurant over the last 2 years, admittedly amongst a good many good ones. One of them seems to be from a disgruntled diner who was irritated by the minimum charge which is now £10.00 and the allegation that the waiters were sullen. But most correspondents seem to be happy with their lot in Brentwood. They speak of good service and good food. The Restaurant's regulars speak of delicious starters such as Mushroom on Puree, spicy mushroom on deep fried puree bread £2.00 Fish Kebab £2.25. Mulligatawny Soup £1.40 "Absolutely delicious." S.T. Rashmi Kebab, a meat kebab prepared with ground minced steak delicately spiced and dressed with an egg net, and of main courses such as Chilli Chicken Masala £3.25, chicken in hot spices (also available in a meat version at the same price), a particularly good Methi Gosht £3.25, a very savoury tasting, herby, spicy dry curry. There is a good choice of vegetable specialities so we are told including Niramish £2.00, a dish popular in Bangladesh prepared with in-season vegetables using the minimum of spices flavoured with garlic and green chillies. The Special Vegetarian set meal for 1 at £8.00 appealed to 1 of our correspondents. "Being a vegetarian is not always easy but at The Viceroy I felt particularly spoilt with the set vegetarian meal which consisted of Niramish, Tarka Dhal, Sag Aloo, Cucumber Raita and Tandoori Bread and if this was not enough my boyfriend treated me to a Vegetable Biriani." A.S. We urge Mr. Majumdar to keep a very close eye on his standards and we ask for more reports please.

POLASH
169, Station Road, Burnham. Tel: 0621 782233
A very good restaurant with a sister branch in Shoeburyness, Essex (see separate entry).

THE ASHA TANDOORI
66 High Road, Chadwell Heath. Tel: 081 590 5695
This is a takeaway only but that doesn't preclude it from going into The Good Curry Guide. We have had several reports about its quality including this one. "Highly recommended good food in quantity at very reasonable prices." I.D.B. That strikes us as being a very reasonable comment.

THE TANDOORI COTTAGE
108 High Road, Chadwell Heath. Tel: 081 590 2503
Here is another standard Restaurant with its clutch of satisfied regular customers. "This is a very nice Restaurant with good decor and service. Nothing wrong with the food quantities, nothing goes back and the plates are always hot, something we regard as important." J.S.K.

THE ROSE OF INDIA
Rainsford Road, Chelmsford. Tel: 0245 352990
This family business opened early in 1985 and has established a good reputation for quality, presentation and food. He have to hand good reports about the Menu and service and we hear of nice touches which include slices of orange after the main course and a rose for the lady. More reports welcome.

CURRY MAHAL
27 Goresbrook Road, Dagenham. Tel: 081 592 6277
A typical town Curry House although a few years ago it had an untypical

fire which gutted it. It was rebuilt although we are told the decor is nothing special. However we do hear "that the food is very tasty and the portions HUGE. King Prawn Masala is generous to a 'T' with prawns and the sauce is thick and tasty. The Jalfrezi is well spiced with huge chunks of meat. We got a free Tia Maria liqueur with the bill." A.F. Sounds like good Restaurant management. More reports please.

THE INDIA PASSAGE
612 Longbridge Road, Dagenham. Tel: 081 597 8331
This 40 seat Restaurant has a lively bright decor consisting of mirrors and animal tapestries and Indian themes. "The Menu produces no surprises and the prices are reasonable with good service." A.F.

COLNE VALLEY TANDOORI
110, High Street, Earls Colne. Tel: 078 75 2983
We received a good number of votes on this one in our, 'name your favourite restaurant,' survey. It serves popular curries at reasonable prices.

KOHINOOR TANDOORI **CC DISCOUNT**
110 High Street, Earls Colne. Tel: 078 75 3714
This Restaurant opened in 1986. It has a reception area and a 50 seat Restaurant which is tastefully decorated with plants suspended between each table. Correspondents talk of a standard Menu, well presented, carefully served at slightly higher than average prices, for example Poppadums are 40p. Chicken Curry £3.50. Pullao Rice £1.50 plus a rather unnecessary service charge of 10%. This Restaurant serves Kansara After Curry Mints and is prepared to offer discounts to Curry Club members at quieter times. See page 288.

THE INDIAN BRASSERIE
15 High Street, Great Dunmow. Tel: 0371 3334
Opened in 1981 as The India Valley Tandoori and it immediately received good reports from our correspondents in the area. In 1989 it changed ownership to Mr. Z. Uddin who renamed it The Indian Brasserie. "It is certainly worth the journey, however the plate of fresh orange segments mentioned in your magazine did not appear on 3 occasions I have been there. However each time there was a free brandy (which frankly is nearer my heart than oranges anyway) plus hot towels and curry mints." D.J.T. We can't promise the free brandy with every meal, presumably you are a regular face, nor can we promise orange segments any more but we do hear that the food is reliable and good. Typical prices are Poppadums 30p. Chicken Curry £3.50. Pullao Rice £1.20. There is no minimum charge, no service charge and no cover charge. Mr Uddin owns The Prestige of Bengal in Wanstead, E11 and the Bay of Bengal in Ilford.

THE HALSTEAD TANDOORI **CC DISCOUNT**
73 Head Street, Halstead. Tel: 0787 476271
A small 34 seat Restaurant in pink and red decor under the care of Mohibur Rahman and has been since it opened in 1977. Over the years it has built up a regular following who tell us that they enjoy such things on the Menu as the Mutton Dhansak £5.40, the Methi Justh (their spelling) £3.60 and the Chicken Tikka Do-Piaza £5.90, diced boneless spring chicken marinated with a touch of spices and herbs grilled on a skewer over charcoal and then cooked in a fairly dry sauce with chopped onions. The Menu itself describes such a dish as "exquisite" which at least 1 correspondent claims is "slightly overstated but he likes it anyway." P.M. Another correspondent raves about the Chicken Tikka Jalfry (their spelling) £5.90. The prices are Poppadums 40p. Chicken Curry £3.25. Pullao Rice £1.50. There is no minimum charge, no service or cover charge. The Restaurant is prepared to give discounts to Curry Club members at lunchtimes. See page 288.

THE INDUS MAHAL
59 East Street, Colchester. Tel: 0206 860156
This Restaurant has been around for quite some time although relatively recently it changed hands. We have been watching for reports and they have been coming in, apparently to the satisfaction of the locals. Here are two "We visited here during a break in our bridge tournament. We were in fact the bridge team and we were in a hurry. The Restaurant was empty, not surprisingly at 6 p.m. and we placed our orders and requested

promptness. This was met. Had the usual Sheek Kebabs and Chicken Vindaloo. The food was quite good without being excellent. The side dishes, Naans, Poppadums etc. were very good indeed and well presented. Prices more than reasonable." M.S. "Always a cheerful welcome. Pleasantly lit decor but comfort a little tight. Spiced Poppadums 35p. Sheek Kebab £2.00. Chicken Jalfrezi very tasty at £3.50. Plentiful Egg Fried Rice for £2.10. Onion Bhajia £1.35 per portion. Mushroom Bhajia disappointing at £1.90. Pesawa Naan £1.35. Moderate service but quality, quantities and presentation all good." M.P.

TARAS RESTAURANT
48 St. John Street, Colchester. Tel: 0206 763495
Tara is a charismatic West Indian with a deep understanding of the cooking of curry. Their Menu is totally idiosyncratic as is her Restaurant which incorporates part of the old Roman wall as a major feature. Be prepared for good food served excitingly sometimes, according to one of our correspondents and "great fun and humour if the lady herself is there. I would like to recommend this Restaurant as my favourite." R.C. "A top class Restaurant in every way, decor, service and food is excellent if on the expensive side. Chicken Korma £4.95. Rhogan £4.25. Lamb Pasanda £9.00, but one of the better meals I have had for a long time." S.P. Another branch of Tarras has opened at Warrior House, South Church Road, Southend on Sea, telephone 0702 619580.

PRINCE OF INDIA
307 Hornchurch Road, Hornchurch. Tel: 04024 48364
Moglai Chicken and Persian Chicken Biriani were equally good. Poppadums were crisp and the Purees and Egg Paratha with egg on the outside were very good." J.S.K.

THE TASTE OF BENGAL **CC DISCOUNT**
194 High Street, Hornchurch. 04024 77850
We have over the years, built up a good collection of reviews and reports from our regular correspondents on this Restaurant, for example "our favourite in the area, great food, friendly service. It is both helpful and quick. The main dishes are prepared with care and fresh coriander is used in abundance. The Bhoona had fresh tomatoes in the sauce and the Prawn Vindaloo VERY hot and tasty. Hot towels and mints with coffee." A.F. Then we got a rather poor report from the same correspondent as the one quoted above telling us that the dishes were bland, that they were unpleasant and almost everything tasted the same and that service was very poor. Normally this would stop us in our tracks and certainly make us think very carefully about taking the Restaurant out of this Guide, but we have subsequently received good reports from other correspondents so we have to assume that this was an off day. We hope so anyway. The owners name is Mr. Jamal Uddin and we suggest that you ask for him by name when you order from the Menu which has many old favourites - Madras, Dhansak, Do-Piaza, Bhoona and Rhogan Josh to name but a few. Some of the specials which have been brought to our attention include the Bengal Thali at £9.50, Lamb Bhoona, Chicken Tikka Masala, Prawn Do-Piaza, Aloo Gobi, Pullao Rice and Naan. The chef's special on offer "rather rich but very nice" £3.30 is Chicken Special cooked with spices covered with cream, almonds and tomatoe and the Bengal Special, meat, chicken or prawn £6.80 cooked with almonds, cream and coconut and covered with egg served with Special Fried Rice. The King Prawn Channa caught the eye of one of our correspondents at £8.50, king prawns served with chickpeas, cream, almond, coconut and served with Special Rice. Face towels are served, so are coffee sweets, flowers for the lady and After Eight Mints. Poppadums are 30p. Pullao Rice £1.20. Chicken Curry £2.90. There is a minimum charge of £5.00 but no service or cover charge. The Restaurant offers discount to Curry Club members at quieter times. See page 288. We hope Mr. Uddin, that the one lapse was just an out of character blitz with an otherwise good reputation.

THE BELASH
89 The Stow, Harlow. Tel: 0279 36096
This Restaurant seems to have become very busy and very popular. "Excellent food - my favourite place in Harlow." We would like more reports please.

THE SIMLA RESTAURANT
301 Ferry Road, Hullbridge. Tel: 0702 231523
We brought this Restaurant to your attention in our last Good Curry Guide mentioning that it is in a converted house about 200 yards from the River Crouch. We asked for your views and got them, plenty of them. You like it, it appears. "We travel miles to get to this Restaurant and every time we go we are not disappointed." C.D. "We live in Southend but we took your advice and tried The Simla and we have been going there ever since." I.T. The Restaurant certainly is unique with an air of intimacy and tasteful blue grey decoration with oak beams running through the rooms. "The place has ample parking which is a big plus factor for us." D.C. Prices are perhaps a little higher than average. Poppadums 40p. Chicken Curry £3.35. Pullao Rice £1.50. Set dinner from £6.95 and a minimum charge of £7.50.

THE BOLAKA
132 Cranbrook Road, Ilford. Tel: 081 554 5395
"We make regular visits and enjoy consistently good food. Above average decor with carpets on the walls. Tablecloths are clean with no marks from previous customers. Hot plates are in evidence. Poppadums crisp and warm with free Mango Chutney. Onion Bhajias equally good with salad and mint sauce. Portions generous and excellent. Try The Bolaka Special at £7.00, worth every penny, must be tried. No wonder this place is firmly established as our regular." J.S.K. More reports on this Restaurant would be welcomed.

THE JALALABAD **TOP 100**
247 Ilford Lane, Ilford. Tel: 081 478 1285
"I feel fortunate to live so close to what is, the best of all to my mind. The standard is still the highest around and the level of trade reflects the esteem in which the Restaurant has held throughout the area." I.B. "The food is excellent, the Vegetable Curry is packed with crunchy, crisp cauliflower, freshly cooked potatoes, peas, crispy ochra, crunchy carrots and tender courgettes, you name it. It is all good with very little sauce but maximum flavour. The prawn and poultry dishes are exceptionally good and the breads large and piping hot." A.F. "Very varied Menu although we would like to see more fish dishes, the quantities are always huge but the staff are always happy to give you a doggy bag. The best Keema Naan we have ever tasted. We visit twice a month, would like to see segregation of smokers and non smokers and an improvement to the horrible lighting. The toilets however, are immaculate." S. & C.M. "It is not hard to see why people speak so highly of the Restaurant." J.S.K. We have other reports which speak highly of this Restaurant and we therefore have decided that this Restaurant goes into our top 100.

THE LEIGH TANDOORI
1337 London Road, Leigh. Tel: 0702 715815
"It is air conditioned which keeps you nice and cool. It serves super curries and accessories. There is never any pressure on you to rush." B.R. This is a typical report on this Restaurant where the food is competent and the prices are reasonable. We would welcome more reports.

THE TAJ MAHAL **CC DISCOUNT**
77 Leigh Road, Leigh. Tel: 0702 711006
This Restaurant opened in 1973 and commenced its present ownership that of Nazam Uddin in 1978. Consequently it has in the intervening years, built up a good solid corps of regular devotees. Decor is described by the owner as an attempt to recreate the Mogul craftsmanship of medieval India and it includes chandeliers, brass plates and royal frescos. But it's the food you go for, not the drawings on the wall and we hear good things about Korai Chicken £4.65, Lamb Jalfry (their spelling) £4.95, Chicken Tikka Masala £4.45 and Lamb Pasanda £4.65. Other typical prices are Poppadums 30p. Chicken Curry £3.25. Pullao Rice £1.35. There is a minimum charge of £6.50 but no service or cover charge. This Restaurant offers discounts to Curry Club members at quieter times. See page 288.

THE CURRY INN
111 High Street, Southminster, Maldon. Tel: 0621 52564
Our correspondents speak well of this Restaurants special The Curry Inn Special at £9.95. Murgi Masalam £7.95. Badam Pasanda £6.95 and

Butter Chicken £6.95. Prices are a little on the high side with Poppadums at 45p. Chicken Curry £2.95 and Pullao Rice £1.40 and a set dinner for 1 person £9.95.

THE TANDOORI GARDEN OF MALDON **TOP 100 & CC DISCOUNT**
24 Mill Road, Maldon. Tel: 0621 52564

Although this Restaurant first started trading in 1983 it was not until 1988 when it became rather special. For it was in that year that it was acquired by Mr. M. Loqueman, the pioneer of Indian cooking in East Anglia. Mr. Loqueman opened his first branch, The Indus Curry of Colchester in 1962 and followed that with the Indus Mahal in the same city. He sold these in 1987 and after a short holiday abroad he came back into the business with the purchase of The Tandoori Garden. Mr. Loqueman is a special person in Indian cooking. He is the author of a small cookery book called "Twenty Two Years in the Indian Kitchen'. Also a very strong advocate of home style Indian cookery which he attempts to bring to bear in his Restaurant. The Restaurant itself seats 64 in the dining area and a further 20 in the reception area. It has a separate takeaway area and bar, and a 14 foot corridor leads to the reception area. Inside the main Restaurant the decor is at a very high standard. In the middle of the main Restaurant there is a large garden of exotic plants giving rise to the Restaurants name and two large fish tanks and two fountains surrounded by seats which are mainly boxed into two and four person cubicles. The Menu is divided into four sections. Starters which includes many old favourites such as Chicken Tandoori, Onion Bhajia, Samosas and Muligatawny Soup. Prices range from £1.20 to £3.00 for starters. A further section of the Menu is called The Traditional Menu and that includes tandoori dishes with a rather special Chicken Sashlic, spring chicken marinated in a spicy sauce skewered with tomatoes and peppers and cooked in the tandoor served with Pullao Rice or Naan and vegetables at £6.95. The Chicken Tikka Masala in this section is also highly spoken of by our correspondents at £6.90 and this too is served with Pullao Rice or Naan and Vegetable Korma. Also in this section is Bagera Baigon a special dish for vegetarians at £6.50 consisting of peas, mushrooms and fresh aubergine cooked with vegetable ghee served with Pullao Rice and Kulcha Naan or Chapatti. In this section also appear five Biriani dishes; Prawn, Chicken and Vegetable and two specials; Special Lamb Tikka Biriani which include pieces of tandoored lamb cooked with rice, vegetables, bamboo shoots and served with Vegetable Curry and Naan at £6.50 and a similar version involving chicken at £5.80. The next section of the Menu covers many old favourites; Madras, Vindaloo, Korma, Bhoona, Do-Piaza, Rhogan, Malaya etc. in chicken, meat, prawn, lobster and vegetables. Prices range from a reasonable £1.50 for vegetable dishes up to £4.50 for Korai Gosht. They average around £3.00. By far the most interesting section of the Menu is what Mr. Loqueman calls his home style cooking. This includes five special dishes; Handia Kebab at £9.50 which is beef steak marinated in yoghurt with selected herbs grilled over charcoal and served with Pullao Rice and vegetables in a creamy sauce. Saslikan Korma; lamb or chicken marinated in yoghurt and mild spices, skewered, grilled in the tandoor and then cooked in a Korma with acme juice (spicy stock) and served with Pullao Rice and vegetables at £8.50. Also at £8.50 is Kurshani Kania which is meat or chicken cooked using a special recipe and served with Pullao Rice and vegetables. There is a special Lobster Masala served with Pullao Rice or Naan at £9.50 and a special hot home style Madras Curry at £8.00 also served with Pullao Rice and vegetables. The reports we have received have spoken very highly of this Restaurant under Mr. Loqueman's ownership and especially of these home made specials. Therefore we are placing The Tandoori Garden of Maldon on our top 100 list. The Restaurant offers discounts to Curry Club members during its quieter times. See page 288.

THE KISMET TANDOORI **CC DISCOUNT**
171 High Street, Ongar. Tel: 0277 362889

52 seat Restaurant in a listed building built in the 15th century. The low white ceilings crossed with ancient beams, walls the original tudor bricks. "The whole thing creates the most fabulous atmosphere." B.C. Attractive light fittings and plants set the scene for what promises to be a first class curry meal. At first sight the Menu doesn't seem to be anything other than a standard Curry House Menu with many old favourites appearing at reasonable prices but we are assured that the quality of cooking is extremely good. Some of the specials include Korai Gosht, mutton

cooked in selected spices, green peppers and fenugreek at £4.95 served in a cast iron Karahi dish. The specialities include Chicken Tikka Masala at £6.95 including Special Fried Rice. Chicken or Mutton Pasanda at £6.95 and Murgi Masalam, a whole chicken for 2 people at £12.95. These dishes are marinated and barbecued and cooked in a sauce made with spices, cream, ghee and nuts to which red wine and selected herbs are added. They are served with Special Fried Rice. Moglai Chicken at £7.45 is prepared in yoghurt and coconut with tomatoes and eggs and cooked in butter and served with Special Rice. The really special chef's meals are Kurzi Chicken for 4 people at £50.00 or Kurzi Lamb for 4 people at £65.00. Whole leg of lamb or 2 whole chickens are marinated for 24 hours which is why 24 hours notice is required. They are gently simmered in spices and herbs to retain their flavour and they are enhanced with spices. They are served with Special Rices and a special sauce made with brandy. "Mr. Ali the owner, says that this was the favourite dish of the Mogul Princess' and with such ancient and wonderful surroundings who are we to doubt him." T.R. Nice touches at the end of the meal include Chocolate Mints, fresh oranges and hot towels. This Restaurant will offer discounts to Curry Club members at quieter times. See page 288. It is advisable to book at this Restaurant.

THE SAFFRON TANDOORI RESTAURANT
32 Eastwood Road, Rayleigh. Tel: 0268 745275
It is a standard Curry House with all the old favourites at reasonable prices and the service is said to be very good indeed. We would like more reports please.

INDIA GARDEN
62, Victoria Road, Romford. Tel: 0708 62623
We welcome the India Garden back to the pages of our Guide. It's there because you tell us it should be. It's very popular and serves all the favourites competently.

THE REGENCY PALACE
55 High Street, Romford. Tel: 0708 722787
Opened in 1989 and is undoubtedly increasing in popularity judging by the reports we are receiving. It is already said to be very good with two vegetable main courses Niramish and Korai, both good value at £2.95. Also Vegetable Thali with Plain Rice, Dhal, chickpeas, spinach, potato, cauliflower and Raita along with Tandoori Rota for £7.00 doesn't look much until you try to eat it. Hot towels and mints and occasionally slices of orange end the meal. One complaint is that the waiters are slow and they often mix up the orders and bills even when they are not busy." A.F. "It has firmly established itself in Romford as a high class Restaurant offering unusual dishes. We ordered Poppadums and were impressed with the selection of chutneys that accompany them. Tamarind (Imli) was one of my favourites, Tandoori Lamb Chop Masala £4.75 is excellent although the rice we were served on one occasion was quite a small portion. The Regency Kulcha, crisp unleavened bread stuffed with vegetables is superb. Service is excellent but when busy, standards drop." J.T.

THE POLASH
86 West Road, Shoeburyness, Essex. Tel: 03708 3989
We are glad to see The Polash retain its place in The Good Curry Guide for the third time running. Its sister branch at Burnham on Crouch is equally good with an identical Menu. In fact the Menu hasn't changed since our last entry and we see no reason, apart from updating the prices, why it should. We said then and we say now, the choice on the Menu is huge, practically at PhD level. Go there as an expert or with one who can decipher the printed words into goodies you will enjoy. But goodies there are. The experts eye will at once spot the rareties. Niramish Curry for example (try it and see) at £1.95 or Lamb Badam Pasanda with cream almonds (£5.25) and their Rowgan Jush (their spelling), is still excellent at £3.70. Another good dish is the Saly Goosht (their spelling), a meat dish garnished with matchstick chip potatoes at £3.70 and continue to be amazed and amused at the names of the special meals which starts with Kims dishes £11.95, for one person, a 3 course meal including Tandoori Chicken, Chicken Masala, Niramish, Rice and Sweet or Coffee. Kiplings Favourite £23.95, for 2 people, which includes Chicken and Mutton Tikka, Tandoori Lobster Masala, Bhoona Gosht, Mushrooms, Pullao Rice and

Sweet or Coffee. The Passage to India, £34.95 for 3 people. The Sunset in the Ganges, £46.95, for 4 people and the Far Pavilion £89.95, for 8 people, which sounds a lot until you realise that it is just £11.00 each. There is a minimum charge of £7.50 per person or £5.00 for takeaway but there is no service charge or cover charge. A thoroughly commendable Restaurant as is its branch at 169 Station Road, Burnham on Crouch, Essex.

THE SOUTHEND TANDOORI
York Road, Southend on Sea. Tel: 0702 463182
Of Southend's 20 or so Indian Restaurants it is The Southend Tandoori which our local correspondents like the most.

RUCHITA
Guild Way, South Woodham, Ferriers. Tel: 0245 323855
Reported as being more than competent and highly reliable.

THE TANDOORI PARLOUR **CC DISCOUNT**
63 Hart Road, Thundersley. Tel: 0268 793786
This Restaurant opened in 1979 and is owned by Mr. Rois Ali. Both sides of the Restaurant have high cabins which can be curtained off with satin curtains to give privacy to the diners. The walls have metallic blue wallpaper and there are temple archways cut in which are lined with plants and flowers. The Restaurant's carpet has its name and logo woven into it and the ceiling is also decorated with plants and flowers. It is air conditioned and the lighting is light and bright with candle lights on the table. The Menu is large and interesting with the full cast list of Indian dishes there to choose from. Some of the house specials are quite interesting. Tandoori Chicken Tikka Masala consists of boneless chicken breast cooked with spiced mincemeat and served in a tandoori sauce with almonds. Some of the other Specials include dishes cooked and served in a Karahi Cast Iron Wok and these include Chicken Tikka Rougon (their spelling) at £5.20. Salli Chicken or Meat at £5.20, which is a curried meat garnished with matchstick fried potatoes. Typical prices are Poppadums 30p. Chicken Curry £2.90. Pullao Rice £1.10. Set luncheon is £5.40 and set dinner for 4 is £39.95 involving the Kurzi Lamb which is a leg of lamb marinated for 24 hours, (requiring 24 hours notice) cooked with tandoori spices and garnished with green salad, served with Special Rice and Vegetable Bhajee. This dish is also available for 2 people at £21.95. There is a minimum charge of £5.00. There is no service or cover charge. Customers get a free hot face towel after their meal and coffee sweets. Every two people get a free coffee, every four people get a free bottle of wine. In addition, pensioners get a 10% and there is a discount available to Curry Club members at quieter times. See page 288.

THE RAJDHANI
272 London Road, Westcliffe on Sea. Tel: 0702 332184
Standard curries at The Rajdhani but well done we hear. "We had a very good lunch choice with excellent quantity and much more than ample quantities, therefore I had a doggy bag (not much work done back at the office after that)." M.S.

GLOUCESTER

THE RAJVOOJ
1 Albion Street, Cheltenham.
Tel: 0242 23970
The Rajvooj has become a very firm favourite in this area. The Menu carries the standard list of curry dishes and the helpings are more than ample we are told. "The food is very good indeed, especially the hot dishes. Rather than being just hot, they have a distinctive flavour." P.C.H.

TANDOORI CURRY INN
Lower High Street, Cheltenham. Tel: 0242 519121
Good curries are available in this establishment. We hear very good things about the Menu and the service. "I did something I have always wanted to do but never have done before - I phoned them up on the day before and ordered the Murgi Masala, Chicken marinated for 24 hours. The wait was immeasurable - I went on a diet and must have lost half a stone. When we got there it was well worth the wait. It made a feast for two and I would do it again." T.H. More reports on this Restaurant are welcomed.

DILRAJ
37 Long Street, Dursley. Tel: 0453 543472
"Attractive green and pink painted decor, better than it sounds perhaps with lots of greenery. The Poppadums were perfect, crisp and hot. The Vegetable Samosas were very good. The portions weren't the largest I have ever encountered and the Chicken Korai was a little bit too subtle in flavour for me. However the lamb was exquisite. The coffee was virtually tasteless but I suppose we don't go for coffee. Basically it is a sound Restaurant providing good value for money." G.R. "This Restaurant is fairly new having opened in September 1989. Generally visit every 2 weeks and we always receive a warm and friendly welcome from the owners Rashid and Rakib. They have transformed a dirty cafe, and ill fated pizza bar into a spacious and tastefully decorated Restaurant. Warm and crisp Poppadums are available and the Onion Bhajias makes a great starter for 3! Karahi Chicken was delicious and plentiful, excellent meat and well spiced. The Naan bread is always piping hot and probably the best I have had anywhere. The vegetables were not outstanding but they are okay. Special mention for Madras Sambar which is very hot. Barfi (Indian fudge) to finish off a good meal." D.R. More reports please.

CONNOISSEUR TANDOORI RESTAURANT
22 London Road, Gloucester. Tel: 0452 417556
This Restaurant has recently come to our attention with a number of good reports. Correspondents tell of interesting starters such as Chicken Chat, light Pakoras and Aloo Dossa which is a pancake with curried potato in it "absolutely delicious. If you don't believe me, try it." P.A. Main courses include Karta Gosht, Jal Feroz, a chicken stir fry dish. Murgh Masala, Koray Murgh Makkony, which is tandoori chicken in a rich red gravy sauce served in a Karahi and Chilli Chicken. This was delightfully hot with fresh green chillies, yet incredibly tasty." N.C.

THE PASSAGE TO INDIA
Old Market, Nailsworth, Gloucester. Tel: 0452 4063
"Fine cuisine, it is mouthwatering. The owners are very friendly and the service first class." N.E. More reports please.

THE PRINCE OF INDIA
5 Park Street, Stow on the Wold. Tel: 0451 31198
Another competent Restaurant with good reports coming in to us, for example "A general excellent ambiance, sensible prices and good food." E.D. More reports please.

THE JEWEL IN THE CROWN
22 Gloucester Street, Stroud. Tel: 0453 765430
A small Restaurant seating about 35 to 40 people, it has built up a regular and loyal following, so much so that it is wise to book. "At 9.30 on a Saturday evening this Restaurant is generally full. To be asked to come back later is common place. It is a bright and smart place with the tables quite close together. Food is excellent with great portions. Lamb Kashmir is laden with fruit and Tikka Masala has a superb flavour. The Bombay Potato and Bringal Bhajee are very good, nice big chunks and not mushy at all. Onion Bhajias are superb and Viceroy, a delicious unique creamy egg custard like sauce served on tender chicken is wonderful. Service is sometimes a little disorganised, it is always friendly and always quick." D.R.

THE MUNIRA **CC DISCOUNT**
69 Church Street, Tewkesbury. Tel: 0684 294353
Located in an olde English timber building which is decorated in pretty whites and pinks with wall mounted lighting to give a soft candlelight glow.

It seats 72 and has come to our notice as an excellent Restaurant. The Restaurant is owned by Nesawor Miah and the cuisine is standard Bangladeshi which means to say it has a Menu with all the favourites there. Established in 1983 the Restaurant clearly has a strong local following who enjoy the Onion Bhajias "so light, so tasty, circular shaped. I wish I could make them like that at home." C.P. £1.10 and King Prawn Butterfly £2.25 "it is so delicately spiced and so beautifully shaped that it makes you hardly want to eat it." T.S. "My favourite here is the Meat Malaya which is spiced meat cooked with pineapple and served with cream on top. Sounds rich, sounds yukky but it is really delicious, £2.95." B.D. Other prices include Poppadums at 25p. Chicken Curry £2.75. Pullao Rice £1.00. A set dinner is available from £9.95. There is no minimum charge, no service charge and no cover charge. Diners get a hot face towel and Suchard Twilight Chocolates. This Restaurant offers a discount to Curry Club members during its quieter times. See page 288. There is a Munira branch at 60 High Street, Cheltenham, 0242 516677 with an identical Menu.

WOOTON INDIAN CUISINE
13/15 Church Street, Wooton Under Edge. Tel: 0453 843628
This Restaurant only opened in March 1990 bringing curry to Wooton Under Edge for the first time. The decor, we are told, is pleasant with good expensive linen and tableware. "The service is second to none. Nothing is too much trouble. We recommend the Nawabi Pasanda and the Prawn Bhoona, they are both great. Good helpings are given and chutneys are always included in the price. Hot towels and orange segments are served after the meal along with unlimited coffee. A great asset to Wooton. We return many times." L.A.M. More reports please.

H & W

HEREFORD & WORCESTER

THE RAJAH
8 Load Street, Bewdley. Tel: 0299 400368
We have only had a few reports on this Restaurant but they're all good. We hear that the Restaurant is very small so it is advisable to book, even on a Monday. "The Lobster Tandoori is delicious." A.G.T. More reports please.

THE ANARKALI
55 Worcester Road, Bromsgrove. Tel: 0527 31936
This is just a takeaway but that doesn't prevent it from going into our Guide if we receive good reports about it, and good reports we do receive. It opened in January 1983 and is operated by Hira Miah who also operates the Shah Jahan in Erdington, Birmingham 23 and the Everest Indian Takeaway at 45 Regents Grove, Leamington. The full cast list of curry favourites is available on the Menu plus a new idea, a selection of frozen curries. That is a good idea and we have not heard of that before. Being located near the Midlands, Balti dishes are available including Balti Chicken at £2.90, Balti Prawn and Spinach at £3.30 and King Prawn Balti at £4.25. An unusual one is Surrya Chicken £2.70, served with banana and Bombay Chicken served with potato and tomato at £2.70, is also an interesting variation on a theme. Musselin Chicken involves chicken breast with green beans at £2.75 and Poppadums are priced at 25p. Chicken Curry £2.80. Pullao Rice 80p. Set dinners range from £11.95 for 2 people to £34.95 for 6 people representing extremely good value.

THE SONALI
1 Worcester Road, Bromsgrove. Tel: 0527 78058
This is we hear, a particularly good Restaurant enjoyed by the people of Bromsgrove. "I use this Restaurant often and can say that it usually is

good. Personally I absolutely adore the Tikka Chicken Masala." B.H. More reports please.

HUSSAINS **TOP 100**
13 Vine Street, Evesham. 0386 47227
The first Hussains was established at Stratford, see entry in Warwickshire. This branch has set itself the same target as its sister branch and the reports that we get about it are extremely good. The Restaurant is named after its founder Mr. Noor Islam Hussain. In a remarkably short space of time (just over 6 years) he has established a chain of Hussains in Cheltenham, Reditch, Evesham and Stratford. The cooking is unashamedly Bangladeshi, that is to say they cook standard Northern Indian curries in the way that we all like them. The Menu offers a selection of starters from £1.95 to £2.10. A favourite of one of our reporters is King Prawn Patia on a Puree, king sized prawns gently spiced, cooked in a sweet and sour sauce and served on putti bread £3.45. The Chicken Tikka Masala, so many peoples favourite, is at this Restaurant "absolutely delicious diced tandoori roasted chicken presented in the most superb red sauce made from fresh tomatoes, ghee, cream and wonderful spices for just £5.60. I could die for it." S.K. There is a good selection of vegetable and seafood dishes and we hear very well of the Luknow Biriani, special basmati rice cooked with chicken, lamb, ghee, nuts and spices and complimented by a fresh vegetable curry at £5.75. The Stratford branch is in our top 100 and so is this one.

THE ALBELA **TOP 100**
40 Widemarsh Street, Hereford. 0432 269191
Our correspondents from deepest Hereford (yes, we do have them there too) tell us that The Albela is an "excellent Restaurant and certainly the best of Hereford's four." R.T. "It would probably be unfair to compare this Restaurant with the West End of London, but it certainly satisfies us simple people out here in the wilderness." S.N. More reports would be welcome.

ESSENCE OF INDIA
4 New Street, Ledbury. Tel: 0531 2328
This 48 seat Restaurant opened on the site of the former Eastender Tandoori Restaurant in June 1989 and it didn't take long before it became known to us. It has a cocktail bar and a reception area and a downstairs Restaurant where they serve a range of Bangladeshi cooked Northern and Southern Indian curries along with the odd Pakistan and Nepalese dish. One of the partners Mr. J. Rahman is often present who ensures things run smoothly. It is a standard Menu with "reasonably good food." N.T. Typical prices include Poppadums 30p. Chicken Curry £2.95. Pullao Rice £1.20. There is a minimum charge of £5.20 but no service or cover charge.

THE ANUPAM INDIAN
85 Church Street, Malvern. Tel: 06845 573814
"This is a very nice Restaurant although it is a little difficult to find being stuck down a small alley off Church Street. The decor is tasteful in greens and pinks and the food is very good. I particularly recommend the Thali for one at £9.95. It is just the right variation and size for someone eating on their own." N.N. "It is more or less a standard Menu but there are one or two nice things such as Tandoori Makal £4.95 and Lassi (yoghurt drink available sweet or salty). There is sometimes Kulfi (Indian ice cream) available for dessert. We think this is brought in probably from royal sweets. None the less, it is nice when it's there." M.A. More reports welcomed.

THE AKASH **CC DISCOUNT**
33 Unicorn Hill, Redditch. Tel: 0527 62301
This Restaurant was established in 1979 by Mr. A. A. Choudhrey and we welcome it to the pages of this Guide following a number of good reports received after the last few years. "We go there pretty regularly, we particularly like the decor, pink and white and the friendly reception we get. I also like the Nargiss Kebab, a kind of scotch egg surrounded by kebab meat at £2.20, not usually found in the run of the mill Restaurant, whilst my husband enjoys Dhal Soup £1.50." R.S. There are some interesting House Specialities including Butter Chicken £6.50, half a

tandoori chicken off the bone, cooked in a liquid sauce of Capsicum, tomato, spices, fresh coriander which is fried in ghee. This dish is supplied with Pullao Rice. Jahi Chicken is Chicken Tikka cooked in a masala sauce, mixed with yoghurt and fried in ghee to give it "an exotic aroma". It includes Pullao Rice, £6.50. An unusual dish is Chicken Capsilla, diced chicken cooked in mild sauce with Capsicum, onion and garnished with an egg net served inclusive of Pullao Rice for £6.25. Poppadums cost 40p each. Chicken Curry £3.50. Pullao Rice £1.35. A set luncheon is good value at £3.50 and a set dinner for 2 is £24.95 which includes starters of Tandoori Chicken and Masala Raan, which is leg of lamb smeared with yoghurt and a mixture of selected spices, marinated for several hours and then roasted with lashings of ghee and yoghurt until the meat is deliciously tender. It is served with Pullao Rice. Side dishes if you need them, are Aloo Gobi and Mushroom Bhajee. "It is absolutely fabulous." C.S. At the end of the meal face towels are supplied along with After Eight Mints. The Restaurant will offer Curry Club members a discount in its quieter times. See page 288. Mr. Choudhrey has 2 branches The Redditch Indian Takeaway, 41 Unicorn Hill, Redditch, Worcestershire and The Taste of India Takeaway, 1240 Aldwich Road, Great Barr, Birmingham.

THE SEVERN TANDOORI
11 Bridge Street, Stourport. Tel: 02993 3090
Standard curries.

PASHA TANDOORI **CC DISCOUNT**
56 John Street, Worcester. 0905 426327
This Restaurant was established in 1987 by Nurulh Haque and our reporters describe it as light and airy with lots of plants and decorated with Laura Ashley wallpaper and booth dividers. "We enjoy this Restaurant for its pleasant, bright decor and its privacy." K.P. The cooking is Bangladeshi, Northern Indian and dishes include "'Snargi's Kufta, an Indian version of the scotch egg with spiced minced lamb, deep fried in batter and served with a light omelette £2.15. Fish Kebab, minced prawns seasoned with onions, fresh mint and herbs with a touch of ground spices and cooked in butter, £1.95. Kebab Platter consists of Sheek Kebab, Lamb Tikka and Chicken Tikka at £2.65. For a main course the Tandoori Platter is a favourite of many. "I really can't eat anything else. The Menu calls it a feast for tandoori lovers, so I guess I am a tandoori lover. It consists of Tandoori Chicken, Tandoori Lamb, Chicken Tikka, Sheek Kebab, King Prawn and is served with Naan Bread, chutneys and fresh salad. A magnificent meal and I am sure that it is terribly healthy." D.L. £6.75. We hear also of the Chicken Hasina, mildly spiced chicken flavoured with dried fruits and nuts and cooked in fresh cream, £4.15 and Chicken Sylhet, diced chicken breast mixed up with minced lamb and hard boiled egg and cooked in mild spices and cream,. Another favourite is Chicken Sabzi Bhuna which is diced chicken cooked in a thick spicy sauce with fresh mixed vegetables at £4.15 and there is another variation of this cooked with chickpeas in place of the vegetables. Lamb Rogon Josh (their spelling) is tender pieces of lamb cooked in a traditional masala paste and garnished with chopped tomatoes, £4.25. The Specials offer a variety of set meals, 2 which particularly stand out for 2 people at £21.95 are the Pasha Fish Special which consists of Fish Kebab followed by Tandoori Fish, Poppadum, Fish Masala, Tandoori King Prawn, King Prawn Bhuna, fresh vegetables, Basmati Rice and Naan and for one person the Vegetarian Thali which consists of Samosa, Onion Pakora, Poppadum, Vegetable Bhuna, Bagan Bhajee (Aubergine), Tarka Dhal, Basmati Rice and Naan. Poppadums are 35p each. Chicken Curry £3.55. Pullao Rice £1.30. There is no minimum charge, no service charge and no cover charge. The meal ends with a hot face towel, coffee, sweets and fresh orange segments. Mr. Haque is often to be found on the premises as he has no other branches and the Restaurant offers discount to Curry Club members at their quieter times. See page 288.

PURBANI TANDOORI **CC DISCOUNT**
27 The Tything, Worcester. Tel: 0905 23671
This Restaurant first opened in December 1979 and it the property of Mr. Abdul Haque. This Restaurant is an old friend of The Good Curry Guide having been in both our previous editions. We continue to get good reports. We particularly like this report. "I was made so welcome with my two children, the staff simply couldn't do enough for us and this was a busy Thursday evening." C.D. Here is another interesting quote "My wife

doesn't like Indian food but the staff made no problem of that. She had a melon cocktail £1.60 whilst I had a delicious Meat Samosa £1.90. Whilst I tucked into The Purbani Special Chicken £5.90, pieces of spring chicken cooked with delicious herbs and fruit along with a Sabzi Biriani (Vegetable Biriani) £5.10 my wife had a massive T Bone Steak cooked to perfection £6.95, served with chips, peas and tomatoes. Honestly I don't think it could have been done better at a top English hotel." F.V. Typical prices include Poppadums 35p. Chicken Curry £3.30. Pullao Rice £1.20. There is a set dinner from £10.50 per person. No minimum charge, no service charge and no cover charge. Face towels and sweets are given to all diners and the Restaurant will offer discounts to Curry Club members at their quieter times. See page 288.

HAMPSHIRE

JOHNNY GURKAH 'S CC DISCOUNT
186 Victoria Road, Aldershot.
Tel: 0252 28773

I suppose you either love Johnny Gurkah's Restaurant or you hate it. Your Editor happens to love it, but it has to be said that we do get the odd bad review about it. First of all, the place is really quite tacky. I am sure Mr. Hari Karki, the proprietor, won't mind me saying this. The Restaurant is situated in down town Aldershot which is hardly known for its charm and beauty. Aldershot, lets face it, is an Army town. Mr. Karki is a Gurkah. He is tough and knows how to deal with the chaps when they come in for a riot. With the Gurkhas themselves stationed not far away at Church Crookham, he can be sure that the Nepalese connections are well appreciated. I have been to this Restaurant with Sue Arnold of the Observer years ago who thoroughly enjoyed it and wrote about it in her column. Go with an open mind, tell Mr. Karki that you are interested in the food rather than the local soldiery who are perhaps rather less interested in it than you are. Keep clear of it after pub closing hours and you should have a reasonable meal. It is advisable to book but ask for some of the Nepalese Specials. The 4 course Rodi-Ghar Special at £13.00 is a good introduction. Typical prices include Poppadums 40p each. Chicken Curry £3.00. Pullao Rice £1.45. The minimum charge is £3.00 and there is a service charge of 10%. Towels, Mango Punch and After Eight Mints are supplied to all diners. The Restaurant is generally very busy but it is offering discounts to Curry Club members at lunchtimes only. See page 288.

THE SURMA
33 Andover Road, Ludgershall, Andover

"A very small Restaurant with very courteous staff. It is reasonably priced and there isn't an ounce of grease in sight. This little town is extremely fortunate to have such an excellent eating house." K.J.P. We are glad to hear that and would like to hear more reports on this Restaurant.

THE PURBANI
2A The Square, Botley, Nr. Southampton. Tel: 04892 3161

This Restaurant which opened in 1983 is the property of Mr. N. A. Khalique and it makes its second appearance in the pages of this Guide. We get good reports about it. Typical prices include Poppadums 40p. Chicken Curry £2.95. Pullao Rice £1.30. A dinner for 2 people is £15.95. Minimum charge is £8.10. Service charge and cover charge are not applicable.

THE MAHARAJA
Fryern Arcade, Eastleigh. Tel: 0703 261444

We get good reports about this Restaurant too, stating that it is a standard Curry House with excellent friendly service where "I have never been disappointed. It is good value for money and the service is good even when they are busy." C.S. We welcome more reports.

THE COVE TANDOORI
Fernhill Road, Cove, Farnborough. Tel: 0276 31091
The Cove has attracted a fair measure of good comments. "It is notable for its extensive Menu, ample helpings, smart, careful service." F.B. More reports please.

THE RAJ PUT
Fleet Road, Fleet, Hampshire. Tel: 02514 6352
Yet again The Raj Put comes out as the best of the three in Fleet. "This Restaurant is more than acceptable, it is the only place I go to." J.S. "The cuisine is excellent and mouth watering. We like it very much." B.P.

LAST VICEROY
4-7 High Street, Hamble
This Restaurant was established in January 1989 on the premises of the former Agra de Luxe. The Manager Badrul Zaman, is in charge of a very attractive Restaurant with white walls and black ceiling beams and elegantly framed paintings. The Menu commences with a very interesting description about the Last Viceroy who was of course, Lord Mountbatten. He was the last representative of the British Empire and handed over his Office of Governor General to the Indians in 1948. The Restaurant has a good selection of, what it calls, popular curry dishes. "There is always so much to choose from, why do I always choose the same thing? I'll tell you what it is, it's Dhansak Chicken £4.75; it is so hot, so sweet and so sour, the lentils blend it and it is so delicious and they serve it with Pullao Rice. My husband by the way, always goes for Jalfrezi, a very hot chicken dish cooked with onions, fresh ginger, fresh garlic, fresh green peppers and a sprinkle of coriander, £4.15." M.P. There are some very interesting dishes called Chef's Recommendation which include Saltan Puri Pullao which is spiced rice with lamb and cashew nuts served with lamb curry £7.35 and Nawabi Thali, a selection of Chicken Tikka, Rhogan Josh, Bindi Bhajee, Pullao Rice and Naan Bread at £8.45. Typical prices include Poppadums 35p. Chicken Curry £3.05. Pullao Rice £1.30. Set dinners are from £9.95. There are no minimum charges, service charges or cover charges.

INDIAN COTTAGE
4 Portsmouth Road, Horndean. Tel: 0705 591408
The Indian Cottage returns for this third time to The Good Curry Guide. Pleased to say that we have had nothing but good reports since the last Guide was published. Service is reported as being "even and warm". The Restaurant is well respected by its local following.

THE JALALABAD
22 Stock Road, Gosport. Tel: 07017 582927
The Jalalabad is respected by a hard core following of regulars who tell us of good cooking, even, competent service and reliable curries. More reports please.

THE MADHUBAN
94 Station Road, Liss, Hampshire. Tel: 0730 893363
This Restaurant opened in the small town of Liss in 1987 and within a year it had expanded to double the size. It is a very elegant Restaurant with an over all colour scheme in blue. When you enter the Restaurant you find a small lounge bar behind which is the seating area which is very spacious. One is struck by 2 very attractive chandeliers and an over all restful atmosphere. Bombay Mix is on the table for you to nibble at while you peruse the Menu. It has a branch, The Pipasha, in the tiny village of Churt.

THE GANDHI RESTAURANT
139 Kingston Road, Portsmouth. Tel: 0705 811966
We hear that this is a smart place and "one of the better establishments in town." N.T. "We had an excellent meal and the service was first class in this spotlessly clean Restaurant." M.S.

THE PALASH **TOP 100**
124 Kingston Road, Portsmouth. Tel: 0705 664045
Strict door control is the way owners Kadir, Mazid and Ullah prevent rowdies from ruining the Palash's image and carefully built up reputation. Portsmouth is home the the Royal Navy, and it is not unknown for the lads

and lasses of the Senior Service to be a bit high spirited. That may be alright for HM SHIPS and even for Pompey's (and Southsea's) other fifty or so curry houses. Indeed Kingston Road itself has half a dozen, who are used to the ten pints of lager and a vindaloo brigade.
But the mindless are not welcomed at the Palash. You must book if you want a table after 10pm and the staff will not admit those who dress or behaviour does not appeal. Fortunately for readers of the Guide that leaves the way clear for the enjoyment of 'a great friendly place, where I always have had the best of everything.' GD. 'The staff continue to care about details. The welcome, the appearance of the place, their obvious job satisfaction and above all - good food.' GR. Families and children are welcomed. The food continues to be reported as 'fresh with subtleties in every mouthful.' The Palash serves all the welcomed favourite curries and Tandooris. Its specials include Mint Gosht, lamb flavoured with spices and mint. Prices here are reasonable and we continue to rate The Palash as the best in the area. It remains in our TOP 100.

THE TANDOORI MAHAL
297 Commercial Road, Portsmouth. Tel: 0705 820835
This is a standard Restaurant with a standard Menu but, we are told, they will cook other items by request. "I wanted a Prawn and Vegetable Dhansak. I asked the waiter and he said it was no problem, it arrived within 10 minutes and was extremely good." W.H. Service is said to be very good and even when the Restaurant gets busy no-one is forgotten and the service is always done with a smile.

THE CURRY GARDENS
10 High Street, Ringwood. Tel: 0425 475075
No surprises, we are told, at this Restaurant but you are in for a fairly safe bet curry meal with all the old favourites on the Menu.

THE DHAKA
16 Onslow Road, Southampton.
The Dhaka gets the thumbs up from its local following. We hear of consistent cooking, friendly service and satisfactory prices.

THE KOHINOOR
2 The Broadway, Portswood, Southampton. Tel: 0703 582770
This is one of two Restaurants owned by Kuti Miah. We have received many good reports about this Restaurant over the years. See next entry.

KUTI'S INDIAN CUISINE TOP 100 & CC DISCOUNT
70 London Road, Southampton. Tel: 0703 221585
Following the success of his Kohinoor Restaurant reported above, Kuti Miah decided he would open a Restaurant which would be better even, than his highly successful Kohinoor. He did this in August 1986 and called it Kuti's Indian Cuisine. We have been inundated with responses about this Restaurant which certainly leads us to believe that it is the best in Hampshire. In fact we include it in our top 100. The Restaurant seats 66 and it has a reception area and the Restaurant proper has cabin type tables for most of the seating. The decor doesn't please all our correspondents however. "This is an upmarket Restaurant but the decor is a ghastly pink colour including the Menu. The waiters appear to be wearing Noel Coward type jackets." J.L. Fortunately this reliable correspondent went on to tell us that the food is pretty good and that is what we hear from everybody else. "The Lamb Pasanda £5.70, was dreamy and creamy, so tender, so tasty, that I wanted to eat it all again, if only I had had enough space for another go." S.L. "We go here regularly. My sister has Korai Murgh at £6.50, which is chicken served in a cast iron cooking implement and I always have Kashmir Chicken £5.20, which is hot and spicy yet sweet and tasty." Many reports go on in the same vane but the price of fame is slightly high. Typical prices are Poppadums 40p. Chicken Curry £3.95. Pullao Rice £1.90. A set luncheon "extremely good, well worth the money (£6.50). I take advantage of this lunch every time I am in Southampton on business." L.S. There is a set dinner from £10.95. There is no minimum charge. There is a 10% service charge but no cover charge. Customers are given face towels and sweets with coffee and this Restaurant will give a discount to Curry Club members during its quieter times. See page 288. In out Top 100.

THE RAJ DUTH **CC DISCOUNT**

4 Bedford Place, Southampton. Tel: 0703 24196

We receive a fair number of good reports about the Raj Duth. We hear that "the decoration is attractive (it is fairly Indian really) with wooden archways, blue upholstery on the chairs and wonderful old prints of things like elephants round the wall." D.C. The Restaurant opened in 1979 and was taken over by Kobir Uddin in 1989. The Menu is fairly standard with all the things you would expect to see on it including 2 which make this Restaurant the first Balti Restaurant in the South of England. Chicken Bulthi or Lamb Bulthi both at £5.50 are cooked in special spices with carrots and served in an authentic Indian dish in Indian style. The dish of course being the Karahi (cast iron wok like cooking and serving implement) and Bulthi presumably meaning Balti. Vegetarians will be pleased with the Vegetable Thali which includes mushrooms, spinach, Tarka Dhal and Vegetable Bhajee at £5.90. The Kabuli Channa (Chick Peas) £1.60, makes an excellent side dish according to more than one of our scribes. Typical prices include Poppadums 40p. Chicken Curry £3.30. Pullao Rice £1.45. Set luncheon is £3.75 and set dinner is £19.50. The latter which is of course for two people appealed to two of our correspondents who went into ecstacies about value for money and quality. This Restaurant offers discounts to Curry Club members during its quieter times. See page 288.

THE ROSE OF INDIA **CC DISCOUNT**

180A Burgess Road, Southampton. Tel: 0703 760959

Good curry Restaurants really have blossomed in Southampton since we wrote our last Good Curry Guide. There are now 30 Restaurants and another one about which we hear good things is The Rose of India. "We particularly enjoyed the Chicken Delight at £6.10. As a curry it was truly a delight and it has become one of our regular favourites." P.R. "I am not a very adventurous person so on one occasion I asked the waiters who are always friendly, what should I choose. This particular waiter said try the Meat Razala so I did at £4.95 and I have never looked back since, it was superb." P.T. Typical prices include Poppadums 30p. Chicken Curry £2.70. There is no service or cover charge and the Restaurant is offering discounts to Curry Club members during its quieter times. See page 288.

THE SURMA

44 London Road, Southampton. Tel: 0703 27492

For many years The Surma was clearly the best Indian Restaurant in Southampton and it is not so much that it has waned, rather that other rising stars have shot past it. However The Surma is the only Southampton Restaurant to have achieved entry into all 3 Good Curry Guides, including this one and it is certainly popular, indeed very popular, with the residents of Southampton. "I have never had a meal in this Restaurant that has been less than excellent. The service is perfectly adequate." S.M.

THE AKASH

99 Albert Road, Southsea. Tel: 0705 750245

The Restaurant is one of Southsea's longer established Restaurants, in fact we are told that those in the know call it 'Georges'. We have two theories put forward as to why that should be, so we will leave you to find out which is the true one. One correspondent speaks of an interesting painted ceiling and cleverly lit murals. The food is good, he says, well cooked and spicy "just the sort of place I like." J.L. Prices are very acceptable with Poppadums at 30p. Chicken Curry at £3.00. Pullao Rice at £1.15.

THE GOLDEN CURRY **CC DISCOUNT**

16 Albert Road, Southsea. Tel: 0705 820262

Apparently the locals call this one Shariffes Golden Curry. We are not totally sure of the reason for this one either because it is owned by one Salim Ullah, but we do hear that it is popular and that it serves very good food. In fact this Restaurant opened in 1979, but has recently been tastefully refurbished in an Indian style and it has air conditioning as well. We have reported before about Portsmouth and Southsea's nightlife. It is one of those places where not much happens, but when it does it tends to happen after the pubs shut. This Restaurant caters for the after pub trade by staying open until 2 a.m. between Monday and Saturday and 1 a.m. on Sundays. Unless you enjoy the atmosphere, language and ribaldry that is invariably part of the scene in any Restaurant which operates in the wee hours, our advice is to go early. If you do we are assured that you will enjoy the food, the service and the Restaurant as a whole. It is a standard Curry House and typical prices include Poppadums 30p. Chicken Curry £2.90. Pullao Rice £1.50 and there are no extra charges. This Restaurant offers a 10% discount for students and 10% on takeaway meals over £5.00. It also offers a discount to Curry Club members who attend in the Restaurant's quieter times. See page 288.

THE KASHMIR
91 Palmerston Road, Southsea. Tel: 0705 822013
The Kashmir retains its place in The Good Curry Guide for the simple reason that it is very popular. We have said it before and we will say it again, we single out The Kashmir not as a brilliantly innovative establishment but one where the food is consistently good. So too is the service and the portions are more than ample.

THE MIDNIGHT TANDOORI
101 Palmerston Road, Southsea. Tel: 0705
Further along the road is The Midnight Tandoori and it is very popular. We receive regularly good reports about this Restaurant. Don't expect miracles here. "The Restaurant was full and I am sure many of the customers were regular. Although the food is above average, I wondered why other Restaurants in the area were empty while this one was full. However the food is good and the service is cheerful." J.L. In fact with 95 seats it is quite a large Restaurant. It has been around since the early 1960's, so it should know what it is doing. Dishes include Sahahi Lamb or Chicken at £5.10 and £5.20. Butter Chicken £4.70. Jeera Chicken £5.10. Tandoori Kasana £7.10 and Chicken Tikka Masala at £4.60. All we hear are very good.

THE STANDARD TANDOORI **CC DISCOUNT**
8 Albert Road, Southsea.
This Restaurant is believed to be Southsea's oldest and it opened in 1959 as the Bombay Indian. As such it was entered into our first Good Curry Guide in 1984. Since then it has been renamed The Standard Tandoori but it is still under the same ownership of Mr. D. Miah who is both the occupier and the owner. We have to tell of a report that we received some time ago which said of this Restaurant "My grandfather enjoyed curry and he brought me here when it first opened and I was 24 years old. Later I brought my girlfriend here and when she became my wife we used it as our regular. I brought my children here and have done for years and very recently, I am delighted to say that I brought my young grandchildren here. 5 generations have eaten in this Restaurant over 31 years." Sadly this report had no name and we do have a faint suspicion that it might be the owner. If it is a genuine report, we ask the writer to identify himself. The Standard Tandoori's longevity has insured that it has built up a very large loyal following. The Menu is quite long and quite interesting with many standard favourites, particularly recommended are Mint Gosht, a medium dry curry cooked with mint and saturated with cream £6.90. Hunde Gosht at £5.60, thin lamb or chicken fillet, first grilled in the tandoor, then cooked with almonds and garnished with tomatoes and special gravy and served in a special silver two handle Hundi (this is also called a Handi or a Karahi - see Glossary). Typical prices include Poppadums 50p. Chicken Curry £3.05. Pullao Rice £1.50. Set dinners range from £7.80 to £47.94 for 4 - this mind you includes wine. This Restaurant also has a fairly useful Wine List and on the Menu it says about wine 'that a meal without wine is a day without sunshine'. In common with other Restaurants in the area, the Standard stays open in the wee hours (2.30 a.m.) every morning. The Restaurant offers a discount to Curry Club members at its quieter times. See page 288.

THE CURRY AND TANDOORI CENTRE
24 Jewry Street, Winchester. Tel: 0962 65603
Winchester now has seven Indian Restaurants and it is The Curry and Tandoori Centre which, for the third time, gets into The Good Curry Guide by a close head. "It is a surprisingly large Restaurant and in many ways slightly old fashioned. Although it is not exactly shabby, it hasn't gone in for appearance. It has concentrated on its food. My Chicken Tikka Biriani £5.40, was very good indeed and my sons Chicken Tikka Masala £4.50, was well above average." J.L.

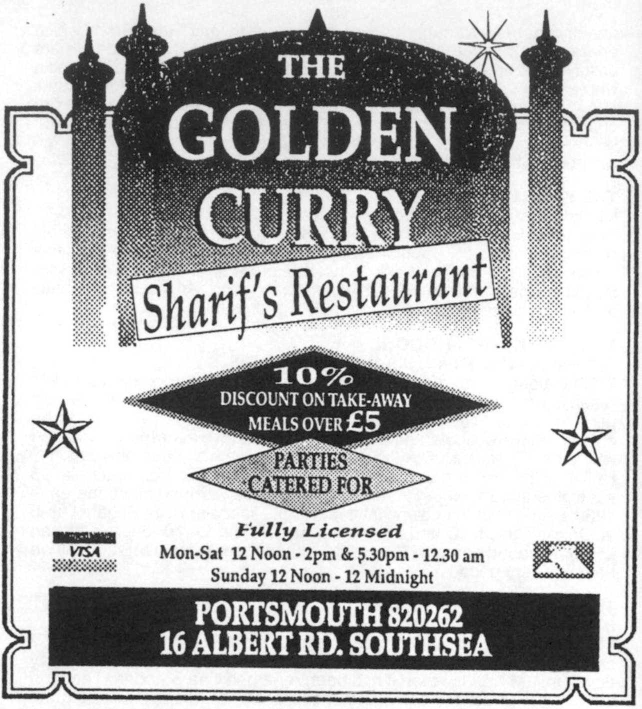

HERTFORD

THE INDIA COTTAGE
7 Northgate End, Bishops Stortford.
Tel: 0279 53513
Recommendations by several of our correspondents puts The India Cottage into this Guide for the first time. We would like more reports on this Restaurant please.

THE SONARGAON
55 High Road, Bushey Heath, Watford.
Tel: 081 950 0475
This Restaurant has been around for quite some time. It appeared in our first Good Curry Guide as the Agra Two. Since then it has been redecorated and renamed The Sonargaon. Its present owner is Mr. Bahir Uddin and as he has no other branches, he is often to be found at his Restaurant. Large chandeliers dominate this 60 seat Restaurant. The Menu is standard Bangladeshi Indian with some nice Specials such as Chicken Safar Khan £5.30 and Chicken Royal Korma £5.30, both mild and tasty. Chicken Kechundi at £6.50 is a fairly hot dish and there is also a Tandoori King Prawn version of that at £9.10. The Lamb or Chicken Green Masala contains chilli and fresh coriander and at £4.15 is enjoyed by some of our correspondents as is the Lamb Arjuman at £6.30. Other prices include Poppadums at 40p. Pullao Rice at £1.40. There is a minimum charge of £5.00.

THE TASTE OF INDIA
33 Salisbury Square, Old Hatfield. Tel: 0707 273933
The best in town according to more than one correspondent. Serving good competent food politely and with good humour. More reports on this Restaurant please.

THE CURRY CENTRE
51-55 Waterhouse Street, Hemel Hempstead. Tel: 07072 42973
Hemel boasts no less than four Indian Restaurants and this one pips the others to the post by sheer numbers of reports we have received over the last 2 years.

MOURI
15 Castle Street, Hertford. Tel: 0992
Formerly the Hertford Tandoori, it was taken under new management during 1989 and it still has "the same standard Menu, with few specialities. But the food surpasses the former excellent standards." P.C.

THE SHAHENSHAH
6 Parliament Square, Fore Street, Hertford. Tel: 0992 51580
This Restaurant has been known to readers of The Good Curry Guide for several years as The Guru Tandoori and it changed hands fairly recently. Of the four in Parliament Square it is said to be the best. Service is said to be prompt and helpful and the quantity and quality well above average. "Over all we had a superb meal, but the prices were high, though I suppose you are paying for quality." P.C. We also heard criticisms about luke warm food although our correspondent did remark that there were 11 people in his party. More reports please.

THE SAAGAR **CC DISCOUNT**
48 The Broadway, Letchworth. Tel: 04626 684952
The Saagar opened in 1987 under the ownership of Motiur Rahman. It did not take long before it came to our attention as a good attractive Restaurant. We hear that the decor is mainly pale green with curtains along the large frontage windows. Mirrors and subdued classical Indian pictures make up the remainder of the scene along with high backed upholstered chairs. Specials that we hear of include The Saagar Special Chicken Tikka, Meat Tikka, Tandoori King Prawn in delicate herbs and spices cooked and served in a cast iron dish at £6.90 and Tandoori Machlay, seasonal trout marinated in herbs and spices cooked slowly on the tandoor and served whole with fresh vegetables or side salad and dressing at £5.10. Typical prices are Poppadums 35p. Chicken Curry

£2.95. Pullao Rice £1.30. There is a set luncheon from £5.95. There is no minimum charge or cover charge but there is a service charge of 10%. However this Restaurant does give an above average amount of nice touch extras. Orange slices for example are given as fresheners between courses. After Curry Mints (Kansara) are given with coffee and what the Restaurant calls 'its digestives tray' (sugared almonds, pan masala and sugar coated aniseed are also supplied). Diners get hot face towels and there is a carnation for the lady. The Restaurant also offers discounts to Curry Club members in its quieter times. See page 288.

THE AKASH
5 Southgate Road, Potters Bar. Tel: 0707 43778
A long established Restaurant, very reliable, indeed it appeared in our first Good Curry Guide in 1984. We are confident that you will always get a good, fair, reasonable priced curry at this Restaurant.

THE BRITISH RAJ **TOP 100**
55 High Street, Royston. 0763 41471
Editors of Food Guides aren't supposed to say this, but I have to tell you I have a very big soft spot for The British Raj. Firstly I must admit I have never been there - something I must put right. The reason I have a soft spot for this Restaurant is that its owner clearly has a sense of humour. Nazir Uddin Choudhury has no other branches and his only interest in Indian Restaurants lies with The British Raj. It isn't a big Restaurant with 47 seats neither is the decor immaculate. It is however very friendly and it is very clean, so say our reporters. I am delighted to say that we continue to get happy and delighted reports about this Restaurant. Mr. Choudhury's mini Menu is like a little book and it is packed full of amusing anecdotes, pictures, cartoons and a writing style which is most entertaining and which I am delighted to see, has remained unchanged since our last Guide. Here are some examples, in the Menu there are some guidelines to eating curry. One of them says "Remember curry enhances your appetite, while you eat unknowingly you find yourself overloaded. Please select your Menu carefully" and again "People often do not know how intimate our Indian food is!" Another line which I adore is "The eating of spicy food promotes perspiration which itself takes your fatness away" - I only wish it did. Elsewhere the Menu tells us that "the tastefulness is terrific". Who are we to doubt it. Judging by the reports we receive, the food is just as good as the Menu. But go on about the Menu, which other Menu do you know which includes a recipe? The Menu tells us "we make good food taste better and you can eat with us (1) at the Restaurant (2) by taking your meals away (3) by you own cooking. Try out the recipe for Mattar Paneer on page 4." It is all wonderful stuff. Choudhury is clearly the greatest showman in the Indian Restaurant business. Choudhury's head chef Bashir Ahmed claims to have been the first chef to introduce tandoori dishes into the U.K. in 1963. He is said to have assisted in the opening of a number of top ranking Restaurants in the U.K. In his time in India he served food to the ex King of Hyderabad and those that have met him say he is a great personality. There are so many dishes on this Menu that the only thing to do is to take a Menu home and study it there before you order. We have regulars that say they have worked their way round the Menu more than once. Perhaps they tried the Giant Tandoori Mixed Grill £7.99 or the Butter Chicken Masala, a full meal and one of the chefs specialities at £8.79 goes big on garlic, recommending it in the Menu as "a way to reduce high blood pressure and prevent heart attacks". A number of their garlic assisted dishes are asterisked such as Garlic Aloo Morobba which is a potato curry cooked in a garlicy, creamy sauce £3.49 or Garlic Palak Capsicum Bhajee which is a vegetable mixture of garlic, spinach, peppers at £3.49 "Try our Garlic Morobba" says the Menu "It could help to maintain a healthy heart and circulation whatever the reason!" This Restaurant is located in the eastern part of Hertfordshire and therefore it lays claim to being geographically in East Anglia. For this reason the Restaurant has made a point of inviting the respective winners of the Miss Anglia Contest since 1978 to come as Guest of Honour to try one of their curries. The Restaurant offers a number of different Thali combinations which they call Thal including a vegetable one at £7.99, a chicken or meat one at £8.99, a prawn one at £9.29 and so on and should you be feeling in the festive mood try the Raj Speciality, the Thalia Shagorana (the wedding feast). The Menu says of this dish that "although it is a wedding feast for the marrying couple, it is overwhelmingly used for VIP treatments on specialised occasions and anniversaries. Why not try it tomorrow

which is something to you, but when ordering please provide us with 24 hours notice because the dish needs careful preparations and cooking methods. Eat your way to intimacy and enjoy the gastronomy of this feast and make the event spicy and full of admiration." What does this feast consist of. It consists of lots and lots of different dishes, enormous quantities by the look of it and a litre of house wine for 4 people. At £39.99 that seems like good value to me. The Restaurant makes no minimum charge, charges no service charge but it does have an absolutely ludicrous cover charge of 19p. All diners get hot face towels, sweets with coffee and roasted supari spices to refresh the breath at the end of the meal. Three more points of interest which we would like to bring to your attention. Firstly, this Restaurant sells Indian beer (Cobra we hope) and Indian Paan liqueur. This is a rather extraordinary liqueur made in India from juice of the beetle nut and this is the only Restaurant I know, which sells it. It is also the only Restaurant I know which offers the diners a fifth course which is a Hooker (Hubble Bubble Pipe). Yes, if you so have a mind you can smoke your way out of a meal in true Indian style. For this and all the other delightful things at this Restaurant I am going to make an idiosyncratic award to this Restaurant by placing it in our top 100. Children are welcome "they get small meals".

THE MUMTAJ
115 London Road, St. Albans. Tel: 0727 58399
The Mumtaj is one of St. Albans longest standing Restaurants. It originally opened in 1962 although it came under the new management of Mr. N. Islam in 1988. The Mumtaj received an entry in our previous Guide and the new management then indeed improved upon the standards of the previous era. An attractive Restaurant with red high backed chairs contrasting with grey stippled walls and white gloss work. Starters include Meat or Vegetable Samosas, Kebabs (various kinds), Tikka (various kinds), Chicken Chaat, thinly sliced chicken served cold in a spicy sauce £2.70 and Onion Bhajee (their spelling for Bhajie) which are onion balls prepared with gram flour, spices and herbs, then deep fried at £1.65. Also they serve Onion Pakura which many Restaurants treat as the same preparation, but this time the onions are lightly spiced and then fried. There is a good selection of Biriani dishes ranging between £5.10 for Chicken Biriani up to £8.95 for Tandoori King Prawn Biriani. Specialities include Mumtaj Special which is barbecued spring chicken with capsicum, onions in a mild sauce £8.50. A King Prawn Delight, tandoori king prawn cooked in a special Pakistani mild sauce enhanced with red wine £9.50 and Peshawari Lamb at £7.50, pieces of lamb fillet cooked in yoghurt sauce with almonds and pistachios, cashews and sultanas. Another House Special is Chicken Charga £6.95, which is barbecued chicken coated in shaheen spices and served dry. The prices inlcude Poppadums 30p. Chicken Curry £3.15. Pullao Rice £1.20 and whilst they don't have a minimum charge or a cover charge, they do have a service charge of 10%.

THE MOHAN
116 High Street, Old Town, Stevenage. Tel: 0438 726419
Rated by our reporters in the area as being the best of Stevenage's five. Reports would be welcomed.

THE GHANDI
13 High Street, Waltham Cross. Tel: 0992 718807
This Restaurant, which opened in 1976 as The Megna became The Ghandi in 1989 when the present management of Mr. Shazad Miah took it over. Prior to the takeover we had several good reports about this Restaurant, for example "We eat here frequently and have had several takeaways. The food and the service is excellent. Between us we have sampled a fair amount of the Menu. The specialities are especially good. It gets busy late on Fridays and Saturdays." T. & A.W. Following the takeover there was, as you would expect, a silence of a few months, then the reports started to come back in again and this means that The Ghandi has won its place back in the heart of its regulars. We are told that the light, airy, spacious Restaurant in pinks, marble and granite, which seats 60, serves good food. One of our correspondents enjoys the Chicken Jalfrezi at £5.95 whilst another raves about the Chicken Chilli Masala. "It is so hot and fresh." A.T. at £3.50. Prices include Poppadums at 35p. Chicken

Curry £3.00 and Pullao Rice £1.50. There is a minimum charge of £7.00 but no service or cover charge. Face towels, After Eights, fresh flowers on the table of which the ladies can take them if they wish, are included for the diners. Mr. Miah has 2 other Ghandi Restaurants, one in Sandy, Beds., the other at Woodford Bridge, Essex.

THE ALI BABA
13 King Street, Watford. Tel: 0923 229793
This Restaurant was formerly The Akash and was recently renamed as The Ali Baba. We receive good reports for it either name, although one reporter says that he found it predictable but pleasing. More reports welcomed.

HUMBERSIDE

AGRAH INDIA
7/9 Seaview Street, Cleethorpes.
Tel: 0472 698669
For the entire existence of the Curry Club i.e. the last 9 years, we have been receiving a 'progress report' from one of The Agrah's regulars. It turns up about 3 times a year and it is rather like receiving a school report. What he says doesn't change very much. He likes the place, he speaks of a thoroughly consistent curry and he enjoys visiting it. Proprietors A. Miah, A. Roof and B. Miah opened this Restaurant in 1980. Because of its seaside location this Restaurant is visited by national television stars and personalities who appear at the local entertainment venues. Given half a chance, any one of the owners will show you their visitors books with signatures of Windsor Davis, Clodah Rogers, Bryan Ferry, Mike Hallet (the snooker player) and many others. "However we don't go for star gazing we go for the food. Our attention is drawn to Shik Kebab (their spelling) and Shamosa (their spelling). The latter at £1.05, the former at £1.25. Unusual Specialities include Burburi Chicken which the owners claim is a recipe from the Emperor Babur's Court and a method of preparation which is especially suitable for meat or chicken, which are briskly fried with fresh onions, black pepper, cinnamon, bay leaves and cardamom, served with Pullao Rice at £5.25. Special East Bengal (Bangladeshi) dishes include Chicken and Mushroom at £3.65, Prawn and Beans at £3.75 and Meat and Bindy (lady's fingers) at £3.80. Another unusual dish is Fillet Steak Masala which is a steak served with peas, tomatoe and chipped potatoes but prepared with oriental spice including garlic. A pure invention but pure heaven." P.D. Prices include Poppadums 25p. Chicken Curry £3.30. Pullao Rice £1.00. Set luncheon £2.50 and there is a minimum charge of £1.00.

THE KOHINOOR RESTAURANT **CC DISCOUNT**
56A Beverley Road, Hull. Tel: 0482 26394
This Restaurant began trading in December 1981 under the management of Mr. S. Miah and some of our regular Hull reporters have asked why it hasn't appeared in The Good Curry Guide before. The answer is simple, you didn't speak highly enough of it before. But now you have and in the last couple of years, we have heard many good reports about The Kohinoor. "It is a clean and comfortable Restaurant with soft background music and friendly service. I asked whether they had a tandoor and I was invited into the kitchen. The food was good and we enjoyed the evening." P.W. We are told that the Restaurant has recently been redecorated and expanded. For the most part the Menu is fairly standard but there are 1 or 2 specials which catch the eye of our regular reporters. How about the Chicken Dilaight (is that pronounced Delight? ed). This is a chicken dish cooked with cream and curry spices at £4.75 and there is a King Prawn version at £5.75. Also highly regarded is the Shahi Chicken, a mild delicately spiced and richly flavoured dish at £3.95 and the Cyclone

EMPIRE OF INDIA

286 High Street, Beckenham, Kent.

Telephone: 081 650 7183

LIGHT OF INDIA

TOWNWALL STREET, DOVER

TEL: 0304 210666

Chicken which is "fairly hot and spicy and cooked with coconut", that's what it says on the Menu but one of our correspondents said "The Cyclone nearly blew my head off but I love it, I would come back for more" £3.55. prices include Poppadums 35p. Chicken Curry £3.45. Pullao Rice £1.45. A Big feature of the Kohinoor is its happy night. On Sunday, Monday and Thursday nights only you can for £7.95, get served a very worthy 3 course meal including, if you are a party of two, a free half carafe of wine and if you are a party of four, a free bottle of Neirsteiner. There are no extra charges and this Restaurant offers discounts to Curry Club members at its quieter times. See page 288.

THE STANDARD TANDOORI RESTAURANT **CC DISCOUNT**
212 Spring Bank, Hull. Tel: 0482 23552
This relatively small 46 seat Restaurant was redecorated in the middle of 1990. Some of the dishes on the Menu are, we hear, quite adventurous. Some indeed are South Indian recipes. There aren't many places for example, where you can get Patravel Bhajia (this is a particular kind of leaf - the Arvi leaf) at £1.40 or Karela Bhajia which is a Bitter Gourd, also £1.40 ("not my taste, too bitter for me.") P.T. They also do Parwal Bhajia, £1.40, another Southern Indian leaf dish. Also Tinda Bhajia which is small marrow at £1.40. They do a Green Bean Curry and a Chickpea Curry, both dishes are £1.40. Also from South India comes the Samber (their spelling). This is a hot and spicy dish with the use of lentils and lemon juice to obtain a sharp distinctive flavour. Prices range from £2.40 for Vegetable Samber to £3.90 for King Prawn Samber. Typical prices include Poppadums 25p. Chicken Curry £3.50. Pullao Rice £1.30 and there is a range of set dinners for 2 people ranging from £15.25 to £17.80. Some of our correspondents rave on about the Banana or Pineapple Fritters, 80p. There is no minimum charge nor is there a service or cover charge and the Restaurant offers a discount to Curry Club members at their quieter times. See page 288. The Restaurant also has a branch called the Bolaka, 133 Chantaland Avenue, Hull.

KENT

THE CURRY COTTAGE,
28 North Street, Ashford. Tel: 0253 20511
"Conveniently located in the centre of Ashford. This Restaurant has a pleasant atmosphere.

EMPIRE OF INDIA
286, High Street, Beckenham. Tel: 081 650 7183
The Empire continues to receive ample praise from our correspondents, which ensure its continuing appearance in these pages.

THE RAJ, **CC DISCOUNT**
187 Main Street, Biggin Hill. Tel: 0959 72459
"One of the great things about The Raj is that it has a car park." C.B. We also hear other good things about The Raj from quite a number of reporters. It is the third time this Restaurant has been in The Guide and as in previous editions, reporters speak of better than average food. Quality of the food and service is excellent with the best and freshest Poppadums ever. Try the Peshwari Naan Bread at £1.20. It is an education to your tastebuds." M.A. This 70 seat Restaurant has a reception area and 2 floors as our reporters J.W. told us last time "The Madras Curry is very fine indeed".Offers discounts to Curry Club members at its quieter times. See page 288.

THE SURUCHI RESTAURANT, **CC DISCOUNT**
466 Bromley Road, Bromley. Tel: 081 698 8626
This Restaurant opened up in Bromley Road in 1980 under the ownership of Mr. S. Dey. We are told that they provide a few unusual treats. The starters for example include Stuffed Mushrooms, filled with a spicy filling

and Nagis Kebab, which are the Indian version of scotch eggs i.e. hard boiled eggs covered with spicy kebab meat, then they are baked. One of our reporters enjoys the Meat Himalayan. Another says of the Rogon Gosht (their spelling) that it is one of the best they have ever tasted. The vegetarian is well catered for here we understand, with "a most delicious mild creamy Korma (Molai Korma) and another wonderful dish, Dhal Masala." B.T. Another person tells us of "delicious Aloo Dumm, literally steamed spicy potatoes which are delicious." Another interesting special is Lamb Chilli Masalla £5.25 and other typical prices include Poppadums 40p. Chicken Curry £3.25. Pullao Rice £1.30. There is no minimum charge and no service or cover charge. This Restaurant is prepared to give discounts to Curry Club members at its quieter times. See page 288.

THE POONA,
High Street, Chatham. Tel: 0634 42906
There is a standard Menu, reasonably priced, very efficient and friendly service and "very well cooked food." B.H. More reports please.

THE BENGAL LANCER,
15 Royal Parade, Chislehurst.
We find this Restaurant a little bit puzzling because we have received reports again and again of its excellence and then every now and then we receive a contradictory and quite negative report. We can say that this Restaurant seems always to be full so it is important to book. It is quite a big Restaurant, full and big can mean erratic service. It has a good atmosphere and we are told that most of the time a pianist enhances the mood of the day. One reporter speaks of Tikkas superbly spiced and succulent. Rhogan Josh that had a personal touch, the hallmark of a good chef. On another occasion the same reporter (J.L.) visited this Restaurant on a New Years Eve when it was jam packed and "the Lamb Vindaloo worked magic, cured me of my flu that had ruined my Christmas." The Restaurant is evidently good with children because we hear of an occasion where the waiter "needed a medal for not murdering my son who decided tonight was the night to display in public his complete repertoire of obnoxious tricks." Good reports continue to flow in but then as we said, the occasional snorter has spoiled an otherwise excellent record. For example, we heard from another reliable reporter N.C. that the service was slow, the waiters ignored customers and chatted amongst themselves, the main course took 20 minutes to arrive and when it did, the Meat Curry was bland although the Meat Madras had good flavour, good meat. Despite this lapse this reporter still reckoned he had a good meal in comfortable surroundings. We think this Restaurant probably suffers a little complacency for being busy much of the time and we would welcome more reports.

THE LIGHT OF INDIA,
Townhall Street, Dover. Tel: 0304 210666
This Restaurant began trading in 1984 and is run by Mr. Nural Islam. Here is a typical report "They gave us ample hot portions well presented. They can cope with a rush of customers late on a Saturday night." B.C. This Restaurant got a Clean Food Award in 1990 from its local Borough Council. Typical prices include Poppadums 40p. Chicken Curry £3.50. Pullao Rice £1.60. It does set luncheons for £4.50 and a set dinner for £10.95. There is a minimum charge of £8.50 but there is no service or cover charge.

THE INDIA, **TOP 100 & CC DISCOUNT**
1 Old High Street, Folkestone, Kent. Tel: 0303 59155
One of our favourites and it is also favourite with reporters both local and those who travel far and wide. More than one tells us how he heads for The India as a port in a storm when he arrives back at the docks from Europe. The reason for this popularity lies in the cooking and the chef proprietor Mr. Ali Ashraf. He was trained as a chef in France as well as in India and has combined French and Indian methods with great flair and originality. He uses cream, wine and brandy in combination with delicate spices to create very original dishes. Mr. Ashraf not only uses unusual ingredients such as crab and duck but his Menu reads like a dictionary of authentic Indian cooking. "The biggest problem I have with this Restaurant is knowing what to choose. All the food looks so enticing and whatever you choose it always tastes enticing too." S.G. We can start with Sabzi Ka Soup at £1.20 which is a freshly made spicy vegetable soup.

Amongst the starters you will find such delights as Crab Kochin (crab with ginger and coriander) £3.15. One correspondent says (J.T.) says of the Sita's Dosha (the India's spelling for Dosa - see Glossary). "This is a pancake stuffed with prawns, mushroom, crab and coriander and spices and it is absolutely delicious." £2.25. Amongst the main courses you will find Chicken Bangalore, boneless chicken in a medium spiced pepper and mushroom sauce and Country Chicken which is a dish from the Anglo community in India, boneless chicken cooked in a light spice gravy with mushrooms, green pepper and tomatoes. The Rogon Gosht £4.50 (their spelling) is very aromatic with nutmeg, mace and pistachio nuts and Fish Masalla is freshwater fish cooked with special spices and herbs £5.50. Rice dishes include Shahjani Biryani which is an ancient Moghul Emperors dish involving lamb and rice cooked with almonds and cashew nuts, £4.95. "Their Pullao Rice is wonderfully full of flavour cooked with ghee, milk, almonds and saffron £1.25." There is a good selection of vegetable dishes of which Channa Masalla £1.70, is "outstanding." D.P. including chickpeas with ginger, garlic, onion and coriander. Mr. Ashraf prepares 3 special dishes requiring 24 hours notice. These are Murog Masallam, chicken marinated in yoghurt, then cooked with fresh cream, poppy seeds and aromatic spices such as cinnamon and bay, £20.95 for 2. Vath, an unusual dish involving duck, cashew nuts, raisins and aromatic spices such as cardamoms and cinnamon, £25.95 - "very highly recommended." D.B. and Raan, a whole leg of roasted lamb marinated and cooked in delicate and tasty flavourings such as saffron, lemon, almonds and raisins at £30.95. There are a whole range of set dinners for 2 people ranging from £16.95 to £22.95 and for 4 people £33.95 to £45.95. These prices include a glass of wine and there are set luncheons between £5.95 and £7.50. It is not a very large Restaurant with just 52 seats and the atmosphere is cosy, light and sociable. The pale walls are offset by some charming miniature paintings and elegant Maharaja style chairs and settees but it is Mr. Ali Ashraf and his lightness of touch which make this Restaurant so special. There is a minimum charge of £5.50 per head. It is advisable to book. There is no service charge but there is a cover charge of 50p a head for which diners get hot face towels, coffee sweets and flowers for the lady. This Restaurant is very deservedly in our top 100 and it offers discounts to Curry Club members at its quieter times. See page 288.

THE CURRY INN, **CC DISCOUNT**
98 King Street, Maidstone. Tel: 0622 56094
We are fortunate in having a number of very good and reliable correspondents in the Maidstone area. Of these, N.G. would perhaps get our Correspondents of the Year for diligence. Every Restaurant which he rates as good and on which he reports, he visits at least a dozen times and reports on each visit. He has done this with The Curry Inn. Another reporter talks of "the Chicken Dhansak served with Pullao Rice at £4.80 as being enormous and highly addictive." B.N. The Restaurant serves a set luncheon for £5.50 and there is no service or cover charge. The Restaurant is also offering discounts to Curry Club members at their quieter times. See page 288.

THE SHAMRAT BRASSERIE, **CC DISCOUNT**
36 Upper Stone Street, Maidstone. Tel: 0622 764961
Maidstone has eight Indian Restaurants and the The Shamrat is the other one about which we receive very good reviews. Our correspondents M.G. has done his wonderful reporting on this Restaurant as well and it backs up the reports we have had from others. In his view, this is Maidstone's best curry Restaurant by a slight head. Does anyone agree or disagree with that? Certainly as far as the Menu goes, it has got some very imaginative dishes. There is a French influence to the cooking, for example, Murgh Flambe O Cognac is £5.50, tender chicken cooked in white wine and herbs with Pernod and Sherry flambed in Brandy. Another similar dish is Murgh Moriche Flambe O Whisky is £5.50, pepper chicken cooked in white wine with herbs, Pernod and Sherry flambed in Whisky. Gosht Flambe O Cognac, pieces of lamb cooked in red wine and Sherry and flambed in Brandy and Chingri Supreme Flambe O Cognac, King Prawns cooked in selective special herbs with wine and Port flambed in Brandy at £8.50. N.G. refers to this dish as a unique masala sauce of the Chicken Tikka Jalfrezi, £5.40 he says "what a choice, tender chicken cooked in a spicy sauce with lots of fresh chillies - phew!" Other people have called the Chicken Tikka Masala "exquisite" and "unmissable". N.G.

and M.S. This Restaurant is highly recommended and booking is advisable. This Restaurant will offer a discount to Curry Club members at its quieter times. See page 288.

THE TASTE OF PARADISE,
Chatham Road, Sandling, Maidstone.

We have been receiving good reports about this relatively recently opened Restaurant. Its Menu consists of well known tandoori and curry favourites but it also has a fair selection of Ceylonese (Sri Lankan) dishes. For example, the Ambul Thyral as a main course, "looks strange but tasted great and Tuna Fish with Peppercorn was quite outstanding. The quality of all the food is reported to be excellent and the quantities also good and it is always served on hot plates. Poppadums are served with a tray of pickles, which is a nice touch and the Tandoori Chicken which is very tasty is, we hear, served with salad and red and green chilli sauce. Prawn Curry was very hot and the Chicken Biriani very tasty and the Naan was the lightest I have had. There was no service charge but we left 10% anyway." M.P. More reports would be welcome.

THE BOMBAY BRASSERIE, TOP 100
Green Street Green, Orpington. Tel: 0689 62906

We have received a number of good reports about this Restaurant. For example this one, "I am becoming a real fan of this smallish Restaurant and I am not alone. I arrived at 6.15 and got the last table. I had never seen such a well organised takeaway service. They do everything well. Their meals have a distinctive, delicious taste. One complaint, I am tired of listening to their tape of The Snowman, EastEnders and The Phantom of the Opera." J.L. It is quite a sizeable Restaurant seating about 100 but it seems to be regularly full quite early, especially Fridays and Saturdays, so booking is advisable. We have several reports to hand that say the meals are outstandingly good and that the service is very friendly. On one other occasion J.L. said of this Restaurant "Their Korai Gosht is still an excellent meal and who cares about the calories, but they produce brilliant breads. It occurred to me that what separates the really top Restaurants from the good ones like this one is their use of herbs. The Bombay Brasserie's Chicken Muli and Rhogan Josh were both well cooked and well spiced but would have benefitted from a few more herbs, something like Fenugreek or perhaps Coriander. But an excellent value for money Restaurant." J.L. This Restaurant appears in this well travelled correspondents top 10 and we have put it in our TOP 100.

THE RAJ OF INDIA,
Crescent Way, Orpington. Tel: 0689 51952

This is quite a recent Restaurant, it opened in 1987 in the ownership of Mr. Muzibur Rahman who also owns The Raj of India, Swanley and The Raj of India, Sittingbourne, Kent. The reports that we receive have been building up progressively and satisfactorily and they speak of an elegant corner site with The Raj of India built into a white and black timbered building, with elegant archways in white with a blue tiled base. The blue theme is carried inside the Restaurant with blue carpets, blue bar fittings, tablecloths and decor, all in all it is a very smart looking Restaurant. The Menu is standard and very comprehensive offering all the favourites that one would expect, including some Raj of India Newabi dishes (meaning the dishes of the Royal rulers) such as Chicken Malaya, chicken cooked in a medium sauce with pineapple, £3.25, Chicken Bombay, chicken cooked with lychees, £3.25 and Sag Mutton, mutton cooked with spinach, garlic and mild spices, £3.25. Typical prices include Poppadums 35p. Chicken Curry £3.15. Pullao Rice £1.40. There is no service charge, no minimum charge, no cover charge and the Restaurant gives each diner a hot face towel, After Eight Mints and fresh orange segments before coffee.

BLACKFEN TANDOORI,
33 Wellington Parade, Blackfen, Sidcup.
Tel: 081 303 0013

It opened relatively recently in a Grade 2 listed building. Both the decor and furnishings are referred to by correspondents as "delightful and sophisticated. You can look into the kitchen through a glass panelled door and see immaculate stainless steel and tiles." D.P. Other reporters talk about good food and their excellent service and we understand this Restaurant has its sister branch The Marden Tandoori, Marden, Near aidstone. "There are a good selection of starters. The Prawn Puree and Samosas are both tasty and the main courses are plentiful in quantity even if you are hungry. The Lamb Pasanda at £6.90 melts in the mouth. The Tarka Dhal is excellent with plenty of onions and garlic. My wife says even the loos are worth visiting." G.P. More reports welcomed.

THE ANGLO INDIAN,
The Pantiles, Tunbridge Wells. Tel: 0892 26633
Reports tell us of a very passable Restaurant serving very passable food. "I was a visitor to the very pretty town of Tunbridge Wells the other day and I passed at least three Indian Restaurants before spotting The Anglo Indian. I felt drawn to it and went in and had a most excellent meal." C.B. This comment is typical of those that we receive. Prices are reasonable. More reports welcomed. This Restaurant has been around for 25 years and it has changed from redflock to pressed leaves a few years ago. It remains extremely popular with a huge, if not exactly cheap, Menu although helpings are gigantic.

THE NEW CURRY CENTRE,
96 Bellgrove Road, Welling. Tel: 081 303 9818
"Service is excellent and fast. The decor is comfortable and well lit. It could do with extractors as kitchen smells and smoke prevaded a bit and it was a little too warm. However the Meat Madras and the Bombay Potato both had good flavours and the Chapattis were very good indeed." M.C. More reports welcomed.

THE SHAPLA,
20 London Road, Westerham. Tel: 0959 63397
This Restaurant which opened in 1978 changed hands in 1986 shortly after it appeared for the second time in our Good Curry Guide. The new owner S. Tarat has maintained standards. The food remains well above average and is highly regarded by our local reporters. The Restaurant itself aims to be simple but exclusive and in this respect it appears to be succeeding. Unusual dishes include Chicken Manturi £6.95 and Chicken Ludhiana at the same price, both of which are "well spicy and tasty." Typical prices include Poppadums 50p. Chicken Curry £3.50. Pullao Rice £1.50 and these already slightly high prices are boosted by a 10% service charge.

LANCASHIRE

THE KIRN TANDOORI,
63 Bond Street, Blackpool. Tel: 0253 46056.
Blackpool is well known for a number of things such as political party conferences, illuminations, trams, its seafront and its sticks of pink coloured rock but is not renowned regrettably for its curries. It has no less than seven Indian Restaurants, yet until recently none came to the fore as being remarkable or let alone worthy of a mention in this Guide. However in 1990 a new Restaurant was opened which immediately attracted considerable attention from our scribes. One report says "I saw an advertisement for this newly opened Restaurant which said 'find us under the Porthole Cafe'. That alone drew me there in a sense of curiosity and we found this Restaurant was indeed under the Porthole Cafe. It was in the basement." S.S. Mr. Mohammed Maqsood owns the ground floor Porthole Restaurant which serves English food. He claims to have been in catering in India for over 12 years and that he opened The Kirn meaning 'sunrays' (and named after his very young daughter) in response to public demand. "The recipes we serve are the recipes we make for ourselves." The Menu includes many well known specialities and apparently they do tandoori particularly well. Other specialities which have come to our notice are The Kirn Karahi Gosht, lamb cooked in herbs and spices, £5.80. The Chicken Lahoree (spicy), the Chicken Jaypuri (medium) and the Chicken Islamabad (mild) are some of the Chefs Specialities are £5.80. "The service is extremely pleasant. We particularly like the young waiter and waitress, seemingly unusual at an Indian Restaurant. We also had a delicious Korma which we were told was cooked in fresh cream, milk, coconut and white wine which would have accounted for an extremely tasty sauce." More reports would be welcomed on this Restaurant please. This quote came from one of our regular Blackpool correspondents "The price structure is a little strange. The starters are cheap £1.50 to £2.30 but main courses average from £4.00 to £5.00. Prawn dishes are around £9.50 with side vegetable dishes at £3.00. Rice and Naans were £1.00 and Poppadums 70p each." B.R.

THE GEETA,
12 St. Peter St., Blackburn. Tel: 0254 677277
Blackburn has a dozen or so Indian Restaurants and picking a good one has proved slightly difficult. It is not that the others are all bad, it is just that nothing particularly stands out about them. However about The Geeta, we have received marginally more good reports than we have for any other so for that reason it gets entry into this edition of The Good Curry Guide. "It is a deceptively large dining area and well decorated. My Chicken Cappsula looked and tasted lovely. The customer is in this Restaurant. I went back the following night and it reinforced my opinion. In all aspects it is good." J.L. More reports please.

THE FAYEZ, **CC DISCOUNT**
82 Victoria Road, Cleveleys 0253 853562
This Restaurant was formerly known as The Kushum. This is a typical report. "The Fayez have extended their considerable Menu. Some new dishes are the Shahi Tora and the Lobster Kebab. The A La Carte Menu includes a 5 course banquet from £9.50 to £11.00. Last Christmas I tried Kurzi Lamb, it was absolutely incredible. A whole leg of lamb arrived just for me!" B.R. We hear that portions are huge and another one of our regular reporters has tried the Kurzi "Our annual lamb Kurzi day (leg of lamb marinated in spices and yoghurt and cooked slowly for 24 hours which costs £14.95 per person). The meat fell off the bone when it saw the knife. Can recommend plenty of Moet to refresh the pallet." D.C. We also hear good reports of the Tandoori Special Biriani £5.75, which gives massive portions with a lattice worked omlette on top. The Restaurant gets busy and the decor is impressive. Our Lancashire correspondents swear that this Restaurant is the best in Lancashire and they have been

known to give discounts to Curry Club members in their quieter times but this could be a bit erratic although we think it is still worth trying. See page 288. A highly recommended Restaurant where booking is advisable.

THE RAMNA, **CC DISCOUNT**
54 Park Road, Chorley. Tel: 0257 74644
The Ramna opened in 1987 and is in the ownership of Mr. N.D. Nawab. He owns no other branch and is often to be found at the Restaurant. It has a reception area and a cocktail bar downstairs and the Restaurant is spread over 2 floors, 72 seats downstairs and an upstairs party room has 30 seats. The colour scheme is pink and green. Crystal chandeliers and oriental art pieces along with cubicles for 2 and 4 and open plan seating make for a very pleasant atmosphere, we are told. The Menu consists of a wide range of favourite curry dishes. "Yakni Murghi, chicken cooked in a thick yoghurt based spicy gravy at £5.85 was delicious as was my wifes Murghi Masala, Chicken cooked with egg, nuts and tomatoes at £5.65. Both these dishes were served with rice." M.D. "One day I went in and asked for a really hot curry. I said it had to be *really, really* hot. The waiter said we can give you Chicken Chilli Masala. It is cooked with green chilli, herbs in hot spices. Fine I said but make sure it is really hot. When it came it was incendiary level and the waiters stood around watching me eat it, offering lager and water free of charge. They couldn't believe I would eat it, but I did." C.P. Also of note is a Vegetarian Thali, priced for 2 people at £12.50 and for 4 people at £24.00 and containing a very good selection of vegetable dishes. A unique feature of this Restaurant is what it calls, its East-West dishes, for example a sirloin steak is cooked with a masala spicy medium hot gravy and served with chips and a salad at £6.95. We also have reports about the 12 course Sunday dinner which is served from 2 p.m. to 5 p.m. on Sundays with prices of £8.50 per adult and £6.50 per child. This Restaurant also serves one Balti dish, Balti Chicken cooked with onions, green peppers and tomatoes is served in a Balti or a Karahi dish - see Glossary. Poppadums are 30p. Pullao Rice 90. There are no extra charges. Diners get hot face towels, fresh orange slices, flowers and the Restaurant offers a discount to Curry Club members at its quieter times. See page 288.

SAJU'S, **TOP 100**
Church Street, Chorley. Tel: 0257 481894
This Restaurant has been a favourite of The Good Curry Guide since it came into being in 1985. The reason we liked it was because here was something totally different. It is an Indian Restaurant in a former converted Church. At the beginning we used to receive a lot of 'witty' correspondence from our reporters who went there, presumably out of curiosity to see whether they would get a culinary uplift from such a sanctified setting. It is worth repeating some of these cracks. "I am not sure of the ethics of all this." D.D. "Where will all this end? Can we expect to receive C. of E. curry or an R.C. Rhogan?" P.L.A. Other cracks pour in from "Vindaloo in the vestry" to "Baptestry Biriani" and "Will they be serving Poppadums with Holy Communion." The only problem was we didn't get very good comments about the food. Fortunately the owner Mr. Mohammed Ali has taken a firm grip on the quality of the food he serves there. Firstly, lets talk about the decor. It is undisputably very plush and very smart indeed and cost a lot of money. Some of the features of the Church still remain including a sweeping double staircase up to the balcony. The plush round backed chairs are grouped round smartly laid tables, the crockery, cutlery and the glassware is immaculate. Indeed, food comes served on Wedgewood. Over the last few years the reports about the food have improved and improved. "I have dined here often and I can say that it is usually good, sometimes very good, sometimes superbly good. Personally I rave over the Tandoori Lamb Masala." A.H. This very recent one "In the three years since I have visited the place things have changed dramatically. I had a truly exceptional meal. My only criticism was I had a long wait for a table, despite the fact we had booked. The Poppadums arrived with a superb array of pickles and chutneys. Vegetable Samosas and Shami Kebabs were excellent. The Chapattis melted in the mouth. The Saju's Special and the Chicken Dupiaza were superb. Large portions of everything, especially the Pullao Rice and Bingel Bhajee. The service was very attentive and the ladies got a flower and the gentlemen weren't forgotten either, they got a lollipop. It really is

excellent." G.W. We are so pleased to hear of the transformation of cooking at this Restaurant and we have had so many good reports on it that we have decided to put the Restaurant into our top 100.

THE PAVILLION,
82 Albert Road, Fleetwood.
Tel: 03917 2790
"Good news for North Fylde, with a new Restaurant being situated in the lighthouse area of Fleetwood. It should do especially well in the holiday season. Managed by Amil and Janni, two very personable Indians. This Restaurant is compact and plain with about 35 covers. The portions are a little small compared to local competition but the quality is superb. The prices including rice £2.50 to £4.00 makes it quite a reasonable Restaurant. A quick tour of the kitchen is often offered which is always interesting." D.C. More reports welcome.

THE PRACHEE,
New Preston Road, Kirkham. 0772 685896
This Restaurant opened in 1981 under the ownership of Mr. M.A. Rob. We mentioned it in our first Good Curry Guide in 1984 and were glad to see it come back into this one. Good friendly standard Restaurant with a branch of the same name in Bradford Road, Whitecross, Guiseley, West Yorkshire. Typical prices are Poppadums 35p. Chicken Curry £3.25. Pullao Rice £1.25 and there is a minimum charge of £5.50.

THE INDIAN COTTAGE,
115 Towngate, Leyland, Nr. Preston. Tel: 0772
This is another Restaurant which our reporters describe as a good, safe, standard Restaurant. The Specials include Murgh Masala, medium chicken curry cooked with yoghurt, ginger, coriander and fenugreek leaves and special spices £5.45. Gost Kata Mosala (their spelling), succulent beef curry braised golden brown with a touch of whole garam masala, £5.45 and Murgh Charga, chicken marinated with yoghurt, ginger, garlic, gram flour, almonds, tomatoes and sultanas cooked in a red sauce £5.45. Typical prices are Poppadums 40p. Chicken Curry £2.60. Pullao Rice £1.10. They also have a branch called The Bengal Cottage, 26 Burnley Road, Bacup, Lancs.

NELSON

SHABANA
62, Manchester Road, Nelson. Tel: 0282 691282
Good food and good use of spices at this restaurant. More reports please.

PRESTON

THE KISMET
20, Derby Street, Preston. Tel: 0772 51880
This unpretentious restaurant returns to the guide because of its useful open hours, (if you are an insomniac and like curry after 2am in the morning). As we said before it very very handy from the M6 and anything is better than Motorway service stations. When this restaurant opened in 1980 is was sited in 'an old transport shack' The owner Abdul Wahid said that himself. A few years latter it was transformed into what some of our readers call an 'extremely Indian, very attractive, warm and friendly place with a spacious lounge bar and restaurant 'I always feel like I'm in an Indian Palace when I come to the Kohinoor' A standard but quite comprehensive menu offering all the old favourites, but new to this restaurant are chicken Jalfrezi and Shashlik, the former being a stir-fried, attractive and spicy chicken dish and the other being a skewered kebab type dish. Prices are very reasonable and the added advantage of the ample car park, but disadvantage of several surcharges, such as pickle charge tray of £1.20, cover charge of £2.50 and 10% service charge. This seems a little bit hefty for Preston. More reports please.

POLASH TANDOORI **CC DISCOUNT**
29, Berry Lane, Longridge, Preston. Tel: 0772 785280
Large 110 seat restaurant opened in May 1988 under the ownership of Runuk Ula. He also has Runuks Bibina Restaurant in Burnley in Lancs. One correspondent writes of the decor which he says is authentic and attractive Indian decor with contrasting light and deep blue tables and a lattice ceiling with grey silk ivy leaves. The tables are a mixture of free standing and intimate cubicles. There is a reception area and cocktail bar. The restaurant displays a notice which invites people to tour their kitchen at any time. 'We took up the offer and were fascinated watching the chefs Chefs prepare tandoori dishes and the speed in which they work amazed us.' CF. 'From the long and extensive menu you can pick out Mulligatawny Soup £1.45 or Tangra Kebab large tender chicken drum sticks cooked in the Tandoor £2.65 or Lamb Cutlets, same price, tender lamb chops marinated in spices and grilled in the tandoor. Kahaliji, is unusual £2.65 it is liver marinated in spices and onions and served with a sauce as a starter and Deshi Pakora, Onions with lentils, potatoes and flavoured spices, deep-fried and served with salad and sauce £12.25 is we hear very delicious.' PT. Their specials include Tandoori Lamb Cutlet Masala, their Tandoori Cutlets are cooked with minced and served with a sauce £7.95. Mogli Chat, succulent pieces of chicken cooked in a special fried sauce of herbs and spices £7.95. Dishes are served with Pullao Rice and Nan and the heat strengths will be varied according to tastes. Other prices include Poppadoms 35p, Pullao Rice £1.25, Set dinner is available from £19.95 for two people. One of our correspondents describes as 'a very filling meal'. This restaurant offers discounts to Curry club members at there quieter times. See page 288.

RAWENSTALL

SURMA RESTAURANT
13, Bacup Road, Rawenstall. Tel: 0706 216185
'Instead of my usual chicken Bhoona at this restaurant which costs £4.35, I tried something really adventurous I had Tandoori Chicken Bhoona at £5.45. You see, I love Bhoona and I couldn't bring myself to try anything else. It was absolutely delicious and I am now a convert.' ED. This restaurant has a branch the Surma I at 69, Photostore Street, Photostore Road North, Westwood, Oldham. Prices include Poppadoms 35p, Chicken Curry £3.95, Pullao Rice £1.35 and set dinner from £16.75. There is a minimum charge of £6.00 put no service or cover charge.

ST ANNES-ON-SEA

ST ANNES TANDOORI
7, Orchard Street, St Annes-On-Sea.
A standard menu of Biriani dishes, Korma, Bhoona, Medium Curry Madras, Vindaloo, Roghan Gosht Do-Piaza, Dhansak etc. A specials from the tandoor includes a Steak Masala, £7.10, 'A big portion of T bone steak is soaked in tandoori marinade, cooked in a Bhoona sauce and served with a green salad and Pullao rice and is my favourite' DK. Typical prices are Poppadoms 30p, Chicken Curry £2.95, Pullao Rice £1.00. Set luncheon £3.25 Set dinner from £16.95 for two.

SHYAMALEE
16, David's Road South, St Annes-On-Sea.
'Bhoona Prawn on Puri was so delicious as a starter and so large it could have passed as a main course. The Sri Lankan Chicken was massive with pieces of chicken in a spicy coconut sauce, but the Pullao Rice was rather plain.' BR. Is this the best in St Annes? More reports please.

WHALLEY

TRISHNA
King Street, Whalley.
'This is a welcomed venue in this charming Lancashire village town near the historic abbey. It is full of nice touches (hot face towels, flowers and lolly pops for the gents) and its cooking is light and careful' PT.
More reports please.

LEICESTERSHIRE

LEICESTER

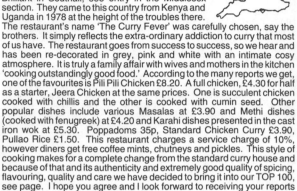

CURRY FEVER TOP 100 & CC DISCOUNT
139, Belgrave Road, Leciester.
Tel: 0533 662941
This restaurant opened in 1978 and it is run by Sunil and Anil Anand. These two brothers are related to the owners of the Brilliant in Southall, see entry in the Middlesex section. They came to this country from Kenya and Uganda in 1978 at the height of the troubles there. The restaurant's name 'The Curry Fever' was carefully chosen, say the brothers. It simply reflects the extra-ordinary addiction to curry that most of us have. The restaurant goes from success to success, so we hear and has been re-decorated in grey, pink and white with an intimate cosy atmosphere. It is truly a family affair with wives and mothers in the kitchen 'cooking outstandingly good food.' According to the many reports we get, one of the favourites is Pili Pili Chicken £8.20. A full chicken, £4.30 for half as a starter, Jeera Chicken at the same prices. One is succulent chicken cooked with chillis and the other is cooked with cumin seed. Other popular dishes include various Masalas at £3.90 and Methi dishes (cooked with fenugreek) at £4.20 and Karahi dishes presented in the cast iron wok at £5.30. Poppadoms 35p, Standard Chicken Curry £3.90, Pullao Rice £1.50. This restaurant charges a service charge of 10%, however diners get free coffee mints, chutneys and pickles. This style of cooking makes for a complete change from the standard curry house and because of that and its authenticity and extremely good quality of spicing, flavouring, quality and care we have decided to bring it into our TOP 100, see page. I hope you agree and I look forward to receiving your reports on this restaurant, meanwhile it offers discounts to Curry Club members at it quieter times. See page 288.

THE CURRY HOUSE
64, London Road, Leicester. Tel: 0533 550688
This is a restaurant of long standing in a city which is awash with curry restaurants and it is the first time it has appeared in this guide. I welcome it to my pages and am pleased to report that it serves standard curries at standard prices consistently reliable and well.

THE CURRY POT
78, Belgrave Road, Leicester. Tel: 0533 538256
This is its third appearance in these pages and it continues to serve good food.

TAJ TANDOORI
259, Melton Road, Leicester. Tel: 0533 662185
We've received a number of reports on the Taj Tandoori, which introduces it to our Guide for the first time. We hear of very tasty competent tandoori dishes and curries at reasonable prices.

THE FRIENDS TANDOORI
43, Belgrave Road, Leciester. Tel: 0533 668809
A new comer to these pages, put there by reporters who say it should be here. It is one of some seven or eight Indian restaurants on Belgrave Road, where competition is stiff, but we hear the food is excellent and it deserves a mention. I welcome your reports.

THE KHYBER
116, Melton Road, Leciester. Tel: 0533 549133
Established in 1984. The Khyber prides itself on having a menu which is slightly different from the norm. Chilli Prawns £2.00 and Chilli Corn £1.90 along with Vegetable Cutlet £1.70 are three interesting starters. Brought to my attention by a reporter. Shahi Nan is a Nan bread with crushed nuts at £1.35 and Palak Chicken at £3.05 is chicken cooked with spinach. You will be able to buy all the standard curries should you want them. Kormas, Dhansak, Madras and Vindaloo, are there as plenty and 'well done too' (HT) and I hear that dishes will be cooked that are not on the menu.

THE LAGUNA TANDOORI
77, Narborough Road, Leicester. Tel: 0533 549133
ML Verma opened this restaurant in 1974. It immediately established itself as an upmarket restaurant and has always been one of Leicester best. It was recently re-decorated in themes of red and black with pink and white tables cloths. The walls are dove grey with Indian Silk painting on the walls. It is a very smart restaurant and is supported by very good cooking. Starters include Boti Kebab, Tandoori roasted lamb pieces at £3.50 and Hasina, Tandoori roast lamb with skewered with capsicum, tomato and onion at £3.80. Speciality for the connoisseur, as it says in the menu, is Lamb Moghuli, lamb cooked in a thick gravy with cream and egg £4.00. Lamb Shah Jehani an exotic prepation of lamb garbnished with mince meat and herbs. £4.00. And we hear good things about the Naw Rattan Pullao which is rice cooked with green peas and garnished with ground nuts £2.50. Popadoms are 30p and standard Pullao Rice £1.20. There are no hidden extra charges.

THE RAJ
95, Humberston Gate, Leicester. Tel: 0533 532860
'This restaurant has very nice surroundings. The upstairs has a large bar area with comfortable seats. A sweeping spiral staircase takes you down to the basement restaurant. The popadoms were lovely dry and crisp. King Prawn Butterfly consisted of two well battered pieces, one was a king prawn the other identical was white fish with a 'tail' incorporated into it. Lamb Tikka Masala, highly red in colour but quite good. Vegetable cutlet was served in a creamy sauce, falling apart but very tasty. Onion Kulcha Nan was really excellent.' DT. 'Chicken chat was a huge portion, delicately flavoured enough for two. King Prawn Bhoona was only so so. But the Okra in its spicy sauce was good. The Raj Rice however, was rotten. The Tandoori Stuffed Pullao was absolutely superb, exceptional infact. Indeed the breads were the strongest part of this restaurant.' TD. More reports please.

THE VISHAL
69/71, Church Gate, Leicester. Tel: 0533 562639
'The Tandoori Prawn was excellent, chosen with Dhall Maknhi and Pullao Rice. The Keema Nan was really first class. Why are all the champion bread makers all in Leciester? Well suported by the local community but lacking in decor and atmoshphere ' TD. More Reports please.

THE RISE OF THE RAJ **CC DISCOUNT**
6, Evington Road, Leicester. Tel: 0533 553885
This restaurant opened in 1985 and immediately became established as a very good curry house. It was too late to be entered into our last GCG but we have received many reports about it since. The decor is a mixture of pink and burgundy with maroon chairs, pinks table cloths and napkins. 'Even the red carnations on the tables seem to match.' CD. Starters include 'one of the nicest Shami Kebabs, minced lamb, grilled in the Tandoori £1.95 that I have ever had.' FH. Delicious Aloo Chat, small pieces of potato spiced with a hot and sour sauce £1.85. Specials include a splendid vegetarian Thali at £6.95 containing Bingand Masala (their spelling for Begam or Augergine) Channa Masala, Sag, Tarka Dhal, Mixed Riata, Basmati Rice, Nan and onion Bhajia, which was 'pure vegetarian so filing and wonderful that I have visited this restaurant lots of times for this dish alone. The food is always superbly home cooked.' JL. Another favourite it the Murgi Jalfrezi, Chicken cooked with green chillies with a strong spicy sauce. £4.95. Typical prices include Poppadoms 35p, Chicken Curry £3.65, Pullao Rice £1.40. The owner Abdul Bashar has no other branches and is often to be found to hand in his restaurant. There is a minimum charge of £6.95 for dinner, and there is a service charge which covers free hot face towels and mints with coffee. This restaurant is prepared to offer discounts to Curry Club members at its quieter times. See page 288.

THE TAJ MAHAL
12, Highfield Street, Leicester. Tel: 0533 540328
It seems hard to believe now with Leicester's 70 plus Indian restaurants that at one time there were no Indian restaurants in Leicester. Indeed the Taj Mahal was the first one to open in the area, which it did in 1961. At that time it was a total novelty. · The nearest Curry House was in Birmingham and there weren't so many Indian restaurants there either.

In those days the editor's work took him around the county and he used to scour cities for curry houses. Imagine now asking for a curry house and receiving blank, puzzled looks, when asking Taxi drivers, Police men and local citizens for their whereabouts. Having found it he used it each time he visited Leicester on business during the 1960's and 70's and on one occasion, following a request for chilli pickle an anxious owner and chef appeared and spent an earnest half hour counselling him against eating hot spices. This restaurant has appeared in both editions of the Good Curry Guide and we are glad to say that it is back for the third time. We must note however that it changed ownership in 1987 and in now managed by Mr Ali Asahaf. There seems little doubt that there has been an attempt to take this restaurant up market, with new decor, a shiny new bar and a brass fan. However, judging by the reports we receive it still remains a 'darned good curry house.' Prices are fair and there is a good collections of Specials, such as the Shai Butter Chicken £5.90, Lamb Badam Pasanda at £5.50. Popadoms 40p, Standard Chicken Curry £3.25 and Pullao Rice at £1.40. There are no hidden extra charges and you will get hot towels and sweets with your coffee.

THE RAJ TANDOORI
96, Humberstone gate, Leicester. Tel: 0533 532860
This restaurant reaches the good curry guide for the first time. This is because we have had had good reports for it from a number of our local correspondants. It opened in 1982 and is owned by Harshad Unadkat. Decked out in reds and grey with gold chairs and flowers the restaurant is quite frankly a standard curry house with perfectly fair prices.' NP. The Chicken Tikka Masala is £4.10, Godum Bahar Chicken is £4.10. The prices are quite reasonable with popadoms at 30p.

THE FAR PAVILLIONS **CC DISCOUNT**
11, Swan Street, Loughborough. Tel: 0509 215235
The Far Pavillion was established in 1987 by Shahid Ali and it is one of about twelve similarly named restaurants established at that period. Following the very successful television movie of the same name based on the novel by MM Kay. This restaurant occupies a dominant corner site and its exterior is very smart, with two floors of archway windows. The attractive blue logo is an unmissable part of the street scene. Inside is a tastefully decorated reception with Indian furniture. The 90 covers are split between two floors, 30 downstairs and 60 up. The blue theme continues throughout the decoration. There are, according to our reports, some very interesting things on the menu. Momos for example, are meat dumplings from Nepal and appear as a starter at £1.95. The Vegetable Cutlets are also well regarded at £1.95. The Raj Chingor Jhol at £6.20 are King Prawns cooked Bengali style, in medium spices. There are a number of fish dishes such as Tandoori Trout. Scampi figures largely and you will meet it in Korma, Bhoona, Biriani, Rhogan, Dhansak and Patia dishes. 'The variety of dishes was extremely good and through out our meal we were guided by the staff.' CF. Typical prices are Popadoms 30p Chichen Curry £3.80, Pullao Rice, £1.30. There is a Buffet Lunch at £4.95 and a set Dinner at £20.00 for two. The minimum charge in the evening is £7.00. There are no other charges. This restaurant offers a discount to Curry Club members at its quieter times. See page 288.

THE JEWEL IN THE CROWN **CC DISCOUNT**
98/100, Leicester Road, Wigston. Tel: 0533 810073
The restaurant opened its doors in 1987. In the last entry we discussed the origin of names, it is interesting to note 'The Jewel in the Crown' is one of over twenty similarly named restaurants that opened their doors following Granada television's successful series of the same name, shown in 1987. The decor is described as simple and the menu is more or less standard, 'though the thing that I liked was the English Dishes section, which includes a Spanish Omelette!' BL. The favourite seems to be Palak Chicken, chicken cooked in spinach and spices £3.80. The Shashlik is £6.96, a kebab dish. Chicken Karai £7.95 and Lamb Karai £8.95, both succulent and creamy dishes. 'I liked the Bangle Bhajee at £3.20 wondering if it could be something we could wear, it turned out to be their spelling for Began (aubergine).' DT. Typical prices include Popadom 25p, Chicken Curry £4.20, Pullao Rice £1.45 and a minimum charge of £7.50 per head. These charges are lifted slightly with the 5% service charge. They will offer a discount to Curry Club members at their quieter time, see page 288.

LINCOLNSHIRE

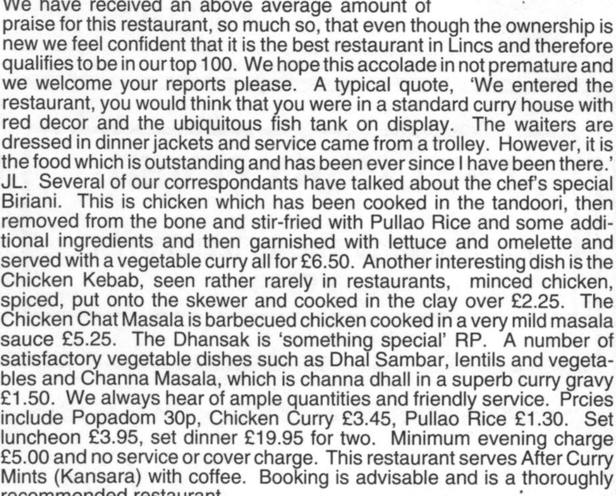

BOSTON

THE STAR OF INDIA TOP 100
110, West Street, Boston.
Tel: 0205 60558

This restaurant opened in 1980. It appeared in our first Good Gurry Guide in 1984, then again in 1986/7, and then in 1988 it drew the attention of the Good Food Guide. In March 1990 it changed ownership to Mr Tanvir Hussain. We have received an above average amount of praise for this restaurant, so much so, that even though the ownership is new we feel confident that it is the best restaurant in Lincs and therefore qualifies to be in our top 100. We hope this accolade in not premature and we welcome your reports please. A typical quote, 'We entered the restaurant, you would think that you were in a standard curry house with red decor and the ubiquitous fish tank on display. The waiters are dressed in dinner jackets and service came from a trolley. However, it is the food which is outstanding and has been ever since I have been there.' JL. Several of our correspondants have talked about the chef's special Biriani. This is chicken which has been cooked in the tandoori, then removed from the bone and stir-fried with Pullao Rice and some additional ingredients and then garnished with lettuce and omelette and served with a vegetable curry all for £6.50. Another interesting dish is the Chicken Kebab, seen rather rarely in restaurants, minced chicken, spiced, put onto the skewer and cooked in the clay over £2.25. The Chicken Chat Masala is barbecued chicken cooked in a very mild masala sauce £5.25. The Dhansak is 'something special' RP. A number of satisfactory vegetable dishes such as Dhal Sambar, lentils and vegetables and Channa Masala, which is channa dhall in a superb curry gravy £1.50. We always hear of ample quantities and friendly service. Prcies include Popadom 30p, Chicken Curry £3.45, Pullao Rice £1.30. Set luncheon £3.95, set dinner £19.95 for two. Minimum evening charge £5.00 and no service or cover charge. This restaurant serves After Curry Mints (Kansara) with coffee. Booking is advisable and is a thoroughly recommended restaurant.

LOUTH

THE HALAL TANDOORI
1, Mercer Road, Louth.
Tel: 0505 607960

This restaurant was established in 1985 in a 500 year old listed building. It is the oldest building in the town and even the interior layout is subject to preservation orders. Oliver Cromwell is said to have slept in this building, one wonders what he would have made of curry, probably he would have banned it in the way he banned Christmas mince pies. (By Act of Parliament, incidentally which has never been repealed, so it is illegal to eat mince pies on Christmas day). However, even Cromwell might have been a convert, judging by the reports that we recieve. Mr Miah also owns the Agra and the New Agra in Cleethorpes. (see entry in Humberside). The Halal is run with a good degree of professionalism in terms of service, presentation and food. The menu contains the normal cast list. One or two specials are Akhini Chicken which is 'preparation of boneless chicken eggs, sultana, almonds, cherries and other flavoursome spices, served with a special gravy,' at £5.10. Although this sounds like a fruit salad with spices, we are told 'it is really unexpectedly delicious'. CH. Another unusual dish is fillet steak masala which is really nothing more than Steak, chip and two vegetables with a spiced up gravy, but is really very good at £6.50. Chicken Biriani is rather special at £6.50, with chicken Tikka pieces stir-fried with rice, coconut, sultanas, almond and garnished with omelette. It is served with a portions of curry gravy. There is also a Lamb version of this at £5.75. Typical prices include Popadoms at 25p, Chicken Curry at £3.30, Pullao Rice £1.00 and set lunch at £2.50. There is no mimimim charge, service or cover charge.

THE SHAHEEN
2, Pinchbeck Road, Spalding. Tel: 0775 67852
The Shaheen evidently serves competent curries at reasonable prices in a friendly and efficient manner. More reports welcome.

STAMFORD

THE RAJ OF INDIA **CC DISCOUNT**
2, All Saints Street, Stamford. Tel: 0780 53556
The arrival of the Raj to Stamford was welcomed in 1982 and got into our Good Curry Guide in 1986/7. We have had good reports from the area, ensuring that this restaurant stays in our current guide. Starters contains the normal range of Prawn Puri, Butterfly, Tikkas and Kebabs. One unusual dish is Curry Soup at £1.10 which we are told 'is delicious'. TK. One dish that catches the eye of a regular reporter is Garlic Chicken, £5.00, while Khatta Meat, a sour dish at £5.25, attracts another reporter. The restaurant's Phall dishes are described as very very hot indeed. The Chicken Tikka Zalfari at £6.00 is only described as very hot. The menu tells you that various dishes con be made hot or mild for 25p extra. Hot I can understand because of the addition of extra chillies and other heat giving indredients, but mild seems rather strange, to they take something out and charge for it? Ah, well this is a small nit pick because clearly the restaurant is very popular. Other typical prices include Popadoms 35p, Chicken Curry £3.70, Pullao Rice £1.30 and set dinner for one from £12.00. No additional charges such as service, minimum and cover. The restaurant gives a 10% discount for takwaway and also offers a discount to Curry Club members at its quieter times see page 288.

STAMFORD TANDOORI
16, All Saint's Place, Stamford. Tel: 0780 55033
The Stamford Tandoori opened in 1985 under the management of Rafique Islam it is evidently already offering active competition to the Raj. Correspondents talk about a delicious Malgateani Soup (their spelling for mulligatawny) ay £1.50 and superb breads including Kulcha Nan at £1.20. The Vegetable Thali includes Bindi Bhajee, Dhall, Onion Bhajia, Rice and Nan at £7.50. A special dish that attracts some of our correspondants is Nawabi Murgh Stick, this is a dish involving chicken in a highly flavoured curry sauce at £5.90. Given 24 hours notice the restaurant will serve Kurze Lamb for four at £45.00, and Kurze Chicken at £35.00. The time is required to allow for marination and the slow cooking that is required for this particular dish. Popadoms are 35p, Chicken Curry £3.75, Pullao Rice £1.25. No surcharges.

GREATER MANCHESTER

AKASH INDIAN
336, Manchester Road, West Timperley.
Tel: 061 973 0697
The Akash was established in 1969, which in Indian restaurant terms makes it quite a long time survivor. It has an immense following, some of whom report to us about it, 'We travel many miles to go to the Akash on a regular basis because we find the food so very good.' TC. 'The cubicles give the restaurant a feeling of intimacy, the copper and brass work and the oriental pictures make it feel very Indian.' GBR. 'We are very pleased to find that they charge only half price for children, particularly good news for us as we had four with us.' FS. 'They let us in at closing time and then muddled our order up, but the food was delicious and we forgave them, particulary because it was Christmas.' DD. Prices are acceptable with Popadoms at 40p, Chicken Curry £4.00, Set lunch at £3.50, dinner for £8.50.

ASHTON

THE LAL QUILA **CC DISCOUNT**
Wigan Road, Ashton-in-Mackerfield.
Opened in August 1986, and we welcome it for the first time to the Good Curry Guide. It is a restaurant that clearly tries hard. 'We particularly like the ten course Indian banquet, on their banqueting night, on the first Wednesday of every month. For £10.50 you can eat yourself through a seemingly endless supply of food, followed by coffee. Booking is essential for this special night.' VW. Sunday lunch is evidently another favourite ritual at this place, served between 1pm and 5.30pm with a choice of eight set meals and children at half price. Each of the eight costs £6.50 and there is surely something for everyone with one purely vegetarian and the other purely English. The everyday menu contains an interesting aray of starters, including Tandoori Trout £2.75. Lamb Chop Tandoori at £2.70. Also available as main course dishes at £6.95 and £7.50 respectively. Two south Indian Thail dishes, a non-vegetarian one is available at £10.75. Somebody asked why restaurants call them non-vegetarian, instead of meat, the answer is non-vegetarian Thails include not only meat, but chicken, dairy based products and eggs, which strictly speaking, true vegetarians will not eat. It also includes a vegetarian Thali at £9.90. They also serve a good range of curry dishes including some vegetable and mushroom main course dishes, based on a standard curry menu you can get Mushroom and Vegetable Biriani, Do-Piaza, Korma, Madras etc. What a good idea. Masud Ahmed is the owner, he has no other branches, so will often be found on site. This is clearly a restaurant that cares, other typical prices include Popadoms 40p, Pillao Rice £1.25. Minimum charge of £6.50, but no service or cover charge. This restaurant is offering discounts to Curry Club members at quieter times, see page 288.

THE BELASH TANDOORI **CC DISCOUNT**
223, Stamford Street, Ashton-Under-Lyne. Tel: 061 339 4908
This is a new restaurant to the Good Curry Guide. It opened in 1987 and it changed ownership in 1989 and now is under the management of Mr Choudhury. It is distinguished by its late operating hours, closing 1am Monday to Thursday, 2am on Friday and Saturday nights and 12.50 on Sundays. It is also distinguished, we're told, by good food, attractive settings and good service. The food is standard Bangladeshi cuisine, as you would expect to find in any stardard curry house. Typical prices are popadoms 35p, Chicken Curry £4.40 with rice, Pullao Rice £1.10. Set luncheon £3.75 and set dinner £15.95. 10% discounts are available to students, OAP's and for takeaways and the restaurant is prepared to give a discount to Curry Club members at their quieter times, see page 288.

BOLTON

THE GANGES
110, St Georges Road, Bolton. Tel: 0204 22862
This restaurant opened in 1981 as the Asia, but changed to the Ganges when it changed ownership in 1989. Its new owner Stuart Ali has maintained good standards at this restaurant, so we hear and it is also distinguished with late closing times on Thurday at 1.30am and Fridays and Saturdays 2.30am. There are private cabins with small archways which enable dinners to have particular privacy and we hear of good food. The Ganges special, for example, consists of chicken, meat prawn, egg and mushroom and bamboo shoot in a medium curry base for £5.35 which includes rice or chips. Other typical prices include Popadoms 30p, Chicken curry with rice £4.05, Pulao Rice £1.05. There is a mimimum charges of £3.55, but there is no service or cover charge. Mr Ali also ownes the Halal Tandoori, 296, Chorley Old Road, Bolton.

THE LENA TANDOORI
131, Bradshawgate, Bolton. Tel: 0204 383255
This restaurant has acheived some remarkable reviews from our correspondents. 'This is probably one of the finest restaurants in the north of England. Glass fronted kitchen walls, allows you to see the chefs at work. Food is incredible. It is difficult not to go over board about it. The Tandoori Quail is excellent, main course is absolutely superb. I was extatic about

my Keema Nan and mixed vegetables. The service is impeccable and Popadoms and Bananas were complimentary.' DW. 'One Popadom each, they sent five extra free of charge, the Tandoori Fish was excellent, the main course was the Chefs special, Chicken, Meat, Lamb, Prawns, Tandoori Mix with rice and Vindaloo sauce, it also had potatoes in it was also nicely spiced and not to hot. The overall impression is that Lena's must be the best in Bolton' RC. 'The food is excellent with original flavours. Adbul Manan, the manager and owner offers seconds free of charge and everyone receives a free liquor at the end of their meal.' TF. More reports are welcomed.

MANCHESTER

THE TONDOORI ROYAL RESTAURANT **CC DISCOUNT**
682/684, Burnage Lane, Burnage. Tel: 061 432 0930
M Hoque opened this restaurant in 1978. It has appeared in both the previous editions of the Good Curry Guide, and we welcome it into this new edition of the Guide. It is a 90 seat restaurant, and in common with many restaurants in the area. It has long hours. It stays open till 1.30am Sunday through to Thurdsay and 2.30am Fridays and Saturdays, three hundred and sixty five days a year. It is an open plan restaurant. I am told that the decor is changed every two years to beat monotoNy. Cuisine is fundamentaly Bangladesh and North Indian, although there are some Southern Indian and other dishes included on the menu. Starters include the rather interesting Lamb Chop Tikka, £2.00 and Gobi (Cauliflower) Fritter, £1.85. Hap-Es (hoppers from Sri Lanka) are tasty pancakes at £1.85. Tandoori Specialities spelt Tondoori throughout this restaurant, include fish at £5.40, served with salad, Pullao Rice or Nan bread and a curry sauce. Tandoori Lamb Chop £5.40. Every dish on the menu has a star rating, one star denotes mild, two medium and three hot. The one star rated Bangalore is a dish cooked in mild spices with cream, coconut and banana. Prices with this dish varied between £4.50 and £5.60, depending on the principal ingredient used. King Prawn Jal Frezi is three star rated and is cooked with green chilli, fresh ginger, capsicum, onion and tomato at £5.90. Madras has three stars, is hot and spicey, cooked in the traditional spices with tomato purQe and again, ranges between £4.50 and £5.60. Vindaloo has no stars but says in brackets extra hot, and 'of course uses a good more proportion of garlic, lemon ginger, black pepper and chilli to create a 'firery taste in the richness of its ingredients', according to the menu. A nice touch we hear at this restaurant is a black board on which are listed specialities of the day. I also hear well of the banana fritters, £1.30. Typical prices for standard items are Popadoms 25p, Chicken Curry £4.30, Pullao Rice £1. There is a minimum charge of £4.30 but no service or cover charge. Diners get a hot face towel, fresh orange segments after eights and flowers for a special occasion. The restauants ofers discounts to Curry Club members at quieter times, see page 288.

CHEADLE

THE ALIGARH
202, Wilmslow Road, Heald Green, Cheadle. Tel: 061 436 8809
'The decor is superb and the service extremely good. The menu is very comprehensive, including these dishes. The starters, Sheek Kebab and Chicken Tikka especially fine. The Chef's special included Chicken, Lamb and Prawns in a dry sauce, it was very nice. There were ample portions of everything.' JB.
More reports please.

CHEADLE HULME

THE CHESHIRE TANDOORI
9, The Precinct, Cheadle Hulme. Tel: 061 485 4557
This small restaurant has always been very popular. It is owned by Mr Sataeami who is formerly the manager of the Manchester Rajdoot. It's a relatively tiny place with just 36 seats, so booking is advisable. We continue to get repeated reports about the quality of the service and the food.

HAZEL GROVE

THE AKASH **CC DISCOUNT**
2, Dorchester Parade, Jackson's Lane, Hazel Grove. Tel: 061 439 1040
This is a one hundred seater restaurant which opened in 1956 and appeared in our last GCG it continues to get good recommendations. They talk of afriendly reception and reliable food. Especially the Akash Special, at £8.00. Typical prices include popadoms, 30p, Chicken Curry £3.70, Pullao Rice 85p. There is a set luncheon at £2.50 and a set dinner at £8.00. The minimum charge is £4.00 and there is a service charge of 10%. However, this restaurant does give discounts to Curry Club members at its quieter times. See page 288.

HORWICH

THE SAAGAR
61, Church Street, Blackrod, Horwich. Tel: 0204 669000
Sufficient good reports have surfaced about his restaurant for us to introduce it to the GCG. More reports welcome.

MANCHESTER CITY

THE ASIAN SWEET CENTRE AND RESTAURANT
77, Wilsmslow Road, Rusholme, Manchester 14.
Cheap and cheerful. Piles of sweets, snacks and curries to eat in or out. Really cheap.

THE ASHOKA **TOP 100**
105, Portland Street, Manchester M1. Tel: 061 228 7550
This restaurant came into being in November 1985. It was just too late for it to enter the last edition of the GCG. Some correspondents call it a copy of the celebrated Rajdoot Restaurant and from the point of view of the decor, menu, style and prices they are similar. Owned by Mr N Hira, the restaurant specifically sets out to be up market. 'No after-pub-closing-time in this restaurant', says one of our correspondents. The 96 seat restaurant is very spacious and attractively designed. There are Indian seats, artifacts, stools, statuettes and pictures carefully placed all around the restaurant. At its centre is a well laid out bar and a reception area where customers can sit and relax with a drink while ordering their meal. Once the table is ready you are taken to your seat in the main restaurant and there is a separate party and function room. Ashoka, was the first emperor of India. He ruled between 273 and 232 BC and was the first ruler to unify that great country. This restaurant specialises in the Northern Indian style of cuisine of the Moghul Emperors, who were to rule Indian over fifteen hundred years later. The starters include Tandoori Fish at £3.10, Aloo Tikki at £2.30, which is a deep fried spicy potato and pea cutlet. 'delicious, unusual, my favourite', VM. The main courses are all said to be excellent. Of note is the Makhan Chicken, a speciality of the house, with Tandoori Chicken cooked in a sauce enhanced with butter and cream at £5.25. Keema Mattar is minced lamb cooked with peas in a herb and spice sauce at £4.95. Kofta Masala, is minced lamb meat balls, cooked in a medium curry sauce. £5.25. We hear that there is a good representative cast list of vegetable dishes such as Aloo Jeera, potatoes cooked with Cummin seed. Makhan Paneer, Indian cottage cheese cooked with butter, cream and tomato and Vegetable Kofta, vegetable rissoles cooked in a creamy sauce, each at £3.50. One of our correspondents talked very highly of the Vegetable Pullao Basmati, which is basmati rice cooked together with mixture of fresh vegetable, served with a curry sauce at £5.25. 'It's a meal in itself.' CP. This is not the sort of menu which heat grades many different types of curry, but for the hot heads the Chicken Chilli which is diced, roasted chicken pieces cooked with capiscum and green chillies - as many as you like for £4.50. The breads are said to be exquisite and desserts include Kulfi £ 1.60, Indian ice-cream flavoured with pistachio nuts and there are other Indian sweets from the trolley at £1.50 per shot. That most Indian of drinks, Lassi is available, sweet or salted, through-out the meal, at 75p. For those of a more alcoholic disposition, the restaurant has a well stocked wine list.

Set dinners are available from £9.50 to £11.50. The buffet luncheon cost £4.50. There is a minimum charge of £7.00, there is no service charge but there is a cover charge of 50p per person. This does however, include bar snacks, chutneys and one free popadom per person. If you advise the restaurant that it is your birthday, they will supply a birthday cake and a free cocktail to the birthday person. This restaurant applies a discount for Curry Club members at its quieter times, see page 288. The Ashoka is definitely a cut above. It is probably more expensive than the average restaurant , but from the reports that we have received it is certainly one of Manchester best restaurants, indeed it rates as one of the top restaurants in the country. So it joins our TOP 100.

THE DEANSGATE INDIAN RESTAURANT **TOP 100 & CC DISCOUNT**

Entrance Longworth Street, Off St John's Street, rear of, 244, Deansgate, Manchester. M3. Tel: 061 825 1888

The Deansgate Indian Restaurant actually is an Indian restaurant. It was opened in 1987, by M. Bhatt, who is a character, an individual and with strong views and a Gujerati. The food is vegetarian and Mr Bhatt's food is very much of the home made style. Mr Bhatt and his wife, Divya, are very charming and they both welcome the opportunity to chat to their customers. He is to be found front of house while Divya is usually in a flowing sari busy cooking and organising activities in the kitchen. 'I felt like I had visited somebody's home, when I went to the Deansgate Tandoori. The owner told me about his family having been in the food business since they went to Africa from Indian in the 1890's as caterers to the Indian tea plantation workers.' RS. The restaurant use to be a congregational meeting hall for Sunday School. The Bhatts are well aware that the decor leaves a lot to be desired and are determined that money and hours will restore the building one day. Meanwhile they welcome student artists to display their work, in a worthy effort to brighten the place up. The Bhatts do not have a printed menu. Because the dishes change from day to day, they prefer to use a word processor and print out their menu each day. The restaurant is first and foremost a Gujarati Vegetarian restaurant. 'It's refreshingly different with simple decor. You don't feel obilged to dress up. It's a healthy looking menu boasting no artificial additives, its low in fat and high in taste. The nutritional data providing information about the calories.' JH. 'The cooking varies from day to day. Its fun to go not knowing exactly whats going to be served.' FW. Mr Bhatt is very strict with his customers about wastage, he doesn't mind what you eat or how much, but if there are left overs on your plate, he will fine you £2.00, which he donates to the third world. The set diner is £6.00, there are no hidden extra charges. Typical dishes include Lasan, Garlic, Ginger, Spinach, Potato, Courgette, Cauliflower and Date Bhajee, home made chutneys, aubergine slices in garlic and chilli sauce. There are other superb dishes, too numerous to mention, all cooked in the home made Gujerati style. 'That's what we go for, the vegetarian food is absolutely different from Indian food that we have tasted.' WP. The restaurant also does meat, chicken and fish dishes. With a menu that changes every day, it is quite hard to keep track of it all, but we hear that on one occassion there was a Bangladeshi fresh water fish called 'Vwal' on offer and on another occassion there was deep fried Patra a leaf only native to Indian, which is rolled up in gram flour like a swiss roll then fried. There is no end of novelty that comes out of this restaurant. The restaurant has experimentally been offering a Sunday lunch where provided ten or twelve people book, you can enter the restaurant at 12.30 and are offered newspapers and books and you tuck into different dishes which are brought out every twenty minutes until about 5pm. The price of this Sunday treat is Vegetarian £7.00, non- vegetarians £8.00. We feel that this restaurant is outstandingly good, making a tremendous effort to bring real Indian food into Manchester, indeed Great Britain. Gujerati food is one of the most outstanding Indian cuisines, and the prices at this restaurant are amazingly cheap. As you would expect their are no hidden charges, such as cover or service. They do offer Students their £6.00 meal for £5.00, not surprisingly they cannot offer a discount to Curry Club members in the normal way with dishes being so cheap. Things can be slightly unpredicable, dishes can run out early and the quality can vary from day to day. However, this final quote sums it all up 'I wish all restaurants were like this one, it inspires me.' TC. We thoroughly recommend this restaurant and wish them well in the future for their bold and innovative ideas. We recommend everybody to visit it and we have included it into our Top 100 for the reasons given. Reports are welcomed.

GAYLORD **TOP 100 & CC DISCOUNT**
Unit 4, Marriots Court, Manchester. M2. Tel: 061 832 4866
The Gaylord started business in 1979 and has an excellent pedigree. The small frontage leads upstairs to a large and attractive 92 seat restaurant. It is Punjabi and vegetarian and it has always been reported as consistently above average. There are four soups on offer, Chicken Shorba, Arbb Gosht, Mulligatawny Soup all at £1.10 and a Vegetable Soup at 95p. Starters include Pakoras, Chicken, Vegetable and Paneer, prices range from between £1.95 and £2.75. An unusual Fish Koliwora at £2.75. There are the usual range of Tandoori dishes, plus one very unusual Paneer Tikka, kebabs of fresh home-made Indian cheese, marinated in Tandoori spices and baked at £2.95. The menu is of course not the standard curry house menu. Roghan Josh is correctly cooked, we hear, with browned onion, fresh ginger, garlic and fresh spices in yoghurt. Not a hint of curry house tomato, capsicum and chilli. The Methi Mazz caught the eye of one of our correspondents, minced lamb cooked Kashmiri style with spinach and fenugreek, £4.75. There is a strong list of vegetable and vegetarian main course dishes, including Tinda Masala, being a small Indian squash, cooked in a spicy gravy, £3.40. Tamal Kukrie, is lotus roots at £3.40 is another unusual Nepalese dish. There is a good selection of Indian sweets from the trolley, £1.50 for any two pieces and corespondents especially like the Special Indian Tea at 95p. Here is a typical quote. 'I was made very welcome (as a single women - not always the case). Advice was offered on the menu, and I was asked if everything was alright after each course. The decor is attractive with the Tandoori kitchen in full view of the restauant through a glass window. The Popadoms were good and the food excellent. The best Paneer dish I have ever had, several pieceS of freshly made cheese in a rich masala style sauce, a lovely change from the usual heavy handed Mattar Paneer. The service was friendly and efficient and it was lovely to be offered Halva and Barfi (see glossary) as well as the more usual desserts.' DRC. Most of our quotes are like that, but we did receive one snorteR, which talked of over spicing and tough meat (JBA). We think that this is untypical and highly recommend the Gaylord. Prices are a little high for such style, Popadoms are 50p, Chicken Curry £4.55, Pullao Rice £1.60. Set Luncheon is £4.95 and set Dinner £9.95. There is no minimum charge or cover charge but there is a service charge of 10%. Pensioners and students get a 10% discount and the restaurant makes available a discount to Curry Club members at its quieter times, see page 288. We have placed it into our TOP 100, see page 25.

THE KAILASH **CC DISCOUNT**
34, Charlotte Street, Manchester. M1. Tel: 061 236 1085
This restaurant opened in 1989 in the former 'Tandoori of Manchester.' This seventy-five seat restaurant is in the basement, which has been attractively re-furbished in pinks, greys and red, to achieve a collective upmarket look. The Kailash now describes itself as a Nepalese and Indian restaurant. Most of the dishes on the menu are indeed Indian, but you are recommended to try the Momota as a starter, £2.50 (a mince meat dumpling). Also the spicy stuffed capsicum, £2.00 and the Vegetable Cutlet for £2.00. We also hear good reports about the Charra Masala, tender chicken cooked in a aromatic Nepalese spice mixture for £4.20. Aloo Tarma is a delicious vegetable dish made with potatoes and bamboo shoots, £2.90. Typical prices include Popadoms 35p each, Chicken Curry £4.20, Pullao Rice £1.00. Set luncheon £4.50, set dinner £9.00. There is a service charge of 10%, however, the restaurant is giving discounts to Curry Club members at its quieter times, see page 288.

THE KATHMANDU **TOP 100 & CC DISCOUNT**
42, Sackville Street, Manchester. Tel: 061 236 6268
We get nothing but praise for this restaurant.
'If a finer restaurant in Manchester exists, will someone tell me?' Marani Chicken is a magnificiant way to start a meal, (it's the chefs speciality of fried chicken with herbs and green chillies at £2.25.) They boast that their Pilaw Rice is good enough to eat on its own, and they're not kidding. The Lamb Pasanda, called Shai Pasanda, which are thin slivers of lamb cooked with onion and tomato, £4.75, is delicately spiced perfection. The Bringal and Bindi were a credit. Nan Bread was cooked as it should be.

The service was excellent. Rhogan Josht melts in the mouth. You are made to feel important. The sheer ambience and the fish pond makes it a night to remember.' GW. 'I recently had one of their banquets, it was a huge meal, all of it excellent, for just £9.50. I don't call that expensive.' AH. 'Excellent breads, Chicken and Vegetables in luxurious surroundings and a very light bill.' PH. This quote comes from a very well travelled correspondents, 'A visit here is always a highlight to my trips to Manchester. It's consistantly of a high standard. Its stunning decor, though the Kohinoor in Glasgow is better. A few years ago I would have considered their prices high, but they haven't increased much since then, so they represent excellent value for money. Try the Special at £10.25, which gives you samples of about eight dishes.' JL. If you were in Manchester, this place is a must. It's spacious, enhanced with ornaments, plants and blue and purple table linen. As you enter the restaurant you will be surrounded with bronze bhudda statuettes, camel stools, Indian tables and a brass net ceiling light. In the main restaurant there are large Venetian paintings, Indian paintings, bronzes and in the middle is a eight foot by four foot fish pond. Kathmandu is the capital of Nepal and this restaurant was opened in 1980 by Gopal Mohan Dantol, himself Nepalese. He delights in talking about the food. 'Some like it hot,' said the menu and for those who do like it hot, you can have Murchi Lamb Kashmiri, where the meat is cooked with chilli and aromatic spices such as cinnamon and there is Chicken Pepper Kadai, which predominently uses black pepper, both at £4.75. Home-made Indian cheese features in Paneer Jeera, this dish is cooked in the clay oven at £1.95, and paneer also features in one of the breads, Paneer Kulcha £1.10. Set meals range from a reasonable £7.50 a head to £12.50 a head for the Kathmandu Special. There is a choice of sweets from the trolley at £1.25 or Kulfi Malai (Indian Vanilla Icecream), at £1.50 or fresh fruits when available and coffee Kathmandu at 80p. Prices at this restaurant are indeed very fair, with Popadoms at 30p, Chicken Curry £3.95, Pullao Rice £1.20. Set luncheon is available at £3.75, there is no minimum or cover charge, but there is a service charge of 10%. The Kathmandu has a specially chosen wine list, by Raymond Green, consultants for the House of Tatelow in London. This restaurant has recently taken to outside catering and recently catered for a wedding for a 1,000 guests. Children under seven years of age eat free and the restaurant is prepared to give discounts to Curry Club members at specific days of the week. You are advised to contact this restaurant direct to find out which days they are, also see page 288. We have no hesitation in maintaining this restaurant in our TOP 100.

THE KISMET
33, Bury New Road, Manchester. M8. Tel: 061 834 7351

The Kismet is believed to be Manchester's second oldest Indian restaurant after the Kohinoor. We have one regular correspondent who said he has been eating in this restaurant for over twenty six years (AH), though it had been going for many years prior to that. He say's 'It's near Strangeways Prison and I was weaned here, (I hope he means the Kismet and not Strangeways), so I'm biased. I always come here for a really good curry.' AH. Nothing more needs to be said.

THE KOHINOOR **TOP 100**
47, Oxford Street, Manchester. M1. Tel: 061 236 5882

'Good news it's back again, and it looks very different from when it closed. It deserves to be restored to the GCG and the food is noticeable better than average. ' JL. We are delighted to maintain this restaurant in the GCG because last time we gave it obituary and reported it's closure. The reports however, were accurate and it has subsequently re-opened. Worthy of note, this restaurant was established in 1938, making it the second Indian restaurant to open outside London (the first was in Oxford, a year earlier), and only the fifth in the UK. The original proprietors were Mr Bahdur and Mr Nazir. Later, Mr Nazir, became famed for canned and bottled goods. It survived the war and the re-building of Manchester and countless competitors and countless recessions. We are glad that it is back and by ignoring its brief closure, it now rates as the UK's third oldest survivor. The food is reported to be very good indeed and for reasons of longevity if nothing else we will place it in our TOP 100. see page 25.

PEPPERS

63, Bridge Street, Manchester, M3. Tel: 061 832 9393

'I must recommend this place the food is brilliant. There is always a wait for space, but that is to be expected, because you can eat as much as you like for £4.95.' MK. 'I lunched there on one occasion and the buffet offered a choice of chicken curry, Aloo Bhajee, Keema Mattar and Tarka Dhal, accompanied by breads, pickles and chutneys. I particularly enjoyed the Popadoms and the Samosas and the seemingly endless choice of Raitas, pickles and chutneys. All this for £4.95 and you can help yourself as often as you like (and many did!). The Rice and Nans are a delight, highly recommended.' AW.

RAJDOOT **TOP 100 & CC DISCOUNT**

Carlton House, 18, Albert Square, Manchester. M2. Tel: 061 834 2176

Rajdoots is one of a chain of four restaurants. Each of which is at the top of its tree. We have already reported about the Rajdoot in Bristol (see entry under Avon). This restaurant is of equal calibre. Managed by Mr Sant Mali, the restaurant recently moved to new premises. The move has given the owner a chance to refurbish and he has maintained the standard of elegance and decor. Apart from one poor report on this restaurant, we have always had good reports. Many of our Manchester friends and members of the Curry Club who dine very regularly at Rajdoots are happy, full of praise and have no complaints. However, when a bad report comes in from a well travelled, well respected correspondent we do take it seriously and we just hope that it is a 'blip'. The menu is identical to the restaurant in Bristol in Avon, which we have described in some depth, please refer to that entry. Typical prices include Popadoms free, Chicken Curry £4.60, Pullao Rice £1.30, set luncheon £7.00 and set dinner £11.00 to £14.00. There is a minimum charge of £8.00 and a service charge, a hefty 12% plus a cover charge of 50p. This restaurant will give a discount to Curry Club members during its quieter times. See page 288. It remains in our TOP 100, see page 25.

ROMILEY TANDOORI

6-7, Precinct, Compstall Road, Romiley. Tel: 061 430 5878

We are told that the Romiley, started in 1979, under Mr MA Ullah, is a very comfortable establishment, with velvet coverings, typical lighting, cubicles with engraved perspex dividers and table candle lights. They are proud of their kitchen and welcome visitors in there. 'We entered the kitchen and were very impressed to see where it all happens. We ate a delicious meal and it was our first visit to a professional kitchen. It seemed very well organised.' CC. The food which emanates from these kitchens, we hear, is of a very high standard. Typical prices are Popadoms 25p each, Chicken Curry £3.65, Pullao Rice 90p, set lunch, is ridiculously cheap at £1.95 and set dinner is £13.95. There are no minimum charges, no service or cover charge.

THE SANAM

215, Wilmslow Road, Rusholme, Manchester. M14. Tel: 061 224 8570

There are infact two Sanam restaurants within one hundred yards of each other. One is at 215, and the other, the larger one at 145-151, Wilmslow Road. 'We went to the larger edition. It is a large restaurant with a busy takeaway, selling marvelous looking sweets. It's very busy with the local Asian clientelle. We had Liver and Kidney Kebabs to start with: very tasty. The fish (cod) Masala was very well spiced. My Tarka Dhal was distinctively buttery. It's cheap, with brisk service and unlicenced, but they don't mind if you bring in your own drink.' AM. This restaurant is owned by Abdul Ghafoor Akhtar and seats a large 150, but such is its success that plans are afoot to increase capacity to 350. It is so cheap that we won't list individual items. You would be hard pressed to spend £4.00 per head in this establishment. You will certainly leave full and well satisfied. A venture of this kind, cheap and cheerful, transport-cafQ-style is always good value and should be investigated when ever possible. We highly recommend this one as being amongst the best on Wilmslow Road.

THE SHEZAN

119, Wilmslow Road, Rusholme, Manchester, M14. Tel: 061 224 3116

Another example of Wilmslow Road superbabilia. 'It's always full to over flowing. They immediately brought pickles and a substantial salad. The Kebab was a bit bland, but the Samosa and Popadoms were good. So too was the main course which was both visually excellent and had a superb aroma. The Madras was, however, slightly underspiced. There were plentiful accompaniments and it made an impressive spread. I don't know why this restaurant is so full, it is no better than others in Rusholme, but it is certainly very good.' AH.

THE TANDOORI KITCHEN
131, Wilmslow Road, Manchester. M14. Tel: 061 224 2329
'The Onion Bhajias and Popadoms for starters were OK, the Keema Vindaloo was superb, the best I've had for a long time, served with a large Naan which was hot and of a fresh texture. My friend's Keema Madras was also very good, but the Pullao Rice was a bit short on portion. Pickles were available at no extra charge. I have yet to be disappointed with Curry Houses in this area, they are all good to excellent and all extremely good value.' AH.

TAVAK RESTAURANT
201, Wilmslow Road, Manchester. M14. Tel: 061 257 3890
This is another little gem on the Wilmslow Road.
'The food is wonderfully delicious. Prices are so cheap and the atmosphere is great.' BS.

THE VICEROY OF INDIA
63, Whitworth Street, Manchester. M1. Tel: 061 228 1839
This restaurant only opened in January 1989. In the same ownership as the Gaylord, Manchester, see entry earlier, this eighty seat restaurant clearly has a very good pedigree. Upwards of that it has some very useful late opening hours, if you work or play in the wee hours, 1am Tuesday to Thursday and 3am on Friday and Saturday. It should be made clear that this restaurant is aiming at a different clientelle than the Gaylord. The menu is simpler, carrying standard curry dishes and the prices are cheaper. Starters include some soups, smaosa, bhajias, fritters and kebabs. There is a full and useful range of main dish curries. Special set meals, Vegetarian Thali £6.95, Viceroy Special £7.95. Popadoms 40p, Chicken Curry £3.75, Pullao Rice £1.25. Set luncheon is £3.95. There is no minimum charge and no cover charge. Service charge, however, is 10%.

LIGHT OF BENGAL
114, Union Street, Oldham. Tel: 061 624 4600.
Well established, and back in our Guide because of your good reports. It has a competence and maturity which comes with experience, and the food is good at reasonable prices.

THE SURMA
69, Featherstall Road, Oldham. Tel: 061 627 0586
We have many reports about this one, which is quite popular with a regular following. Reports welcomed on this one too.

THE INDIA GARDEN TANDOORI **CC DISCOUNT**
411, Bury Old, Prestwich. M25. Tel: 061 773 7784
This restaurant in the north west suburbs of Manchester is a favourite haunt of some of our correspondents that tell us that it is a darned good standard curry house. It commenced trading in 1985 under the direction of Surabur Rahman. Prices are reasonable, Popadoms are 30p, Chicken Curry £3.30, Pullao Rice at £1.35, set luncheon at £4.95 and a set dinner at £10.20. There is no mimimum, cover or service charge at this restaurant, but they are prepared to offer discounts to Curry Club members at their quieter times, see page 288.

THE TANDOORI GHAR
64, Drake Street, Rochdale. Tel: 0706 46296
This restaurant was opened in 1985, by its owner Dhirendra Dey. It is his only restaurant and it follows the standard curry house formula, right down to a numbered menu, with no less that one hundred and seventeen items on it. There are no particular surprises but you should be able to find everything that you want on the menu. The 48 seats are split over two floors and it has alcove seating surrounded by Indian ornaments. Prices, Popadoms 25p each, chicken Curry £4.00 (including rice), Pullao Rice £1.00, set luncheon £3.75 and set dinner £8.45 to £8.95.

THE CURRY COTTAGE **CC DISCOUNT**
394, Washbury Road, Sale. M33. Tel: 061 973 8199
Owned by Mr FA Syad, this restaurant opened in 1982 and is described as cottage style in colours of burgundy and gold. Infact there are three Curry Cottages, all owned by Mr Syad, this one, The Curry Cottage in Radcliffe, Lancashire and The Curry Cottage in West Didsbury. The menu at all three is identical and comprehensive. They serve a standard selection of starters and Tandoori dishes and main curries.Prices are very reasonable ranging from £2.40 to £4.00 for these dishes. popadoms 20p, Chicken Curry £3.40, Pullao Rice £1.00. Set luncheon is £3.50 and set dinner £9.50 each. There are no cover, minimum or service charges. The restaurant will offer discounts to Curry Club members at their Didsbury branch only, see page 288.

STANDARD INDIAN
Higher Road, Urmston, Manchester. Tel: 061 747 5788
For a decade the Standards Indian restaurant has been serving, standard Indian dishes to an adoring public who like chips as much as rice with their curry. The curries however, are competetent and one or two specials include Nizam Chicken, £2.90 and Nargiss Kebab £1.45. The restaurant doesn't go in for King prawns, it prefers to serve different types of scampi curry, which make a change. The highlight of the week at the Standard is its Indian banquet, which is held every Sunday. Here the chef's Thali consisting of seven different dishes with house wine, Indian sweets and coffee for two is just £14.00 and for four is £27.00. This is served between 2pm and 7pm, but you must book for the set meal. Other prices include Popadoms 35p each, chicken curry £4.60, Pullao Rice £1.75. There are no extra charges.

THE GREAT KATHMANDU
Burton Road, West Oldbury, Manchester. M20. Tel: 061 434 6413
They say that the Great Kathmandu supplies the best curries in the local area. More reports please.

MERSEYSIDE

BIRKENHEAD

THE MANZIL **CC DISCOUNT**
67/75, Grange Road, Birkenhead.
Tel: 051 647 9911
It is a pity that this restaurant is in such a dilapidated area, it definitely holds it back, as it deserves better. The decor is quite tasteful and quite successful. The food is good, indeed above average. 'The Dhansak was excellent.' JL. Abdul Mumin opened the Manzil in 1981. It is open for all 365 days of the year till 3am, which gives it a reputation locally ... 'Last orders are at 3.30am, well, that's a new one on me. I've heard of it still being open at 4.30am. Infact one of my friends told me 'I didn't know it closed.' Despite the crazy hours the food is definitely well above average. Mixed Kebab as a starter £1.60, Chicken Biriani £3.20, Chicken Curry £2.50, Pullao Rice £1.30. set dinner is £18.00 for two. There is a minimum charge in the restaurant of £4.50. This restaurant offers a discount to our Curry Club members at its quieter times, see page 288.

LIVERPOOL

ASHA
73, Bold Street, Liverpool. L1. Tel: 051 709 4734
This restaurant was the first to be set up in Liverpool in 1964 and the editor remembers well asking taxi drivers, policemen and general members of the public where Liverpool's only curry house was, during that year. No

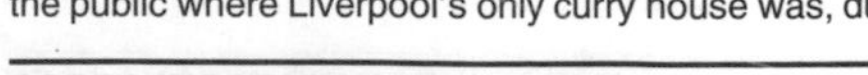

one knew, infact no one knew what a curry was in those days and it was only by chance that I found it in Bold Street and throughly enjoyed my curry there. The restaurant still has an excellent reputation, despite there now being at least fifty other up starts all around it, the competition in Liverpool has become very fierce. 'I had an excellent meal in a good restaurant. The Popadoms were well done and the Lamb Pullao was absolutely superb, although the vegetables were a little watery.' JL. 'Altogether an excellent meal.' TLP. Dishes on the menu remain totally individual, Tondoori (Tandoori), Vazi Bhaji (Bhajia) and Rogoun Gosht (Rhogan Gosht), this only adds to the charm, its the food that matters.

THE DILSHAN
544, Aigburth Road, Liverpool. L19. Tel: 051 427 2273
We have received a good many recommendations for this restaurant, which its regulars claim to be one of the best in Liverpool. They all talk of... 'Excellent food, friendly and helpful service from the waiters and very acceptable prices, with a menu that suits all diners.' PD. More reports will be welcomed.

THE MAHARAJA
73, Renshaw Street, Liverpool. L1. Tel: 051 709 2665
'This restaurant has a very well thought out design, in a long and thin premises. The bar and the foyer are just behind the front door, there is a small flight of stairs which leads to a well decorated dining room, with the waite'rs table positioned, so he can respond instantly to your request. The food is very good indeed, I had the set menu, the day that I visited and I was very impressed.' JL. 'First class Chicken Tikka Masala and everything else to.' PH.

THE RAZ INDIAN TAKEAWAY **CC DISCOUNT**
93, Rocky Lane, Anfield, Liverpool. Tel: 051 260 2301
Your typical Bangladeshi/Indian takeaway. It is owned by Saddk Miah and is one of the newist in town, having opened in 1990. We hear good reports about it. It is competetant and friendly with good food and relative prices. Popadoms are 25p each, Chicken Curry £2.60, Pullao Rice £1.50, set dinner is £7.80 and there is a minimum charge of £5.00. The Raz offers discounts to Curry Club members at its quieter times, see page 288.

NEWTON

THE TASTE OF INDIA
56, Market Street, Newton-Le-Willows. Tel: 092 52 28458
This restaurant which was formerly 'The Bilash', was restyled, refurbished and had a tandoor fitted. That was in 1988. The Taste of India was relatively unknown until Rick Astley hit the Popular Music charts in a big way. This is his town and this is his restaurant and the cooking is exceptional, service is good and portions are generous. 'Usually it costs around £14.00 for two.' BM. More reports welcomed.

THE SHAMRAT **CC DISCOUNT**
8, Stanley Street, Southport. Tel: 0704 30397
This restaurant was formerly known as 'The Garden of India' and appeared in both the previous GCG's. It became the Shamrat in 1989. According to one reporter. 'It's carrying on the good work that was established by the Garden.' GT. Menu is varied and comprehensive. 'I like the Green Chilli Masala dishes. The always seem very fresh, the green chillis and the fresh tomato, giving a luster to the dish.' BRR. 'Onion Bhajia at £1.50 is nearly a meal in itself and they were scrumptious. We were very impressed with this small restaurant.' MS. Typical prices include Popadoms 40p each, Chicken Curry £3.35, Pullao Rice £1.25. There is a minimum charge of £5.00 but no service or cover charge. Regular clients are often given a coffee and a liqueur free. This restaurant is prepared to give discounts to Curry Club members at its quieter times, see page 288.

THE TANDOOR MAHAL **CC DISCOUNT**
24/26, King Street, Wallasey. Tel: 051 639 5948
This restaurant appeared in the previous GCG and subsequently received satisfactory reports, until it's greatest fan, sent a report with just

slightly less than his usual enthusiam. 'The outside tends to be a bit scruffy, but the inside is well decorated. The service is very pleasant although it attracts pub and club throw out clientelle. Chicken Tikka is done to Madras strength, is consistently good but there is room for improvement. Our meal cost us £14 for the two of us.' DB. We know that DB likes this place because in the last GCG he said that this restaurant has become his HQ, along with his cricket club. We decided to keep this restaurant in the GCG but we would certainly like more reports. Typical prices are Popadoms 40p, Chicken Curry £3.95, Pullao Rice £1.15. There is a minimum charge of £3.50 per person, but no service or cover charge. They give Pensioners a 10% discount, children are half price, Takeaway meals also get a 10% discount and Curry Club members will also get a discount at their quieter times, see page 288.

THE HESWALL TANDOORI
52, Pensbury Road, Heswall, Wirral. Tel: 051 342 8614
'This is a small and quaint restaurant, with a generous car park. Chicken Tikka and Roghan Gosh are excellent. Pullao Rice was a good large portion. I ordered a Madras curry and a pot of the hottest sauce that they did. The Madras curry was rather bland, and the hot one was what a Madras should be. Looking forward to our next visit.' DB. His next visit was OK, judging from his report and those of others who enjoy this restaurant too. If uou have a comment about this restauant, please send in your report.

WIRRAL

THE WIRRAL TANDOORI
18, The Village Road, Bromburgh, Wirral. Tel: 051 334 0024
'I felt spoilt for choice in this small and friendly restaurant. The Chicken Chat starter is a must. Three recommendations on the main menu are Tandoori Mixed Grill, £7.55, Nawabi Sticks £4.90 and Sumit Tandoori, £6.20. The Tandoori Chicken is served sizzling with brandy poured over and flambed just before serving, a must for any curryholic.' AJK.
We have received complementary remarks about this restaurant but we would like more reports.

MIDDLESEX

Middlesex is no longer officially a county. Maps now refer to it as greater London. Residents still refer to it as Middlesex however and so do we. It contains such eminent locations as Southall, Heathrow airport, Twickenham and Enfield. Post-codes only to add to the confusion. Barnet, for example, has an Enfield postcode - EN4, and is in Herts. Waltham Abbey is EN9 and in Essex. Enfield itself is Middlesex which does not exist so it is in London!!!

BARNET

THE ANUPAMA **CC DISCOUNT**
9 Church Hill Street, Barnet. Tel: 081 441 0577
This restaurant is managed/owned by Mr C Uddin and it opened in 1983. It has a standard menu, with the regular and popular curry dishes on offer. Typical prices are Popadoms 30p each for plain, 40p for spiced, Chicken Curry £2.80, Pullao Rice £1.25. Set dinner is £40.00 for two. There is a minimum charge of £10.00. This restaurant serves 'After Curry Mints' by Kansara and we hear of a service charge of 10%, however, this will be eased out because the restaurant offers to Curry Club members at its quieter times, see page 288.

THE SHAPLA
37, High Street, Barnet. Tel: 081 499 0046
This restaurant appeared in the previous two GCG's and has being in business since 1972. It changed ownership in 1980, to Mr S Ahmed, who is the current proprietor. We get regularly good reports about it. It was completely refurbished, recently, with an area being set aside for take-away customers only. Comfortable chairs with tables set in pleasant surroundings and the large ubiquious fish tank at the rear of the restaurant. Typical prices include Popadoms 40p, Chicken Curry £2.95, Pullao Rice £1.40. Set dinner at £8.50, there is a minimum charge of £7.80. There is no service or cover charge.

ZAIQA
7D, High Street, Barnet. Tel: 081 441 6375
This restaurant was formerly the Curry Centre and it opened in 1970. It appeared in our first GCG with very good reports. However, popularity wained and it was taken over in November 1987. It is currently managed by Manarol Haque. The decor is quite elegant with round backed chairs, in brown, set against magnolia walls on which there are framed Indian paintings. The restaurant seat 56 and is clearly very popular in the area. The menu is a standard Bangladeshi, North Indian and inbludes Tandoori Lamb Chops at £2.25 as a starter along with Bombay Aloo Cocktail, boiled potatoes and tomatoes mixed with a spicy, tangy sauce for £1.95. Aloo Chat, small pieces of boiled potato mixed with fresh coriander, green chillies and tamarind sauce at £1.95. One of our correspondants raves about the Vegetarian Thali, a selection of mushroms, bringal, aloo Gobi, Dhal, Tarka, Pullao Rice and mixed raita and Rotie bread at £8.50. Other typical prices are Popadoms 35p, Chicken Curry £3.65, Pullao Rice, £1.70, Set luncheon at £3.50.

KUTTA BILAI TANDOORI **CC DISCOUNT**
211, High Street, Brentford. Tel: 081 560 4394
'The Keema Mattar was good, with a lemony tang.' JL. 'The Chicken Tikka Masala, has to be the best I've had anywhere.' CD. On the form we sent Mr AR Khan, the owner, we asked how many floors have you, eg: upstairs/downstairs, he replied, 'none' but we presume that this 106 seat restaurant manages to accommodate itself some where. Typical prices are not as cheap, Popadoms 59p, Chicken Curry £3.10, Pullao Rice £1.50, set luncheon £5.00, set dinner £10.50. Minimum charge is £12.00 and all this is boosted by a massive service charge of 12%, plus a cover charge of £2.00. This restaurant is offering Curry Club members a discount at its quieter times, see page 288.

EASTCOTE

SHAPLA TANDOORI
166, Fieldend Road, Eastcote. Tel: 081 866 4747
This restaurant remains extremely popular and we continually get quotes about it being one of the best in the area. We need not say more. Reports welcome.

CANNON TANDOORI
7, Station Parade, Whitchurch Lane, Edgware. Tel: 081 952 2501
'Good selection of food is always found here and the portions are large. The curry dishes are tasty and there is a selection of English foods for those who don't like curry, also Indian wines and beers are available. Recommended.' SY.
Reports welcomed.

ENFIELD

RAJ
57A, Church Street, Enfield. Tel: 081 367 7492
'We arrived just before midnight and didn't leave until 2am, we were last out. (what a surprise!!) Despite our late arrival, the waiters didn't show at any moment that they wanted us out and the service was really good, considering. The food quality and quanities were reliable and above average, particularly the Dhansak, which was hot and spicy.' TC.
More reports welcomed.

GREENFORD

TIKKA CENTRE
1298, Greenford Road, Greenford. Tel: 081 422 4911
Situated in a small shopping parade, this restaurant first opened in 1982 and it changed hands in 1987, now to be managed by Mr A Ahmed. I had a very impressive Meat Thali, consisting of a large quantity of Pullao Rice, a delicious Medium Curry, a bowl of plain yoghurt, a small coleslaw type of salad, Nan bread, Popadoms, plus two pieces of Tandoori Chicken (breast and leg) and four enormous chunks of Chicken Tikka, six pieces of Lamb Tikka and a Sheek Kebab, with a choice of a sweet and a coffee, what a feast.' AD. The meat Thali is currently priced at £12.00, other typical prices include Popadoms at 30p each, Chicken Curry £3.20, Pullao Rice £1.40, set dinners start at £8.50. There are no hidden charges, no minimum charge, no service charge and no cover charge. They give a 10% discount for takeaways.

MONAF'S
119, Station Road, Hampton. Tel: 081 979 6021
We've received a number of good reports about Monaf's which ensures its first-time entry into this Guide. We hear of good quality food served in a friendly, confident and conscientious establishment.

THE SOPNA **CC DISCOUNT**
175, Hampton Hill, Hampton. Tel: 081 979 2977
One correspondant delights over the Mulligatawny soup, prepared, he told us with lentils, red chilli, ginger, turmeric and other spices at £1.30. Another correspondant adores the meat Phal, which he says is exceptionally hot at £3.20. Three Shopna Specials which are well spoken of are, Special Biriani £6.80, Gost Khara Masala - leg od spring lamb, boned, diced and braised in golden brown sliced onions, ginger, garlic and whole Garam Masala spices, £4.80. Bara Kebab Masala - young lamb chops, marinated and served with a sauce of fresh cream and tomatoes at £5.80. All said to be superb. Good prices include Popadoms 35p ,Chicken Curry £3.10, Pullao Rice £1.30 and there are no minimum, cover or service charges. Customers are provided with a hot face towel, fresh orange segments and after eights at the end of the meal, and the restaurant is offering discounts to Curry Club members at its quieter times, see page 288. The discount also applies to the restaurant's branches, Bilash Tandoor Restaurant, 4, Broad Street, Teddington, Middx and The Barn Tandori Restaurant, 188, Castlenau, London. SW13.

HARROW

THE NEW TAJ MAHAL
23, Station Road, Harrow. Tel: 081 427 1279
'If you love red flock wall paper and red velvet chairs, pictures of the Taj Mahal and waiters in dinner jackets and a multi heat graded menu, then you'll love this one. The food is not culinary it is liquid engineering. Was is cooked in 'Castrol GTX' or ghee. Where would we be without these enchanting little establishments.' AS. 'We do need these places. I had butterfly King Prawn, which was OK, followed by a really delightful Persian Lamb Biriani, the one with the omelette on top. It was very delicately spiced and served with a good wholesome vegetable curry. The Paratha was beautifully made and round. They were most friendly and helpful. On this occasion, I was on my own and was offered newspapers and magazines to read. I have been here, on and off for about ten years and it is now a really worthwhile high street local.' AD.

The editor of The Good Curry Guide welcomes your views on restaurants we list in this guide and on any curry restaurants or take-aways you visit. Please send them to: The Curry Club, PO Box 7, Haslemere, Surrey, GU27 1EP.

SITAR
174, Station Road, Harrow. Tel: 081 863 2080
This is a Gujerati, vegetarian restaurant. It opened in 1986 and is owned and run by two sisters. Hansara is the cook and the restaurant's specialality is home-style Gujarati recipes. If the style is new to you. Try the Special Thali for £5.25. 'There is a wealth of dishes to try.' AS. 'This is a spotless clean restaurant and the food is really, really good and worth a try. It offers a limited selection of wines and lager.' AD.

THE VINTAGE RESTAURANT
207, Station Road, Harrow. Tel: 081 427 7960
'What is outstanding in this restaurant is that the owner, Mr Patel, cooks most of the time and will discuss any methods in detail with any client. I was shown the kitchen. It was spotless and the food was absolutely fresh. I have been here 'umpteen' times, it is always good and occasionally superb, especially when Mr Patel does the cooking the results can be spectacular. I had Lamb Dhansak and my colleague, Chicken Dhansak, plus accompaniments. It was knock out. The balance of lamb and pulses (eight different kinds) and vegetables linked with perfect spicing.' AD. Strongly recommended to people who appreciate good food. Try to go on a Monday, when Mr Patel personally cooks. More reports please.

HILLINGDON

THE ROYAL TANDOORI **CC DISCOUNT**
2, Mercies Road, Hillingdon. Tel: 0895 32294
This restaurant was established in September 1979, by Mr Nazir Uddin Choudhury, despite this relatively long run, we have only just recently started to receive good reports. They talk of standard Bangladeshi cooking which is very competetantly done by a friendly crew. Typical prices are Popadoms 45p, Chicken Curry £3.30, Pullao Rice £1.30 and set dinner at £9.50. There is a minimum charge of £6.00 and the restaurant is offering discounts to Curry Club members at its quieter times, see page 288. They also operate the Romna Tandoori, 20/2, The Broadway, Bucks, where the discount is also applicable.

HOUNSLOW

THE ANAPURNA **CC DISCOUNT**
47/49, Spring Grove, Hounslow. Tel: 081 577 2266
The menu carries the full range of dishes that you would expect and we hear good things about the Chicken Tikka Masala at £3.90, the Karahi Lamb Tikka, tender lamb tikka cooked with special spices, with onion, tomato and capsicum and served in a cast iron pan, £4.90. Akhny Gosht, is tender spring lamb diced and cooked in ghee with spices, mixed with rice and served with vegetable curry £5.20 and Anapurna Chicken, the house special, ccoked with ground almond, cream and garnished with egg, a mild dish at £3.90. Other typical prices include Popadoms 30p, chicken Curry £2.80, Pullao Rice £1.40. There are no extra charges. Mr Miah is ofering discounts to Curry Club members at his quieter times, see page 288, it also has a branch, the Anapurna at 101, Chiswick High Road, London. W4, where the discount is also applicable.

ICKENHAM

THE ICKENHAM TANDOORI **CC DISCOUNT**
89, High Road, Ickenham. Tel: 0895 679300
This restaurant is quite a newcomer to the scene, opening in 1989. It is the property of Mr Rakbi Ali, who also owns the Tropical Curry in Beconsfield, Bucks (see entry). The inside of this restaurant is decorated attractively with oriental style cabins and has already started to attract good reports. We hear of a superb Chicken Tikka Masala, £6.80, which includes Basmati Rice or Naan, as do all the other specials. Murghi Masala £6.95, Chicken Jal Preazi (they're spelling for Jal frezi), a hot dish, cooked with green chilies and extra fresh spices, £6.80. Typical prices include Popadoms 25p each, Chicken Curry £3.60, Pullao Rice £1.15, set luncheon £4.90. There is an evening minimum charge of £7.50 a head but there is no service or cover charge. Customers will receive hot face

towels and After Curry Mints (Kansara). The restaurant is offering discounts to Curry Club members at its quieter times, see page 288.

ISLEWORTH

THE OSTERLEY PAVILION **CC DISCOUNT**
160, Thornbury Road, Isleworth. Tel: 081 560 6517
This is another relative new restaurant, coming onto the scene in 1989. Again we have been receiving good reports, which justify entry into our GCG. The decor we are told is quite smart with light green wall paper, flecked with gold, a deep red carpet and white table cloths with light green patterns of the chairs. The food is Northern Indian and the waiters are Bangladeshi. From Chefs Special Soup at £1.70 through to Tandoori King Prawn at £3.95. There is standard range of Tandoori Specials , including Chicken Shashlik, diced chicken mildly marinated with tomatoes, capsicums and onion, barbecued on skewers and served on a bed of salad for £4.95. The menu carries the standard range of heat graded dishes. Typical prices include Popadoms 35p, Chicken Curry £3.50, Pullao Rice £1.50, set luncheon £8.50, set dinner £9.95. There is an evening minimum charge of £9.95, but there is no service or cover charge. Hot face towels, sweets and flowers and served and the restaurants is offering a takeaway discount only to Curry Club members, see page 288.

PINNER

AJANTA
410, Uxbridge Road, Pinner. Tel: 081 428 9727
The Ajanta caves were discovered in Indian about 150 years ago, almost by accident, when a British soldier stumbled apon them, revealing wall paintings and some stone scuptures, painted over 2,000 years ago. The Ajanata is somewhat newer than that, but is old enough to have got into both the previous editions of the GCG. It also attempts to re-create a cave like atmosphere, from the exterior to the interior. Reports we get about this restaurant are all consistently good and we hear about a standard menu, with a wide, heat graded choice and acceptable prices.

HATCH END TANDOORI
284, Uxbridge Road, Pinner. Tel: 081 428 9781
'It was a warm summer evening in June. Six of us went for a 5km fun run, followed by a takeaway. With a large party you can really go to town on the order selection. The food was excellent, I always try to find something original, the Chicken Green Masala was best, fresh coriander gave a superb taste. It was like a cross between a Curry Club 'Club Night' meal and Veeraswamy's opening night.' AS. 'Very nicely decorated, opened four years ago, but not very well known outside the area. Staff give you a welcoming and very positive attitude. A tasty chicken Pakora was followed by a delicious King Prawn Patia, and Special Pulao Rice, multi coloured with fried onion and beated egg. A rare vegetable dish was Mali Kupto (there spelling for Malia Kofta), two fried lentils cakes in a spicy sauce of cream and other vegetables. Very good and extremely filling. A very substancial addition to the area.' AD. 'A pleasant surprise: the bill. It was only £11.00 each for loads of excellent food.' HL.

THE NEW ASHOKA
32, Bridge Street, Pinner. Tel: 081 429 0474
'The service was exceptionally friendly particularly from the more junior staff. I started with Chicken Tikka, this was somewhat better than average. The Popadoms were partially fried and then grilled, with onion salad and mint sauce. The Lamb in the Dhansak was a little tough, but the lentil sauce was excellent. It was hot, sweet and sour. I also had a Palak Aloo (Spinach Potato) not over shadowed by excessive spicing. One of the best of our local restaurants.' AD. More reports welcomed.

THE RUISLIP TANDOORI **CC DISCOUNT**
115, High Street, Ruislip. Tel: 0895 632859
It opened in 1983 and has been in both the previous GCG's. It has been owned from the beginning by Mr KB Raichhetri who is from Nepal. You will find Nepalese dishes on the menu with Northern Indian dishes.

Settees and chairs, mahogany ceiling, white walls, painting and coloured lights make up this restaurant. Our experienced curry freaks talk of going for the Nepalese dishes: for example Meat Kalia, Gete Masala (Chicken Chilli Masala), Karahi Specials and Chicken or Meat Nepal. There is also a Chicken Kathmandu Tandoori dish and a Vegetarian Nepal. There is a mild curry with Mango, most of these dishes average £5.00 and other typical prices include Popadoms 30p, Chicken Curry £3.85, Pulao Rice £1.40. There is a set luncheon at £5.25, set dinner, is £10.95. Evening minimum charge is £6.00. There is no service charge and no cover charge. The restaurant supplies face towels, sweets with coffee and it will offer discounts to Curry Club members at its quieter times, see page 288.

SOUTHALL

OMI'S **TOP 100**
1, Beaconsfield Road, Southall.081 571 4831
A small sit down licensed restaurant slightly off Southall's beaten track but really well worth seeking out. It is highly popular with the Asian community. I was taken there by a well known Indan Journalist, KN Malik, who promised to show me Indian food at its best. He was absolutely right. At Omi's we were swamped with a wealth of dishes, each chosen from the blackboard behind the serving counter. I cannot single any one out in particular. They were all great. A memorable meal in fascinating company at what seemed like very reasonable prices all washed down with lassi and Indian beer. It undoubtedly must go into our TOP 100.

BRILLIANT **TOP 100 & CC DISCOUNT**
72/74, Western Road, Southall. Tel: 081 574 1928
No way can this restaurant be called elegant, but what is can be called is darned good, efficient with a very high turn round, confident, highly relaxed, very informal and very informed. As soon as you come in and sit down, one of the waiters serves you with small glass dishes of chutneys, one is carrot with vinegar and spices, the other mint with chilli, both are absolutely fresh and delicious. What you do is order Popadoms and chew your way through these chutneys, the waiters don't mind if you finish them, they will replenish them. You can then get down to the serious eating. The menu looks quite small but don't be put off by that, also don't expect standard curry house food here. What you get is superbly cooked, perfectly spiced dishes, where every spice counts and every taste matters. If you want your food ultra spicey, or ultra hot, tell them, they'll do it for you. One very good piece of advice: do not over order. Old hands at this restaurant will often be heard ordering starters only and tell the waiter that they will order main course dishes later. There is no pressure on you to do anything else and believe me, the starter will probably fill you up anyway. The point about the food at this restaurant, is that it is like Indian home cooking. The 'piece de resistance,' is the Butter Chicken and the Jeera Chicken, both are available as starters only and are priced for four persons at £9.00, for a whole chicken, and for two persons £5.00, for half a chicken. We can tell you that the result is huge chunks of succulent chicken, stir-fried in massive amounts of butter ghee, the first with red spices, the second, Jeera, with cummin, and the third, with fresh green chillis. The Aloo or Onion Bhajia are onion delicately spiced in fresh batter and the Aloo Tikka, is a potato rissole, £2.00 each. Other interesting starters are Mogo Fried and Chilli Corn at £2.00 and Meat or Vegetable Samosas at £1.00 each. Should you find that you have room for main course, try the Methi Chicken £4.50, chicken cooked with fenugreek, or the Masala Chicken, a spicey chicken dish, cooked on the bone at £4.00, in a curry gravy. Alternatively Palak Lamb, £4.50, is lamb cooked with spinach. Keema Panner, is another interesting dish, minced lamb with peas at £2.75. However, it should be pointed out that both the mince and the lamb are Halal, and has a distinctly different taste to English lamb. This adds greatly to authenticity, it can affect people's judgement, if they're not used this particular taste. The vegetables at this restaurant are of course superb, you can get a mixed vegetable curry for £2.50, Aloo Cholaa (chick peas) for £2.50, and Mattar Paneer (Indian cheese and peas) at £3.00. Bindi Curry is freshly cooked as is Mushroom Curry, one at £3.00 the other at £2.50. The breads are delightful. The restaurant has an extensive wine list, unusual for Southall, which includes Omar Khayyam (Indian Champagne) at £14.95 and Cobra Lager. The Brilliant is perhaps a little hard to find, it is situated in a back street, but is worth searching out. There you will find Mr Anand senior behind the till,

72-74 WESTERN ROAD
SOUTHALL, MIDDLESEX

FULLY LICENSED
INDIAN RESTAURANT

Reservations: -574 1928

Also take away service provided

Also take away service provided
Catered for Royalty
Frequented by Connoisseurs and Indian Film Stars
Recommended in the Sunday Times – Good Food Guide
Time Out

Partners:
K.K. ANAND & D.K. ANAND

- Background music
- Air conditioning
- Outside catering

"THE ONLY ONE OF ITS KIND"

Curry Craze

Tandoori Restaurant

Fully Licensed

Superb authentic, home cooked East African — Indian cuisine. Caterers for wedding receptions and parties.

Take away service available.

8/9 Neeld Parade
The Triangle, Wembley.

Reservations Tel: 902 9720

Open Monday to Saturday
12. –2.30 p.m. and 5.30–11.30 p.m.
including Bank Holidays.
Last orders at 11.30 p.m.

Take-Away Service available.

119 Station Road, Hampton,
Middx. Tel -979 6021/1421.

supervising operations, while the waiting is carried out by members of his family. This restaurant is decidedly in our Top 100. Standard prices are Popadoms 30p, Chicken Curry £4.0, Pullao Rice 80p, set luncheon £7.50, set dinner is £10.00. There is no mimimum charge and no cover charge, but there is a service charge of 10%. The restaurant will offer discounts to members at its quieter times, see page 288.

MADUS BRILLIANT **TOP 100 & CC DISCOUNT**
39, South Road, Southall. Tel: 081 574 1897
This restaurant commenced trading in 1980. It is owned and operated by Sanjay and Sanjeer Anand, the former sees to the customers, the later tends to the cooking. The owners are the sons of the owner of the Brilliant restaurant, but would emphasise that the two restaurants have no trading connection whats so ever. Madhus Briliant was established five years after the Brilliant and was set up as a result of a dispute between the two brothers, when they disagreed about the instalation of a Tandoori oven. Trade in both restaurants boomed.The Brilliant closes on Monday; Madhus closes on Tuesday. Madhus Brilliant is situated on South Street, which is easier to find, than the Brilliant. It is noticeable by its plate glass window and is set back in the middle of a parade of shops. The restaurant occupies two floors and seats 102 people. The tables are quite large, canteen style, but nobody minds sharing a table. People come and go through out opening hours, having a quick snack and going rapidly and others staying the whole evening. There is never any pressure to vacate. Like the Brilliant, it is a true social meeting place for the local Asian community and for others who travel in from miles around, we're told. It also now attracts at least 30% non-Asians, who have come to enjoy Madhus Brilliant, as much as their Asian counterparts. It has a spiral staircase which takes you to the first floor which is decked out in shades of blue, it has a separate bar and the toilets are located up there too. Madhus Briliant specialises in outside catering and holds a contract with Heathrow Park Hotel. The restaurant is proud of its visiting celebraties: Tina Turner and Ian Botham for example. If this interests you you should ask Sanjay to see the photo album. This restaurant goes into our Top 100. Typical prices are Popadoms 30p, Chicken Curry £3.75, Pulao Rice £1.25. There is no minimun charge or cover, but there is a service charge of 10%. The restaurant will give discounts to Curry Club members at their quieter times, see page 288. See also page 7.

SAGOO AND THAKAR - THE ROXY **TOP 100**
114, The Green, Southall. Tel: 081 574 2579
See below

SAGOO AND THAKAR - THE ASIAN TANDOORI CENTRE
157, The Broadway, Southall.
'Mr Sagoo and Mr Thakar joined forces years ago to establish a restaurant. They soon afterwards opened a second branch and the two restaurants are operated by Mr Sagoo in one and Mr Thakar in the other. Don't ask me which one is which, I don't really know, the fact is that both of these restaurants have been the editors favourite Southall restaurant for many a year. The style and the method of the menu in both restaurants is almost identical. The Roxy is the larger of the two. They are very much the preserve of the Asian community and both are unlicensed. As far as I know they have no objection to bringing in your own alcohol although I have never seen the need to do it. Through their windows you will see huge piles of colourful Indian sweetmeats, Jalebis, Gulab Jamuns, Barfi of many colours and Halvas. Don't feel intimidated about going in. The welcome here is always guaranteed. You queue at the counter and tell the staff what you want. You put it on a tray and take the tray to a table and you sit and eat. All the dishes on offer are priced and written on the wall menu. You walk past the chill cabinet, containing Indian sweets, then the hot cabinets containing the curries. Behind the counter are piles upon piles of Bombay mix, Chewda, Cashew nuts etc, manufactured and packaged by Sagoo and Thakar. As both branches the staff have remained unchanged for as long as I have known it. They are open 10am until 11.30pm, which is the hours which the shops of Southall seem to operate. The restaurant offers a representative selection of Tandooris and kebabs and tikka and meat curries. Be prepared for chicken and meat on the bone although they do do it off the bone. The distinctive tatse is of the meat is Halal mutton, which is not to everybodie's taste, but the most exceptional curries are in my view the vegetarian curries. Stacked

high are huge piles of Indian breads, Paratha, Naan, Chappatis and they will include the unusual Corn flour Roti. I have been into both of these branches, many more times than I can count at all times of day and have never found them empty. Sometimes you have to stand in a long queue, but its worth it because the portions are enormous and the word of advice is do not over order. Prices are ridiculously cheap. One of my favourite meals is Aloo Tikki Channa, which is a potato rissole covered with a chick peas curry topped with yoghurt and carrot chutney, Paratha, followed by for example Shahi Korma and Makhi Roti. It would set me back £2.50. I would be filled to bursting. About that Carrot Chutney, incidentally, it is a must in both restaurants, and consits of matchsticks of carrot, immersed in a sweet and sour tamarind/imli sauce. This chutney is supplied at no charge if you place an order. You must have it, it is superb. Such unpretentious restaurants are typical in India but very rare indeed in the UK. They may not of course be to everyone's taste, being unlike the regular curry house, but the editor enters them jointly into his TOP 100.

THE SHAHANSHAH VEGETARIAN RESTAURANT
60, North Road, Southall. Tel: 081 574 1493
See below

THE SHAHANSHAH **CC DISCOUNT**
17, South Road, Southall. Tel: 081 571 3110
Opened in 1984, and owned by Baljinder Gill. Both are pure vegetarian , that is to say they don't cook with butter, eggs, cheese or any dairy products and obviously meat, poultry or fish. The restaurant offers takeaway facilities and supplies chilled vegetarian Indian sweets as well. The cooking is Northern Indian and you will find such delights as Paneer Samsosas at 55p, Mexican Mixture Samosas 40p. Vegetable curry at £1.50 and Veggie Burgers at 45p. There is no written menu, but in the true Indian Southall style, dishes do vary from time to time and are displayed on the board. Popadoms 25p each, Pullao Rice £1.20, set luncheon from £3.00 and set dinner £3 to 4.00. There are no miminum charges, no service or cover charges and the restaurant offers a discount to Curry Club members at their quieter times, see page 288.

TANDOORI KEBAB CENTRE **CC DISCOUNT**
163, The Broadway, Southall. Tel: 081 574 3571
You can't miss it, because outside you will see a traditional horse cart, out on the pavement. Inside it is typical style. It is a large clean cafe type establishment, with brass ornaments. It has one trapping unusual for Southall, but normal in standard Indian restaurants: a fish tank. It is a large restaurant seating 150 on two floors. Typical heaps of Jalebies, Ras Malai, Rasgulla and Barfi and other Indian sweets. The food is uncompremisingly Pakistani halal and while there are certainly dishes for everybody, there are some which might be a little off putting for those not used to it, such as Pypa, lambs trotters still on the bone, in a rich curry sauce. Meat on the bone is widely respected on the sub-continent, Indians and Pakistanis say that the bone enhances the flavour of the dish and is one of the most exciting points of eating. For £2.80 you can do this to your hearts content. Other dishes at £2.80 include Karahi Gosht, Nagaz (brains) and Nahari. You can have mutton curry on the bone for £2.00 and Chicken Curry for £2.30. Mutton Kebabs, tasty large and free from artificial colouring cost 45p. There is a varied selection of vegetarian dishes from £1.20 to £1.80. Popadoms are 30p, Pullao Rice is £1.50, set luncheon £5.50 and set dinner £6.50. Discounts will be offered to Curry Club members at their quieter times, see page 288.

THE TANDOORI EXPRESS ON JALEBI JUNCTION **CC DISCOUNT**
93, The Broadway, Southall. Tel: 081 571 6782
This branch of the well established Tandoori Kebab Centre, opened fairly recently and has a ruddy bright pink neon sign outside, with a bright inviting frontage. As you can tell from its name, it is not particularly aimed at the regular Southall population, who go for the straight forward and not the exotic. According to its owners, the Choudhury brothers, it is aimed at the trendy Asian youths. 'They have got a lot of money to spend and they think quite differently from their parents. They wear western clothes, they do to the disco. There are also a lot of them and this restaurant is designed for them.' They seem to come in their tens of dozens and the restaurant is lively, busy and full. The menu is similar to the one described at the Tandoori Kebab Centre, the mandatory piles of sweets and snacks

and there are curries on show in the hot counter. Make your choice, tell them what you want and they will bring it to you. As with so many places in Southall the food is very cheap. The prices the same as the Kebab centre. However, we have got reports that say the portions are smaller. The restaurant stays open from 9am till 11pm and it is very much a family place with reduced prices available on childrens portions. Mr Choudhury and the staff are encouraged to act as baby sitters. The adults can then get down to the serious business of eating and there is a separate room for parties. This restaurant gives a discount to Curry Club members at its quieter times, see page 288.

STANMORE

THE TAGORE TANDOORI
899, Honeypot Lane, Stanmore. Tel: 081 952 5727
A number of good reports get sent to us about this restaurant. 'This is my favourite restaurant, so I could be biased. It is tidy and comfortable and well lit with attentive waiters, although on busy nights they may need a little prompting. The chicken Chat is out of this world and the Dhal Masala is the best' TAS. More reports welcome.

TEDDINGTON

THE BENGAL BRASSERIE **CC DISCOUNT**
162, Stanley Road, Teddington. Tel: 081 977 7332
This restaurant also receives reports of haute cuisine above average. This sixty six seat restaurant is owned by Mr Ali Aftab and he has no other branches. They opened in 1986 and the decor browns, beiges and greens, plenty of plants, with flowers giving a cool and fresh feel. There are cabins for privacy and the service is commended as extremely good. There menu contains all the 'correct items and a good few others besides' DM. The starters side include Tandoori quails, £1.90, and Channa Chick Peas on hot Puri, £1.90. To be recommended, Chicken Tikka Musalla, £4.90. Scampi figures in certain dishes such as Scampi Bhoona at £5.50. They do Phal dishes, which are extremely hot and although we had this comment from one man, who I think was trying to be macho, 'I ordered their Chicken Phal, which I didn't think was hot enough, so I asked them to take it back and make it hotter, they did it and it came back and I could hardly finish it, it was so hot.' AC. (Serves you right - Ed). For the less hot headed you will find an admirable array of vegetable dishes including Niramish, £2.20 which is a mixture of fresh and tinned curried vegetables, fairly hot Bombay Potato, a mild Chana Masala, Chick Pea, and a rather good idea of the Mixed Vegetable Tray, chef's choice of three different vegetable dishes at £5.00. There are plenty of sorbets and ice creams, fruit and sweets. 'My favourite is the Banana Fritter at £1.30. 'There is a minimum charge of £6.50 in the evening and no cover or service charge. And hot face towels, orange segments and After Curry Mints (Kansara) with coffee. This restaurant is offering discounts for Curry Club members on their quieter times, see page 288.

TWICKENHAM

SHISH MAHAL
21 London Road, Twickenham. Tel: 081 892 3303
This restaurant opened in 1982, it was featured in our first edition of the GCG but dropped out of the second edition. Since then we have received protests to put it back, so here it is. This forty two seat restaurant is described as cool and refreshing with magnolia walls and blue curtains, with matching table cloth and napkins. Indian art pictures surround the walls and lighting is by candle table light. When we checked with Mr Monaf about his restaurant, we asked 'do you have any special dishes', he replied, no there is nothing special at present, all dishes are special at the Shish Mahal. So, Mr Monaf, it would seem that you loyal following wouldn't disagree with that. They particularly liked the House special Thali, with Kebab, Murgh Mukhani, Lamb Pasanda, Mushroom Bhajee, Brinjal Bhajee, Egg Rice, Kulcha Naan and Popadom at £8.95. There is an equally good Vegetarian Thali, at £7.25. One correspondent particularly likes two dishes, the Chicken Shasarkhan, which is chicken mari-

nated and cooked in a thick almond creamy sauce, £4.35 and Methi Mahz, minced lamb, cooked with spinach and fenugreek leaves for £3.95. Other prices include Popadoms 40p, Chicken Curry £3.05, Pullao Rice £1.35. There is a minimum price of £8.50 per head, but no service or cover charge.

WEMBLEY

CHETNA'S BHEL PURI HOUSE **TOP 100**
420, High Road, Wembley. Tel: 081 900 1466
Under the ownership of Mukesh Patel, the menu is simple but effective. Of course it is quite different from the standard curry house, being all vegetarian and being based on Bombay and South Indian cooking. It also has a rather comical pizza department which 'suits my boyfriend admirably, because he says he doesn't like curry, though I am still working on him.' BD. There are two other main sections on the menu, one is called 'Seaside savouries' the reason is Bombay's street snack sites are on the seaside. (Bombay is made up of islands which are connected by bridges). 'Bhel Puri is a mixture of puffed rice (mamra) Sev (thin crispy stick snack in appearance it looks like vermacelli), small Puri (crispy biscuits) and onion with three sauces, tamarind, coriander and chilli. This is all topped off with yoghurt. Potato Puri is the same served with small chunks of boiled potatoes and green chillies and imili chutney. Aloo Papri Chat is crispy puri with chick peas, potato, imli, yoghurt and a garnish of spice condiments. (Roasted Garam Masala and Indian Black Salt). Puris, also known as Gol Goppas are slightly smaller than a golf ball, cooked so that they puff up into balls, these are served with a different bowl of chick peas, moogn lentils and a masala sauce. To eat them correctly you should ask for Jal Jeera (cummin water) a spicy drink which accompanies the puris. Dahi Potato Puri are small crispy puris, with spicy potato covered with natural yoghurt which is garnished with chilli and spices. Dahi Wadiais a lentil lentil fritter coated in a mixture of spicy yoghurt and chutneys and garnished with spices. Idlies are south Indian steamed cakes made of lentils served with delicious coconut chutney. An Idli Sambar is idlies served in a hot vegetable purQed lentil sauce. Other starters include Bhajias (pakoras) Vegetable Cutlets, Vegetablo Samosas and Kachoria which are spicy green beans, rolled into balls, covered in pastry and fried. The restaurant has a selection of Dosas served with coconut chutney and some stuffed with various curries. This restaurant has a clearly defined following of both Asians and non-Asians and we have had already had a good many reports from both communities. It is not licensed, of course, but you can buy sweet or salty lassi, fresh passion fruit juice, and fresh squeezed orange juice. We can throughly recommend this restaurant and we wish their were many more like it. Reports on it are very welcomed. Prices are extremely cheap, therfore we feel it not necessary to make a comparison, you can eat you fill for under £4.00. In our TOP 100.

THE CURRY CRAZE **CC DISCOUNT**
9, Neelam Parade, Wembley. Tel: 081 902 9720
The Curry Craze is located in a triangle, created by Wembley Hill Road and Wembley High Road. It began trading in 1980 and is owned by husband and wife team, Subodh and Shashi Malhotra who are East African Asians, being expelled from Nirobi as were other Asians, in the late sixties. The name the Curry Craze reflects, according to the owner, the popularity for curry and it serves butter chicken, Chilli Chicken £12.00, (half portion £5.50) and Jeera Chicken £8.95 (half portion £4.75), which are whole chickens served on the bone, quartered. The Butter Chicken £8.95 is reddened like Tandoori, the Jeera cooked with cummin seeds, and the Chilli Chicken with chillies, capsicums and mushrooms. A fourth variety is Methi Chicken, £10.00 (half portion £5.00), on the bone with fenugreek leaves. Starter dishes include vegetable tikkie, mixed vegetable cutlets floating in yoghurt £1.75 and chilli corn, hot corn on the cob pieces served on a bed of salad £2.45. There is also a variation of this called Makhi £1.20. Plenty of choice for vegetarians including the unusual Masala Tinda, a medium dry Punjabi squash vegetable, in appearance resembling a goosberry at £2.75 and the Tinda, which is native to both Indian and Kenya at £4.75. There is also Lambs Trotter, on the bone, chewable and suckable for £4.75 and we point out, as we did we did with previous entries, that in authentic restaurants like this, lamb really means mutton and there is a distinctive taste to the Halal

meat. Mr Mahoutra is aware that some English people find his food different. He says that people have been brainwashed by traditional Bangladeshi currys and he would like to introduce his style of cuisine to a wider audience. Well this is the way to do it, Mr Mahoutra, and you'll certainly find no more appreciative curry diners that read this Guide. A discount to Curry Club members is offered at their quieter times, see page 288 for details.

THE MOGHUL BRASSERIE
525, High Road, Wembley. Tel: 081 903 6967
In 1985 the celebrated Amin Ali (see Jamdani, W1 and Red Fort, W1) became assocated with the opening of various sophisicated restaurant around the country. His magic touch is very much in demand with well heeled entrepreneurs and the Moghul Brasserie as an innovation for Wembley being the first up-market restaurant in a suburb already well endowded with cheap Asian curry houses. If Wembley High Street is known for anything it is known for its traffic jams at all times of day and night and the sheer impossibility to park. The owners of this restaurant have solved this problem by supplying you with a vallet. You drive to the restaurant the vallet takes your car from there and parks it for you somewhere mysterious, only known to himself. A very American and convenient service. The restaurant is light and airy with padded cane furniture, sumptuous hand painted paintings of Moghul origin. Prices are above average. More reports welcomed.

WOODLANDS **CC DISCOUNT**
402A, Wembley High Road. Tel: 081 902 9869
Woodlands is part of a chain of three vegetarian restaurants. The second being in 77, Marylebone Road, W1 and the third in 37, Pantone Street, SW1 (see separate entries). Originally from South India, they are all vegetarian restaurants and are to be found all over the sub-continent. The English three, are under the Managing Directorship of Mr Ranjit Sood. Full details about the menu appear in the London SW1 entry. All branches are to be equally recommended. The prices are two Popadoms £1, Vegetable Korma £3.25, Pullao Rice £2.95. Lunch or dinner is £9.75. There is a minimum charge of £5 and service charge of 12%. This restaurant and its two UK branches give discounts to Curry Club members at its quieter times, see page 288 for details of this offer.

NORFOLK

KINGS LYNN

THE KISMET
41, St James Street, Kings Lynn.
'This restaurant has a very expensive menu which is interesting and adventurous. It includes Mass Bhajia, whole trout marinated in spices and fried and we tried Shath Kora Gosht, lamb cooked in Bengali lemon, this we thoroughly enjoyed even though there were in all sixty seven main course dishes to chose from.' PAK. 'Menu is extensive and informative, seating is comfortable and the staff friendly. Every time I visit the standard gets higher. 'No tables warmers meant that the meal was cold by the end. I did not like their stunt of 65p ice-creams on the menu and then saying that only £1.50 portions were available. Our kids now think that their father is very hard hearted and mean. Where Indian restaurants are not easy to find this one is quite acceptable.' JL.

NORWICH

BOMBAY
43, Timber Hill, Norwich. Tel: 0603 20305
This restaurant owned by Mr Miah Siraj, in 1977 in an olde world Tudor style building. Before long the 54 seat restaurant was a great success and Mr Siraj, opened in the course of the next few years three other Bombay branches, two in Norwich at 9, Magdelen Street and at 15, Prince of Wales Street and one in No:1, Exchange Square, Beccles, Suffolk.

Finally he recently opened The Taste of Bombay, 82/84, Prince of Wales Street, Norwich. The menu in general terms in each of the restaurants is the same. We hear about very good service and polite waiters and reasonable prices. 'The starters, Chicken Tikkas and a Skeek Kebab were not very hot, heat wise, and only a hint of spices. The main course, however, made up for them, the Meat Dhansak, Ceylon, Chicken Jal Frezi and the Korai wre all very highly spiced and tasty, although the meat was rather tough. Vegetable dishes were very good, and the pea. Typical prices are Popadoms 35p each, Chicken Curry £3/20, Pullao Rice £1.35.

THE TASTE OF BOMBAY
82/84, Prince of Wales Road, Norwich. Tel: 0603 617835
Until about three years ago, this was called the Agra Tandoori, about which we had received some extremely good reports but equally some reports that were less good. This is relevant because, when this restaurant was taken over by Mr Miah Siraj, (see entry on Bombay, Norwich), he inherited the kitchen, waiting staff and a very beautiful restaurant. 'The decor is very comfortable complete with water fountains.' NP. The menu and the prices are the same as the Bombay, Norwich. More reports are welcome.

THETFORD

INDIA GARDENS
17, White Hart Street, Thetford. Tel: 0842 761270
The India Garden is really taking the lead in terms of Thetford reports. 'It has an extensive menu which includes some English dishes, it also has an adequate wine selection. Portions are nothing short of delicious. The layout of the restaurant is smart simply and clean and thoroughly recommended.' RT. Your reports please.

WYMONDHAM

SHAPLA
22/26, Town Green, Wymondham. Tel: 0953 601114
This town is between Thetford and Norwich on the A11 and is popular with travellers and local people alike who write to us from time to time of the excellence of the Shapla. 'If you are in Norwich and want a good curry it is worth travelling for. It has maintained a very high standard and we eat here nearly every week. The level of service is just about right. Most dishes are good, some are excellent and individual.' BE. More reports welcomed.

NORTHAMPTONSHIRE

IRTHLINGBOROUGH

TANDOORI NIGHTS
48, Station Road, Irthlingborough.
Tel: 0933 652675
Housed in an old Tudor building, and a, 'A warm welcome was given to us in the reception of this L shaped restaurant. I chose the Non-vegetarian Thali which consisted of meat Bhoona, Chicken Tikka Masala, Sheik Kebab, Mushrom Bhajee, Vegetable Curry, Pullao Rice and Naan. All that food for £9.95. The portions must be small, I thought, I waited for twenty minutes for my meal to arrive and when it did, the portions were huge.' DM. We have other similar reports to hand and would welcome others.

NORTHAMPTON

THE BOMBAY PALACE

9/11, Welford Road, Northampton. Tel: 0604 713899

This restaurant we hear 'the service is excellent, even when they are busy on a Saturday night, including an apology for a delay which we hadn't noticed. The Korai and the Shashlik dishes were both very good. The Thali was excellent and the Naan, one of the best I've ever tasted. The prices are reasonable and this restaurant will produce serious competition for other Northampton establishments.' DB. 'Nicely and cleanly decorated and attractively laid out tables with freshly starched napkins. There was a warm welcome with prompt service. The sauces were spicy with good cuts of meat.' PM.

THE ROYAL BENGAL

39, Bridge Street, Northampton. Tel: 0604 38617

The Royal Bengal was established in 1975 in premises across the road. It continues to attract loyal customers and we recieve loyal reports. We hear great things about the Tandoori Masala dishes, the Karahis and the Baltis. Yes, Balti has reached Northampton from the Midlands (see glossary). Papadoms 25p each, Chicken Curry £3.50, Pullao Rice £1.10, set dinner £21.95 for two. There is no minimum, cover or service charge. The proprietor has branches at Coventry (The Dhakar Dynasty, 294, Wallgrave Road) and Kingthorpe, Northampton (The Bombay Palace, 9, Walford Road)

THE TAJ MAHAL

7, Marefare, Northampton. Tel: 0604 31132

This restaurant has maintained its position in the Guide, firstly, because it is Northampton oldest, having opened in 1952, indeed that rates it with the country's ten first Indian restaurants. Secondly, its hours of opening, Friday and Saturday night, are remarkable, closing at 3am. This is typical Curry House, nothing more and nothing less. With nigh on forty years in the business, you would expect them to be good at the job. I can't imagine why they find it necessary to stay open till 3am, but for those who hound up and down the M1, yes there are some of us that do in the wee hours, they are just a hop and a jump away from Junction 15 and 16. Anything is better than motorway food, anytime of day or night. As for the quality of the food, who cares at that hour of the morning?

THE AKASH

36, Cambridge Street, Wellingborough. Tel: 0933 227193

The Akash began trading in 1979, it is a fifty four seat restaurant doing a good solid job for the citizens of Wellingborough. We are told by our reporters that it is the best of the three in the town and specially recommended are the Korai Chicken or Meat which prior warning must be given, we had a wonderful meal.' TE. Other recommended dishes are Chicken Tikka Masala, Lamb Pasanda. Typical prices include, Popadoms 30p each, Chicken Curry £2.85, Pullao Rice £1.15.

TOWCESTER

THE NEW BEKASH

100, Watlings Street, Towcester. Tel: 0327 50505

We understand this restaurant does particularly well on race days, hardly surprisingly. Other than that we have heard very little about it, we did, however, receive one plea, rather than a report, 'We have eaten here on a number of occasions and they serve a wonderful selection of creamy dishes and orange and lemon sorbet after the meal. One or two of the dishes are delicious. You have very few restaurant in your GCG for Northampton and we suggest that this should be tried and added to your list. We hope this is helpful.' PMP. We hope it is too, we would appreciate some more reports.

NORTHUMBERLAND

ALNWICK

ALNWICK INTERNATIONAL TANDOORI
Market Street, Alnwick.
'We travelled twenty miles for this one and we figured it was well worth the journey. The Rhogan Gosh was very authentic, the Naan very light and sweet.' PG. More reports welcomed.

BERWICK

THE MAGNA
39, Bridge Street, Berwick Upon Tweed.
Tel: 0289 306229
We have heard that this is the port in the storm for the rock group 'Lindisfarne', it is also a good place to go if you go to Holy Island and the sites of Lindisfarne. Futher up the A1 road is The Magna and we have received a few reports about this restaurant. It is a standard curry house with the usual heat graded menu, the food can be good, but is limited in choice. 'At least it's there.' KP.

MORPETH

TANDOORI MAHAL **CC DISCOUNT**
17, Bridge Street, Morpeth. Tel: 0670 512420
Morepeth has at least three curry houses and this is the best of the bunch, we hear. It was establishjed in 1980 by Kaptan Miah. Last year it was refurbished with co-ordinating colours of green and gold. A new bar was built with plant boxes and screens and the walls are decorated with Moghul art, including shelf displays of Indian ornaments. The menu is quite exTensive with the standard range of starters, including the usual Chicken Chat or Channa Chat £2.05. Chicken Pakoras caught the eye of one of our reporters £2.05. 'We loved the Tikka Chicken Chum Chum,' £5.25. Imli Chicken (Tamarind fairly hot for £5.25). Another correspondent talks well of the Malayan Chicken, with banana and pineapples for £3.80. There is a single Balti dish on the menu, which means this trend is spreading from the Midlands. The greatest bargain in this restaurant must be the set lunch costing just a remarkable £1.95. A minimum charge of £4.00, but no cover or service charge. Branches are at The Lalquila, Cramington, and The Tandoori Takeaway at 10, Chantrey Place, Morpeth. They are giving discounts to Curry Club members at their quieter times, see page 288 for details of the offer.

PONTELAND

PONTELAND TANDOORI
11A, Main Street, Ponteland. Tel: 0661 860292
This restaurant opened in 1988 to the delight of the people of Ponteland, who live on the A696, the road out of Newcastle, past the airport. Although Newcastle is very well served for Indian restaurants the outskirts aren't. We hear good reports from locals and travellers about Sirag Miah's restaurant. Hand carved Italian chairs, pressed fan shaped serviettes, chandliers, Greek arches and a grand father clock. Despite all this we are assured it is an Indian restaurant and the Chef Special at £5.00 (a fillet of chicken with cashew nuts at £7.20) is very good. Chilli Chicken Masala £5.30. Popadoms 30p each, Chicken Curry £4.20, Pullao Rice £1.65 and a set luncheon at £2.50. There is an evening minimum charge of £8.00.

NOTTINGHAM

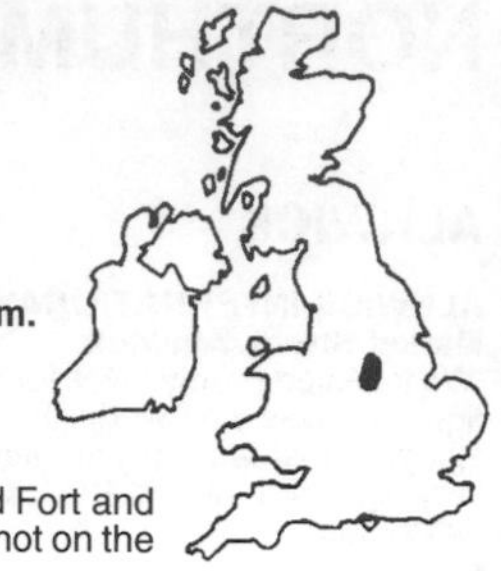

LENTON

THE TASTE OF INDIA
55, Abbey Street, Lenton, Nottingham.
Tel: 0602 784957
Ref: 9499
At this restaurant we hear that the food is well cooked and the portions are large. The owner used to work at London's Red Fort and there are always ready to make any dish not on the menu.' CA. More reports welcomed.

NEWARK

THE ASHA, **CC DISCOUNT**
Studman Street, Newark. Tel: 0636 702870
This restaurant has been in existance for several years ansd it has recently been refurbished. Standards are now first class and no expense has been spared. It gets particulalry busy at weekends when booking is esential and is extremely comfirtable, byut the service is individual even when they are busy. One reporter speak of the food, always being well prepared and well presented and they are very generous with their portions. One reporter says this is propbably the best restaurant I've ever used, I eat there at least twice a week.' TW. He is a local and probably bias, but view that the restaurant is good is aired by others. Typical prices Tandoori Chgicken £4.20, Meat Rhogan £3.50, Pullao Rice £1.23 and Chappatis are 65p each.
We hear that there is a Newark Curry Club which has been going for about six years. It meets on the first monday of each month at The Asha and the correspondent is the menu co-ordinator, this involves chosing and negotiating (for a discount) the menu. Usually about twenty five people turn up on their Club evenings. Besides eating curry together they raise money for charity (over £600 last year). This sounds very interesting and I'm sure your members and ours would like to get together. The restaurant is giving a discount to all Curry Club members, see page 288 for details. We look forward to hearing more reports on this restaurant.

CHAND TANDOORI **CC DISCOUNT**
26, Mansfield Road, Nottingham. Tel: 0602 474103
First opened in 1979 and was taken over my new management in December 1989. We are pleased that the new family business cares very much for their restaurant. It has been redecorated, apparently with some advice from its customers and it now has a colour scheme, 'to match the uniform of the staff, to look like the Moghul Empire.' Seating is split over two floors. Proprietor Mohammed Aslam described the menu as, 'one that leaves nothing to the imagination and omits nothing.' 'Great effort is made for vegetarians with 'V' marks against suitable dishes.' GM. 'If you have nobody to impress the next day try the Garlic Nan at £1.50 or the Garlic Chappati at 95p each, or better still both.' GC. Prices are a trifle on the high side with Popadoms 50p, chicken Curry £5.45, Pulao Rice £1.50, set luncheon is a reasonable £2.99, set dinner for two is £16.80. There is a minimum charge of £6.50 with a service charge of 10%. The restaurant gives discounts to Curry Club members at its quieter times, see page 288 for details.

KRISHNA
144, Alferton Road, Nottingham. Tel: 0602 708608
This restaurant is owned and run by a brother and sister team. They specialise in Gujarati pure vegetarian cooking. The menu is a revelation for Nottingham, offering a complete break from the traditional heat graded curry menu. This is not just because it is vegetarian, but the food is so very different. Anybody who enjoys curry will enjoy themselves wading through the recipes. You are helped by small colour pictures which show how appetising the dishes look. Prices are reasonable, starters all of which are served with Tamarind Sauce, salad with lemon wedge. Serves

Bhel Puri (see glossary) for £1.50. 'They make exceptionally good Dosas.' CR. For £3.95 you will be served a huge flour and water pancake filled with a dry curry, rolled up and accompanied by a different curry in gravy, yoghurt and coconut chutney. Jeera Rice £1.90. Their care with cooking deserves to be commended and we wish them well. We look forward to hearing more about this restaurant.

LAGOONA TANDOORI
43, Mount Street, Nottingham. Tel: 0602 411632
Over the last few years, reports have been a bit patchy. However, following marked improvement, we would be loth to take this restaurant out of the Guide, since it has been there for the previous two editions. Typical comments 'Peshwari Nan was unlike any other I have tasted it was round with crushed nuts not the usual almonds and sultanas, it was excellent. The Ladies Finger (bhindi) was firm and not flabby, served in a good sauce.' JT. We look forward to receiving more reports on this restaurant.

MOGAL-E-ZAM **CC DISCOUNT**
79, Goldsmith Street, Nottingham. Tel: 0602 473820
Opened in 1970, by Mr Sheik. Had a period of brilliance with nothing but great reports received. In the 1980's other restaurants overshadowed it, but it is now making it back to the light. Prices include Popadoms 30p, Chicken Curry £4.70, Pullao Rice £1.20, set luncheon £4.25 and set dinner £8.90, evening minimum charge is £10 a head and Mr Sheik tells us that he gives free channa and ganthya (Indian nibbles) at the bar, hot face towels, mints and supari and a flower for the ladies and the bill for the gents. With your Curry Club membership card you will receive a 10% discount, see page 288. We would appreciate more reports on this restaurant.

NOOR JAHAN **CC DISCOUNT**
39/41, Manchester Road, Nottingham. Tel: 0602 476449
This restaurant is another old hand, it opened in 1971. Changed ownership in 1989, to Mutahr Khan. New ownership can sometimes rock the boat but not on this occassion. Standard menu, but for a dish called Mumma Cook, medium hot curry £4.40. Popadoms are 30p each, Chicken Curry £4.20. Pullao Rice £1.10, set luncheon £4.75, set dinner for two £18, minimum evening charge and service charge of 10%. The restaurant gives discounts to Curry club members at its quieter times, see page 288 for details.

SAAGAR **TOP 100 & CC DISCOUNT**
473, Mansfield Road, Sherwood, Nottingham. Tel: 0602 622014
Owned by Mohammed Khizer, opened in 1984. He eclipsed some of the well established restaurants in Nottingham. Infact you tell us it is the city's best restaurant. Setting is English empire. Head chef is Pakistani. Menu contains all the old favourites that you would expect to find, plus a few treats. 'King Prawn Pakora is fabulous with garlic/lentil sauce for £3.20. Chicken Pakora, being very light and crispy. Mukani Kofta balls, spicy mince meat balls cooked in ghee, 'just fabulous' TS. £3.05. Saagar Roast Chicken £6.40, served with rice, vegetables and curry sauce. Hussaini Chicken or Lamb, medium curry chicken pieces cooked with keema mince meat , lentil sauce for £6.40. Balti dishes are available here, served in a sizzling wok and are cooked with capsicum, tomato, onion fenugreek leaves making them very spicy but not hot. (£6.70). Their menu touches South India: Kallan is a good example, chicken, meat or prawn. cooked with mango, coconut and fresh spices, the end result is a sour yet very tasty, delicious dish. All main meals prices include rice, popadoms and chutnies. No minumun, service or cover charges. 'Why aren't all restaurants like the Saagar.' CB. The Saagar goes into our TOP 100. Curry Club members are allowed a discount at lunch times only, see page 288.

TRENT BRIDGE TANDOORI
London Road, Nottingham. Tel: 0602 864935
Here is a comfortable, normally decorated restaurant. Recently changed ownership, which has not effected standards. Service is always with a smile. 'Free popadoms and chuntneys, this says much'. CN. A small restaurant with a standard menu with a good and varied choice. More reports welcomed.

KHYBER PASS
46, Kings Street, Southwell, Nottingham. Tel: 0602 012640
'The food here is always high quality and at a very economical price. It has a cosy atmosphere but is hardly the Ritz. The restaurant is in a converted terrace house, with seven tables downstairs and similar up. It is best to book on Friday and Saturday night. Meals are of a high standard a taste freshly prepared. 'The food was tasty, hot and competively prices. Three popadoms were served with each meal and for a change rice is included in the price of the curry.' LW. More reports welcomed.

SUTTON-IN-ASHFIELD
83, Outram Street, Sutton-In-Ashfield, Nottingham. Tel: 00623 559955
'Wood panelling everywhere, rather like being an olde worlde train, lets hope they don't get death watch beetle.' AF. A compact 52 seater restaurant, there are penty of plants around to ease the extensive woodwork. We hear that the quality of the cooking is 'really quite exceptional. I visited here with a local friend, and I thought the standard here was better than my local Hammersmith restaurant.' BR. The cooking is standard Bangladeshi. The menu includes all the regular dishes with no surprises at all. Howover, it is quite clear that everything is done competetantly, with panache and friendliness. Typical prices are Popadoms 30p, Chicken Curry £2.75, Pullao Rice £1.10. Set dinner for two people £ 16.00. There is a minimum charge of £5.50. The restaurant is usually very busy, so booking is advised. However, they have consented to give discount to Curry club members of 10% on takeaways only, see page 288. 'I decided in a rash moment to go into this restaurant with three young fractious children. Husband was away on a business trip and I was simply yearning for my curry fix. I have never been into a restaurant with my children on my own. It was half full, but the staff were simply marvelous. Handed out the menu, the children at once looked like little angels and behaved themselves. On the menu is the most attractive picture of a swan and an Indian couple, riding on its back on a lake floating in a lake, with little frogs and birds. This captured the children's minds and the restaurant staff did the rest. They even only charged me for two portions, I got two children free. Aren't they marvelous.'

OXFORD

ABINGDON

THE PRINCE OF INDIA
20, Ock Street, Abingdon. Tel: 0235 523033
One of a chain of twelve Prince of India's. 'Everything was good with nothing actually standing out. It is well decorated if slightly garish. The best was the Channa Masala, which I'm becoming very fond of. No reason to avoid it if you are in the area.' JL. More reports welcomed.

BANBURY

MOGHUL TANDOORI
58, Parsons Street, Banbury. Tel: 0295 51920
We continue to hear about a nicely placed restaurant in a charming town. High standard of decor and enjoyable food. More reports welcomed.

SHISH MAHAL
45, Bridge Street, Banbury. Tel: 0295 66489
We had a report a short time ago, that this restaurant had taken on two new chefs, Nepalese brothers who had both worked at the Salttee Oberoi, Kathmandu (the capital of Nepal). We did hear that the cooking had improved remarkably and that it is a very popular restaurant. We would dearly like to hear more, especially about those Nepalese chefs.

'First time I had ever had a curry listening to 'The Archers'. The food, decor and the staff were all excellent. When we arrived at 7pm on a Saturday night, we were the only customers, by 8pm the place was packed.' KPT. The restaurant has recently been refurbished in brighlty coloud woven fabrics, showing scenes of India. Mr A Ahad is the manager and he has recently introduced a Sunday lunch buffet which he hopes will attract the whole family. Indeed this restaurant is rather keen on children, (at half price) and Mr Ahad believes that the wall decorations will intrigue them.

DIDCOT

THE PRINCE OF INDIA
26, The Parade, Edinburgh Drive, Didcot. Tel: 0235 819555
Didcot is a relively small town and had no Indian restaurants at all at the begining of 1990 and now has three. We wish them all well of course. We are able to bring one to the attention of our guide readers straight away. It is part of the ever expanding group. See other guide entries for the style and menu of this chain. Reports are welcomed.

FARINGDON TANDOORI
19, London Street, Faringdon. Tel: 0367 21896
In 1986 this restaurant was known as the Madhumeeta and it was mentioned in our first GCG. In 1987 it changed name to the Dilraj, change of ownership meant standards went down hill before going up again. Another ownership and name change, and we get nothing but praise about it. One of our regulars says it must be one of the best in Oxfordshire. Extensive menu. Chicken Phall was met with satisfaction 'The quality, quantity and service all were well above average and it has become a regular haunt of mine.' KJP. Another says, 'This is a small pleasant restaurant, not too elaborate, which has a good atmosphere. They have a large and varied menu which will suit everyone and make more of an effort to help customers choose their dishes than most. We had onion chutney with the Popadoms and fresh coriander leaf was being used which was excellent. Main Dishes were King Prawn Tandoori Masala £7.35 and King Prawn Dhansak £5.95, both were tasty and portions good. Vegetable Pullao Rice £1.45, portion was a little small. I live in Durham, but staying with my boyfriend, who lives and works in Farringdon. We were the last to leave and it was nice to see the chef and waiters sitting at one of the tables having their own supper, a huge pan of boiled rice and an even larger pan of some curry.' DD. Reports welcomed.

HEADINGTON

MIRABAI **CC DISCOUNT**
70, London Road, Headington. Tel: 0865 62255
Opened in 1984 and is owned by Mr Laskar, who ownes no other restaurants. It did not take long before we were getting regular reports about this restaurant. Not large, seats 46, 'tastefully decorated with attention to small details.' TS. 'Menu is physically enormous, practically needs a table to itself, but its list of contents isn't that overwhelming. I was glad to see that all my old favourites where there and I was about to order my usual, when the waiter came and made a recommendation. As this was my first visit to the Mirabai, I heeded his advice. Thank goodness it was wonderful and I'm now a convert. Try their Kashmiri Roghan Gosh, although far from authentic (it had sultanas and pineapple in it), £2.70, it was very nice indeed.' SG. 'Akhni Pullao is another favourite at £5.90, a really tasty rice dish with chick peas in it.' ST. They also do a 'mean Chicken Tikka Masala for £4.90.' TS. Typical prices are Popadoms 30p each, Chicken Curry £3.60, Pullao Rice £1.35. Set luncheon £5.30, dinner from £7.50 to £13.50 per person. There isn't a minimum charge, there is a service charge of 10% and the restaurant offers discounts to Curry Club members at it's quieter times, see page 288. Free home delivery service within five miles.

KIDLINGTON

OVERSHIRE TANDOORI **CC DISCOUNT**
11/13, Oxford Road, Kidlington. Tel: 08675 2827
Opened in 1983 and connected to The last Viceroy, Bourne End in Bucks. Managed by Mr Bari, who says he has, 'a very smart restaurant,' and we

don't disagree with him. It is outstanding. Brown wooden arches offset against panelled windows and a white frontage. The interior carries the same colour and design, with mahogany backed velvet chairs, discrete lighting and arched booths. 'There is an extensive menu with extremely good service, and the food is delicious and highly recommended.' NH. Specials include Chicken Nawabi Masala at £7.20. Lamb Pasanda at £5.35 and Lahore Lamb Chana at £5.75. Other prices are Popadoms 35p, Chicken Curry £3.20, Pullao Rice £1.65. There are no extra charges in this 80 seater restaurant, and they are offering a 10% discount on takeaways to Curry Club members, see page 288.

JAMAL'S TANDOORI
108, Walton Street, Oxford. Tel: 0865 310102
'I was introduced to this restaurant by a business colleague and I was very impressed. The pink and mauve decor is perhaps a little garish by day, but by night the ambience is good. There is an extensive menu but I found the food a bit on the mild side for a serious curry eater. I requested that my Chicken Phall was made hotter. It was and it was superb. The quality was excellent and the portions more than adequate.' KP. We hear that this restaurant recently took over the shop next door and now has a capacity of eighty. It still fills up, especially on Friday, Saturday and Sunday nights. prices are reasonable, more reports please.

MODHU BON
16, Turl Street, Oxford. Tel: 0865 000000
I am pleased with the opening of this restaurant because it is vegetarian and that often spells good cooking. Reports have improved greatly over the years, so I feel confident now that this restaurant deserves an entry into The Good Curry Guide. 'This was the first time that we had tried a vegetarian restaurant and we were well satisfied with the meal. We shared Pullao Rice, Spinach and Potato with sliced peppers and a Mushroom with onions curry, all the spicing was just right. There is no attempt in the decor to give the restaurant an Indian appearance. We were the here for the food.' PM. More reports welcomed.

THE MOONLIGHT TANDOORI
58, Cowley Street, Oxford. Tel: 0865 240275
This Pakistani restaurant has a mainly student clientele. We hear of good quality food. 'The restaurant gets very busy and booking is essential. Go at early evenings to avoid waiting for tables. Large portions are served.' DC. The restaurant was recently enlarged to include a conference/ private party room. 'The food however, is still as good as ever offering a great variety of dishes and many vegetarian choices.' DK. More reports welcomed.

THE POLASH RESTAURANT TOP 100 & CC DISCOUNT
25, Park End Street, Oxford. Tel: 0865 250244
The best restaurant in the city. A forty four seat restaurant that opened relatively recently, 1988. Is owned by Abdur Rouf. He has no other branches so he is able to spend considerable time nursing this restaurant into excellence. Described as the only up-market restaurant in Oxford. The decor is 'tasteful in pale dark grey set with pink tablesclothes and peach flashes across the walls and a pale green ceiling hung with crystal chandaliers. Mahogany chairs do not give the impression thjat one is in India.' VL. This is Banglasdeshi cooking, with the choice of dishes and the expertees of chefing shows an experienced hand. 'Everything on the menu sems to be done well. It is a bit expensive but I have been in here many times. I just love it all.' SL. Nargiss Kabab, £2.20, which is a hard boiled egg, covered with spicy mince kebab meat, then baked and fried, attracts a lot of attention. 'It is really like a scotch egg, I have never seen this before.' ML. Sobjee Samosa, £1.95 (standard Vegetable Samosa) has excited more than one of our correspondants. 'They are so fresh and so tasty.' CW. 'I did something that I have never done before in an Indian restaurant, in fact any restaurant. I said to the waiter, 'I don't know what to choose, I leave it to you.' 'Of course you can sir, how much do you want to spend.' That was a clever answer. There were four of us, so I said make it fourty five pounds, but make the dishes very unusual. He did and brought us Horan Masala, which was venison baked in the tandoor and then cooked with onions, tomatoes and green pepper in a dry sauce for £7.25. Batak Masala, tandooried Duck in a coconut and spicy sauce for £6.45. Buaal Masala, Indian fish, a Bangladeshi dish with tomatoes and

onion, £5.40. Kofta Masala, £4.80, ground meat balls cooked in a spicy sauce. The rest of the meal was made up of breads and rice and accompaniments. The whole meal, with drinks and coffee came to exactly £45.00. I was very impressed.' GC. 'An excellent restaurant, the menu is so different from anywhere else, they even do Pheasant on occasions. The Sunday Special Buffet at £6.75 a head, represents good value.' KS. This establishment gets very busy and booking is recommended. They are offering discounts to Curry Club members at their quiete times, see page 288. We see this as a very good restaurant, and we have decide to include it into our TOP 100.

WALLINGFORD

THE PRINCE OF INDIA **CC DISCOUNT**
31, High Street, Wallingford. Tel: 0491 35394
As we have mentioned in the Abingdon entry, that THE PRINCE OF INDIA has several branches in the area. This is one, 'It has a varied menu including one or two unusual dishes, including Tandoori Rainbow Trout and Special Beef, a steak in a spicy sauce. Chicken and lamb House Specials were quite delicious and the quantities were generous, quality is extremley good and service friendly, efficient and good. We have never been disappointed with a meal here and it is becoming increasingly popular so reserve your table, a must on Friday and Saturday evenings. Booths are wonderfully private for two but cramped for four. My only critisism is that I wished they did tea. It is expensive but worth it.' VBK. Prices are the same at all branches of The Prince of India, with at Popadoms 55p, Chicken Curry £3.95, Pullao Rice £1.50, Set dinner for two £32. There is a minimum charge of £5.00 per person, but no service or cover charges and all branches will give Curry Club members a discount of 10% on takeaway meals only, see page 288.

SHROPSHIRE

BRIDGNORTH

THE EURASIA TANDOORI
21, West Castle Street, Bridgnorth. Tel: 07462 4895
This is a safe bet with no surprises on the menu, but with everything you would expect to find. The service is competant and the prices are fare.

THE OLD COLONIAL
3, Bridge Street, Low Town, Bridgnorth. Tel: 07462 66510
This is a restaurant with a difference it is set in an old English tudor beamed cottage and serves dinner only. 'The food is attractively presented and served and we use this place regularly.' AF. Has one other note worthy asset which could well be unique in the UK, a takeaway service with a difference, they will come out to your home with a complete meal, serve you and do the washing up. What a service!. It is hard to know what to call this service, perhaps a 'bring away service.' 'We use it from time to time, it does cost more than usual, but it gives you a wonderful sense of luxury and well being and is worth an entry in the guide just or that.' DM.

LUDLOW

THE SHAPLA TANDOORI
17, Tower Street, Ludlow. Tel: 0584 2033
'This is a scruffy place with grubby carpets, tablecloths and plonky Indian music. It was a third full, and we got a warm welcome. My starter was Chicken Tikka pieces which took twenty minutes to arrive and looked

harrased when it did. But with the assistance of the hot paprika and pepper sauce which was very piquent and tasty, I forgave it. The main meals arrived, chucked onto the plates in lumps, my Bombay Duck was as wooly as old socks, but the main meals were delicious. There was plenty of meat, it wasn't fatty and there were lots of fascinating spicy flavours, over all wonderful. Finally the coffee, this was the worstl have ever had bar one, perhaps they were using sterlised milk or sterilised coffee. We weren't charged for the coffee. Scruffy presentation, poor drinks, but amazing food.' RC. Other reports have included, 'It has an exquisite menu with generous portions. They are always busy, a good idea to book at weekends.' 'Starters were very light and crispy, Samosas and the Chef Specialities of Korhai and Chicken Masala were both served sizzlingly hot. Nan Bread, Raita and Bhajias were all excellent.' B and JW. We would like more reports please.

SHREWSBURY

THE CURRY HOUSE
29, Nardol, Shrewsbury. Tel: 0743 56035
This restaurant has been in the Good Curry Guide Pages before and your reports describe it as a reasonable restaurant, probably the best in Shrewsbury.' AN. More reports please.

TELFORD

THE JEWEL IN THE CROWN **CC DISCOUNT**
51, High Street, Dawley, Telford. Tel: 0952 502729
This restaurant opened in 1986 and supplies the needs of the people of Dawley with a good standard well cooked and presented curry. 'We went there when it first opened, and have been going ever since, the manager always recognises us and the staff are very friendly, full marks for them.' RR. This restaurant is offering 10% discounts to Curry Club members at their quieter times, see page 288.

MISTER DAVE'S BALTI HOUSE
2, Burton Street, Telford. Tel: 0952 503955
Mr Dave we are told is an English man who opened his first Indian restaurant in Lye, West Midlands (see entry) in the mid '80's. This his second branch, opened in 1987. Balti dishes are pre-prepared stir-fries using the Indian cooking implement the 'Karahi' and you can have any combination of ingredients served in your 'balti', thus leading to an apparently long and comprehensive menu. Mr Dave's restaurant is unlicenced, but you are encouraged to bring in your own drink. It has very basic decor, but is very clean. Prices are extremely reasonable, there is no cutlery on the table but you can ask, otherwise use your Nan or Chappati and scoop it up in traditional Indian style. 'The food is very delicious, very filling and very cheap, service is so friendly it is like eating in your own home.' RLR.

SOMERSET

FROME

BELASH TANDOORI
8, The Bridge, Frome. Tel: 0373 63567
Whilst there are very few Indian restaurants in the county of Somerset we are blessed with a good number of regular correspondents. They tell us that the Belash serves standard curries in the standard way and with reasonable prices.

THE RAJ TANDOORI
29, High Street, Glastonbury.
The small town of Glastonbury is celebrated for its Druid Summer Solstice. However, there is another reason that our correspondents wish to draw it to our attention The Raj Tandoori, is exceptionally good and doing remarkable business considering it is in such a small town. Indeed, we reported about it in our two previous Good Curry Guide's and following that it appeared in the Good Food Guide. It seems to have coped well with all this notoriety with the food remaining above average, the prices remaining reasonable and the service, as always, friendly.' PJ. More reports welcomed.

TAUNTON

THE GANGES **CC DISCOUNT**
93/95, Station Road, Taunton. Tel: 0823 284967
This restaurant is part of a small chain of six Ganges restaurant which became established in the West Country during the 1980's. They have branches in Plymouth, Torquay, Tavistock, Truro and Penzance, see separate entries. Their latest venture brings to Taunton a new standard of restaurateuring. 'This must be the best decorated restaurant in Somerset, it really looks expensive. The front seems to be pure marble with marble extended into the bar and takeaway reception area. The restaurant, itself, is well bestowed with mirrors, hand painted pictures, furniture and light fittings imported from Portugal. With its air conditioning it is very smart, very comfortable and very lush.' DS. The management at this sixty seat establishment have taken the sensible decision of not opening at lunch time so concentrating only on their evening trade, seven days a week. The menu is the standard type, cooked by Bangladeshis with northern and Southern Indian dishes on it. 'We went as a party of four and thoroughly enjoyed the Special Curry, Special Biriani, Shai Akbori Chicken and the Tandoori Mixed Grill which came with all the trimmings. We stayed for three hours, drunk as much coffee as we could. Hot towels and sweets were provided. All that for under £10 a head.' CL. Other typical prices include Popadoms 40p, Chicken Curry £3.75, Pullao Rice £1.75. There are no extra charges such as service or cover and the restaurant offers a 20% discount for takeaway meals only to Curry Club members, see page 288.

Our correspondents tell us of three other standard curry houses dotted around in the county's main towns, where you will be warmly received and you'll be served good standard currys. These are: The Akash, The Parade, Minehead; The Shalimar, 59, High Street, Wellington and The Taj Mahal, 100, Middle Street, Yeovil.

STAFFORDSHIRE

CODSAL

THE RAJPUT
The Square, Codsal. Tel: 090 74 4642
Codsal is a small town on the outskirts of Wolverhampton. It is near the airport and the racecourse, but is just sufficiently far away from that big city to be in the county of Staffordshire. The Rajput has been brought to our attention by several of our correspondents: 'It is in an old tudor building making it an unlikely Indian restaurant. There is a small comfortable reception area with a bar, where you can get Papadoms and nibbles. Upstairs is the restaurant, where you will find a nicely decorated beamed dining room. The menu seems to be

quite limited and contains none of the hotter curries, but the waiter assured us that the kitchen could make virtually any dish that we liked. On the whole the meal was delicious, except for the Chat which lacked definition.' More reports welcomed.

GNOSAL

RAJIES
High Street, Gnosal.
With a population of just over 3,000, it seems unlikely that this village would have an Indian restaurant. But, it has, so it just goes to show that the 'every village has one' syndrome is upon us. Even though it is such small place we get correspondence about it. (There aren't many Indian restaurant in the UK about which we don't). 'I knew the manager from the Rajput in Codsal (see previous entry) he recognised us immediately and welcomed us. We purused the menu. It was the same as the Rajput, when the food arrived it was the same quality too, superb; the chef had moved with the manager. We declare it to be amongst the best Indian meals that we have had.' SA. 'The Indian waitresses here were dressed in sarees, which makes a really pleasant change. The restaurant is built in converted old time building and we'll visit again.' MM. More reported wanted.

LEEK

ALMINAR
17, St Edwards Street, Leek. Tel: 0538
As we said last time, the former 'Empress of India', Queen Victoria, sets the scene at the Alminar as she watches the proceedings along with Indian Royals, in the form of paintings on the walls. The menu remains extensive, serving the many curry and tandoori favourites, heat graded from one star - mild, to six star - very hot. 'And it is very hot, very very hot.' SR. The prices are very reasonable and the service is 'more than friendly' and as we also said last time, some will be pleased to know that the world champion darts player, Eric Bristow, uses this restaurant as his local. More reports welcomed.

LICHFIELD

THE EASTERN EYE **TOP 100 & CC DISCOUNT**
19, Bird Street, Lichfield. Tel: 0543 254399
This restaurant opened in 1985. Reports flow into our office on a regular and prolific basis about this restaurant. Within a year it found itself in the pleasant position of having to extend from its relatively small size to a larger eighty seats. The first thing to say about this restaurant is that its owner Mr Abdul Salam, winces when ever he hears the word curry. This is reflected on the menu which is as far from the standard Indian menu as you can get. The word curry does not appear on it, indeed, says Mr Salam, 'we don't serve curry here, all our food is individually spiced and special'. It is quite a big claim but judging by the reports that we receive it is a fair claim. The menu selection is carefully put together with 'unusual' dishes from all over India. All the dishes are carefully described and they say from which part of India they come. For example: Vhoojelo Gosht comes from Kashmir, and this is barbequed lamb with fresh Papaya which is widely used in many parts of the world for tenderising meat. This recipe is given extra 'zing' by the use of Worcester Sauce, £7.50. The starters include Tandoori Machchi which is a Bengali fish dish, £3.95 and Buttey Kebab, (their spelling for Boti and not for a meat sandwich). It is described as a delicately spiced Lamb Kebab cooked in the tandoor, £2.95. The Banquet is well worth investigation. It consists of a huge number of dishes. Mr Salam himself is usually there and enjoys a chat about the food. He and his staff will warn you that you may have to wait a litle, because the food requires enough time to cook properly and that's why the food is unique. We highly recommend the place, infact we think its exceptional.' BW. The Good Curry Guide agrees with you and we are putting this restaurant amongst our TOP 100. It is advisable to book as it is normally busy and despite this it will offer a discount to Curry Club members on Sundays only, see page 288 for details.

LICHFIELD

JASMINE
20, Bird Street, Lichfield. Tel: 0543 262581
The arrival of the Eastern Eye has undoubtedly caused the Jasmine to try even harder to appeal to its clients. We heard in the last GCG of a reporter who took up the commonly quoted restaurant addage 'that if a dish isn't on the menu, we'll cook it.' The reporter asked for a Dream' dish which included all sorts of ingredients, eg: prawns, chicken, lamb etc, cooked in a particular style. Our reporter said, 'this dish was produced enthusiastically, at little extra cost.' It evidently fired off a spate of copiers, because we have had other reports about this 'dream' dish, not just here but at other restaurants too. 'The Jasmine has an extensive menu, the quantities are extremely generous and the service good. Fifteen of us visited, starters included almost one of everything, Tikkas through to Bhajias, they were all nice and succulent. The main course included Veg Biriani, Tikka Masala, Vindaloo, Medium dishes and Tandooris. It was one of the best meals that we have ever had. The food was all brought together and with burners to keep it warm. At the need of the meal they gave us free Tia Marias with our coffee and mints. For fifteen people the food came to £113, the drinks £13 and the service £4.00. Extremely good value for money.' PV.

STAFFORD

THE CURRY KUTEER
31, Greengate Street, Stafford. Tel: 0785 53279
We receive an above average number of reports on this restaurant, for example 'This is a cosy, split level restaurant with seating for about 50 people. We had a delicious Biriani. We were happy in all aspects.' DR. At one time the Curry Kuteer and the Purbani (see next entrant) were owned by two partners, The Parbani was the upmarket establishment and the Curry Kuteer somewhat down market, but attracted enough customers. The partnership split up, taking a restaurant each. Since the split about four years ago the Curry Kuteer's menu has gone from strength to strength and it definitely takes the edge.' ET. Reports welcomed.

THE PURBANI
14, Bailey Street, Stafford. Tel: 0785 46800
'When ever I feel like going out for an Indian meal in town, I go to the Purbani. Over recent years it has expanded its somewhat restricted menu and the variety of food competes admirable with the Curry Kuteer (see previous entry). I have recently had an excllent Chicken Karahi and a Prawn Dhansak there and I always enjoy their Mulligatawany Soup and the Kathi Naan Bread. Companions have spoken highly of the Tandoori Chicken Salad.' PT. Reports welcomed.

STOKE ON TRENT

AL SHEIKH'S BALTI CENTRE
15, Howard Place, Shelton. Tel: 0782 285583
'This restaurant has pine and tiles decor and it is unlicenced, but you can bring your own. If you decide to wait at the pub around the corner, ask the waiter to call to fetch you when your table is ready. A unique service, surely? The Liver Tikka was unusual and delicious and came with a chilli and garlic sauce as well as the usual raita. Naan breads were enormous, three of us failed to finish two even though we had no rice.' PV. More reports welcomed.

SHAHEEN **CC DISCOUNT**
24, Sandon Road, Meir. Tel: 0782 319620
The Shaheen opened in 1987 and has taken the crown of honour in Stoke by becoming the town's most popular restaurant. Our correspondents tell us of a smartly presented restaurant with 'a very enjoyable cocktail bar' AH and a fully comprehensive menu. It contains over twenty starters, and every type of curry from very mild Korma to extra hot Tindaloo, with prices between £3.25 and £4.75. The restaurant has a Balti section with prices

ranging from £3.55 for meat and £5.85 for King Prawn. Prices include Popadoms 25p each, Pullao Rice £1.15 and there's a minimum charge of £4.80 per head. The restaurant operates an evening trade only and closes at weekends at 2.30 in the morning. Just to prove that there are people that use restaurants at this time: 'Sometimes the canteen gets very dull and we like to go and get a late night takeaway, when we are on night shift. The Shaheen, fits the bill perfectly, not only for its hours, but for the food. I got six different curries for me and my mates and I got the surprise of my life when another customer walked in and ordered four different takeaways, all of which were English, steak, chicken, omlettes, salads, apple pies, the lot. It stuck me as being rather funny.' DL. The restaurant offers discounts to Curry Club members at its quieter times, see page 288.

STONE

THE CROWN OF INDIA
Hilton House, Market Square, Stone. Tel: 0785 814911
This is a relatively newly opened restaurant which is not to easy to find. 'This is a funny little place located in the upstairs of a building at the back of Market Square. The food is good and reasonably priced, so it is definitely worth a visit when you are in the area.' NN. More reports welcomed.

TOWNSTALL

THE KASHMIR GARDEN, **CC DISCOUNT**
257, High Street, Townstall. Tel: 0782 839366
This restaurant opened in 1989, it is attractive and elegant with a red brick archway facade, and a colour scheme of saffron yellow, contrasting with brick red napkins and velour mahogany chairs. It has a fully comprehensive but standard curry house menu. It links itself to Kashmir, by Chicken Kashmir, a dish prepared with fresh fruit and cream for £4.30. Its Balti dishes are served in a traditional Karahi £4.50. Other specials include Chicken Tikka Mossala £4.30, Chicken Jalfrezi 34.30, Tandoori Trout £4.90. Popadoms are 25p each, Chicken Curry £2.95, Pullao Rice £1.20. There is no minimum charge, service charge or cover charge and the restaurant is offering discounts to Curry Club members at its quieter times, see page 288 for details.

UTTOXETER

THE INDUS TANDOORI
Queen Street, Uttoxeter. Tel: 0889 5023
This restaurant appeared in our first GCG in 1984 and we are glad to see it back again in this edition as a result of regular reports. 'This place takes some beating we have been regular customers of a number of years and have always been satisfied. The staff are always very friendly.' N and GD. More reports please.

SUFFOLK

BECCLES

THE BOMBAY RESTAURANT
1, Exchange Square, Beccles.
Tel: 0502 717610
This restaurant opened in late 1983 and was immediately popular. It appeared in both our previous GCGs. It is one of a similarly named chain (see Norwich). The menu and prices and general

standard of the restaurant are identical to that of the Norwich branches. Therefore, prices are reasonable and the service friendly and competetant.

BURY

THE SHAPLA
29, Mustow Street, Bury-St-Edmunds. Tel: 0284 60819
'Curry is more popular than you think in Bury. To prove it we have a very good restaurant, named the Shapla.' DF. No, this quote wasn't from the restaurant's owner, because we have had many reports like it. Correspondents speak of the Shapla being their favourite, tidy, attractive with good food. More reports welcomed.

HADLEIGH

THE ROYAL BENGAL
High Street, Hadleigh. Tel: 0473 823744
This restaurant is in the same ownership as the Royal Bengal, Woodbridge and the Royal Tandoori, Stowmarket. (see separate write-up). 'The meal and the service at this restaurant is always impeccable. We often eat in a party of four and don't expect to may more than £40 complete with trimmings and drinks. Always a great night out.' RDC.

IPSWICH

THE BOMBAY RESTAURANT
60, Orwell Place, Ipswich. Tel: 0473 251324
This restaurant was formerly, The Rajastan. It was taken over by the Bombay of Norwich Group, in 1988. See The Bombay under Norwich for full details of menu and prices etc. 'The food and presentation are excellent. It was the best Onion Bhajia I have had and I have never seen a Keema Naan with so much meat. The service was impeccable.' RDC.

THE IPSWICH TANDOORI
46a, Norwich Road, Ipswich. Tel: 0473 257207
Most restaurants with any measure of competelence attract a regular hardcore following and the Ipswich Tandoori is no exception. 'We find everything about the Ipswich just right, it's cheaper than its rivals, better than some of them, they know us well and we feel at home. We visit at least once a fortnight, sometimes once a week, we don't bother to go anywhere else.' TA. 'I have noticed when I have used the takeaway that the portions are larger.' RDC.

LOWESTOFT

THE BOMBAY RESTAURANT
Pier Terrace, Lowestoft. Tel: 0502
Another restaurant in the Bombay Norwich chain. See entry for full details of menu and prices. 'I was on holiday here visited here no less than three times in two weeks, it was excellent.' CSJ.

THE SOMRAAT TANDOORI
30, Old Station Road, Newmarket.
This restaurant has a sound and loyal following. 'I can't fault it, the service was prompt, friendly and polite. The food, well, the food is simply gorgeous. I am a great fan of King Prawn Jalfrezi which is not on the menu, but, Hey Presto! you ask for it and it will be delivered to your table. The portions are so big, I've gained six pounds in weight since the restaurant opened last year. I can highly recommend the Garlic Naan and the King Prawn Karahi, both are superb.' SS. More comments are welcome.

THE ROYAL TANDOOR INTERNATIONAL
16, Tavern Street, Stowmarket. Tel: 0449 615143
In the same ownership as the Royal Bengal, Hadley and the Royal Bengal, Woodbridge. See separate entries for full details of menu and prices. One of our most regular correspondents says 'excellent, can't

fault it. We expected a lengthy wait and indeed it was an hour before we ate anything, but it really was worth the wait, high quality curries and the Kansara After Curry Mints were a really nice touch.' ND.

THE ROYAL BENGAL TANDOORI **TOP 100 & CC DISCOUNT**
6, Tuay Street, Woodbridge. Tel: 0394 7983
In the same ownership as the Royal Bengal, Woodbridge and the Royal Tandoor, Stowmarket. This branch opened in 1982 and is managed by Mr Khan. 'It is a medium sized restaurant (52 seats), with an nice Indian style atmosphere, with plants and paintings.' NO. In our first GCG we described this restaurant's menu as being one of the most attractive that we have seen. Fortunately they have not changed the menu. It's a large laminated card, its cover features a beautiful tiger, inside are pale grey drawings of Indian wild life - elephants, deer, monkeys etc, surrounded by trees and flora. Inset is a description of the dishes. 'I know you can't eat the menu, but please don't change it.' RG. One of our correspondents particularly likes the Tandoori Chicken Biriani, which is tandooried chicken chunks prepared with Pullao Rice, tossed in ghee and seasoned with various spices, brown onion, tomatoes and served with curries vegetables. 'A massive meal in itself, for £7.00.' Other favourite specials include, Chicken Tikka Masala £6.45, Meat Karahi £5.25, Chicken Jalfrezi (hot) £5.35. The Royal Bengal discourages the after pub drunks, with careful door control. Children under six are not admitted at certain hours, but those under fourteen are served children's portions and are charged accordingly. 'Excellent, can't fault,' says RDC, and we have many other reports of the same ilk. We have decided, therefore, to admit this restaurant to our TOP 100. It is advisable to book at this busy restaurant and they have consented to give Curry Club members discounts at their quieter times, see page 288 for details.

SURREY

ASHSTEAD

THE MOGHUL DYNASTY
1, Craddock Parade, Ashstead.
Tel: 03722 74810
We have received many recommendations about this relatively new restaurant, which opened in 1988. We understand that the decor is plain but refreshing, modern and pleasant and there is Bombay Mix on the tables. 'All the food is excellent, but the Tandoori Lamb Chops with Prawns, served in a pineapple shell, was among the best I've eaten there (and that's a lot) and it's so unusual. At the end of the meal they serve hot towels and pan seeds. Very good service with much more humour than normal. Very popular so book at peak times. Prices are average, and is probably our best local' DLC. and this for an area that is particularly rich for good quality restaurants.

THE CURRY HOUSE TANDOORI
61A, Street, Ashstead. Tel: 03722 77432
This restaurant is equally popular judging by reports. 'We get served good curry from a menu that contains all the curry favourites that you would expect to find, plus a few more. The Tandoori Chicken Pachanta, involving red wine at £6.25, Bamboo Shoot Bhajia (rather novel) for £1.99. Other typical prices are as follows, Chicken Curry £3.85, Pullao Rice £1.30, Popadoms 35p each. Children are welcome and special arrangements are available for private celebrations of parties from two people upwards. The Curry House, Ewell is a sister to this branch. PS. The Ragan Joosh £4.35, is not the ex American President at a Barmizva. It is the enchanting house spelling of Rhogan Josh.

BRAMLEY

THE CHAMPAN
High Street, Bramley, Nr Guildford. Tel: 0483 893684
The Champan opened in 1988, in the relatively small village of Bramley. It is located in an olde worlde, oak beamed, English Tea Shop type of building. It is tiny, split between two rooms on the ground floor. It is a branch of the longer established 'Trishna' of Haslemere, (see separate entry). It is a very cosy place, which 'has a habit of going from empty to bustingly full in a remarkable small space of time, so it is advisable to book.' DD. The Chicken Tikka Masala (DD's favourite) is £5.80, Pullao Rice £1.80 and Popadoms 45p each. It is altogether a very pleasant restaurant and an asset to the village, the only slight drawback is it's a difficult place at which to park.

CARSHALTON

THE ROSEHILL TANDOORI **CC DISCOUNT**
20, Rythe Lane, Rosehill, Carshalton. Tel: 081 644 9793
The Rose of India is owned by Mr S Rahman and it has been described as, 'An establishment where the decor is plain and simple, but where the food isn't.' RE. We hear of 'Complex spices and juicy chicken pieces in dishes such as Murgh Makhani £3, fragrant Onion Bhajias at £1.' TD. Other specialities which are highly regarded by the restaurant's followers: Gosht Palak, meat with spinach, £3.50, Gosht Pasanda £3, Jinga Masala (Prawns), Niramish (fresh vegetables cooked in minimal spices), Bhindi Do Piaza, ladies fingers with plenty of onions £1.80. Popadoms 30p each, Chicken Curry £3.00, Pullao Rice £1.30. There is a minimum charge of £6.00 but no service or cover charge. This restaurant is prepared to offer discounts to Curry Club members at its quieter times, see page 288 for details.

CROYDON

DEANS TAKE-AWAY
241, London Road, Croydon. Tel: 081 684 0239
Hours 11am till midnight. Run by a Mr Dean, who has plans to open branches all over the place with a bright modern image, with fast food service, a La Wimpy Bar or Kentucky fried Chicken, with Pakoras, Samosa, Tandooris and Sweet meats. He has branches at South Wimbledon and in Tooting. The prices are extremely reasonable with Pakoras at 60p per quarter, Samosas 45p for meat and 40p for vegetable. Chicken Curry £2.50, Pullao Rice 95p. Their best seller remains their three and a half ounce Lamb Kebab with lettuce and tamarind sauce (imli) wrapped in a chappati sort of Doner Kebab. We predicted four years ago that the day cannot be far away when big business cottons on to the potential of Indian fast food and there is a franchise Pakora Bar on every high street. Let's face it, India has been producing fast foods for thousands of years. However, the explosion has yet to happen, meanwhile visit Deans.

THE KHYBER,
204, High Street, Croydon. Tel: 081 686 1729
'You are not to expect anything earth shattering or out of the ordinary at this restaurant,' LD. It has been around for many a year and has been in both of our previous editions of our Good Curry Guide. 'It is just a regular curry house where everything gets into gear and works in perfect order.' MD. 'The staff take pleasure in your pleasure.' As an example they call two of their set piece dishes 'the menu of discovery and the menu of tasting.' Make the discovery and tell us your conclusions.

ROYAL ASIA TANDOORI **CC DISCOUNT**
91, Lower Adiscombe Road, Croydon. Tel: 081 656 7818
Has been open for nearly five years and has built up a very strong and good reputation. The owner is often to be found on site and enjoys a good natter, especially about his food and the personalities that have visited his restaurant. He will tell you with great pride that Bernard Wetherall (former speaker of the House of Commons visited there, and that Eric Bristow the

The editor of The Good Curry Guide welcomes your views on restaurants we list in this guide and on any curry restaurants or take-aways you visit. Please send them to: The Curry Club, PO Box 7, Haslemere, Surrey GU27 1EP.

darts champion has been known to roll in to stoke up. But for ordinary mortals like you and me they tell us of a very popular restaurant. It's not much to look at from the outside, but on the inside it is very tasteful and so is the food.' PK. Actually Mr Ali has a partner to the restaurant, his cousin, the chef. Some of his specials include Bangladeshi Fish Curry £5.95, Prawn Jal Frezi or Chicken at £5.50. Two set meals, called 'Discovery' for two £23.95 and £27.95. They engage a three piece sitar band from time to time, which greatly adds to the sense of the occasion. They will offer discounts to Curry Club members at their quieter times, see page 288 for details of this offer.

EGHAM

EGHAM TANDOORI
231, Pooley Green Road, Egham. Tel: 0784 451856
SHIRAZ Miah opened this restaurant in 1983. It has proved to be very popular in the local area. It operates a standard Bangladeshi Northern Indian menu with reasonable prices. Papadoms 40p, Chicken Curry £2.90, Pullao Rice £1.10 and set luncheon £6.90. Diner for one £10.90. Kurzi Lamb for four £42.00. Minimum charge is £8.00 per person and service and cover charge do not apply.

FARNCOMBE

THE FARNCOMBE TANDOORI
18, Farncombe Street, Farncombe. Tel: 048 68 23131
It has a wide and spacious and elegant frontage with expanses of glass and tiles set off against a stainless steel top. Inside there is a moulded ceiling and an overall theme of browns and white, but it is the establishment's foliage that receives the comments. 'Baby evergreen trees outside, it's like stepping into a jungle. The walls are papered with skeletons of leaves and there are hanging plant boxes everywhere.' LK. It has established a pleasant atmosphere, however, with dimming spot lights and candles on the tables. It is a standard Bangladeshi Northern Indian menu. Prices are reasonable, Popadoms 40p each, Chicken Curry £3.15, Pullao Rice £1.25. There is a two course dinner for two at £18.00. They have a sister restaurant, The Romna Curry Centre, 340, Regents Park Road, Finchley Central, London, N3.

FARNHAM

THE DARJEELING RESTAURANT
25, South Street, Farnham. Tel: 0252 714322
Farnham's Darjeeling restaurant exoludes a confidence which is strong enough to make it Farnham's most popular restaurant judging by the number of reports that we receive. The restaurants cooking is 'delicately spiced and always tasty.' JD. 'Service is so smart and friendly.' 'When ever I go for a curry it is always full, no matter what day of the week it is.' Perhaps for this reason, the restaurant opened a sister branch in Farnham called the Banares in Down Street.

FETCHAM

THE FETCHAM TANDOORI
248, Cobham Road, Fetcham. Tel: 0372 374927
This restaurant is very well established and very well attended and it is not only popular with its locals but it seems to achieve a regular amount of press. We also receive good comments about it, for example, 'offers the best Phall, the hottest curry, we've ever tasted - we often drive from Bromley just to visit this place. If you like curries that are so hot that you can only just finish them, this is the place. Sag Bhajee is the best we've had, fresh spinach not at all slimy!. We've been visiting this restaurant regularly over the last ten years.' A & DB.

GODALMING

THE GODALMING TANDOORI
143, High Street, Godalming. Tel: 0483 426084
This restaurant which was formerly called The Shapla and is Godalming's favourite. It serves a typical menu of curry favourites. One correspondent raves over the Korma and the Naan bread.' SS.

THE RAJAH TANDOORI
Headley Road, Grayshott, Hindhead. Tel: 0428 73 5855
'I had a craving for a curry that night, it was dark and misty and as I got out of the car I had a vision across the street of two white turbaned, white apronned kitchen workers, possibly chefs. They were so clean they hadn't done a stroke of work, but they were cleaning up a mass of spilt litter. It appears that a lorry had backed over their litter sacks earlier in the day. The restaurant is long and thin and decorated in hues of blue. The ceiling is like a canopy of tents. Popadoms 35p each were warm and crisp, chutneys cost 40p but were not removed during our meal, the Chicken Tikka Masala at £4.75, contained large chunks of chicken breast which had been skewered from the tandoor. The Prawn Vindaloo £3.85, which was Madras strength swam with prawns. Nans at £1.20 were buttery and fluffy. The Pullao Rice £1.35, was well cooked but a small portion - they must have been concerned that I didn't eat too much carbohydrate. Bombay Potato £1.85 was not too hot and was made from a concentrated onion base - lovely. All that and a drink or five for £30 for two.' DD.

GUILDFORD

THE SHAHEE MAHAL **CC DISCOUNT**
50, Chertsey Road, Guildford. Tel: 0483 572572
This restaurant opened in 1970 which makes it Guildford's earliest and it has a rather patchy standard. Sometimes we receive good reports and sometimes not so good. It's owner Mr Uddin, is very much aware that the menu is a cliche and is concentrating on a new menu and new decor. We welcome reports on the new style Shahee Mahal. Meanwhile, Popadoms are 40p, Chicken Curry £3.10, Pullao Rice £1.40, Minimum charge of £8.00 a head. There is no service or cover charge and the restaurant will offer discounts to curry Club members at its quieter times, see page 288 for details of this offer.

HASLEMERE

THE SIMLA RESTAURANT **CC DISCOUNT**
84, Weyhill, Haslemere. Tel: 0428 643885
Haslemere is the home town of the editor of this Guide, and in common with every other restaurant goer, he had his old habbits and his old favourite local haunts. The Simla is one of them. In our last guide, we said that in the small town of Haslemere there is an abundance of Haute Cuisine. It still exists with a string of very expensive restaurants of all nationalities, many of which regularly get themselves to the Good Food Guides. In the face of such rarified atmosphere, it is perhaps not suprising that Haslemere Indian restaurants, of there are three, are also quite good. The Simla was the last of the three to arrive in the town and its decor is perhaps the best, with individual booths divided by hand engraved, back lit tinted window screens and skeleton leaves wall paper. The service is always exceptionally friendly, even if you have a takeaway, you sit in a comfortable lounge area, eating as many Bombay Mix nibbles that you care to eat, whilst you sup a drink. The menu contains all the old favourites, the cooking is generally very good with rich creamy tasty sauces. From time to time, however, the standards can be a bit patchy, maybe on the main cook's night off. This restaurant is prepared to offer discount for Curry Club members at its quieter times, see page 288 for details of this offer.

THE TRISHNA TANDOORI
64, Weyhill, Haslemere. Tel: 0428 643854 **CC DISCOUNT**
The food at this restaurant at times, particularly early in the week, can be very very tasty and good indeed. At weekends, when the pressure is on the quality seems to slip a bit, but it is still acceptable. It also happens to

have two branches, The Mowchak Tandoori, 207, Havant Road, Drayton, Portsmouth in Hampshire and The Champan Tandoori, Bramshot (see entry), which are both very acceptable restaurants. However, the editor was at the Trishna very recently when an incident occured which in all probability should exclude this restaurant from this guide. A diner on the table next to mine found a hair in her main course meal, she at once complained to the manager who loudly disclaimed all responsibility. 'It's a long hair,' he said, 'My chef's have short hair, therefore it can't be from my chef's.' The diner demonstrated that she didn't care who's hair it was, that fact was that it was there and it was unpleasant. A very loud and ugly row ensued, the bill was asked for, adjustments were made by the diners, not the manager who said, 'don't come to my restaurant again,' shutting the door behind them. The moral of this restaurant is that no matter how good the food it is very easy to turn off a restaurant full of eager customers, one of whom may be a food editor, and most of whom will probably never go there again. Reports welcomed. The Trishna gives discounts to Curry Club members at its quieter times, see page 288.

KINGSTON

THAMES SIDE TANDOORI
54, High Street, Kingston. Tel: 081 549 6216
'Excellent decor, with friendly and efficient service.' Specialities of the house are well worth asking for, the Chicken Jal Frezi and the Tandoori King Prawn Masala are both excellent.' KP.

NEW MALDEN

HAWELLI INDIAN **CC DISCOUNT**
1, St Georges Indian, High Street, New Malden. Tel: 081 942 2858
There are three in the chain, this one, another at Feltham and the third at Sutton. The New Malden branch is the newest and we're told it is already a great favourite with regulars in this district, which is already very well endowed with Curry Restaurants. 'The outside is fairly plain and perhaps leads you to believe that there will be nothing special inside. However, when you do step over the threshold, you'll find a very expensive airy restaurant which I like to visit as much at lunchtime as in the evening.' MF. The menu contains all the regular items you'd expect to find, in addition there are a dozen or so Hawelli Specials, 'Lamb Pasanda is my favourite, it is cooked with cream and coconut, almonds and sultanas and red wine.' EH. There is a particularly nice nutty dish called Badami, cooked with cashew nuts and another cooked with chilli which I adore.' SH. Particularly popular is the Sunday buffets which at £5.95 for adults and £4.50 for children enable diner to eat as much as they like and go back to the buffet as often as they like. Popadoms 35p each, Chicken Curry £3.05, Pullao Rice £1.35. There are no additional charges and this restaurant is prepared to give discounts to Curry Club members at their quieter times, see page 288 for details.

PURLEY

THE ARALYA **TOP 100**
11, Purley Parade, High Street, Purley. Tel: 081 660 3654
The Aralya is a Sri Lankan restaurant and there aren't to any of those around anywhere in the UK. Sri Lankan food has some resemblance to the food of South India. There is great emphasis on cooking in coconut with lentils and rice flour, there is no use of wheat, chillies are predominant and vegetable and fish dishes are very popular. There are no restrictions on beef, mutton or pork. The cooking at the Aralya, is, we understand extremely good and it is certainly unlike any standard curry house that you will find in the country. 'When we first came to the restaurant, we were not sure whether we would like the food. We did and now we come as regulars.' EL. The food will certainly be unfamiliar to most diners but the staff are told extremely helpful in deciphering the menu. Starters include Devilled Beef or Pork, Sate, Mala Vade which are fish cutlets. Four people can enjoy the Arayla Special Platter which includes a number of starters with a salad. String Hoppers are a kind of Sri Lankan noodle made from rice flour, six cost £1.65. A plain hopper is a plain flour

pancake costing 70p, an Egg Hopper includes an egg in the middle for £1. Plain Godamba are square pancakes folded in at £1.30 and an egg version is £1.50. Koltu Roti is a rice flour bread enhanced with coconut and tomato. Fish dishes include Amul Thail which is tuna fish curry at £3.60. Pava Malu is a white jack fish served in a coconut curry for £3.60 and Badun is a blue runner fried with spices for £3.60. There are a good selection of vegetable dishes, all are fresh, none from tins, say the management. These include Fried Potato Curry, Pumpkin and coconut milk Green Beans. We very highly recommend this restaurant and are pleased to include it into our TOP 100, see page 25.

THE INDIA PALACE TANDOORI **CD DISCOUNT**
11, Russell Parade, Russell Hill, Purley. Tel: 081 660 6411
For a more conventional kind of curry house, Purley has on offer the India Palace. It's menu is perfectly standard and includes all the curry favourites which according to our correspondents are served particularly well. Typical prices are popadoms 40p each, Chicken Curry £3.20, Pullao Rice £1.50. The restaurant offers a 10% discount on takeaways and is also prepared to offer discounts to Curry Club members at their quieter times, see page 288 for details.

SANDERSTEAD

THE DIWANA
49, Limsfield Road, Sanderstead. Tel: 081 651 1121
This is a very well established restaurant with a regular following. 'It is well furnished with smart decor, the service is prompt and very attentive. The food is very tasty, although the portions are relatively small. However, the quality is usually fine. The Mixed Biriani, £6.35 is very nice, and so it should be at that price. The rice is outstanding and the restaurant is worth visiting anytime.' TD.

SHALFORD

THE VICEROY
2, Kings Road, Shalford, Nr Guildford. Tel: 0483 300239
This relatively newly opened restaurant is typical of the newer restaurants, that it is placed in a very small village with a population of less than 3,000, in the unlikely location opposite the village green. The outside appearance is very inviting and so is the interior. It is an attractively decorated restaurant, the service is extremely friendly, the food, while not outstanding, is cooked competetently and very tasty. More reports welcomed.

SURBITON

THE AGRA
142, Ewell Road, Surbiton. Tel: 081
There are many good curry houses in this area of Surrey and the Agra, it appears is one of the most popular. 'It is one of these places that always seems to be busy and where they have the formula just right.' JD. That formula consists of attentive service which is, 'never over the top, yet they never keep you waiting and never flap when they are busy, which they frequently are.' KR. It has a standard menu, with all the old favourite and no surprises that you can be sure of a reasonably priced good curry night out.

MANTANA **CC DISCOUNT**
9, Claremont Road, Surbiton. Tel: 081 390 3361
The Mantana formerly the Pattaya is a Thai restaurant which opened in 1985. This makes it one of the earlier Thai restaurants in the UK. The restaurant seats approximately sixty and the decor is pale blues and pale pinks with Thai tapestry wall hangings and plants. The tables consist of Laura Ashley linen with curtains to match. The atmosphere is gentle and sutble and light music plays in the back ground. It is a pleasure to review Thai restaurants as the food is usually so refreshing and spicily different. The Mantane is no exception and we have received many a review from our Surbiton reporters. Starter include Crab Claws £2.95, Sate £3.25,

Pu-cha (deep fried crab meat with pork and carrot) £2.95. It also includes snails, mussels and prawns. Three Thai soups and four cold appetisers, which include a squid salad. As is so often with Thai restaurants, the staff a number of women, including the owner Miss SP Weerapan. There is a minimum charge of £3.50, for a quick lunch, set dinner from £8.99 to £14.50. Surcharge of 12%. The restaurant is prepared to offer a discount to curry club members at its quieter times, see page 288.

SUTTON

THE HAWELLI **CD DISCOUNT**
135/137, Epsom Road, Stonecot Hill, Sutton. Tel: 081
This restaurant is relatively new, opening in Summer 1990. It is set in the former Epsom Steak House, and is the sister to branches in FeLtham and New MaldEn. It appears that this restaurant has become just as popular as its sisters in a remarkably short space of time. We have received many applauding reports. The decor is soft and pinky. Velvety furniture is enhanced with mirrors on the ceiling and chandeliers. Two quite large fish tanks are beside the baR. The waiters are more than used to ribald jokes about the Tandoori Fish that swim in the tank. The owner Mr Mozu Choudhury, is often on hand and enjoys talking to his customers about the food. He will tell you that his head chef Harun, has been in the business for twenty years and enjoys preparing special dishes which are not on the menu. The Specials, which are oN the menu include Chicken Rezalla £5.50, Lamb or Chicken Pasanada, cooked with almonds, coconut, sultanas and butter for £5.50, Tikka Korai Lamb, lamb marinated in various spices and cooked in butter with a thick sauce, also avaliable as a chicken version for £5.25. Kebab Cocktail Masala, as assortment of kebabs in a mild sauce for £6.25. Popadoms are 35p each, Chicken Curry £3.05, Pullao Rice £1.35 and Sunday Buffet is good value at £5.95. There are no other charges. The restaurant gives face towels and coffee sweets to its guests and is prepared to offer a discount to Curry Club members at lunch times, see page 288.

THE SHAPLA **CD DISCOUNT**
77, Stonecot Hill, Sutton. Tel: 081 644 6340
This popular restaurant opened in 1985. It is fully air-conditioned and is decorated in a pink scheme with plants and candle lights, pink table cloths and napkins. The menu contains a number of starters including tikkas and kebabs, samosas and soups. They serve the regular range of tandoori dishes and chef's specials include a Shahi Lamb or Chicken Korma for £4.75, chunks of meat cooked with cream and yoghurt, garnished with pistachios and almonds. Butter Chicken is highly spoken of where chicken pieces are cooked with cream, almonds, ghee and coocnut for £4.75. The Shapla Special includes a curry with fruits, such as pineapple, lychee and eggs and served with Pea Pulao Rice, for two people £20.15. Popadoms are 40p each, Chicken Curry £3.10, Pullao Rice £1.30. There are no extra charges and the restaurant is prepared to offer discounts to Curry Club members at its quieter times, see page 288.

TADWORTH

THE KHYBER RESTAURANT
2, Water House Lane, Kinsgwood, Tadworth. Tel: 0737 52813
This restaurant, which has been running for ten years is well established and has recently been redecorated. The menu has the usual wide choice of tempting dishes, two of which are Raj's Murgi £6.50, Begum Bahar £5.10, both are popular chicken dishes. Popadoms are 35p each, Chicken Curry £3.60, Pullao Rice £1.40. There is a minimum charge of £5.50.

THORNTON HEATH

TANDOORI NIGHTS
442, White Horse Road, Thornton Heath. Tel: 081 684 4736
This smart newish restaurant has captured the imagination of the locals and it is becoming very popular and well reported. The cooking, it

appears, is careful and subtle, the ambibence is excellent and 'The restaurant is an asset to the district.' SL. More reports welcomed.

TOLWORTH

THE JAIPUR
90, The Broadway, Tolworth. Tel: 081 399 9165

Right from the beginning when this relatively new restaurant was built it was going to be different. The exterior decor is unmissable, largely because of its huge ornate pillars. Incidentally, not initially popular with the local council who decided they were ugly. But ugly this restaurant is not. It is very striking. Jaipur is a city in Northern India, in which in every single building is pink, this is a tradition that started because the natural building material was pink sand stone. Even new buildings today are painted various hughes of pink. Naturally, the Jaipur in Tolworth is decked out in colours of pink. 'I have been here a few times and have enjoyed it very much. The most amazing sugar pink decor, dancing ladies seemed to be sculpted out of the walls.' DD. 'It seats 49 people and was empty when we arrived but not for long. Our onion Bhajia came in four separate pieces, the Chicken Madras was not that hot but was excellent. I hope it remains as good.' TB. Starters include Chicken Chat Puri, spicy chicken and chick peas served with puffy fried bread. £2.50. Jingre Dhal Soup, prawns in a spicy soup £2.50. Main courses include Chicken or Lamb Jafrani £5.25, barbecued and cooked with nuts in a spicy sauce. Chicken or Lamb Palak £4.95, cooked with spinach. There is a good selection of vegetable dishes are this restaurant is to be thoroughly recommended.

WALLINGTON

THE AKASH TANDOORI
145, Stafford Road, Wallington. Tel: 081 647 5592

The Akash has been trading in Wallington since 1978. It is attractively decorated and seats 58 people. The menu is comprehensive and includes Bhoonas to Vindaloos, with a normal cast list of sundries. Non vegetarian Thali £9.55 and Tandoori Mixed Grill at £6.55. Other prices are Popadoms 40p each, Chicken Curry £3.20, Pullao Rice £1.30. There is a minimum charge of £8.00.

WARLINGHAM

THE WARLINGHAM TANDOORI
14, The Green, Warlingham. Tel: 088 32 2362

'I particularly enjoyed the Tikka Masala, the Madras being too hot for me. My colleague commented that it was nearly as hot as a Vindaloo. (so it should be if correctly cooked - Ed). The Garlic Nan struck us as really special.' RT.

WEYBRIDGE

THE GAYLORD
73, Queens Road, Weybridge. Tel: 0932 842895

We have not noticed any decline in this restaurant's popularity, despite the opening of competitiors in the Weybridge area. It is a small restaurant and as we said before in the previous GCG it is essential to book a table. 'Be prepared to wait when they are busy, but also be prepared for really good food.' ET.

GOLDEN CURRY — CD DISCOUNT
132, Oatland Drive, Weybridge. Tel: 0932 846931

This restaurant manages to break the mould by having green flock wall paper instead of red. But the menu is fairly standard stuff, with nothing missing. 'The menu says on request we can serve other Indian dishes not included on this menu, I particularly wanted a King Prawn Pullao, so I asked for it and within ten minutes, I got it, it was absolutely delicious.' TD. Another reporter tells of the excellent King Prawn Masala at £9.95. Other prices include Popadoms 40p, Chicken Curry £3.40, Pullao Rice £1.70

and there is a rather steep minimum charge of £10.95. However, the restaurant is interested in offering discounts to Curry Club members at its quieter times, see page 288 for details.

SUSSEX

BEXHILL

THE SHIPLU
109, London Road, Bexhill-On-Sea.
Tel: 0424 219159
This Bexhill branch is the newest of three Shiplu's situated in East Sussex. It opened in 1989 to popular acclaim, especially of their sizzling dishes of which PR says, 'I thought Concorde was landing when they served my Tandoori Mixed Grill at £7.50 and it tasted just as good.' Their menu describes the Tandoori Musalla (their spelling) as being served in a quiet and mild sauce (SC calls it 'delicious') and it also describes their medium hot dish as 'mild spices'. The other two Shiplu's are at the same standard in 5, Norman Road, St Leonards on Sea and 177a, Queens Road, Hastings. All three restaurants offer discounts to Curry Club members at their quieter times, see page 288. Typical prices are Popadoms 35p, Chicken Curry £2.75 and Pullao Rice £1.05. Set dinners are from £8.00.

BILLINGHURST

TANDOORI VILLAGE
42, High Street, Billinghurst. Tel: 0403 784735
We have had years of satisfactory reports such as 'Can always count on good quality food. Not the cheapest but excellent value for money,' PF and 'Has deservedly become my favourite in a wide area,' LT. Just recently we received a report on cold food 'which the waiter offered to put in into the microwave', BM. We believe this to be untypical although the service has remained 'leisurely' for years. The setting is unique being in an Olde English 15th century converted forge and there is a large car park.

BOSHAM

THE WISHING WELL
The Main Road, Bosham Nr Chichester. Tel: 0243 572234
New to the Guide because it opened since our last edition but it quickly became acclaimed and popular. 'It turned out to be large and airy - we tried it on spec - the decor was a bit pub like - but the food and service deserves praise.' FM. We have many such reports telling of a 'pleasant atmosphere, good food and staff happy to try and meet suggestions not on the menu.' NA. Chicken Curry with Pullao Rice £7.00. Set meal £9.00 to £45.00 (Kurzi Lamb for Four).

BRIGHTON

THE BLACK CHAPPATTI **TOP 100 & CC DISCOUNT**
12, Circus Parade, New England Road, Brighton. Tel: 0273 699011
'Well with a name like that I just had to try it.' BW. It opened in 1987 and immediately came to notice as well above average. Their secret lies in the cooking. It is 'fresh and varied right down to the home made chutneys and pickles.' CR. Perhaps the fact that one of the proprietors, Steve Funnel, is the chef ensures high standards. The other partner, L Alker tells how 'We do not limit ourselves to one particular style - we tend towards North Indian in winter and the lighter South Indian in the summer.

We have also been known to cook Burmese, Malaysian and Thai - infact anything which is spicy and tastes good.' The menu reads like a good Indian cookbook and in itself is mouthwatering.' BM. 'I'm vegetarian - their Thali at £7.25 was so tasty and surprisingly filling.' CS. It is rare to find authentically prepared Vindaloo, The Shikar Vindaloo at £8.25, follows Goan tradition and uses pork, marinated in freshly ground hot spices and coconut vinegar. It is then slow baked and served in an iron karahi.' Today's specials' are always worth perusal. For example Tandoori Macchi at £7.75 featured red mullet and on another occasion The Viceroy's Venison at £8.95 was on offer. Another dish described as 'particularly fine', by VM is 'Chicken Hyderbadi at £7.95. Diced breast cooked with coconut, almonds yoghurt aromatic spices and fresh mint - 'The perfect marriage of Moghul and South Indian cuisine. The restaurant serves Pullao Rice, Papadoms and chutnies, included in the 10% service charge the average meal price is £15-£20. The Sunday lunch buffet at £5.95 for vegetarians and £6.95 for carnivores is remarkable value. Booking here is essential. This restaurant offers discounts to Curry Club members at quieter times (see page 288). Because of its particular care we put it into our TOP 100, see page 24. Note: Special hours, evenings only Tuesday to Saturday plus Sunday lunch.

BURGESS HILL

CURRY INN
187, London Road, Burgess Hill. Tel: 0444 232124
This establishment has been around for ages. We have mentioned it in a previous Guide. This description by I and NC sums it up. 'A real local, no trimmings just substantial good curries.'

INDIA GARDEN
199, Church Road, Burgess Hill. Tel: 0444 246501
'Not the classiest of the four in town but it's our favourite. We go again and again. The Onion Bhajias are the best ever - the Dhansaks superb. You can go in the kitchen to watch them prepare your meal.' I and NC.

CHICHESTER

AKASH
Old Swimming Pool, Eastgate Square, Chichester. Tel: 0243 775978
The Akash continues to satisfy its customers and it is good to see it retaining its place in this guide. Located near the heart of the beautiful pedestrianised cathedral city of Chichester, although itself a rather drab building sited above the local swimming pool.' But don't let that put you off - the decor inside is typically Indian with pink and gold table cloths, plants, pictures and Moghul style windows.' MAM. 'It is normally very full at night and has a very large menu. The papadoms were lovely and crisp and the chicken Tandoori Masala (£5.05), had a very good flavour although its bright red was off putting. The Naan was excellent and Bringal Bhajee super.' MC. Papadoms 35p, Chicken Curry £3.40, Pullao Rice (their spelling Pulaw), £1.25 and set meals from £9.05.

CROWBOROUGH

ROSE OF BENGAL
3, Crowborough Hill, Crowborough. Tel: 0892 653183
'A rose by any other name could not better our local', says one enthusiast, PH, and Moshud Ali's Rose seems to be very popular. Correspondents talk of good service and unusual specials. 'I had not heard of 'Shad' dishes before. They are curries cooked with almond, peeled tomatoes and butter in a creamy sauce. You can get a Tandoori Chicken Shad £5.45 or Tandoori King Prawn version at £8.95. The restaurant has a sister branch the Star of Bengal in Ukfield. Papadoms are 50p, Chicken Curry £3.00 and Pullao Rice £1.35. Thali meals range from £9.50 to £11.50. There is no service or cover charge but there is a minimum charge of £5.95.

EAST GRINSTEAD

SHAPLA
94, Railway Approach, East Grinstead. Tel: 0342 327655
Takeaway only at 'reasonable prices with generous helpings.' LT.

NIZAM
42, High Street, East Grinstead. Tel: 0342 323462
'With a few hours to kill we ended up here for three enjoyable hours under no pressure to vacate. Generous portions, service excellent, endless Irish Coffees.' RD. Branch at Nizam Tandoori, Haywards Heath.

EAST WITTERING

RAJA **CC DISCOUNT**
5, New Parade Shore, East Wittering. Tel: 0243 673635
A Rahman's Raja has been dispensing curries at the seaside for 11 years. The food is good, we hear. Papadoms are 40p. Chicken curry £3.15 and Pullao Rice £1.35. Discounts are available to Curry Club members at their quieter times, see page 288.

EASTBOURNE

MAHARAJAH
6, Susan's Road, Eastbourne. Tel: 0323 32325
'This restaurant should be in the Guide. It's not upmarket butis excellent. I especially enjoyed the Meat Moglai Chana and Naan bread.' IB.

HALISHAM

RAJDUTT
48, High Street, Hailsham. Tel: 0323 842847
Under the ownership of Abdul Salik for over a year now, the Rajdutt serves all the usual goodies one expects from a Bangladeshi curry house at standard prices.

HASTINGS

SHIPLUS **CC DISCOUNT**
177A, Queens Road, Hastings. Tel: 0424 439493
See Bexhill Shiplu.
Discounts available for Curry club members at their quieter times, see page 288.

HOVE

CURRY MAHAL
171, Portland Road, Hove. Tel: 0272 779125
The wide frontage gives way to an elegant interior - white Taj Mahal arches clad with brass, pink and burgundy tables and chairs. Prices are reasonable with a good array of specials.

KARIMS
15, Blatchington Road, Hove. Tel: 0272 739780
Voted one of the best in the area.

SWAN TANDOORI
56, The Drive, Hove. Tel: 0272 772210
'A little expensive - you pay for the decor. It's in a large house which was formerly a French restaurant. Windows open to floodlit gardens with terrace and statues. You can enjoy your coffee there when the weather allows. It's all very acceptable with tasty food, though the portions are a bit small.' I and NC.

LEWES

GHANDI
20, Fisher Street, Lewes. Tel: 0273 477340
Voted the best in Lewes by our correspondents.

MIDHURST

ASHA
Rumbolds Hill, Midhurst. Tel: 073 081 4113
A very good standard of service and food.

RYE

CHILKA HOUSE
4, High Street, Rye. Tel: 0797 226402
Unusual food cooked to a high standard.

ST LEONARDS ON SEA

SILVERHILL **CC DISCOUNT**
375, London Road, St Leonards On Sea. Tel: 0424 439436
Some restaurants are demonstrably proud of their appearance and their product. Judging by comments received, A Rouf's establishment is one of them. One correspondent raves over the Chicken Chilli Masala at £6.50, whilst another delights over the Special Biriani at £5.25.' PD and RC. Discounts are available to Curry Club members any lunchtime, see page 288.

SHIPLU **CC DISCOUNT**
5, Norman Road, St Leonards On Sea. Tel: 0424 439273
See Bexhill Shiplu.
Discounts available for Curry Club members at their quieter times, see page 288.

STEYNING

MAHARAJAH **TOP 100 & CC DISCOUNT**
High Street, Bramber, Steying. Tel: 0903 814746
At 150 seats this is large restaurant by any standards. Does it cope with such a scale? The answer, it appears is 'yes'. Some of the dishes are unique. Marango for example is Lamb or Chicken cooked with spices, mango, mushroom, beans and bamboo shoots all for £7.95. AL Mashriqui dishes involve the tandoor and a rich sauce with spinach topping for £7.95. 'The menu is especially tempting, and one to return to frequently, to try new things.' VR. 'Leave room for banana, pineapple or apple fritters at £1.60 to round of a great meal.' RM. The Maharajah is Redwan Choudhury's sole restaurant and is highly recommended. In our TOP 100 see page 25, and offers discounts to Curry Club members at its quieter times, see page 288.

STORRINGTON

COTTAGE TANDOORI
25, West Street, Storrington. Tel: 0903 743605
We got regular reports of enjoyable meals here. 'It is in a cottage (quite common it seems in Sussex - Ed) and the atmosphere is perhaps a little twee and incongrous. But the food is excellently cooked, spicy and flavoursome'. CN. One reporter was critical of the dish 'the chicken was cold and the sauce mediocre' BAS, but this is in isolation. More comments welcomed.

WORTHING

SHAFIQUES **CC DISCOUNT**
42, Goring Road, Worthing. Tel: 0903 504035
Shafiques is attractively decorated in a light colonial style with cane

furnishings and lattice partitions and a ceiling fan. The menu carries the usual wide range of curry choices. Some of the specials have caught the eye of our scribes. Jehangir is a medium curry at £8.95, Shah Nauz Shikar for £7.95 and Fawzia at £8.95 'are all worth trying'. BC. Papadoms are 40p each, Chicken Curry £3.50, Pullao Rice £1.55. Set lunch from £6.00, dinner from £15.00. Discounts are available to CC members at quieter times, see page 288.

TASTE OF BENGAL **CC DISCOUNT**
203, Heene Road, Worthing. Tel: 0903 211357
The Taste of Bengal is a takeaway only which appeals to the tastes of our reporters who tell of a standard menu with a good wide choice, and reasonable prices. Popadoms are 35p each, Chicken Curry £2.60, Pullao Rice £1.10. There is a 'sister' restaurant at Golden Bengal, 40, Lyndhurst Road, Worthing. Discounts are available to Curry Club members at their quieter times, see page 288.

TYNE AND WEAR

GATESHEAD

BILLQUAY TANDOORI **CC DISCOUNT**
78, Station Road, Billquay, Gateshead.
Tel: 091 496 0270
'Not the cheapest, not the largest portions, but the quality is excellent. Try the Sri Lankan Chicken Breast for £2.80.' IF. This is a smart take-away only establishment. Syed Ali also owns The Last Days of The Raj, Gateshead. Good prices and offers 5% discount for Curry Club members, see page 288.

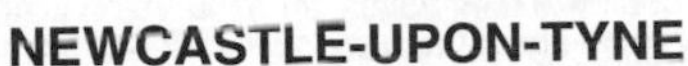

NEWCASTLE-UPON-TYNE

DARAZ **CC DISCOUNT**
4, Holly Avenue, Jesmond, Newcastle. Tel: 091 291 8431
Shahi Turkra (meaning the Royal Piece) is fillet of Lamb marinated in a rich sauce for £5.95 and is typical of the 'delicious and highly merited specialities to be found at Imran Choudhury's Daraz.' HC. 'My husband always likes to try the Curry of the Night.' says TC. 'It's their version of dish of the day.' Prices are reasonable with papadoms at 35p each, Chicken Curry £4.25 and Pullao Rice at £1.25. There are no extra charges and a discount is available to Curry Club members, see page 288.

BRIGHTON HALAL TANDOORI
8, Brighton Grove, Newcastle. Tel: 0
A no frills takeaway, only with good food and straight forward prices. Recommended by BC and others.

SIMLA
39, The Side, Bottom of Dean Street, Newcastle. Tel: 091 232 1070
Another extremely good restaurant very popular with Newcastle curryholics. 2.30am closing weekdays, 3am weekends.

SACHINS **TOP 100**
Old Hawthorn Inn, Fourth Banks, Newcastle. Tel: 091 261 9035
Sachins has attracted more than average attention since it opened. It is unusual because it is owned by Liam Cunningham a Scot, who continues to describe his establishment as being 'one of the few to serve Punjabi food'. The fact that nearly all the UK's curry houses base their culinary efforts on Punjabi dish does not deter Sachin's afficionados who flock there as if drawn by an unseen hand. It is a good place to star gaze. Elton

John, Midge Ure and Dire Straights always go there when they are in town. But don't be surprised that prices are slightly above average. The food is for the most part above average, though don't expect the unexpected on the menu. Book, avoid the latter part of the week and ask for the main room.In our Top 100.

RUPALI **TOP 100 & CC DISCOUNT**
6, Bigg Market, Newcastle. Tel: 091 232 8629
The Curry Club has been extolling the virtues of the Rupali for years, so it is with pleasure that we saw it go into the Good Food Guide. Fortunately this has had no adverse effect on the restaurant's lively charismatic owner, Abdul Latif. Of the many complementary reports we get, most mention Mr Latif. Some complain about the decor being 'tacky' and 'it would benefit from being redecorated.' NS and such like. Even the GFG talks about 'flock wallpaper and close packed tables with paper cloths.' Frankly, who cares? Indeed one might advise Mr Latif to keep everything just as it is. For what he has, is a highly successful restaurant. The food is definitive standard curry shop fayre - not a jot more, not a jot less. The curry gravy stock pot is much in evidence, and Latif himself can be found as much at the cooker as front of house. The result is the standard curry done to perfection. It I were asked to name the Bangladeshi Indian Curry House which most sums up expectations, the Rupali must be it. But there is more. Latif is an enterpreneur always dreaming up press catching gimmicks. For example he has 'Happy Night' every Thursday where a three course set meal with a glass of wine and coffee liqueur costs just £6.95. Lunch and meals before 7pm cost £0.00. The gimmick which I enjoyed the most was the Rupali's hot curry challenge. Eat the whole of the Rupali's hottest curry and you don't pay. Beware though, Mr Latif uses extra hot chilli powder and plenty of it. 'You can feel the great atmosphere as soon as you climb the stairs, and as far as prices go this must be one of the best value places anywhere.' DD. For all these reasons I have put the Rupali in our TOP 100, see page 24. There is an additional bonus too. Discounts are available for Curry Club members at selected times, see page 288.

VUJON **TOP 100 AND CC DISCOUNT**
29, Queen Street, Quayside, Newcastle.091 221 0601
If restaurants are rated by the quality of their toilets, then the Vujon is at the top. One correspondent raved on about them so much that we really believed he would prefer to eat his dinner in three. There is a serious point here of course, if front of house is immaculate, you can be sure 'back stage' is too. Matab Miah claims to work in the kitchens, and he is happy to show customers around.
The restaurant is unashamedly up-market. Vujon means in Indian languages 'gourmet dinner' and the menu aims to reflect this. There is a careful balance of starters (Tomarta Shuru £1.80 is spicy tomato soup and main courses Chilli Rashan Chingri £5.80 is a hot prawn dish. Naram Duck £6.80 is roasted duck glazed with spicy honey. There are many other equally interesting choices. Expect to pay higher than average prices, of course. £20 to 25 a head with a drink or two should be anticipated. There is a ten course dinner called Vhandaris Surprise at £40 for two. A decidely good restaurant in our TOP 100, giving discounts to Cury Club members at their quieter times, see page 288.

TANDOORI NIGHTS
17, Grey Street, Newcastle. Tel: 091 221 0312
Well acclaimed and competent restaurant with reasonable prices.

THE NEW BENGAL
232, High Street, Gosforth. Tel: 091 285 6706
Good quality standard curries at fair prices.

MOTI-JHEEL
4, Waterloo Street, Newcastle. Tel: 091 232 7952
A long standing favourite in Newcastle but recently we've heard that it has lost its edge. It still gets good reviews though, and its unusual menu with

such delights as duckling and Indian steaks with 'Light and delightful spicing.' JB.

MOTI-JHEEL TANDOORI
36/38, Station Road, Gosforth. Tel: 091 284 1028
Not to be confused with the previous entry, this relatively new takeaway only establishment, opened in 1988 and in 1990 it was taken over by a consortium involving the owners of the Verandah in Edinburgh and the Rupali in Newcastle, (see separate entries). That particular pedigree has helped partner chef, Karim Shahid to produce takeaway only food at a very high standard. The menu contains the many favourites you'd expect, with some interesting unusuals. 'Chicken Wing at £1.30 is a starter, 'roasted Bangladeshi style.' 'Chasni Massallam' at £3.35 is a main course dish incorporating kebabs in a sweet and sour mango pickle based sauce. Popadoms are 30p, Pullao Rice £1.20. If you're feeling lazy (or adventurous depending how you look at it) you can order the 'Chef's Special' for £13.50, set meal for two containing his choice of starters, main dishes, side dishes and desserts. 'Stunningly good value.' JD.

SOUTH SHIELDS
Better ones include the NASEEB at no: 90, 'They charge 20p for doggy bag.' TB.

STAR OF INDIA **CC DISCOUNT**
194, Ocean Road, South Shields. Tel: 091 456 2210
Of the many Ocean Road curry houses this one comes highly praised. It's even on BC's list. Inside are plants and alcoves, green wallpaper and velour chairs. Proprietor Mohammed Faruque has set heroic hours, 2.30pm till 2am daily (1am Sundays). 'Choose from a plentiful list and the qualities were equally plentiful. Their Jalfrezi at £3.70, was melt in the mouth stuff'. NS. 'The service was a little too quick which might suit some, but the food was delicious and fresh.' ED. Papadoms 25p each, Pullao Rice, 95, Chicken Curry £2.80. Proprietor Mohammed Faruque also owns the Royal Bengal, Prince Regent Street, Stockton-On-Tees and The Shapla, 192, Northgate, Darlington. Discounts are available for Curry Club members at all three branches at their quieter times. See page 288.

SUNDERLAND

BENGAL LANCER **CC DISCOUNT**
15, North Bridge Street, Sunderland. Tel: 091 564 0527
A large restaurant on 2 floors, seating 140. Abdul Shohid's Bengal Lancer has become popular in the two years since it opened. We have good reports about the food. The Tandoori and Tikka Specials are well appraised as are 'the Zeera Chicken or Lamb at £4.80, enhanced with cummin and the Butter Chicken or Lamb for £4.80 is a good alternative to Tandoori being cooked in ghee. The menu selection also ofers Sri Lankan, Nepalese and Malay dishes as well as Indian, and vegetarians have a wide choice too. Papadoms are 30p each, Pullao Rice, £1.40 and Chicken Curry £3.30. Set lunch is from £4.95 and set dinner £34.95 for four. Discounts are available to Curry Club members at quieter times. See page 288.

FULWELL TANDOORI CHEF **CC DISCOUNT**
119, Fulwell Road, Sunderland. Tel: 0783 5496016
Takeaway only and 'the best around for miles' RPC. A full menu with 'something for everybody'. Prices are already good Papadoms 20p each, Special Brahman Vegetarian Thali at £3.95 might asppeal to some whilst the Special Tandoori Mix for £3.90 is equally popular. Pullao Rice 85p and Chicken Curry £2.20. They are offering discounts to Curry Club members, see page 288.

GRANGETOWN TANDOORI KITCHEN
1, Stockton Terrace, Sunderland. Tel: 0783 5655984
Another popular takeaway only establishment. It too does the Brahmen Special, 'We introduced this dish to the area', Shofuzul Islam, partner, which is a vegetable dish for £3.10. Other unusual dishes from the ample choice on the menu include Makoni for £3.50, Chicken Tikka in a rich

reamy sauce, and Maya Kalia for £2.85, beef with bhuna spices. Popadoms are 20p each, Chicken Curry £2.25 and Pullao Rice 95p. 'The meal for 8 contains an amazing 19 dishes plus, 8 popadoms and 8 breads all for £38.00, just £4.75 a head - it never seems to end.' JL.

WHITLEY BAY

SHAHEN SHAH
187/9, Whitley Road, Whitley Bay. Tel: 091 297 0503
Fairly new to the town this clean well decorated restaurant has freidnely srvice and smartly dressed staff. The starters were delicious and main courses memorable. Hot towels helped us refresh ourselves after our feast.' DD.

WARWICKSHIRE

LEAMINGTON SPA

ASHOKA
22, Regent Street, Leamington.
Tel: 0926 28272
TOP 100 & CC DISCOUNT
The Ashoka is celebrating a massive 30 years in business in 1991. No mean achievement! When it opened there were just 300 curry houses in the UK of which not even 20 were in the Midlands. The editor remembers visiting here not long after it opened and a rare treat it was. I'm pleased therefore that it keeps its place in the Guide as a good, reliable establishment. It has changed a lot since the red flock early days - since I was last there, so I wouldn't know the place. But our correspondents do. 'I've been using the Ashoka for the last 12 years and have never been disappointed.' AH. It now has the simple and elegant look in both its upstairs and downstairs rooms. Since 1975, the Ashoka has been owned by MR Choudhury, an experienced restauranteur as the menu shows. It contains all the regular favourites fairly priced. Popadoms 30p each, Pullao Rice £1.10, Chicken Curry £4.50. But it is the specials which should be tried. There are no less than 27. They average at £7.50 and include rice or bread. They range all over the Indian sub-continent with, for example Gurka Specials (with green herbs), Chatt Sylheti, (spring chicken with Bangladeshi Vegetables), Surati Halim Lamb with lentils and Shakuti a Goan speciality cooked in coconut water. The Mahi (Bengal Fish) Tandoori at £7.50 is another dish worth trying and included in the price is salad, mixed vegetable curry, Pullao Rice or Bread and its 'sensational in terms of value and quality.' SJF. For its menu, its longevity and for sentimental reasons (why else be editor?) I am including this restaurant in our TOP 100. It has a 'sister' branch, the Tandoori Restaurant, 31, Silver Street, Coventry. Both restaurants offer discounts to Curry Club members at their quieter time, see page 288.

LEAMINGTON

POPPADOMS
21, Bath Street, Leamington. Tel: 0926 450986
From the oldest to a new arrival in Leamington. Poppadoms is a vegetarian restaurant and the 'Food and the service is delightful. The spicing was excellent and the rice was moist. We'll certainly go again, although not vegetarians, we enjoyed our meal.' AH.

RUGBY

DILRUBA **CC DISCOUNT**
155, Railway Terrace, Leamington. Tel: 0788 542262
Another regular entrant to the pages of the Good Curry Restaurant Guide, the Dilruba's menu offers a comprehensive selection of curries and accompaniments. 'You always tell us to go for the specials,' says BW (not actually true, Ed.), 'but I always go for a stonking good Vindaloo for £4.25 and stonking good it always is.' And who can argue with that? Maybe I'll just dare suggest you try the 'super finger likin' Butter Tikka Chicken for £6.25. It puts the colonel on his bike.' BR. And there's much more, believe me. Azir Uddin also owns the Bombay Palace in Coventry, (see West Midlands). Both restaurants give discounts to Curry Club members, see page 288.

STRATFORD UPON AVON

HUSSAINS **TOP 100**
6A, Chapel Street, Stratford. Tel: 0789 205804
Noor Islam Hussain opened this, his first restaurant, in Stratford in 1985. Hussains got off to a fast start, as we said last time, 'with thespians and curryholics alike.' One of our regulars tells of the stars who frequent the place, 'Ben Kingsley, for example, uses it when he appears at the Royal Shakespeare Theatre.' PR. Since appearing in our last guide Hussain's has become much acclaimed in other guides and more importantly by our members. Noor Hussain's success is reflected by a small chain of Hussain's restaurants newly opened in Cheltenham, Redditch and Evesham. They all run to the same formula... smart, upmarket premises, 'nice comfortable place with attractive decor,' and service 'a bit erratic but at least they apologise.' LC. The menu is quite short, as you'd expect, none-the-less it contains such familiars as Bhuna, Korma, Dhansak, Madras and Pathia. 'The Chicken Makhani at £6.25 is one of the best I've tried. Succulent Tandoori Chicken saturated in super lush sauce.' RD. Prices reflect the restaurant's local being slightly higher than the norm. Papadoms are 30p each, Chicken Curry (sorry Bhuna) is £4.75 and Pullao Rice is £1.60. Minimum charge is £7.50. Set meals from £8.95 (vegetarian) to £25.95 for two. 'The menu says 'each dish has its own distinctive flavour and aroma which cannot come from any curry powder but from spices and herbs specially prepared by ourselves.' 'I for one believe them.' SA. The tributes flock in, and in our recent request to our members to name their favourite restaurant(s), Husseins got so many nominations that I am putting it into our TOP 100. Their opening hours are noon to 11.30pm, which reflect the fact that Stratford is a busy tourist town. Hussein's is a further reason to visit.

LALBAGH
3, Greenhill Street, Stratford. Tel: 0789 293563
'Visited on first night of opening (Feb '89) to find a very good menu and an offer to make things not listed. My Balti dishes were good but not spectacular. My little girl aged seven 'cleaned' her plate of the Chicken Tikka and then Mixed Tandoori leaving nothing but the salad, both times!' (The Lalbagh can thank her for this entry which your editor couldn't resist). 'Outstanding service, £70 for five makes it a little expensive, but it will proove popular.' Mrs P. Reports please.

STUDLEY

PEPPERS INDIAN CUISINE
45, High Street, Studley. Tel: 052 785 3183
'A rather good restaurant, I thought, which I came upon whilst on my business travels. It has a fresh name, fresh green look and fresh food.' TD. The menu offers many favourites plus some nice touches such as Quail Dhunger at £6.55, Stuffed (meat or vegetables) Peppers at £1.85 and Lassi drink for £1.15. Papadoms are 35p each, Pullao Rice £1.25 and Chicken Curry £4.25. 'Not the cheapest, but value for money - and you don't get stung on the drinks.' BP.

INDONESIAN
73, Alcester Road, Studley. Tel: 052 785 7207
'Traditional Indonesian food here. The staff are good for advice. Dips and crackers are on the table to start with. There's satay on the menu, of course and Perkedel (sweetcorn cake with sweet and sour sauce). Lumpia is a crispy vegetable roll. Main course dishes include an interesting mixture of sweetish, hot and sour dishes, and there are a couple of curries.' BP. Reports welcomed.

WARWICK

BHARATAM **CC DISCOUNT**
24, Smith Street, Warwick. Tel: 0926 491736
Sam Chakravarty, boss of the Bharatam goes to great lengths to explain that his restaurant is Indian (as opposed to Bangladeshi). (Bharatam means 'from India),' and that his clients come as much for the food as the atmosphere. It opened in 1988 and won the praise of a number of our scribes. 'Certainly one of the best we've come across.' GI. 'My husband and I celebrated his 50th birthday here. The tables were tastefully presented and included fresh flowers. The food was excellent and they gave us free liquers.' AH. One couple (J and BW) reported slow service and cold food, but we believe this not to be the norm. Unusual dishes include Fish Fry chunks of a salmon-like Indian fish served for as starter as spicy steaks for £2.25 and Fish Bengali at £6.00, Paneer (Indian Cheese) dishes are prevalent and people speak well of the house Thali set meal non-vegetarian at £9.95 and Vegetarian Thali for £8.95. This restaurant offers a discount to Curry Club members at its quieter times, see page 288.

WEST MIDLANDS

BIRMINGHAM CENTRAL

BRISTOL STREET TANDOORI
26, Bristol Street, Horsefair, B5.
Tel: 021 643 5723
CC DISCOUNT
This restaurant (formerly the Shah Bagh) opened in 1989. 'Pick your way through an enormous choice.' CL. Some of the specials merit a mention. Chingri Johl at £7.95 is King Prawn oven cooked. Kotmi Ka Salan for £4.95 is lamb combined with potatoes and cauliflower. The restaurant offers a discount to Curry Club members at quieter times, see page 288.

DAYS OF THE RAJ **TOP 100 CC DISCOUNT**
51, Dale End, B4. Tel: 021 236 0445
This was formerly the Gurkah. It opened in 1986 and the new owners P. Kulair and B Singh spared no expense on their masterpiece. 'The first floor dining area features a waterfall as its centrepiece.' PM. The kitchen can be viewed through a window and the airy cane furniture, light walls and contemporary sepia Raj photographs give a suitable evocation of those long gone days. The menu is refreshingly short, with just four starters, and an average of four main dishes under various headings such as Lamb, Chicken, Tandoori etc. There is also a wine list, carefully selected to balance the subtlety of the food. The menu leaves you in no doubt as to what to choose with its clear description and 'the waiters assist with unpatronising advice if you need it.' DC. 'I've tried everything but I think the Jalfrezi (Chicken £5.95, Prawn £7.25) is best served sizzling in an iron karahi. After the meal you take coffee in a lounge which allows for a constant flow of people.' AD. Even at lunch the restaurant is busy - the haunt of local businessmen (set lunch is £5.95). Another dish which

appeals is King Prawn Goa (£6.85). 'The Prawn was huge and meaty, the spicing - it was all there ginger, garlic, cummin, coriander and the rest - yet none predominated. It was amazing.' PE. 'They give Papadoms, chutneys, mint sauce and fudge with the coffee at no extra charge. Why don't they all do that.' BW. Amid a literal sea of praise the occasional whimper does come through. 'I find their use of rich creamy sauces to be much too rich.' PM. Regulars talk of the gourmet evenings, which operate from time to time with a pre-booked sitting from 7.30pm till late. The overwhelming opinion expressed by a great many respected correspondents is that this is the best restaurant in the Midlands. It therefore goes into our TOP 100. The Days Of The Raj is offering discounts to Curry Club members at its quieter times, see page 288.

KOH-I-NOOR
28/29, Horsefair, B1. Tel: 021 662 2053
'One of the best and one of the oldest in town. I do like the food but the oddest feature is the huge centrally placed plastic tree with coloured lights.' JL.

MAHARAJAH **TOP 100**
23, Hurst Street, B5. Tel: 021 622 2641
One of our reporters travels the whole country in pursuit of his job, and he delights in taking lunch or dinner in Indian restaurants. His opinion is as good as any professional food inspector, but he seems to have one foible - pink. 'In spite of its pink table cloths and the enormously high prices (£19 for food for one is over the top!) the decor gives the impression of being spotlessly clean, and Is enhanced by paintings and ornaments. The many waiters are friendly and welcoming and seem able to strike a rapport with all customers, even those they turn away because the tiny place is usually over crowded.' (The unfortunate side effect of regular Guide reportage - Ed). The menu offered a sensible range of goods. I ordered Roghan Josht which looked, smelled and tasted superb.' JL. We've not had reports recently of the edible silver leaf or gold leaf which this restaurant used to serve over its Birianis years ago on its early days. Does it still do that? Even if it doesn't, we've enough evidence to support its remaining on our TOP 100 list.

RAJDOOT **TOP 100 & CC DISCOUNT**
12, Albert Street, Central Birmingham. B4. Tel: 021 642 8749
Bristol, Manchester, Dublin and Birmingham are the cities which have branches of Des Shada's small chain of up market restaurants. The Birmingham branch was opened in 1971, following a successful venture in London in 1966 (subsequently sold) pioneering an upmarket approach to the Indian restaurant complete with tandoor. Mr Shada has reason to be proud of his small empire, which has dominated every food guide for two decades. But he must not become complacent. As at Bristol and Manchester the Birmingham branch gets many reports singing its praises. 'I chose a set meal and it was a pleasure to eat.' BR. 'Expensive, yes, a little, but the set meals are good value (lunch around £8 and dinner £13) but I've never been disappointed.' ST. The Rajdoots went through a period about two years ago when we received one or two bad reports about each branch. Recently its been back to the old form, with many recommendations and I'm pleased to maintain Birmingham's Rajdoot in our TOP 100. This restaurant offers a discount to Curry Club members at its quieter times, see page 288.

MANZIL
110, Digbeth Road, Central Birmingham. B5. Tel: 021 643 9589
Opening hours are 6pm to 4am, 365 days a year. This restaurant is for insomniac curryholics.

BIRMINGHAM EAST

ASAH
2250, Coventry Road, Sheldon, Birmingham. B26. Tel: 021 743 6572
'There's a happy hour for drinks and 10% off between 5pm and 10pm. It gets busy after then till late. Go straight for the Balti dishes. They're enormous. I recently ordered Chicken And Mushroom Balti. The waiter suddenly whisked it away. When it returned he apologised becasue they had forgotten to add the chicken. I hadn't even noticed.' DE.

TITASH
2278, Coventry Road, Sheldon, Birmingham. B26. Tel: 021 722 2080
Birmingham has a wealth of extremely good curry restaurant of all types as this Guide indicates. The Titash is a Bangladeshi standard curry house with a sprinkling of Balti. Prices are reasonable with Papdoms 25p each, Pullao Rice £1.10 and Chicken Curry £3.80.

YEW TREE COTTAGE
43, Stone Lane, Yardley, Birmingham. B25. Tel: 021 784 0707
An old favourite of our members and this Guide, the Yew Tree Cottage in its barn-style setting, continues to dispense high quality Tikkas, Tandooris, Baltis and curries. Monday to Sunday 5pm to 1am, Friday and Saturday 2am.

BIRMINGHAM SOUTH EAST AND SOUTH

ADIL TANDOORI AND BALTI HOUSE **TOP 100**
148/150, Stoney Lane, Balsall Heath, Birmingham. B12
Tel: 021 449 0335
When we first praised the Adil back in 1983 it was unabashedly a cafQ for the local Asians. It is open from midday to midnight and always seems to be busy. Clientelle is still mainly local Asians, but, as with Southall and Bradford, it is also becoming increasingly popular with the white population. Remember if its your first time this is the real macoy. Use a chapatti or three to mop up the curry - that's the Indian/Pakistani way. They will supply cutlery on request but not alcohol. They don't mind if you bring your own and neither do they charge corkage. 'All the food is Balti - Adil's opened in 1976 and was the first to serve this particular style of food. Balti literally means 'bucket' or cast iron cooking pot. The Balti craze has began to spread like topsy. Initially, and for years, it remained the craze of Birmingham and surrounds. Now it is spreading far and wide. Anything can be served on the flat bottomed two handled balti (called a karahi elsewhere). Meat, Chicken, Prawns, Vegetables in any combination. Adli's has over 50 choices including some truly ethnic vegetable dishes. 'The Karela gourd was too bitter for me but my friend from Lahore adored it.' GR. 'I like Katlama and Tandoori Fish, which is filling and hot. And how about the mega-size Nan, 18 inches by 12 inches tear shaped. We're usually too full to eat a dessert so we take home superb Kulfi or fresh Gulab Jaman.' PM & JS. 'Undoubtedly the best curry house in Birmingham.' GGP. Of it's type, we won't argue with that opinion, so we'll put Adil's into our TOP 100. Incidentially there is now a branch at Adil's (2), 130, Stoney Lane, equally good.

DILSHAD
618, Bristol Road, Selly Oak, Birmingham. B29. Tel: 021 472 5016
Another restaurant for insomniacs. Opening hours are 5.30pm to 4am, 356 days a year.

J JAYS
1347, Stratford Road, Hall Green, Birmingham. B28. Tel: 021 777 3185
'Did they take a Terance Conran home decorating course? Every method of painting is to be found inside and out. The food is good with certain unusual vegetables such as lotus roots in evidence.' NR and PJ. We hear of a service bias towards locals. Reports please.

KABABISH
29, Woodbridge Road, Birmingham. B13. Tel: 021 449 5556
Good Balti place and generally busy.

PLAZA
278, Ladypool Road, Balsall Heath, Birmingham. B12. Tel: 021 449 4249
'Good Balti/curry house in what was and is surely a two up/two down terraced house. It's tiny but we enjoyed the Chicken Mukhnee £3.95, cooked in the clay oven - tasty and mild.' GP. 'It's Indian run in a predominantly Pakistani area. The staff wear turbans.' BP. Closed lunchtimes. Ask for cutlery. Take your own booze.

WELCOME
FOOD

Omar's

RASOI INDIAN KITCHEN **CC DISCOUNT**
321, Stratford Road, Sparkhill, Birmingham. B11.
This is becoming increasingly popular with the Asian community which is a testiment to good quality and freshly cooked food. Discounts are offered to Curry Club members at their quieter times, see page 288.

ROYAL AL FAISAL **TOP 100**
136/140, Stoney Lane, Sparkbrook, Birmingham. B12.
Tel: 021 449 5695
A top quality Balti house. 'A trip here is an absolute must. Its very rough and ready with the tables covered with sheets of paper which are changed after each customer. It's not licensed, but they don't mind you bringing your own. No cutlery, of course, but they'll supply it if you ask. Balti dishes are served in woks and Naans are used to mop up (not cutlery). The Naans here are amazing. They come in three sizes small (usual size) medium (large dinner plate size) and family size (brought to the table between two baskets and literally three feet by one-and-a-half feet!' AF. 'Quality superb.' JB. 'From an huge and innovative amount of different balti dishes I chose Balti Tropical which combined just about everything in one wok - chicken, meat, prawns, mushroom, peas and other vegetables. It was enormous and excellent value at £4.00.' GGP. One of Birmingham,'s best so it goes into our TOP 100.

BIRMINGHAM WEST

OMARS KASHMIRI **CC DISCOUNT**
167, Hadley Road, Ladywood, Birmingham. B16. Tel: 021 454 7104
Omar's is striking. Its bow front emphasised with marble walls and huge bow windows with Laura Ashley floral Austrian blinds. The elegance continues inside where there is a small reception area. The walls have white marble with inset black marble patterns, and there is much evidence of real mahogany around the bar. Authentic ornaments include carved walnut screens and 'the biggest engraved brass hookah (Kashmiri smoking pipe) you've ever seen.' JR. The restaurant itself is tiny - with just 36 seats, although the party room upstairs seats a further 30. Omar's opened in 1987 and belongs to two Kashmiri Moslems - Messrs Bader and Zaman - hence the absence of wine list. 'Our customers are welcome to bring their own - we don't charge corkage.' he says. On the relatively short menu you'll find some Indian dishes and a sprinkling of the inevitable Balti dishes, but there are many from Kashmir. Roghan Josh, Qorma (Korma) and Shahi Kofta - meatballs (each £4.95), Kaalia (£5.50) is aromatic lamb curry to which cauliflower and potato are added. Bhattak Orange Massala at £8.70, is duck enhanced with Cointreau. Omar's four Birianis are infused with saffron and are 'dum' (slow steam) cooked to allow the flavours to permeate. 'Despite its name the Hyderbadi Pucki Biryani £6.95 based on lamb is a superb meal on its own and the waiter have heard all the jokes about it before!' AS. We've enough reports to place this restaurant in our TOP 100, see page 25. Note: it's evening only hours 6 to 11pm, Monday to Saturday and Sunday 1pm till 3pm, lunch buffet £8.50. There is a service charge of 10% 'But you do get free Papadoms, Pickles and Chutneys.' Omar's gives discounts to Curry Club members at its quieter time, see page 288.

BIRMINGHAM NORTH

ALI SHAAN
90, Hawthorn Road, Kingstanding, Birmingham. B44
Takeaway only served between 5pm and midnight every day. Many Curry and Tandoori dishes and a few Balti's are on offer at reasonable prices. Papadoms are 25p each, Pullao Rice 90p, Chicken Curry £2.45. 'My favourite is the Beef Chat Mossala at £2.85, it has a sharp sour taste - delicious.' CM.

CAMELLIA
Churchill Parade, Birchfield Road, Birmingham. B19. Tel: 021 551 4829
6pm to 3am (last orders 2.30am) are the hours. Regular choice of curries supported by some rare Specials. Ruhi (Indian) fish curry at £6.60 and Sally Curries for £3.50 served with Potato Straws are two examples.

CURRY GARDENS
16, York Road, Birmingham, B23. Tel: 021 373 7173
A thoroughly reliable curry house which appeared in our first Guide. It's back because of reports received. All tell of good food, good ambience and respectable prices.

LAL QUILA
34, High Street, Erdington, Birmingham. B23. Tel: 021 382 7620
In the view of one of our regulars it is the best in the northern Birmingham suburbs. 'The menu is fairly short and includes some which were new to us, which we have since worked our way through. Nice touches including orange segments after the main course.' JB.

COVENTRY

BOMBAY PALACE **CC DISCOUNT**
64, Earlsdon Street, Coventry. Tel: 0203 677851
Under the same ownership as Rugby's Dilruba (see Warwickshire), the Bombay Palace offers 'workman-like curries crafter with generous gravies and acceptable accompaniments.' TR. Prices are very reasonable with Papadoms at 30p each, Pullao Rice £1.20 and Chicken Curry £3.20. You can get a three course dinner for £24.00 for four people. The restaurant offers discounts for Curry Club members at its quieter times, see page 288.

FRIENDS CORNER
547/9, Foleshill Road, Coventry. Tel: 0203 686688
In our first guide and our last edition, it was one of Coventry's best. Then it lost popularity and closed and now its back again. The new Friends Corner has a takeaway section downstairs and the restaurant has moved to new quarters upstairs (good idea!). The menu ranges across a wide choice of dishes including some varieties. Fish bhajia (£1.90) and Murghi Dum Boona (£3.60) tender chicken pan fried in spices then steamed to a conculsion with a spicy tomato gravy. Asians eat there which is always a good sign for quality and price, indeed a meal for two with booze need not exceed £25.00. Reports please.

NOOR BRASSERIE
6, Hales Street, Coventry. Tel: 0203
Got the most Coventry votes in our 'Name your favourite restaurant' poll. 'The Onion Bhajia was succulent and had a beautiful spicy sauce. The Vindaloo was not so hot that you couldn't taste the delicate mixture of spices.' GGP. 'Not the cheapest, but we think the best.' CP and JD. More reports please.

RAJDOOT **CC DISCOUNT**
29, City Arcade, Coventry. Tel: 0203 223195
This very large restaurant (140 seats) opened in 1976 and made our first Guide but not the second ('Why not' aksed one of our regulars?). It's back this time but is not related to the Birmingham Rajdoot. The quantities are plentiful. Prices are fair. The food is competent. It's all standard stuff as we said before, with the recent addition of Balti which they describe as 'Ancient Iron Skillet dishes.' Sensibly they don't bother with a lunch trade preferring a 6pm to 2am slog (3am Saturday and 1am Sunday) instead. They offer discounts to Curry Club members at their quieter times, see page 288.

KING WILLIAM IV PUB **TOP 100**
Foleshill Road, Coventry. Tel: 0203
Once upon a time there was Coventry without any Indian restaurants. Then in 1961 they opened the first one. I know because I worked in Coventry. A filling meal cost 3/9d (19p) if I remember. What I can't remember is the name of this erstwhile water hole. Is it still there? What is it's address? Please help me somebody! Anyway, the point of this story is to say that today no one could contemplate Coventry without its complement of 30 or so curry restaurants. So it may not be surprising to find that a Coventry pub serves curry. Many do these days. But this one is different. Firstly the landlords are an Indian couple, Pele and Jatinder Bains. They've been in the business for years and it seemed quite natural to them to offer Indian food. We first mentioned this phenomenon in 1986.

Since then Pele and Jatinder have been featured in that publication, The Camra Good Beer Guide. They also recently won the Michel and Butler East Midlands Pub Lunch award, beating 200 other pubs. So we think it's high time the King William got into our Guide. At any rate our reports have demanded it 'What a great idea - authentic Indian restaurant food in a pub.' DC. 'If only my local did it - imagine real ale and favourite curry!' LP. The food is, we're assured very good. You'll find Tikka and Tandoori, Birianis and Bhoonas, Mediums and Madrases, and even Vindaloos and all at typical pub prices. As experienced Landlords, the Bains even know how to handle lager louts. We're delighted to welcome this establishment to our Guide and for their particular enterprise and obvious excellence we're putting them in our TOP 100. See page 25.

DUDLEY

LIGHT OF ASIA **CC DISCOUNT**
98, High Street, Dudley. Tel: 0384 56778
This restaurant opened in 1967 making it an early arrival in the Midlands. This has given it ample time to establish itself. As time has gone by it has added and improved. Tandoori dishes in the 1970's and Balti in the '80. In 1989 it changed ownership to Messrs Matlib, Ali and Ali. Now, with 130 seats and smart decor the restaurant's hours recognised customer demand. Sunday to Thursdays are 6pm to 1am and Fridays and Saturdays to 2am. They don't open at lunchtimes. The recognised curry favourites are at reasonable prices. Papadoms are 30p each, Pullao Rice £1.20 and Chicken Curry £3.50. From the 19 specials, some are unusual - Podina Ghoust (£4.50) for example is meat cooked with fresh mint. The restaurant offers discounts to Curry Club members at specified times (see page 288).

KNOWLE

ELLORA
1661, High Street, Knowle. B930564 6400
Deserves a mention. An excellent 'Curry House' providing first class food (especially Bhoona and Patia). I'm surprised it has not been mentioned before but I suppose if nobody writes about it you cannot know it exists.' JH. (Quite right Sir! - Ed).

LYE

MR DAVE'S BALTI RESTAURANT
15, High Street, Dudley. Tel: 0384 56778
Mr Dave himself is an Englishman, who enjoys his currys (sounds familiar). He enjoys them so much that he opened his own restaurant as chef-proprietor. It's menu 'caters for vegetarian and meat eating customers. The portions are large and filling and the service quick and pleasant. It's a place to visit.' KW. Buty don't go for the wine list (it's unlicensed), nor for the decor which is simple, cheap and cheerful. More reports welcomed. (See also Telford, Shropshire).

STOURBRIDGE

INDIA HOUSE **CC DISCOUNT**
22, Lower High Street, Stourbridge. Tel: 0384 393361
Standard menu, reasonable prices good portions and quality and a discount for CC members at their quieter times, see page 288.

DILSHAD TANDOORI **CC DISCOUNT**
132, Hagley Road, Stourbridge. Tel: 0384 372762
Again, a standard menu, with the addition (normal in the Midlands) of Balti dishes, of which there are some 32 (which average £3.50). Balti chicken, for example is £2.90 and is straight forward but in order to get to 32 the combinations are massive - how about Balti Bhoona Tandoori Chicken at £3.95, or Balti Keema Madras Bhoona at £3.20. Phew - I thought there were four dishes there! I think the translation for those of us not in the Midlands Balti swim is Balti (cooked in a cast iron vessel, Keema (mince),

Madras (hot), Bhoona (dry fried). The Dilshad offers a discount to Curry Club members (see page 288). Note the hours: 5pm till midnight, 7 days a week.

SEDGLEY

REDFORT **CC DISCOUNT**
Unit 2, Bull Ring Dudley Street, Sedgley. Tel: 09073 71759
If you enjoy speciality spotting on the menu (and trying them too), papcila £5.15, is chicken or lamb cooked with capsicums and tomatoes, Tikka Mince Masallah £6.50, involves Chicken Tikka cooked with a spicy mince lamb sauce, with Pullao Rice. Muchamon at £4.05, involves chicken and green peppers. Popadoms are 30p each, Pullao Rice £1.20 anD Chicken Curry £3.40. The restaurant is offering Curry Club members a discount at its quieter times, see page 288. Note the hours Sunday to Thursday 6pm to midnight (Friday and Saturday 1am).

SUTTON COLDFIELD

INDUS **CC DISCOUNT**
11, King's Road, Newoscott, Sutton Coldfield. Tel: 021 355 5089
Harun Miah will tell you a great deal of thought goes into running his Indus restaurant. He delivers takeaways free (£25 orders at 6 miles, £20 orders at 3 miles). He'll supply them frozen if required. On Sundays he'll give a six person booking a free bottle of wine, and of course he gives discounts to Curry Club members at quieter times (see page 288).

MAHARAJAH **CC DISCOUNT**
272, Highbridge Road, Boldmere, Sutton Coldfield.021
Takeaway only establishment open between 5pm and midnight. Its 101 dish menu includes many standard items and 'it deserves at least an honourable mention for the consistently high quality of its cooking and its generous portions. The Chicken Muchommon £3.25, is marinated then cooked with vegetables is outstanding. Our experiences with items not on the menu, but cooked to order have been mixed. A Methi Gosht turned out to be most acceptable whilst a lamb Pasanda was a disaster.' JB. Papdoms are 25p each, Pullao Rice 90p, Chicken Curry £2.50. This takeaway offers Curry Club members discounts at its quieter times, see page 288.

SONAR GAW **CC DISCOUNT**
14, Queen Street, Sutton Coldfield. Tel: 023 354 2063
Starters, Tandoori, Bhoona, Pasandas, Kormas, Pathias, DoPiazas, Jal Frezis, Baltis, Dhansaks, Rice and Sundries, and Sweets. 122 dishes well defined medium to hot and representing the standard Bangladeshi Indian restaurant curry house menu. To any of the curry dishes you can ask for heat to be added (to Madras, Vindaloo and Phal levels) and hey presto you'll satisfy any self respecting curryholic the UK over. Prices are reasonable and they offer a discount to Curry Club members at their quieter times, see page 288.

WALSALL

THE DILSHAD TANDOORI
24B, Anchor Road, Aldbridge, Walsall.
Goyas Miah opened his Dilshad in 1981. It's another standard menu takeaway only, operating from 5pm to midnight daily. Papadoms are 25p each, Pullao Rice 90p, Chicken Curry £2.80.

SHAHI GRILL **CC DISCOUNT**
89, Bridge Street, Walsall.
Another Midlands restaurant who sensibly dispensed with a minimal lunch trade to concentrate on 6pm to midnight every day. It's standard menu completely provides all your needs. Papadoms 30p each, Pullao

Rice £1.40, Chicken Curry £3.80, minimun charge £7.00, set dinner for four £39.95. The Shahi Grill offers discounts to Curry Club members at its quieter timers, see page 288.

WEST BROMWICH

TANDOORI KITCHEN **CC DISCOUNT**
385, High Street, Carters Green, West Bromwich.
The Tandoori Kitchen is a caring restaurant. Pink is theme which even extends to the menu. 'Tandoori Mixed Grill is good value at £5.80 and so is the fresh mango at £1.00, compared with other restaurants.' DC. Papadoms are 25p each, Pulla Rice 90p, Chicken Curry £2.75. A discount is available for Curry Club members at quieter times, see page 288.

WOLVERHAMPTON

BILASH
2, Cheapside, Wolverhampton. Tel: 0902 27762
'Small, but intimate candlelight atmosphere. The Bilash serves generous quantities with good service, if a little slow when the place is full. Prices are competitve.' JB.

THE DILSHAD **CC DISCOUNT**
41, Berry Street, Wolverhapmtòn. Tel: 0902 23481
'What no Wolverhampton restaurant in your previous Guide?' The Dilshad is worth recommending, located opposite the stage door of the Grand Theatre. A welcome at the door leads to a spacious reception area. Service is attractive and the menu, comprehensive and well priced. The restaurant is made up of three rooms which fill up in sequence as the evening gets busier. Hot towels were served between the starter and the main course and again before the pudding. Flaming Gulab Jamuns and coffee rounded off a perfect meal.' DD. Discounts are available to Curry Club members at their quieter times, see page 288.

WILTSHIRE

CHIPPING SODBURY

SULTAN
29, Horse Street, Chipping Sodbury.
Tel: 0454 323510
In an English house built in 1660 said to have a ghost (spiritual type) but now dealing Rhogan Goshts !
An extremely good restaurant. See inside rear cover.

DEVIZES

DEVIZES TANDOORI
1, Sheep Street, Devizes. Tel: 0380 77697
As soon as it opened (in 1987) we heard about it. Almost every report we have tells about extremely friendly service. The chicken Jalfrezi (£4.50) is particularly liked 'it's nice and hot with fresh chillies, yet not harsh.' H and VP. 'The Onion Bhajias are ampong the best I've tasted.' JW. The kitchen is in view and it is very clean. 'A dish which we've not heard of before is Chilli Conkani (£4.00). It turned out to be curried minced meat served with rice, a novel Bangladeshi version of chilli con carne? Good none-the-less.' GC.

SALISBURY

ASIA **CC DISCOUNT**
90, Fisherton Street, Salisbury. Tel: 0722 27628
'Clean crisp and comfortable and they make you feel at home. King Prawn Puri (£2.50), massive and delicious. Vindaloo (£3.80), very hot and spicy. The Pullao Rice portion was too small. Prawn Moltan (£3.75) is an original, tasty curry, smooth and creamy with finely sliced mushrooms.' NG. This restaurant has been in business since 1963. During all that time it has remained consistently above average. For that we've included it in our TOP 100. The Asia offers discounts to Curry Club members in their quieter times. See page 288.

GOLDEN CURRY **CC DISCOUNT**
7, Minster Street, Salisbury. Tel: 0722 27330
A standard curry house with no pretentions and a menu with a good wide choice of favourites, completely cooked. Discount for Curry Club members at their quieter times, see page 288 for details.

SWINDON

THE BIPLOB **TOP 100**
30, High Street, Highworth, Nr Swindon. Tel: 0793 763794
We were quite stunned at the number of recommendations the BIPLOB got when we conducted our 'name your favourite restaurant' survey. It definitely had a bad patch about 3 years ago but following a change of management it's back to its former high standards. It's located on the A361 about 5 miles north of Swindon in 17th century beamed cottage, built before the Raj found India. Who could have imagined that today Highworth would support a population of 8,000 and that one of its oldest buildings would contain one of the UK's best Indian restaurants? 'The starters were big and superbly spiced, succulent and sizzling. The main course - Chicken Kashmiri for Marion and Duck Tandoori Mussala - arrived after a surprisingly short wait. The duck was outstanding, with lots of fresh ginger and lots of strong sauce which got all over my face and fingers. The Chicken Kashmiri was a complete contrast with lychees and other fruits nestling beneath a rich sweet and sour sauce. Marion preferred my duck (so did I, but I'm a gentlemen at heart). There was a Mogli Paratha (also a novelty) which filled with fresh coriander leaves, egg and vegetable pieces. The texture was firm but not too oily. Yum. The single portion of Pilau Rice was saffron and clove flavoured, good texture (until it started to dry out on the hot plate) and yellow. The Mixed Vegetable side dish was a bit boring, but we were full by then anyway. To finish, all visitors were receiving a dish of sliced oranges (a brilliant idea which I have never come across before) plus some of that scented straw stuff, just for fun. Marion also got her red carnation to take away.' RC. The quality of the food is always above average with exceptionally tender meat, fresh cooking and enormous portions. Regular reports like these have elevated the BIPLOB to our TOP 100.

CURRY GARDEN **CC DISCOUNT**
90, Victoria Road, Swindon. Tel: 0793 521114
With no less than seven curry restaurants on Victoria Road one could be spoilt if not confused for choice. Fortunately our scribes have worked their way through them all and their collective conclusion leaves us with the Golden Curry. Its a standard curry house with a long 'definitive' menu. Papadoms are 30p each, Pullao Rice £1.25, Chicken Curry £3.00. Discounts are on offer to Curry Club members at their quieter times, see page 288.

WARMINSTER

AGRA
32, East Street, Warminster. Tel: 0985 212713
The Agra opened in 1979 has remained consistant in quality since then. Reports please.

NORTH YORKSHIRE

RICHMOND

RICHMOND TANDOORI KITCHEN
32A, Market Place, Richmond.
Tel: 0784 850338

The pretty town of Richmond is dominated by its castle, and the Green Howards. Its cobbled market place is home to the new (1988) Richmond Tandoori Kitchen. (prior to that it was the Kamal). In Bangladeshi ownership (they also own the Shagorika, Seburn and the Moti Raj, Sunderland). The Richmond 'have more types of Nan Bread than I've seen before - seven all together - Plain, Keema, Peshwari, Kashmiri, Egg, Tandoori and Gasklick (95p to £1.05)'. PK. Note: the hours are 6pm to midnight every day. Big discounts on takeaways.

SCARBOROUGH

SCARBOROUGH TANDOORI
50, St Thomas Street, Scarborough.
Tel: 0723 352393

Ahead on points. 'It has become our favourite curry place. The Pasanda £4.30, our favourite curry dish.' G and PB. 'A good average restaurant, the most amusing feature of which is the toilets - 'The Elton John' and the 'Olivia Newton John'. Never mind the food is acceptable.' JL.

AAGRAH **TOP 100**
Devenshire Place, Keighly Road, Skipton.

See entry under Aagrah, Shipley, Bradford, West Yorks.

TAJ MAHAL
18, Court Lane, Skipton.
Tel: 0756 793960

Technically in North Yorkshire, but actually quite near Bradford (therefore not in West Yorkshire - sorry we upset RL with this error in our two previous guides), market town Skipton's Taj Mahal has regularly been reported as being competent. All the more surprising therefore to get a poor report. We've given the Taj the benefit of the doubt. They will give Curry Club members discounts at their quieter times, see page 288, so reports are welcome. Note: hours 5.30pm to midnight.

TAJ MAHAL
7, King's Snaith, York.
Tel: 0904 653944

'Add it to my list of favourites. It has a lovely view over the river Ouse, which makes up for its rather plain decor. They are good with children.' JL. One regular reporter tells of two occasions where they left the credit card payment slip open despite taking a service charge - a detestable habit which almost took them out of this Guide - Ed. But 'tender Roghan Josh, lots of chicken, large portions and first rate Aloo Ghobi all unquestionably good.' BR. Some intersting starters including chickpea mixture on puri - delicious.' DM. Reports please.

RISE OF THE RAJ
112, Micklegate, York.
Tel: 0904 622975

Rising in popularity. Reports please.

YORKSHIRE - SOUTH

BARNSLEY

INDIA GARDENS
16, Peel Square, Barnsley.
Tel: 0226 282612
'Red flock wallpaper and the sort of restaurant that is a God send for curry afficionados. Nothing particularly good or bad about it, but every town should have one.' Reports please.

DONCASTER

INDUS **TOP 100 & CC DISCOUNT**
24/26, Silver Street, Doncaster. Tel: 0302 323366
The Indus was Doncaster's first (1969) and we welcome it back to our Guide. Owners Karim and Rauf Din from Pakistan have taken steps to maintain their no: 1 position in town, and the Indus' 'now has a smart new image and a short menu for the discerning.' GL. 'My partner had his normal stinking stonker (Chicken Vindaloo - £4.90, and make sure it's really hot please) whilst I tried to maintain sobriety by ordering a special Chooza Masala at £6.50 a whole small chicken cooked with spices and almonds. The Kulfi £1.80 went down equally well.' RC. It is a large place (180 seats) and that requires discipline both in the kitchen and on the restaurant floor, but our scribes have given it their vote. On the strength of that we've put it into our TOP 100 (see page 25). The Indus gives discounts to Cury Club members at their quieter times, see page 288 for details.

SARADA
17, Hallgate, Doncaster. Tel: 0302 326406 **CC DISCOUNT**
Formula curries here, but done well. Papadoms 30p each, Pullao Rice £1.10, Chicken Curry £3.70, Set lunch from £2.50 and dinner from £9.00 and they give discounts to Curry Club members, see page 288 for details.

ROTHERHAM

SAAGAR **CC DISCOUNT**
55/57, Sheffield Road, Rotherham. Tel: 0709 377432
'An excellent restaurant it was comfortable with Austrian blinds. The menu contained a more than fair share of unusual ingredients - quail, liver and kidney - reflecting a more adventurous approach to cooking which was first class. Prawn Puri, Chilli Chicken, Karahi Gosht, all was super and not one bit of excess oil. We couldn't eat it all - it was far too much. It was also convenient to get to - we can go by bus so we can relax and drink. They give discounts to Curry Club members at their quieter times, see page 288 for details.

SHEFFIELD

ANILA'S
Division Street, Sheffield. Tel: 0742 722861
Not even 30,000 pea bulbs in its night-sky canopy can get it into this guide, but reports of good food at reasonable prices does. It stays open until 1am weekdays and 2.30am Fridays and Saturdays.

ISLAMABAD
61/63, Attercliffe Common, Sheffield. Tel: 0742 445586
Since appearing in budget eating out guides Kifayt Shah's Islamabad has gone up market. Tablecloths, cutlery and, yes, red flock wall paper is now in. It must be one of the few Indian restaurants to have re-decorated with red flock. And people flock there for miles around according to reports received because 'the food is so darned good.' BW, and 'it's so cheap.' LMcF. reports please.

NIRMAL'S **TOP 100 & CC DISCOUNT**
189/193. Glossop Road, Sheffield. Tel: 0742 724054
It is Mrs Nirmal Gupta who does the cooking which proves that this is an Indian restaurant (you'll not see a woman chef in a Bangladeshi or Pakistani restaurant). Infact in Indian itself it is not uncommon to encounter female chefs, and we know of a few others in the UK. Nirmal's is celebrating its tenth anniversary this year. Many of those years has seen it in Food Guides including our own. It has virtually doubled in size since we reported on it and now has 80 seats, a reception area, cocktail bar and two floors. Its recent revamp in pink has created a new image but the famous blackboard, the Special Board, upon which are chalked the dishes of the day fortunately remains. The technique would hardly merit a mention in 1001 bistros up and down the land, but it's rare if not unique in the world of curry. Nirmal herself makes appearances on the restaurant floor 'and enjoys talking about food.' PM. And there is plenty to talk about. We have streams of good reports to choose from. Almost everyone, regulars, of which there is clearly a large loyal following, and visitors alike, tell of the specials. Some however don't get further than the menu. It's northern Indian and on the face of it, just a standard curry house menu with Tandoori, Tikkas, Kormas, Bhunas, Madrases, Vindaloos and the rest. They'll all there and they're all cooked 'superbly and how I imagine they'd be cooked at an Indian home.' GA. And there's more! 'Nirmal's special Soup £1.00 and 'Potato Chops £1.25 are amazing mashed potato rissoles with a central stuffing of spicy lentils topped with almond tarka. The vegetable dishes prove the point that this is exceptional cooking. The paneer is always light and fresh , and stuffed Bhindi (Okra) is always the test of the good chef - they can so easily go sappy! I've not seen that happen here.' BR. The Lamb Masallam £45 for six, requires 2 days notice much of which is for marination. It is slow roasted 'falls of the bone and melts in the mouth.' DC. For price comparison, Papadoms are 30p each, Pullao Rice, £1.05 and Chicken Curry £3.95. Lunch snacks start at £2.75 and there are some 'great' set dinners from £25.00 for two. There is a service charge of 10% but Nirmal's is offering a discount for Curry Club members at their quieter times, see page 288 for details. Closed Sunday lunchtimes. Unhesitatingly this restaurant remains in our TOP 100 selection.

SHIRAZ
216, Fullwood Road, Sheffield. Tel: 0742 661894
'The menu is small but the quality is consistently high. Dishes are delicately spiced but fiery when necessary. When we visit for a takeaway we are given a glass of wine whilst waiting and the children get a coke free of charge.' LC.

TAJ MAHAL **CC DISCOUNT**
177, West Street, Sheffield. Tel: 0742 720596
Well presented, comfortable sized (40 seat) restaurant permitting them to do the job properly. The menu offers all the old favouriteS at sensible prices. Papadoms 25p each, Pullao Rice 90p per portions, Chicken Curry £2.75. They offer discounts to Curry Club members at their quieter times, see page 288. Nights only 7pm to 2.30pm (Sundays 12.30am).

YORKSHIRE - WEST

BRADFORD

Wow! Did I get into trouble with Bradford in our last guide? The venerable Bradford Telegraph and Argus took me to task for 'missing out on the scores of Bradford restaurants and concentrating on those in the south.' The tourist office

rang me up in anguish and sent pages of information, and I got scores of letters. Well I'll take the rap on the knuckles like a man - but I'm here to tell you my Grandpa was born and lived in Barnsley. I did my flying training at RAF Church Fenton and I've visited Bradford on numerous occasions to work and play. Bradford describes itself as the curry centre of the UK and yes, Bradford does have a lot of curry houses. To put things into perspective London has over 1400, Birmingham has nearly 300, Manchester 160, Glasgow 150 and then comes Bradford with 140. Before Bradford reaches for its collective pen, we must look deeper into these statistics. How many head of population per curry house? The national UK average is 7857. London as a whole 4229, Birmingham is 3779, Manchester 2670 and Glasgow a surprisingly high 5319. Bradford with a population of 300,000 and 140 restaurants has 2142 people per restaurant - the highest density ratio in the whole UK. I am very pleased indeed to announce that Bradford is indeed the curry centre of the UK. It takes a creative mind for a city to capitalise on this and full credit goes to Maria Glott of Bradford City Council's Tourist Office for putting Bradford on the map for curry afficionados. They publish an illustrated guide to the city's curry restaurants and ethnic shops and advise about tours of Bradford. Very interesting stuff. So what has Bradford to shout about? Here are twenty four reasons:

AAGRAH **TOP 100**
27, Westgate, Shipley, Bradford. B18. Tel: 0274 594660
and 483, Bradford Road, Pudsey, Leeds. Tel: 0274 668818
There are three Aagrahs in this chain. Shipley was established first (1977) followed by Pudsey (1986) and the newest Skipton, North Yorkshire. They are all managed by the Sabir Borthers. As they have everything in common we'll deal with all three together. Firstly, let's dispense with the local comics. The name lends its self to strangled cries about heat levels and Pudsey, built on the site of a former petrol station has the added bonus of 'fill'em up' and 'gas' gags. And 'is it spelt like that to get it first into the phone book?' does not have the waiters rolling on the floor with laughter. They've heard it all before, but they take it all in good natured stride. Jokes aside the Aagrah's are extremely good restaurants, all three. Decor is smart, although it too has its moments - Axminster, oldie beams and crazy paving walls contrast with the Indian brass and silks but it's the chairs which captivate almost everyone. Beautiful chairs from Kashmir hand carved, hand painted and each with sixteen tiny bells gives the restaurant a continual tinkling like soft rain. The menu is a confident expression of the Indian restaurant culinary art. 'All dishes are prepared daily from fresh ingredients, not frozen stock.' The truth of that declaration is bourne out by yards of satisfied testimonials: 'Sheekh Meat Kebabs £1.75 which melt in the mouth.' HN. 'An amazing Kashmiri Kebab £1.75, a soft spicy meat filling encased in mashed potato and fried.' CP. 'The waiter glided in with our Special main course dish, Raan (22.50 for two). It is leg of lamb marinated then slowly roasted until it falls off the bone (which is removed prior to service). It came with lemon rice and all the trimmings. I've not had Raan like this since I was at home in Delhi.' MT. 'There are so many specials which are new to me and as a vegetarian I felt spoilt for choice.' GR. The restaurants have the Vegetarian Society award and they were nominated Best Indian Restaurant (all three) 'dazzling vegetables' by the Yorkshire Post in their 'Restaurant of thre Eighties Award (December 1989), and this in the face of fierce competition in Leeds and Bradford. One regular customer at all three of the Aagrah's claims to be able to detect 'differences in degree' in the cooking but describes them as 'virtually indistinguishable.' One of our foremost reporters says, 'worth trying if you are trying to impress somebody but not a patch on some of the Bradford cafes for value and honesty.' PH, But because it is in a different market and primarily because of unsolicited the volume of praise from you we've placed the three Aagrah's in our TOP 100, see page 25. Hours vary slightly from branch to branch but all are evening only.

ALMANZIL **CC DISCOUNT**
29, Briggate, Shipley. Tel: 0274 594249
'The school aged son was the waiter shouting advice to mum and dad in the kitchen. The menu preliminary but wide ranging, with prices ranging from £2.00 to £4.00. The Shami Kebabs were the biggest I've ever tackled like huge red cowpats! The Keema was an utter delight.' PG. (Thank you for that appetising description - Ed). 'Spicy hot bhajias, juicy

meat curries containing huge chunks of tender meat. All excellent.' CB. It's an unlicensed evening only (6pm to 2am) curry house with no frills but reliable food, and it allows discounts to Curry Club members at its quieter times, see page 288 for details.

BHARAT **CC DISCOUNT**
502, Great Horton Road, Bradford. Tel: 0274 521200
Although Mohan and Jayantilal Mistry describe their restaurant as Gujarati (it's their home state) its menu is standard with more meat items than vegetarian. Look carefully and you will find one or two Gujarati Specialities - Patra £1.75, Kolrabi Colcasia leaves rolled in besan batter and fried or Patisse £1.85 spicy mashed potato balls rolled and fried. Note everyone is thinking veggy. 'Their Jeera Chicken £5.50 simply melted in my mouth with its delicate dhania and cummin overtones.' MB. 'The Meat Bhuna was light and careful and you can tell so much from the rice - this Pulav Rice £1.25 was as individual as its grains. Watch for their vegetarian nights every couple of months or so around £10 for their set 3 courses and 'more than remarkable in every department.' RT. The restaurant offers a discount for Curry Club members at their quieter times, see page 288 for details.

BOMBAY BRASSERIE
Simes Street, Westgate, Bradford. Tel: 0274 737564
The decor remains remarkable. One scribe likened it to a film set erected inside the former St Andrews reform church. But reports on food from the former Sheik's restaurant have not been uplifting. More reports please.

COMMONWEALTH **CC DISCOUNT**
51, Cheapside, Bradford. Tel: 0274 731794
Simple, cheap and cheerful unlicenced place. Papdoms are 20p each. Chicken Curry £2.70. Useful hours for curryholic insomniacs - 5pm to 3am - 1am on Sundays. Discounts are available to Curry Club members at their quieter times, see page 288 for details.

DARR
10, Lynthorne Road, Frizinghall, Bradford. Tel: 0274 487987
'The food is consistently at a high standard - a delight to the palate inexpensive and all main dishes were accompanied by a salad free of charge. The portions are generous so go easy on the chapattis or you won't have enough room to finish. Ask to see the spotless kitchens.' GH.

HANSA'S GUJARATI VEGETARIAN **TOP 100 & CC DISCOUNT**
44, Great Horton Road, Bradford. Tel: 0274 730433
Our long entry about Hansa's in Leeds applies to the relatively new Bradford branch. Behind an imposing frontage, with its first floor bow window, you'll find the most impressive vegetarian food which may make you wonder what you need meat for. See Hansa's, Leeds for details of the menu. Deservedly in our TOP 100, and Hansa's welcome Curry Club members who will get discounts at their quieter times, see page 288.

INTERNATIONAL TANDOORI **CC DISCOUNT**
40/42, Manville Terrace, Bradford. Tel: 0274 721449
Lunch trade and late hours - 6pm to 2am at this licensed Pakistani owned restaurant (Bashir and Rehman), with two 40 seat floors which are 'frequently busy and buzzing and all your old favourites at Bradford prices.' Papadoms 20p, Pullao Rice 85p, Chicken Curry £2.80, Discounts for Curry Club members are available, see page 288.

JUNIOR'S **CC DISCOUNT**
44, Highgate, Heaton, Bradford. Tel: 0274 491610
Another standard Bradford Pakistani restaurant one of whose claims to fame is 'the biggest Naan in the north. It's one by one-and-a-half feet in size. It came with their Kipling Table (£30.95 for four). Marinated roast lamb cooked with Keema, enhanced with a drop of Napoleon brandy and served with starters, Pullao Rice, Sweets, coffee and wine. Exceptionally good value.' ST. Papadoms are 20p, Chicken Curry £2.20 and Pullao Rice just 70p make 'this place very reasonable.' CT. Discounts are available to Curry Club members at their quieter times, especially between 6pm and 8pm (happy hour) see page 288.

KARACHI **TOP 100**
15/17, Neal Street, Bradford. Tel: 0274 732015
'This totally unpretentious, unspoilt, unhurried, unlicensed, semi-apologetic all-day cafe is not for the business man trying to impress a visiting client. Thank goodness or we would have to book in the afternoons to get one of the 40 seats.' PH. Despite its recent flirtation into and out of The Good Food Guide it has survived as the cheapest and the best of its type in Bradford. We had it in our first guide but took it out last time (a mistake). 'Learn to eat with your fingers and for heaven's sake avoid the loo's - they're still pretty grim.' JD. Otherwise enjoy 'onion Bhajia's for 35p, which look strange but are the best we've eaten. Raw chillies were brought on request and nine of us ate for an incredible £27.' RCE. 'Bhunas consistantly outstanding £2.50. A lot of meat on the tikkas £1.70. Papadoms 10p each, The standard three chapattis are made behind the counter.' PH. Goes into our TOP 100.

KASHMIR **TOP 100 & CC DISCOUNT**
27, Morley Street, Bradford.
Tel: 0274 726513
The Kashmir is Bradford's earliest curry house. It was established in 1955 at a time when there were only about 100 Asian curry restaurants in the whole of the UK. Its location places it conveniently between the University and the Alhambra and the Museum of Photography. Originally it catered specifically to the small but growing Pakistani community. It still does, but now its clientelle ranges much further, racially and geographically, including tourists drawn to the city by the efforts of the tourist Board. The restaurant now seats a massive 200 on two floors. 'On more than one occasion I've been here even the babes in the pushchairs were shovelling down spicy food.' GLM. There is absolutely nothing pretentious on the menu. It is formula curry. Indeed this restaurant was one of the pioneers of the formula. 23 chicken dishes, 19 Keema, 19 meat, 15 vegetable and 5 biriani, 3 prawn and some sundries comprise the menu. Don't expect tandoori dishes, this restaurant doesn't have such a mod con and they don't serve alcohol - but you can take your own. Prices are unbelievable. Papadoms 20p each, Chicken Curry £1.80, Fried Rice 80p. On top of this they'll give a discount to Curry Club members at their quieter times, see page 288. At your request (literally dozens) it goes into our TOP 100. Note: The hours 11am to 3am daily. Reports please.

KEBABASH
234, Wheatley Lane, Bradford. Tel: 0274 499985
It remains consistently good at Bradford's sensible prices.

MUMTAZ PAAN HOUSE **CC DISCOUNT**
386/392, Great Horton Road, Bradford.
Tel: 0274 571861
This is a branch of the Royal Sweets Bombay Halva Group of Southall and the Mumtaz is a place to go to purchase Indian sweets, Barfi, Halva, Jalebi, Gulab Jaman, Ras Gulla and Ras Malai (see glossary). You can also get samosas and Bhajias and Tikkas and Kebabs to takeaway or eat in. There are curry and rice dishes as well but Paan may be totally new to you. Chances are you won't like it. It's a bitter green leaf in which is wrapped a mixture of shredded betel nut, aniseed, sugar coated fennel seed, sunflower seeds, to which a sharp (lime) paste or sweet syrup is added. An acquired taste. The Mumtaz gives a discount to Curry Club members at their quieter times, see page 288.

NAWAAB **CC DISCOUNT**
32, Manor Road, Bradford.
Tel: 0274 720371
Formerly the Barbar, the Nawaab opened in 1988 as a smart, licensed 120 seat (over three floors) upmarket restaurant. The extensive menu covers the entire curry spectrum (including Balti from the Midlands) and each dish is exceptionally well explained. Prices are slightly high for Bradford but reasonable for elsewhere and they give discounts to Curry Club members at their quieter times, see page 288.

OTTOMANS SULTANS **CC DISCOUNT**
10, Commercial Street, Shipley. Tel: 0274 58662
'We went here expecting Turkish food', said one of our regulars. Imagine our surprise when we found Indian food. we stayed and it was just fine.' J and PR. Yes it is confusing, but it was previously Turkish. It is giving a discount to Curry Club members at its quieter times, see page 288 for details. Reports please.

PATWHAR
66, Oak Lane, Bradford. Tel: 0274 491040
'Mouthwatering food with extremely courteous, speedy and efficient staff. Nothing is too much trouble.' JH. 'Flavoursome food in the right quantities. Good news for vegetarians.' JR. 'My favourite is the Chef's Special Achari Gosht - lamb cooked in a pickle based sauce - delicious - just delicious.' LW.

SABRAAJ
20, Little Horton Lane, Bradford. Tel: 0274 724317
'It's inside a porta-cabin. You are met with a very warm and friendly atmosphere with a fantastic aroma tantalising your tastebuds. Meats lean and tender, subtle in flavour and devoid of a sea of ghee. Pullao Rice cooked to perfection and the prices very reasonable.' NS.

SANAM
50 Beckside Road, Lidget Green, Bradford.
Standard menu standard prices, 4pm till 2am daily. Reports please.

SHAMA **CC DISCOUNT**
2a, Commercial Street, Shipley. Tel: 0274 582312
There are four Shamas this one in Shipley, which opened in 1978. The others are in Bingley precinct, Fleece Street, Keighley and Maynell Avenue, Rothwell. All have open plan in view kitchens and are takeaways (the first two are restaurants as well. Their all operate in the evenings only 5pm to 1am daily. All offer discounts to Curry Club members at their quieter times, see page 288.

SHEESH MAHAL
St Thomas, off Westgate, Bradford.
This is a typical Bradford cheap and cheerful place with the usual downmarket atmosphere, formica tables, threadbare carpets and apalling loos. No cutlery is provided, though a spoon can be mustered on request. Starters all come with lashings of raw onion and mint sauce. The Bhajiias were a little on the greasy side but fresh. I tried Maghaz (curried sheeps Brains) which took courage but after the initial tenative investigation it indeed proved tasty.' AH.

SHIRAZ THE RESTAURANT **CC DISCOUNT**
113, Oak Lane, Bradford. Tel: 0274 490176
Since appearing in our first guide (1984) the Shiraz has drifted two points upmarket. Gone is the sweetshop/samosa take out image and in is THE RESTAURANT (and a new owner, Gul Bahar). The hours have also moved two points later and 3.30am is, we believe Bradfords, latest opener. The menu is standard (with a Balti dish) and prices Bradford average. No licence. Gives discounts to Curry Club members at its quieter times, see page 288 for details of this offer.

SWEET CENTRE AND RESTAURANT
110, Lumb Lane, Bradford.
In the takeaway you'll get Samosas and Pakoras, (£1 for 1lb) and all types of Indian sweets. Downstairs the restaurant is open sometimes, with a terrific atmosphere when full of local Asians. Curries average £2.50 with two filling rotis. Quail curry is £3.50 and Balti mutton on the bone £5.50.

TAJ MAHAL
25, Morley Street, Bradford. Tel: 0274 724947
Another long established venue (Bradford's second?), cheap and cheerful, with unusually and alcohol license. 'The service was excellent and the very good meal for four, including 8 pints of lager came to £20.00. No fuss, no frills.' MR.

TAKDIR **CC DISCOUNT**

West Riding House, 31, Cheapside, Bradford. Tel: 0274 729358

Twenty one this year, Hafiz Bhuiya's Takdir continues to 'motor on quietly and without fuss just as reliable motors do.' MT. It has always been 'upmarket by Bradford standards with highly competent standard curries.' GRS. Portions are generous. Prices fair: Popadoms are 25p each, Pullao Rice £1.20, Chicken Curry £3.00, set lunch £2.50. Discounts at both establishments are available for Curry Club members, see page 288.

BRIGHOUSE

THIPTI

6, Huddersfield Road, Brighouse. Tel: 0484 719818

Evenings only for this typical standard curry house (6pm to midnight, Fridays and Saturdays to 1am). Reports please.

THE SHEZAN

6, Lord Street, Halifax. Tel: 0422 353727

The Shezan is one of those places which motors on and on. We recommended it in our first Guide (when it was Ghani's Place) and again last time. It continues to get the formula exactly right with a regular flow of contented reports.

HUDDERSFIELD

SHER-E-PUNJAB

70, John William Street, Huddersfield. Tel: 0484 542357

A very smart up market establishment which is part of Hazrat Shah's 'Kismet' chain. (He has Kismets at Bradford, Sowerby Bridge, Ilkley and even Paris). Impressions at the Sher-E-Punjab start with the uniformed staff and smart decor. The service and the food place this restaurant above average.

SHABAB

37, New Street, Huddersfield. Tel: 0484 549514

The four Shababs have clearly gone through a bad patch during the late 1980's, resulting in the removal of the Harrogate and Leeds branches from our Guide. Harrogate's Shabab was a TOP 30 restaurant last time. Its decor, to this day is outstanding. But enjoy it though we may, we can't eat the decor. I sincerely hope I'm right in keeping this Huddersfield branch in the Guide, following sufficiently good reports to warrant it. I'd like reports on all the Shababs please. I'm certain they can get back into form.

LEEDS

SHUBA INDIAN CUISINE **CC DISCOUNT**

68/70, Abbey Road, Leeds. Tel: 0532 757170

Well reported with good quality food and that all important factor, generous portions. One regular says, 'it's our favourite from a huge choice in the area. They are good with children and my five year old adores the place. She particularly enjoys Shami Kebab and a Papadom.' TB. The Shuba gives discounts to Curry Club members at their quieter times, see page 288 for details.

DARBAR

16/17, Kirkgate, Adjacent to Littlewoods, Leeds. Tel: 0532 460381

Robert Cockroft had us in stitches with his review of the Darbar in Style magazine.

'It is impressive not merely from the moment you enter its front door but from about five seconds beforehand. This is roughly the time it takes for a beezer looking halfway between Father Christmas and Ivan the Terrible to leap forward, rip the door open and proffer a salute. He is the gateway to a spacious dining room which contains a great deal of fretwork, some French-style chairs and , against a far wall, a huge, elaborately carved panelled door. 'Does it lead anywhere?' one innocent guest inquired. 'No,' said the waiter, 'but the wall was the only place we could put it.'

Game, set and match to the vanishing art of logic. Darbar (otherwise, royal meeting place) is regally swish: creams and golds, cool tiles, humming fans, sweeping figs, smart loos. The senses recoil somewhat at the declaration that 'our curry is as subtle as Socrates and as mild as May.' Rice and breads are better than competent; one drawback remains the prodigious employment of ghee. It is disconcerting when dishes begin to masquerade as the Alaskan oil spill after five minutes on the candle-fired hot plate. Service is elegant if slowish; prices are reasonable with most starters under £2, most specials under £6 and curries around £4. With beer, two can escape , fed, watered, towelled and saluted by Santa for under £25.'
Thanks Robert and Style for letting us use that. Anytime you need a favour!

GULSHAN
1, Club Row, Albert Square, Yeadon, Leeds. Tel: 0532 506638
Surely one of the smallest restaurants in the world, seating just 12. It does a good takeaway trade, of course, but the restaurant has a huge following too. 'If you wish to get a seat, it's best to visit early. The Kebabs are spicy and the curries are served in ample quantities although they can be on the mild side.' TB.

HANSA'S TOP 100 & CC DISCOUNT
72/74, North Street, Leeds. Tel: 0532 444408
Gujarat is a state on India's west coast, north of Bombay. The first Englishman to set foot in India on official duty, Captain James Hawkins, an emissary from King James I, did so in Gujarat in 1608. Hansa's set foot in Leeds in 1986, as the first Gujarati restaurant in the north. Gujarat is one of India's foremost vegetarian states. Its style of food is quite different from that other bastion of Indian vegetarians - the South, which goes for watery pungent curries based on coconut and lentils. Gujarati spicing, whilst delicate, is satifying and individual dishes, though more substantial than their southern counterparts are none-the-less light of touch. All of Hansa's dishes are vegetarian most are Gujarati (one or two are from other parts of India) and some are vegan (containing no dairy products or eggs). If the thought of a vegetarian restaurant does not appeal, think again and give it a try. Over 75% of Hansa's customers are non vegetarian (as is 85% of the UK population). The restaurant has been a great success since it opened. The exterior is quite elegant. The restaurant ceilings are draped, giving a tented effect, plain fresco wall papers are adorned with stencilled artwork along the upper portions. Family photos are hung throughout to give the room a homely feeling. And so to the menu. It contains a carefully balanced selection of vegetarian specialities. Many could well be unfamiliar for this menu bears no resemblance to the standard curry house document. Each item is well described and help is at hand from the staff who are used to explaining to first timers at Hansa's, many of whom try one or two complete Thali meals (£6.95 or £5.50). Those who adventure further will find much to praise. Starters include Patra £1.95 - colcasia leaves and gram flour, batter rolled and sliced (Swiss roll style) then deep-fried. The Special Bhajiya (their spelling for Bhajia) - £1.75 - is described as wickedly spicy. 'It nearly blew my head off at first, then it was a magical delight.' JT. Dhebra £2.50 is a pancake spiced with fenugreek leaves and served with yoghurt sauce. Amongst the main courses the Ondhiya £4.05 is Gujarati Mixed Vegetable Curry. 'I chose this and with it I took Bhagat Muthiya £54.25 chickpea Koftas and Roti Bread. 'What a remarkable explosion of tastes and so filling'. GB. 'Even the wine list is different. Veena £7.25, Indian wine, Omar Khayan £13.25 Indian Champagne and there are 'additive free' wines.' 'There are so many new experiences at Hansa's that I could write a book on it.' JW. So could I and our recommendation is that you go out of your way to try Hansa's. We are quite happy to welcome it to our TOP 100. To tempt you to try it (or to go more if you are already a regular) Hansa's are offering a discount to Curry Club members at their quieter times, see page 288 for details.

THE LAST VICEROY CC DISCOUNT
141/145, New Roadside, Horsforth, Leeds. Tel: 0532 374035
This basement restaurant is decked out like an Arabian tent with a curtained ceiling in one dining room and ye old beams in the other. 'The interior is a delight - the food more so, even at peak times the service was top notch.' GH. 'Madras had huge chunks of chicken and a powerful

sauce £3.25 TB. 'It was my 21st and they gave me and my four girl friends small boxes of chocolates - what a nice touch.' LP. Popadoms are 20p each, Pullao Rice 95p, Chicken Curry £2.95, Set dinner from £8. There is a service charge of 10% but they give discounts to Curry Club members at their quieter times, see page 288 for details.

THE MANDALAY **TOP 100 & CC DISCOUNT**
8, Harrison Street, Leeds. Tel: 0532 446453
It's been at the top for many years but there is little doubt it is teetering a bit. 'It is very well appointed and you can be sure of a courteous welcome and departure., The head waiter was friendly and polite.' ST. Many reporters enjoy the Tandoori Chef in view behind a glass enclosure. The grand piano is still there complete with pianist from time to time. The Mandalay's seeks every opportunity to take its patrons into fantasty world. Even the menu is entertaining with witty short stories on alternate pages. There is a souvenir mini replica menu which diners can take-away. 'The starters were hot and fresh. The meat tender and sauces rich and well flavoured. Portions were so generous that we could share. It justified our expectations after reading the Good Curry Guide's recommendation.' JL. 120 miles from home, we went there on your commendation. The Roghan Gosh was excellent and Tandoori Mixed Grill first class. It was nice to find a restaurant that lived up to its reputation.' PM. In the same week we received a report which talked of the Murgh Massalum going 'overboard with red food colouring and Rhogan Gosh mediocre to taste.' Dr and Mrs PRD. Could this be the same restaurant? More recently we had one of our ace travellers say that he went 'on a very bust Saturday night, everything was very good but the Malai Kofta was outstanding. Compares favourably with the top London establishment.' AD. Prices are less than some people expect for the quality of the surroundings, Murgh Madras is £5.25, Pullao Kesri (Saffron Rice) 95p, Nan 80p per bread and Kulfi £1.45. Our decision after very careful pondering is that this restaurant is well above average but it is human. It will remain on our TOP 100 catergory but we hope the management will think carefully about maintaining the very high standards they set for themselves. We urge you to take the Road to Manadalay, particularly as the restaurant is offering a discount to Curry Club members, see page 288 for details. Reports please.

MOGHUL INDIAN **CC DISCOUNT**
8/9. The Green, Town Street, Horsforth, Leeds. Tel: 0530 590530
Seating just 42 this popular, up market restaurant is regularly full and this leads to reports about it being a little cramped. The food is clearly good enough to off set that problem. They offer discounts to Curry Club members, see page 288 for details.

NAFEES
69A, Raglan Road, Leeds. Tel: 0532 453128
12pm to 3am daily should sort out those needing a curry fix right down to the flock paper. It's the haunt of students from the nearby University and owner Mohammed has a woman chef. Large cheap portions.' DN.

SHEESH MAHAL **CC DISCOUNT**
348, Kirkstall Road, Leeds. Tel: 0532 304161
Azran Chaudhury tells us that Karahi Chicken £3.50 is their most popular dish, followed by mix Kebabs £3.00 and Royal Lamb Gosht £6.00 with Pullao Rice. Its visiting card tells us it is Indian Restaurant 'between the Cardigan Arms and the Rising Sun.' You tell us you like it, so everyone will be happy that the Sheesh Mahal gives discounts to Curry Club members, see page 288 for the offer details.

MUMTAZ MAHAL
44, Bondgate, Otley. Tel: 0943 464301
'It used to have a reputation for being a late night haunt for Lager Louts. Now with a bit of competetion it has taken a quantum leap upwards. We enjoyed a basket of Papadoms, huge Samosas with a substantial salad and a pool of raita - almost a meal in itself and perfectly presented. The main course had us cowering for mercy - it never stopped arriving. Special Rice with whole spices, chicken and meat, vegetables in a tangy dryish sauce, sliced mushrooms, bathing in delicate aromatic ghee - based sauce, and Bindhi flavoursome and tender. All of this and more mopped up by a glazed mattress of a Naan bread at least a foot in

diameter. Needless to say after shifting that lot, the waiters had to lift us out of our seats. They watched with true job satisfaction as we waddled to the door.' PG.

RAJPOOT
134, Kirkgate, Wakefield. Tel: 0924 371215
'Not an out of the ordinary menu but the food is a cut above.' PRDW. 'I was impressed with this comfortable restaurant. The Naan was superb and supplied on request at no charge. Fresh green chillies are available too.' RCE.

TASTE OF INDIA **CC DISCOUNT**
22, Brook Street, Wakefield. Tel: 0924 361779
Also well spoken of, this relatively new place is offering discounts to Curry Club members at their quieter times, see page 288 for details.

Owners of restaurants selected to appear in this guide are invited to advertise. We thank those who have done so – it helps keep the price of the guide as low as possible.

ISLANDS

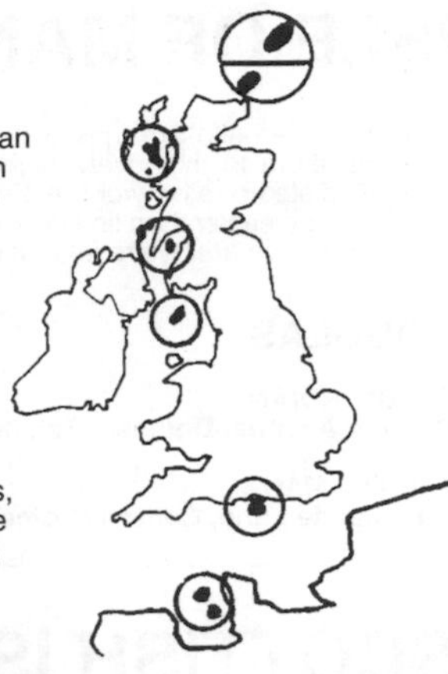

England, according to Napolean was an island of shopkeepers. Had he been around today, he might have observed that Britain is a collection of islands and that the Brits are a nation of curry eaters!
Dotted all around the British Isles are small islands. Some have no curry houses (eg: Lundy, The Scillies, Uist, Mull etc), others do and for neatness of filing we group them together.
Lerwick, capital of the Shetland Isles, has our most northerly curry house (and probably that of the whole globe). It is 800 miles from London and 1,000 miles from our most southerly in St Helier's, capital of the Channel Islands of Jersey. A neat but useless fact for you to mull over while contemplating your curry.

CHANNEL ISLANDS

GUERNSEY

SHANIS
The Fermain Hotel, Fort Road, St Peter Port.
'A group of us had THE most superb meal here. Prawn Puri was £2, Chicken Korma £4.24, Tikka Masala £5.50, Pullao Rice £1.25, Naan Bread £1. Kaleen the owner made us most welcome.' JG.

THE TASTE OF INDIA
Sunset Cottage, L'Eree. Tel: 0481 64516
On the west side of the island and 'yes you can watch the sunset then enjoy tandoori and tikkas, birianis and bhoonas.' JWR.

JERSEY

THE NEW RAJ
8, Burlington Parade, St Saviours Road, St Helier. Tel: 0534 74131
Over the years we have received only one poor report on this restaurant and that was ages ago. It has otherwise received a consistency of reporting, including fair prices.

ISLE OF WIGHT

Technically part of the county of Hampshire, we treat the Isle of Wight as a separate entity in this guide. This, despite a resident telling us that she and her husband travel to Portsmouth for a 'serious curry.' MM. For those with less stamina each of the Island's five main towns - Cowes, Newport, Ryde, Sandown and Shanklin has curry houses. Reports please.

ISLE OF MAN

If you don't say 'hello' to the pixies they won't bring you good luck, and you may not return to this lovely island to enjoy horse drawn trams, the celebrated steam railway or the TT races. Or to try to spot a minx cat, which may be easier than finding a good curry house. Of the few on the island these two are, we're told, reliable.

DOUGLAS

SEPOY INDIAN
Walpole Avenue, Douglas. Tel: 0624 76651

THE TAJ MAHAL
3, Esplande Lane, Central Promenade, Douglas. Tel: 0624 74741

SCOTTISH ISLANDS

Mentioned in this Guide because they are there, rather than for any gastronomic feats. Mind you, it is a feat in itself to find a curry in such remote and wonderful places.

ISLE OF ARRAN, WESTERN ISLES

Kestrel Restaurant
Brodick, Arran.

ISLE OF ORKNEY

SHAKTI INDIAN RESTAURANT
25a, Bridge Street, Kirkwall, Orkney. Tel: 0856 2933

ISLE OF SHETLAND

RABE INDIAN RESTAURANT
26, Commercial Road, Lerwick, Shetland. Tel: 0595 3349

ISLE OF SKYE, HEBRIDES

BAGDAD RESTAURANT
Trinton Hotel, Kyleakin, Skye.

NORTHERN IRELAND

Since our last edition a few new curry houses have opened, but the fact remains that curry does not figure largely on the diet of the residents of Northern Ireland. These few are the pick of a small bunch. Reports from Ireland, North and South, are as scarce as their curry restaurants so we will greatly welcome your opinions.

BELFAST

ASHOKA
365, Lisburn Road, Belfast. Tel: 0232 660362
Established for several years now, the Ashoka has carved a good reputation for itself.

BITHIKA
133, Lisburn Road, Belfast. Tel: 0232 381009
A newer restaurant in the city.

MANZIL
18, Shaftesbury Square, Belfast. Tel: 0232 326677
A good standard.

MOGHUL INDIAN
60, Great Victoria Street, Belfast. Tel: 0232 243727
Diljit Ramas also owns the Ashoka and the Moghul's reputation is equally established.

RAJPUT
461, Lisburn Road, Belfast. Tel: 0232 662168
'Certainly one of the best in the city.' TJ.

LONDONDERRY

THE TAJ
59, Strand Road, Londonderry. Tel: 0504 264768
Reports please.

NEWTOWNARDS

GANGES INDIAN
69, Court Street, Newtownards. Tel: 0247 811426
Reports please.

PORTADOWN

GAYNOR
3, Church Lane, Portadown. Tel: 0762 337117
Reports please.

SOUTHERN IRELAND

All quoted price are Irish currency.

DUBLIN

EASTERN TANDOORI **TOP 100 & CC DISCOUNT**
34/35, South William Street, Dublin.
Tel: 01-710428/710506
The Eastern Tandoori was established in 1984 and it brought a new concept to Dublin - Indian cuisine presented in the smartest surroundings and cooked to the highest standards. Feroze Khan has maintained this reputation building a sufficient customer base to allow him and his wife to open two further Eastern Tandooris at Deansgrange Court Dublin and at 263, Avenue Louise, 1050 Brussels, Belgium. The menu is familiar enough to regular curry diners 'and being up market the word curry appears only four times in small print. New to us were Tandoori Crab Claws £8.95 and Salmon Massalla £7.95. I was not sure that salmon would curry well, but the lightness of touch ensured a memorable dish.' JO'D. 'My wife prefers beef and I prefer lamb. I believe this to be the only

Indian restaurant where you have a choice. She had Beef Jalfrezi and I had Lamb Chilli Massalla both at £7.25 we both tested each others and sure enough the meats were different, and both done to perfection.' ALC. Prices include Papadoms, Pickles and Chutneys. Pullao Rice is £1.25, set luncheon £6.50, Dinner from £11.95 (vegetarian Thali). There is a service charge. All three restaurants offer discounts to Curry Club members at their quieter times, see page 288. More reports welcome but this restaurant is good enough to be in our TOP 100.

RAJDOOT TANDOORI **TOP 100 & CC DISCOUNT**
26/28, Clarendon Street, Westbury Centre, Dublin 2.
679-4272/4280
As with Rajdoot's three other branches in Bristol (Avon), Manchester and Birmingham, (West Midlands), we receive plenty of superlatives about this place. One veteran reporter has made a point of visitng them all. 'I do believe Dublin has a greater choice on the menu. It has that Irish quirk of offering either beef or lamb dishes and you'll find Mackerel and Crab as well. On one occasion I had Tandoori crab £3.85, the Kidney Massalla £6.25 with Pullao Rice £1.35 and Dal of the day £3.75 and beef/garlic nan £2.65 the latter stuffed with mince. I concluded with Earl Gray Tea. There are some meals which stay with you for life as a measure of what should be. This, as with so many new things, was one of those.' ARA. I'd heard that Rajdoots, had won an award for Best Ethnic Vegetarian Restaurant, and I had a vegetarian friend to entertain. I'm a confirmed carnivore and a curryholic to boot. Without a hot and spicy meat dish I feel deprived. But this time I thought I'd follow suit. We had a ball with Panir Shashlik £3.15 and Vegetable Cutlet £3.65 starters and the waiter's selection of four wonderful and totally different dishes mopped up with onion Kulcha (1.35) the fluffiest cumulo nimbus punctuated with fresh coriander leaf and diced onion. With that we tried Chilean red wine 14.85 and it married quite compatibly. Our entire meal came to 53.,75 for two but we lacked for nothing.' BS. It is unsolicited responses such as these which keeps Rajdoots in our TOP 100 (see page 24). Prices are high, boosted by 12% service charge but things are improved for Curry Club members who are given a discount at quieter times (see page 288 for details).

CORK

KASHMIRI
Frances Street, Cork.
Reports Please

SCOTLAND

BORDERS

With a total population of 60,000 in an area the size of Kent it is not surprising that we do not hear too much about the few restaurants in this county. From what information we have received, we'd say these are satisfactory standard curry houses.

HAWICK

LAHORE TANDOORI
4, Station Buildings, Doumont Place, Hawick. Tel: 0450 73313

It is the purpose of a guide to report trends, note the bad things, praise the good, and to compare prices. Entry into any guide, big or small, famous or little known, can affect a restaurant, sometimes adversely. But a guide can do no more than report facts. Clients ultimately are the lifeblood of a restaurant. And clients should make their views known – praise and complaints alike-to the restaurant there and then, not next day. They should also inform us of their views.

Owners of restaurants selected to appear in this guide are invited to advertise. We thank those who have done so – it helps keep the price of the guide as low as possible.

The editor of The Good Curry Guide welcomes your views on restaurants we list in this guide and on any curry restaurants or take-aways you visit. Please send them to: The Curry Club, PO Box 7, Haslemere, Surrey GU27 1EP.

GALASHIELDS

GANDHI
43, High Street, Galashields. Tel: 0896 3450

CENTRAL

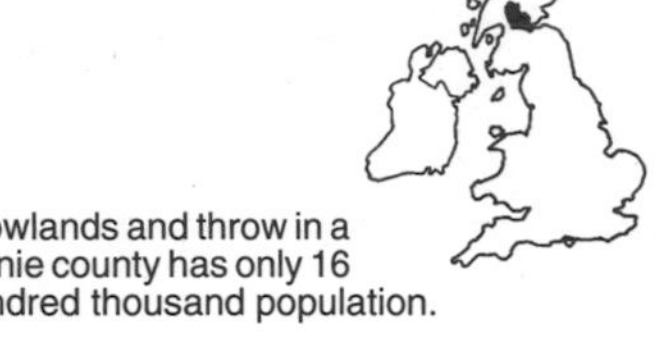

Where the highlands meet the lowlands and throw in a little bit of Loch Lomond this bonnie county has only 16 curry restaurants for its few hundred thousand population. We mention two.

DENNY

OMAR KHAYYAM
1, Church Walk, Denny.
Tel: 0324 825898
Chicken Malaya £3.75 which is not on the menu in many restaurants is my favourite, consisting of huge chunks of chicken with pineapple, lychee, coconut and cream. The quanitites are always huge and the quality very good.' CM.

FALKIRK

WISHING WELL RESTAURANT
4, Wier Street, Falkirk.
Tel: 0324 22010
Formula curries. Popadoms 30p, Pulao Rice 90p, Chicken Curry £3.20. Set lunch £1.95. Dinner £17.95 for two.

DUMFRIES AND GALLOWAY

D and G is home to Gretna Green, but to fewer people, fewer restaurants and fewer reports even than Borders. More always welcome.

DUMFRIES

JEWEL IN THE CROWN
50, St Michael Street, Dumfries. Tel: 0387 64183
Robbie Burns wrote 'Aul Lang Syne' and is buried in this historic Royal Burgh. The Jewel is 'clean and on the small side with a peculiar baco-foil type mirror effect wallpaper, but the services and food were good.' BR.

STRANRAER

SHISH MAHAL
41, Hanover Street, Stranraer. Tel: 0776 3987
The town is surrounded by beautiful countryside and Loch Ryan is

popular with tourists for yachting and fishing. It also has the ferry for Northern Ireland, paddling pools, a rock garden and, amongst others, this curry house, reported as the better one. Reports please, from all you curryholic visitors.

FIFE

Once the home of Scotland's Kings, and sprinkled with more castles, probably more than curry houses, this low population county has none-the-less produced a TOP 100 restaurant.

DUNFERMILINE

ROSE OF BENGAL
10, Guildhall Street, Dunfermiline.
Tel: 0383 725300
The former capital of Scotland for six centuries, and home to Robert-the-Spider-Bruce, Andrew Carnegie, later to become the American millionaire, tartan factories and more latterly the Rose of Bengal curry house, said by our reporters to be the best of the town's three.

GLENROTHES

NURJAHAN
Cos Lane, Woodside Road, Glenrothes. Tel: 0592 630649
Standard curry house

KIRCALDY

RANAS
Charlotte Street, Kircaldy. Tel: 0334 74825
Another standard curry house.

ST ANDREWS

THE NEW BALAKA **TOP 100 & CC DISCOUNT**
3a, Alexandra Place, Market Street, St Andrews. Tel: 0334 74825
Beautiful ancient seaside town named after Scotland's patron saint whose relics are said to be buried here. Better known for its university, Scotland's oldest, and of course the golf. The game was founded here and it accounts for an insurgence of tourists. St Andrews has a small crop of Indian restaurants, but one stands out. It is the New Balaka owned and run by Hilton trained Adbur Rouf. Located in the large basement room of a late Victorian sandstone hotel building. It was refurbished in 1990 to a high standard, resulting in a spacious marble-tiled entrance which leads to a cosy reception and bar area. The dining area is decorated in pastel brown - pink linked to blue carpeting with circuitous hand stencilling. Banquettes seats with Indian tapestry covering wood and wicker partitions divide the space and Bengali silk tapestries are on the walls. 'The menu is a good entertaining read.' EP. 'Starters include the usual range of goodies. But I'd not heard of Chat Pat Chicken £1.95 which turned out to be tandoori chicken Wings, smoky and very succulent too.' RJT. The Mulligatawny Soup £1.85 is reported as 'nutritiously lentilly, spicy, slightly hot and swept with the sour taste of tamarind.' SB. The King Prawns are imported from the Paddha river in Bengal and are a massive five inches in length. They appear in tandoori form £9.95 and many curries. Popular specials include Mas Bangla £6.50 featuring Scottish Salmon (a passable substitute for the Bengali freshwater fish - rohi) marinated in lime juice and spices then fried in mustard oil (much used here) with garlic tomato and aubergine. Lemony Chicken £6.50 lemon, ginger and heaps of coriander leaf 'which we grow in our own garden. Remarkably it has flourished all year round and greatly increases the subtlely of our curries,'

said Mr Rouf. 'There are many choices on the menu, with little omitted,' he continued, 'but any special curry of your choice not included in our menu may be prepared at the discretion of our chef who is armed with both the expertise and the ingredients necessary to create an infinite variety of Indian savouries.' Mr Rouf and his team operate their restaurant with pride and care, welcoming both a burgeoning trade from their local following but from visitors too. We are pleased to place the New Balaka in our TOP 100 UK restaurants (see page 24). They give discounts to Curry Club members at their quieter times, see page 288 for details of this offer.

GRAMPIAN

Aberdeen is the principal city with 200,000 population and over twenty restaurants. The whole of the rest of Grampian has around 100,000 population and a dozen curry houses in Banff, Buckie, Elgin, Ellon, Forres, Frazerburgh, Invervie and Peterhead. We have insufficient correspondence on these to make qualitative judgements on them. You'll find them easily enough and we welcome your reports.

ABERDEEN

LIGHT OF BENGAL
13, Rose Street, Aberdeen. Tel: 0224 644693
Popular. Prices higher than UK average. Papdoms 45p. Pullao Rice £1.60. Chicken Curry £4.70, but these seem to be Aberdeen's average.

RAJ DULAL
11, Dee Street, Aberdeen. Tel: 0224 587980
Decor above average with 'interesting ceiling and brass pillars. The food is fine but they're not subtle on their desire to part customers and their money.' JL.

SHEHBAAZ
19, Rose Street, Aberdeen. Tel: 0224 641786
One of the town's better restaurants in comfortable surroundings.

SHEZAN
48, Bridge Street, Aberdeen. Tel: 0224 575634
Shares our reporters 'best in city' vote with the Shish Mahal.

SHISH MAHAL
468, Union Street, Aberdeen. Tel: 0224 643339
As above.

FRASERBOROUGH

TANDOORI CHAT HOUSE
19/21, Saltoon Square, Fraserburgh. Tel: 0346 26901
Chat means street kiosk snacks in the Indian languages. But the food at Fraserburgh's Tandoori Chat House is, we hear, rather more substantial. It serves all the regular tandoori and curry favourites. Special dishes include Chicken Kandhari, Chicken Marango, Akbari Cham Cham and Fish Shajahani amongst others. Prices are reasonable and service friendly. More reports welcomed.

HIGHLANDS

Rocky wilderness, Ben Nevis, deer, heather, serene beauty, Loch Ness, John O'Groates and just 21 curry houses. Reports are as elusive as Nessie so please let's have 'em rolling in. This is what we know.

FORT WILLIAM

INDIAN GARDEN
88, High Street, Fort William. Tel: 0397 5011
Nestling at the mouth of the Loch Ness canal and the green foot hills of Ben Nevis, visit the museum to see Bonnie Prince Charlie and a reconstructed crofter's kitchen. For the real thing go to the India Garden a 'popular local with reasonable prices and service.' IB.

INVERNESS

The Highland mountains surround this prehistoric and now elegant town. Home to 40,000 people and five curry houses. Of those, you have recommended the following (more reports eagerly awaited).

CANAL RESTAURANT
85, Telford Street, Inverness. Tel: 0463 220311

GULISTAN
38, Eastgate, Inverness. Tel: 0463 231075

ROSE OF BENGAL
4/6, Ness Walk, Inverness. Tel: 0463 233831

LOTHIAN

EDINBURGH

ASHA TANDOORI
8, West Maitland Street, Edinburgh. Tel: 031 220 0007
Reports are coming in increasingly about this smart and organised restaurant with its good cuisine. More reports welcomed.

BALLI'S TANDOORI
89, Hanover Street, Edinburgh. Tel: 031 226 3451
'The welcome on arrival was more than adequate, though after that the service, although efficient, was civil but impersonal. The decor is very attractive, blue and pinks with pretty china. The onion chutney which accompanied was particularly spicy and it came, without having to ask for for it. The lager was supremely cold - a delight to my husband. The whole meal was good. The coffee came in a cafetiere, good try but it was so weak it was just coloured water. The entire meal was under £30 for two.' CC.

BANGALORE **CC DISCOUNT**
52, Home Street, Edinburgh. Tel: 031 229 4554
5pm to 1.30am daily
This smart upmarket restaurant is in the same ownership as The Himalaya (see next entry). Prices are the same. Usefully sited opposite the King's Theatre. Useful hours for the curryholic insomniac. Offers discounts for Curry Club members at their quieter times, see page 288.

HIMALAYA **CC DISCOUNT**
171, Bruntsfield Place, Edinburgh. Tel: 031 229 8216
The Himalaya was the first of Gracian Rebello's two restaurants to open (1975). Unlike the Bangalore, it operates a lunchtime trade as well as evening. The menu is similar. We have had good reports about Indian Garlic Chicken £4.50 and Kathmandu Massallum £4.25 'a tender meat curry combining the savoury of spices and the sweetness of fruits.' JMcT. Prices are typical for Edinburgh - Papadoms are 40p each, Pullao Rice £1.60, set dinner £9.50 for vegetarians, £11 for non-vegetarians. Offers discounts to Curry Club members at their quieter times, see page 288.

KALPNA **TOP 100 & CC DISCOUNT**

2/3, St Patrick Square, Edinburgh. Tel: 031 667 9890

Batiks and Indian miniatures adorn the grey and brick red walls, enhanced by fresh plants and flowers, at M Jogee's Kalpna. The restaurant is distinctly upmarket (it does not do takeaways) and it is exclusively vegetarian with specialist dishes from Gujarat, Bombay and South Indian. This type of food is as far removed from the 'definitive' Bangladeshi (Punjabi standard curries) as India is from Scotland. After a decade at the top of Edinburgh's culinary tree there can be few local curry lovers who have not been to the Kalpna. 'Go whether you are vegetarian or not for a decidedly educational experience.' says one correspondent who is not, but has 'become a regular there.' JG. So at the risk of preaching to the converted... but hopefully converting new followers to one very authentic style of Indian food, here is our appraisal. The menu comprehensively explains itself right down to reminding you that the world's largest animal is a vegetarian. There are eight starters including samosas, and pakoras plus two further types of rissole (Tikkia and Bateta Vada). The Bhel Poori is served cold, crisp and crunchy, contrastingly sweet an sour and savoury. All these plus plain Dosas (rice pancakes) come at £1.50. Add Sambar curry to a Dosa and pay £3.50. Of the eighteen main course dishes (averaging £4.00 each) the advice is 'To go with someone you're comfortable with, share three or four dishes rice and bread. Enjoy the company, place and food and look forward to returning.' RST. Good advice for any restaurant really, and particulary, it seems, at the Kalpna. We have no hesitation in retaining the Kalpna in our TOP 100 restaurant list (see page 24). The Kalpna gives discounts to Curry Club members at their quieter times, see page 288.

KUSHI'S

32C, Broughton Street, Edinburgh. Tel: 031 556 8092

Located in the university area, it has the affections of many a student past and present. This type of place is very common in Bradford or Birmingham but unique in Edinburgh. 'Kushi's gives plain, no nonsense Indian cookery produced to a high standard. Portions generally over estimate appetites at very reasonable prices. The decor is the plain, no table cloths, wooden bench category, but the informality gives the place a welcoming feeling.' BE.

LANCERS **TOP 100 & CC DISCOUNT**

5, Hamilton Place, Stockbridge. Tel: 031 332 3444

This is the third of Wali Uddin's small but exclusive chain of restaurants, established in 1985. We placed it in our top listing in our last edition and have no hesitiation in keeping it there. It is not enough to 'spare no expense' on your decor, but it must be kept that way. At Lancers it would be hard to improve on the rosewood, suede, brass and leather look. Ceilings often let the side down, but Lancers moulded ceilings are quietly unobtrusive, yet are a carefully considered design attribute. It is unlikely that anyone notices the ceilings because first impressions (starting outside with the huge arched window and painted cavalry man) are of regimental presentation, spotless cleanliness and attention to detail. The place gleams. Each table is as laid with the accuracy of the parade ground. Gilded place mats, Wedgewood china, chrystal goblets, containing knife-edge-creased pink napkins and substantial cutlery at attention awaited the arrival of its diners. Downstairs is an inner sanctum - the Officer's Club - where a vast 'Chippendale' table seats 20 for private functions. Before we turn to the food, the wine list deserves a mention. As happens elsewhere in Edinburgh, it gives copious advice including an expert specific match of particular wine to particular dish. We are so impressed we've reproduced it our introduction section. The menu contains a sensible selection of Tandoori dishes, with classic curries: Kurma, Bhuna, Pasanda, Biryani and enough vegetable main dishes to make the place a favourite with vegetarians. The place is always inviting, the service assured and friendly and despite its very up market positioning the prices are Edinburgh norm - Papadoms 45p each, Pullao Rice £1.65, Chicken and Lamb dishes £4.95. Set luncheon is £5.95 and dinner £11.95. Discounts are available to Curry Club members at their quieter times, see page 288 for details. As we said earlier, it is in our TOP 100.

MONSOON **CC DISCOUNT**

13, Dalry Road, Edinburgh. Tel: 031 346 0204

The second of Wali Uddin's small chain, its small size (forty seats) suits its style well. Old hands tells us they prefer the raised area. It is smart and usually packed. The food is all above average under the direction of

Bangladeshi chef Abdul Haque. Wali welcomes Curry Club members to whom discounts are available at their quieter times, see page 288.

SHAMIANA **TOP 100**
14, Brougham Street, Edinburgh. Tel: 031 288 2245
'Although we hadn't booked at this very busy restaurant they put us onto a 'reserved' table asking us to leave at a certain time. The decor is modern and totally unIndian with black and white floor tiles and discreet Indian prints on the walls. The Papadoms 40p each, were the thinnest and crispiest I've ever had. Tandoori Quail (£4.95), Panir Pakora £2.00) and all of the meal added up to the best Indian meal we've had this year.' MC. The change of ownership does not seem to have affected standards. An exceedingly good restaurant worthy of our TOP 100 (see page 25).

INDIAN CAVALRY CLUB
3, Atholl Place, Edinburgh. Tel: 031 228 3232
Shahid and Bilquis Choudhury's restaurant evokes an age gone by with its decor and uniformed waiters. 'who unfold your starched linen napkin and place it in your lap.' TW. 'The menu is different from the usual, extremely filling and very good quality.' HFD. Reports, whilst mainly positive, have suggested a slight uneveness of late. Of the Garlic Naan were told it 'Appeals to garlicholics for its combination of softness and strength of flavour.' KC. 'The Lamb Pasanda shone through like a beacon.' PST. Edinburgh prices. Reports please.

SULTAN
157/9, Lothian Road, Edinburgh. Tel: 031 229 1000
Standard curries are the business of the day here, or rather the night, because Iqbal Mirza's Sultan operates an evening trade until 2am daily. (weekend lunchtimes as well). The decor is an attractive combination of Victoriana and Indiania complete with beams. The food is well above average. They hold Gourmet Evenings with unusual dishes from time to time at around £10 per head. Edinburgh prices - Popadoms 40p each, Pullao Rice £1.35 and Chicken Curry £4.25.

THE VERANDAH RESTAURANT **TOP 100 & CC DISCOUNT**
17, Dalry Road, Edinburgh. Tel: 031 337 5828
The majestic circulating colonial fan, wicker chairs, pine table and wood slat blinds. A humid night and tantilising smells. Only the absence of a backing track of crickets and jungle noises prevents one from transporting straight to the pages of a novel by Somerset Maugham. This was the first of Wali Uddin's small chain (see above) and when it opened in 1981 it set a new standard of restaurateuring amongst Edinburgh's curry houses. That the city now has a very high ratio of top quality restaurants is in no small part due to Wali, an energetic 36 year old, Edinburgh's only Bangladeshi JP, and more at home in a kilt than Dacca. The kitchen is under the direction of partner chef Kaisar Miah. The menu contains a representative selection of the best of Indian and Bangladesh. 'Papadoms 50p, were particularly good and the chutneys fine. The Lamb Kebab £2.75 superb with excellent sauce. Bringal Bhajee £2.75 and Sag Panir Malai £3.95 both fresh with lots of fresh panir. The Gulab Jaman £1.25 dessert spoilt the meal. It was dry and sprinkled with hundreds and thousands!' MCF. As with Lancers, and copied elsewhere in Edinburgh the Verandah's comprehensive wine list gives wine for specific dish suggestions and we reproduce this in our introduction. Despite a few ripples the reports on this restaurant are enthusiastic. For innovation, sincerity and professionalism we are delighted to place the Verandah in to our TOP 100. Wali welcomes Curry Club members to whom he will give a discount to at their quieter times, see page 288.

STRATHCLYDE

GLASGOW

Glasgow, the third most populous city in the UK (760,000), Shipyards, the medieval cathedral, the underground metro, Sauchiehall Street, European Cultural

City. It's not quite curry city UK (see Bradford entry), but it does have 150 curry houses, some at the top of the tree.

TASTE OF INDIA
Unit 2/3, Main Street, Thornlibank, Glasgow. Tel: 041 638 3080
Brought to our attention by our Scottish reporters who tell of tasty curries at the Taste at reasonable prices.

ASMAN
22, Bath Street, City Centre, Glasgow. Tel: 041 331 2575
Smart and exclusive. 'Darned good food in enjoyable atmosphere.' TJ. They give discounts to Curry Club members at their quieter times, see page 288.

ALI SHAN
250, Battlefield Road, Battlesfield, Glasgow. Tel: 041 632 5294
Popular Indian cuisine at popular prices is what we hear. They give discounts to Curry Club members at their quieter times, see page 288.

BALBIR'S ASHOKA — TOP 100 ^& CC DISCOUNT
108, Eldershie Street, Glasgow. Tel: 041 221 1761
Balbir Singh Sumal opened this, his first restaurant, in 1982. From small beginings it rapidly proved popular. Now, with 140 seats (on two floors) this is one of the largest in the city. Indian murals adorn the walls - the Himalayas upstairs, the Moghuls downstairs. 'It was very busy, large and tastefully decorated.' DD. Balbir's wife, Paramjit, masterminds the menu and the kitchens, and the intensely Punjabi cooking. 'Where else, I ask you, can you find a choice of ten pakoras? The only answer was to go for a mixed platter £3.15.' LC. Punjabi Massala dishes are a house speciality in the karahi with fresh ginger, garlic, onion, peppers, chilli and spices. There are a dozen of these on the menu £5.15 to £7.85. Five Kormas including Ceylonese (Coconut) Kashmiri (fruit and yoghurt) Mughlai (cream) Gujarati (lentils) and Shali Bahar (ground and flaked almonds and cream). Fish dishes are to be found in the Tandoori £3.15 and curry sections. The menu continues in this expensive way and the food is undoubtedly. The three Balbir restaurants, go collectively into out TOP 100 (see below).

BALBIR'S INDIA BRASSERIE — TOP 100 & CC DISCOUNT
Cornor of Sauchiehall Street & Eldershie Street. Tel: 041 221 1452
Balbir's success with the Ashoka (see above) led in 1988 to the opening of a smaller 72 seat up market version. It was soon expanded by 50 more seats. The interior transports the diner to a colonial age of grandeur and elegance from the blackamoor statue, standing guard at the entrance to the large square classically proportioned room with its 'marbled' walls and ceilings, shining brass chandeliers, swagged curtains, simplistic furnishings and crisp linen table-wear. The menu here contains a mixture of Ashoka favourites with new items proportionately more expensive 'such a setting is hardly inexpensive.' (Balbir). 'Mussel Massala £2.65 for starter, Sali Boti (Parsi Lamb) £6.15 Goa Fish £6.15 wrapped in vine leaves. The staff are well trained, the service terrific and the food superb. Had a glimpse of the kitchen... it was sparkling.' BN. The three Balbir restaurant go collectively into our TOP 100 see page 24.

BALBIR'S VEGETARIAN ASHOKA — TOP 100 & CC DISCOUNT
141, Elderslie Street, Glasgow. Tel: 041 248 4407
The third of Balbir's trilogy opened in 1989 and is the smallest (48 seats) and the bravest (or so it was thought) venture for Glasgow. The menu provides the best of Gujarati, Bombaya and Southern Indian food. 'The funny thing is there is a greater choice of starter than at conventional restaurants. We fooled the waiters by having a meal composed of starters only. Stuffed peppers £1.60 Karchori stuffed pastries £1.25, spiced mushrooms £1.25, Bhel Poori £1.50 and the extraordinary Pani Poori Gol Guppa £1.75 crispy biscuits discs filled with spicy water - they showed us how, Brown Rice and washed down with Salty Lassi, all superb.' SJS. The three Balbir restaurants collectively go into our TOP 100. They all offer discounts to Curry Club members at their quieter times, see page 288 for details.

THE CAFE INDIA
171, North Street, Glasgow. Tel: 041 248 3818
'The food more than made up for the poor welcome. A large, well lit simple

spacious restaurant, very popular and buzzing with atmosphere. The Papadoms were very crisp, the Mushroom Pakoras were light and finely spiced, the Lamb Pasanda, the best I've tasted and the Chicken Bhoona incredibly tender. £24 for two, no drinks.' IR.

GANDHI INDIAN **CC DISCOUNT**
331, Sauchiehall Street, Glasgow. Tel: 041 332 0055
'A truly satisfying selection on the menu,' (PRC) at this Indian (not Bangladeshi) restaurant run by Devinder Bassi. Papadoms are 50p, Pullao Rice 95p, Chicken Curry £3.75, set lunch from £3.00. Special Gourmet Nights are run every Monday (two sittings, 7pm and 9pm), where for £8.50 you can eat your fuill from dishes not normally on the menu. Branches at the Viceroy, 27, Oswald Street, Glasgow and the Amritsar, 9, Kirk Road, Bearsden. Discounts at all three are available for Curry Club members, see page 288 for details of this offer.

GULISTAN RESTAURANT **CC DISCOUNT**
4, Beech Road, Bishbriggs, Glasgow. Tel: 041 772 3008
Open Noon to Midnight (Sunday 2pm to midnight) the Gulistan proffers the standard menu. Buttered Chicken £6.80 is a popular special. Papadoms are 45p each, Pullao Rice £1.20, Chicken Curry £4.50. A home delivery service is available at nominal charge. It has a branch - The Gulistan, 7, Market Street, Kilsyth and both are offering discounts to Curry Club members at their quieter times, see page 288.

KOHINOOR
225/235, North Street, Charing Cross, Glasgow. Tel: 041 339 1232
Glasgow's oldest curry restaurant established in 1961, we find it considerably under reported, despite it appearing in our two previous guides, with an EXCELLENT tag. Prehaps the 'rather seedy outside' discourages the serious diners, who if they ventured in would find it 'successfully upmarket inside. The set meal was superb, reasonably cheap, looking good and enormous - the Naan was the biggest I've seen. The service was considerate and they weren't trying to get every last penny out of you - One of the best I've ever visited.' JL. We receive the latter remark quite frequently about many a restaurant and we generally consider the comment to be subjective and insufficient in itself to be taken further. In this case however, it is one of our best travelled, most reliable reporters saying it. We urgently need more reports and plenty of them.

ZHAMILS ZHIVAGOS AND ZICOS **CC DISCOUNT**
178, Ingram Street, Glasgow. Tel: 041 552 0055/0876
In 1987 Tony Ghani, owner of the popular and already smart Shah Jahan, decided it was in need of a redec and a new image as far removed from 'Vindaloo Valley' as it is possible to be. Recognising that Glasgow, like everything else in the UK has a thriving population of under 24's, earning good money and, as yet, free of matrimonial shackles, he set out to create a fun factory where these young trendies could regularly spend a chunk of their disposable income and have a sophisticated long night out, free of lager louts. The three venues (referred to in one report from a visiting American as 'the three Zees'. JMc), consist of Zhamils an Indian restaurant, Zhivagos, a bistro lounge serving fast food steaks and pizzas, and Zicos disco. The whole place is 'Fairly lively especially at weekends when it fairly throbs.' NP. The restaurant is 'decked out in greens and golds with leafy trellis booths. It is huge (220 capacity) and the food is as good or better than before.' GT. Tony Ghani wants his fascinating venu to be used by all discerning diners and discounts are available to Curry Club members, see page 288. Reports please.

SHISH MAHAL
41/47, Gibson Street, Glasgow. Tel: 041 334 7899
One of Glasgow's earliest restaurants, the Shish opened in 1964 (the second to do so?) with a ridiculous five seats. With its Punjabi based menu it followed the successful formula established in London, but it pioneered many new things in Glasgow. It was the first to go up market with its white green and red decor and attention to detail, its restaurant cookbook, 110 seats and food good enough to make it one of the first curry houses in Scotland to reach Good Food Guides status, and to stay there for years. It has been in both our previous Guides as 'the best in

—THE—

KOH-I-NOOR

Restaurant - Function Suite - Lounge Bar

235 North Street, Charing Cross, Glasgow G3 7DL

Telephones: 041-221 1555 and 041-204 1444

THE DIAMOND

The most famous of all diamonds, the Koh-I-Noor was found at GOLCONDA in INDIA towards the end of the 13th Century. Originally, it weighed 186 carats. This immense stone was held by the Mogul Emperors and later by the Indian Princes. In 1849, the Koh-I-Noor was presented to Queen Victoria. It was re-cut to 106 carats and since then has featured prominently in Britain's CROWN JEWELS. The Koh-I-Noor was included when a new crown was made for Queen Elizabeth, the Queen Mother - it can be easily recognised in the cross that occupies the front of the crown. Meaning literally, 'Mountain of Light', the Koh-I-Noor is traditionally supposed to bring good luck to a woman who wears it.

SCOTLANDS ORIGINAL INDIAN

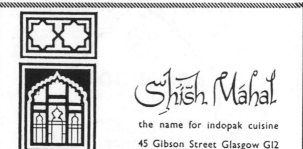

Glasgow,' and in our TOP 30. A wave of disappointing reports have given us the unenviable decision of de-listing the Shish Mahal. In view of its outstanding past record we have retained it as a general entry. Your opinion will determine our next move, so please keep those reports flowing in.

FAISAL SWEET CENTRE
119, Great Western Road, St George's Cross, Glasgow.
Tel: 041 332 7664
Samosas, Bhajas, Pakoras and Mounds of Indian sweets. Takeaway only.

ROYAL SWEETS
286, Woodlands Road, Glasgow. Tel: 0
A franchise branch of the country's largest Indian sweet maker, sells not only heaps of brightly coloured sweets but savouries as well to take out.

HAMILTON

PIR MAHAL **CC DISCOUNT**
78, Brandon Street, Hamilton. Tel: 0698 284090
This popular restaurant, established in 1978 has undergone an extremely Moghul redec. Gilt edged white archwayed walls reveal colourful Moghul scenes, complete with elephant. The brass lanterns and hand painted blue and red chairs are especially admired, having been imported from Pakistan. Good reports received so far. More requested. It has a branch, The Omar Khayan in Hamilton (see entry). Both give discounts to Curry Club members at their quieter times, see page 288.

SHABAB INDIAN DINER **CC DISCOUNT**
4, Barrack Street, Hamilton. Tel: 0698 284379
Despite being a Pakistani restaurant the Shabab, opened in 1989, distinguishes its cooking by the judicious use of wine where appropriate. The special Massala dishes use red wine as well as egg and cream. As with all the Shebab's dishes you have a choice of lamb, beef, veal, scampi amongst the more normal ingredients. £6.96 to £8.75. This smart place has attracted a number of reports in our post bag, and by the infamous restaurant reporter Diner Tec, whose Dragnet-style clipped-tongue-in-cheek reports enthral this editor (I thought I'd get that in) and the many readers of his column in the venerable Glasgow Herald. It has a branch, the Asmaan Tandoori at 22, Bath Street, Glasgow and both are offering a discount to Curry Club members, see page 288.

THE BOMBAY CLUB
The Pump House, Queens Dock, 100, Stobcross Road. Tel: 041 221 7222
An upmarket conversion in the 1877 listed building ajacent to the River Clyde. Good reports but more needed please.

PAISLEY

OMAR KHAYYAM **CC DISCOUNT**
30, Well Meadow Street, Paisley. Tel: 041 889 5121
Tandooris, Karahis and traditional curries, 'served cheaply and incredibly well.' GT. Prices are a bit below the norm for Strathclyde, Papdoms are 40p each, Pullao Rice 75p, Chicken Curry £3.90, set lunch £2.55 and set dinner from £14.50 for two. The Omar has a branch in Hamilton - The Pir Mahal (see entry). Both give discounts to Curry Club members at their quieter times, see page 288.

SHEZAN TANDOORI
82, Glasgow Road, Paisley. Tel: 041 889 6485

SHISH MAHAL
New Street, Paisley. Tel: 041 887 6877
We're told both the above are better than average. Reports please.

PRESTWICK

TAJ INDIAN
141, Maqin Street, Prestwick. Tel: 0292-77318
Standard curries.

STEWARTSTON

FAR PAVILLIONS
50, Holm Street, Stewmarton. Tel: 08687 85149
A well reported house.

TROON

SHABAB TANDORI
42, West Portalnd Street, Tron. Tel: 0292 311797
Good meals here.

TAYSIDE

COUPAR ANGUS

MADRAS
The Cross, Coupar Angus. Tel: 0828 28393
The spread of new restaurants continues to smaller and smaller towns, around the whole of the UK is well demonstrated at Coupar Angus, which new has a curry house for a population of 2,200! More reports please.

DUNDEE

Marmalade in jars, Marmaduke in the beano or is it the Dandy comic and HMS Unicorn. As to curry, plenty of restaurants, but a dearth of good reports, More welcomed.

ANARKALI INDO PAK
34, Gray Street, Broughty Ferry, Dundee. Tel: 0382 480777
'Popular, busy place with friendly service. The food is cooked to order so be prepared to wait. The mixed Tandoori Special is highly recommended and the Naan bread the largest around - no one has ever eaten one solo!' GAS.

SHEZAD TANDOORI
24, Castle Street, Dundee. Tel: 0382 201686
'We had a 'business lunch' here for £1.95. It was limited choice, but very good and excellent value.' JH and TR.

FORFAR

RUPALI
3/5, Queen Street, Forfar. Tel: 0307 64480
Standard curry house.

PERTH

SHALIMAR TANDOORI **CC DISCOUNT**
56, Atholl Street, Perth. Tel: 0738 34204
Kirpal (Paul) Chima's Shalimar remains in this Guide because the standard he set has remained as constant as the day he opened it. Naan breads with super stuffings £1.95 and huge in size, Scottish style Papadoms are 40p, Pullao Rice £1.10 and Chicken Curry £4.25. Discounts are available to all Curry Club members at their quieter times, see page 288 for details of this offer.

Owners of restaurants selected to appear in this guide are invited to advertise. We thank those who have done so – it helps keep the price of the guide as low as possible.

WALES

CLWYD

LLANGOLLEN

SIMLA
4/5, Victoria Square, Llangollen. Tel: 0978 860610

Generally good reports about the Simla, 'The food was of a high standard with large portions which I failed to complete.' BR. One reporter tells of Tandoori 'Too smokey to be palateable, but on another occasion Chicken Jalfrezi and Beef Vindaloo were a definitive sucess. The service can not be faulted. You are left in peace in this small (50 seat) cosy restaurant? Prices are Clwyd average, Papadoms 25p, Pullao Rice £1.10, Chicken Curry £3.50.

RHYLL

AYSHA
47, Wellington Road, Rhyll. Tel: 0

This 'extremely clean restaurant (with spotless toilets) opened in 1989. Despite the place being small (35) there are always sufficient smartly dressed staff to provide immediate attention and helpful advice. On regular visits, I've found the food quite excellent and standards remaining high whilst the prices are Clywd average.' VT.

SEALAND

AMANTOLA
Welsh Road, Sealand. Tel: 0244 811324

'So far so good. Their Chicken Tikka is spot on.' 'Following your good review in your Curry Club Magazine we eventually located this restaurant (its about 5 miles North West of Chester just on the Welsh side of the A548 Ed) and yes we concur it's good.' NK. 'their Chicken Tikka is spot on.' PG. Reports please.

WREXHAM

CURRY MAHAL
Bridge Street, Wrexham. Tel: 0978 261273

Wrexham, the industrial capital of North Wales also has the highest density of population (45,000) and four curry restaurants. The Curry Mahal continues to be reported as the best in town.

DYFED

ABERYSTWYTH

LIGHT OF INDIA
34, Eastgate, Aberystwyth. Tel: 0970 615040

Aberystwyth is known for its seaside, scenic railway and its university (Prince Charles went there). The resultant fluctuations in populations of tourists and students are taken in it's stride by the Light of Asia.

LLANELLI

DILSHAD
31, West End, Llanelli. Tel: 0554 774262

'Went here when the rugby team was in there singing and ravenous. Our curry remained calm and tasty.' GO.

PEMBROKE

PRINCESS OF INDIA **CC DISCOUNT**
3-5, Bush Street, Pembroke Dock. Tel: 0646 685394

'After the castle - a curry. I don't know which I preferred. Both were memorable.' RT. 'It has the usual tandoori - curry house menu and prices are fair.' PJ. Papadoms are 30p each. Pullao Rice £1.15, Chicken Curry

£3.10. Discounts are available to Curry Club members at their quieter times, see page 288 for details of this offer.

GLAMORGAN

For the purpose of this guide, we combine South Mid and West Glamorgan.

ABERDARE

HALA CURRY
31, Victoria Square, Aberdare. Tel: 0685 871814
A safe bet standard curry house.

BARRY

MODERN TANDOORI
290, Holton Road, Barry. Tel: 0446 746787
Well established takeaway only establishment. Cheap enough. Papadoms 20p each, Pullao Rice 70p, Chicken Curry £2.25 and they give discounts to Curry Club members at their quieter times, see page 288 for details of this offer. It has a branch in Cardiff, The Ganges (see separate entry).

SHAHI NOOR **CC DISCOUNT**
87, High Street, Barry. Tel: 0446 735706
Pink marble, pink ceiling, pink menu, everything pink. Good substantial food. Chicken Curry £3.45, set lunch £4.95, set dinner £8.95. Minimum charge £7. Discounts are available to Curry Club members at their quieter times, see page 288 for details of this offer.

CARDIFF

Capital of Wales population 300,000. Home of the Taff (the river Taff that is), University and Rugby. Elegant municipal buildings in spacious parklands, and a choice of over forty curry houses, the standards of which have risen in the last few years. The trend up market and therefore up price has not impressed all of our correspondents, so we include a representative selection.

EVEREST **TOP 100**
43, Salisbury Road, Cardiff. Tel: 0222 374881
It was the Everest which, in 1981 opened to bring in the era of the up-market restaurant to Wales. 'The decor is very smart, we wore ties and would have felt out of place if we hadn't. All aspects were excellent - service, presentation, appearance, spicing (subtle) taste and quantities. It was all a real treat. And the prices? Yes high, but in comparison with similar restaurants, not through the roof.' JL. We are pleased to retain the Everest in our TOP 100.

GANGES TANDOORI TAKE-AWAY **CC DISCOUNT**
14, Crwys Road, Cardiff. Tel: 0
The other side of the coin. Reliable formula curries and tandooris for takeaway only at sensible prices. Papadoms 20p each, Pullao Rice 70p per portions, Chicken Curry £2.34 and they do a discount for Curry Club members at their quieter times, see page 288 for details of this offer.

INDIAN OCEAN **TOP 100 & CC DISCOUNT**
290, North Road, Cardiff. Tel: 0222 621349
Abdul Munim's smart restaurant has become popular since it opened in 1987. We've had many good reports on it from the beginning. The fun begins with the cocktail list 'the Ocean Wave - blue, of course, and the Raja's Ransom aptly describing the effects it had on my pocket.' RST. (Cocktails all £3.50 each). The wine list is a little pedestrian but the menu leaves nothing to be desired.' MB. It has a sensible selection. Quail, trout and lamb chops, are there as delicacies. 'Butter Chicken at £5.50, dripping with naughty ghee, cream, nuts and Lamb Saagwala at £4.50, chunks of tender meat intertwined with tasty spinach were simply superb.' JB. Our price check reveals the upper

Cardiff levels - Papdoms 40p each, Pullao Rice £1.40, Chicken Curry £4.25. Set lunch or dinner from £11.95. The Indian Ocean gives discounts to Curry Club members at their quieter times, see page 288 for details of this offer. A very good restaurant deservedly in our TOP 100.

INDO CYMRU
173, Cowbridge Road East, Cardiff. Tel: 0222 344770
Standard curry house, well reported.

TANDOOR GHAR
134, Whitchurch Road, Cardiff. Tel: 0222 615746
Owners Shamsul and Tahmina Khan are a Bangladeshi husband and wife team. He cooks on view in his open kitchen. 'He clearly delights in performing in there and he seems genuinely pleased when customers show an interest. Whether it's because we do that everytime we go or whether it's always superb, I can't say. But it is.' SM. 'Get him to cook things not on the menu. I had a remarkable chicken dish which he 'knocked up', I'm not sure what is was called though.' RJ. A very good restaurant on.

BANGLADESH TANDOORI
25, Alfred Street, Neath. Tel: 0639 630043
The menu is not extensive, neither were the quantities huge. Prices slightly above Glamorgan average, but the quality is excellent.

PAKISTAN
37, Mill Street, Pontypridd. Tel: 0443 402609
'A cracking meal at a cracking price in this popular place.' AM. Papadoms 20p each, Onion Bhajia 85p, Chicken Curry £3.50.

SWANSEA
The second largest city is Wales, population 200,000 virtually rebuilt since 1945. University, docks, Mumbles and the beautiful Gower. Choice of 35 curry restaurants.

ANARKALI **CC DISCOUNT**
80, St Helens Road, Swansea. Tel: 0792 650549
Competent place with late hours for the insomniac curryholic (2am weekdays, 3am weekends). 'Onion bhajias £1, huge, the sice of hockey balls and very tasty. Kebab £2, a bit bland. Chicken Tikka £2, massive and very tasty.' GB. Pullao Rice 95p per portion, Chicken Curry £3.10. Discounts available for Curry Club members at their quieter times, see page 288 for details.

BENGAL BRASSERIE
67, Walter Road, Swansea. Tel: 0792 641316
Competent standard Bangladeshi curry house.

MOGHUL BRASSERIE
81, St Helens Road, Swansea. Tel: 0792 475131
Another well reported competent curry house.

MONSOON
91-92, Mansel Street, Swansea. Tel: 0792 642560
Again, popular and competent.

ROYAL TANDOORI **CC DISCOUNT**
80, Mansel Street, Swansea. Tel: 0792 472084
Good food and they give discounts to Curry Club members at their quieter times, see page 288 for details of this offer.

SANAM TIKKA
68, St Helen's Road, Swansea. Tel: 0792 466824
Swansea's curry alley (St Helen's Road), 'has this gem amongst the upmarket fat wallet places.' RL. 'It is an unlicensed, bring your own cafQ where I've always had a good meal at decent prices.' IR.

THE VICEROY OF INDIA **CC DISCOUNT**
50, St Helen's Road, Swansea. Tel: 0792 466989
Another honest-to-goodness Bangladeshi curry house with very late hours.

Evenings only 6-2.30am. It has been in our guide since we began (and when the competition was far less). We are glad to keep it here. 'I work a night shift and from time to time I take 'lunch' here at 2am. It makes the hottest Bangalore Phal £3.30. I know.' JRS. Prices are reasonable. Papdoms 25p each, Pullao Rice 90p each, Chicken Curry £3 and they give discounts to Curry Club members at their quieter times, see page 288 for details.

GWENT

BAGAN TANDOORI
35, Frogmore Street, Abergavenny. Tel: 0783 4790
'Well appointed, smart establishment. Whole Lobster Dilruba £13.50, Tandoori Duck and Quail (each £7.50). Popadoms 30p each, Pullao Rice £1.25, Chicken Curry £3.55.

BLACKWOOD TANDOORI
2, Pentwyn Road, Blackwood. Tel: 0495 225081
'A very good restaurant in this valley town.' CB.

KNIGHT OF BENGAL
60, Newport Road, Caldicot. Tel: 0291 425112
Smart and upmarket so expect to pay a bit more.' CB.

THE NAWAB
25, Victoria Street, Cwmbran. Tel: 06333 74272
Regularly reported as good.

BAY OF BENGAL
9, Priory Street, Monmouth. Tel: 0600 4940
The outside is a bit grotty. The inside has been refurbished and the food is good.

NEWPORT

Submerged in docks and industry is the Norman cathedral and the unique car-carrying cable-slung platform-bridge. Also, in Newport a 10,000 strong Moslem community and 20 curry houses.

AGHIRRA
63, Commercial Road, Newport. Tel: 0633 57769
In this Guide for its night owl hours (2.30am wekends, 4am weekends).

KOH-I-NOOR **CC DISCOUNT**
164, Chepstow Road, Maindee, Newport. Tel: 0633 58028
Nothing has changed at the Koh-i-noor since we first reported favourably on it in our first Guide (1984). It is a definitive standard curry house offering 'heat - graded' curries. From 'hottest' curry, through 'favourite curry' to 'fruity curry', and they offer discounts to Curry Club members at their quieter times, see page 288.

MEGALAYA
6, Bridge Street, Usk. Tel: 02913 3372
Even tiny Usk now has its own (a curry house) and is reported to be 'spot-on with excellent food.' NW.

GWYNEDD

one of the smallest county populations (little over 100,000) and 17 curry restaurants.

THE ROYAL TANDOORI CC DISCOUNT
111, High Street, Bangor. Tel: 0248 364664
Cabins and floral decor, face towels a free glass of sherry (unique I think) and a flower for the lady are the nice touches here. Currylovers will find Tandoori and Sizzlers, Kormas, Roghans, Dhansaks, Madrases, and all the rest at reasonable prices. Papdoms are 30p, Pullao Rice £1.20, Chicken Curry £3.10, set lunch £5.00, Dinner £10.95, Discounts are available to Curry Club members at their quieter times, see page 288 for details of this offer.

NASEEB TANDOORI
High Street, Aberconwy. Tel: 0492 593818
Standard curries.

THE GHANDI
11, Palace Street, Caernarfon. Tel: 0286 76797
Beneath the castle walls lies the Ghandi. A sitar and Indian table drums adorn the bar wall. Cubicles and flowers decorate the 50 seat restaurant. The food is highly respected. 'The Chicken Shashlic £5.75 was of the melt in the mouth variety.' VT. The menu 'dares the adventurer into the hotter flavours of the Vindaloo. I dared a Chicken Tikka Vindaloo for £4.50 and enjoyed the adventure.' RSM.

BENGAL DYNASTY CC DISCOUNT
1, North Parade, Llandudno. Tel: 0492 75928
This fairly new restaurant (1988) in Wales' largest holiday resort, and we've received good reports from locals and holiday makers alike. One correspondent enjoyed the Bengal Fish Curry £4.50 which 'was carefully spiced with spices and tomatoes. Our standard price check reveals average prices. Popadoms are 40p Pullao Rice £1.30, Chicken Curry £2.95 and they give discounts to Curry Club members at their quieter times, see page 288.

GANDHI CC DISCOUNT
40, High Street, Llangefni, Anglesey. Tel: 0248 722595
'Remarkably good - the decor with its marbled wall paper, green and gold velvet seating and wood crafted wall pictures - the service and the food.' GT. Ali Iqbal's restaurant produces the familiar cast list of tandoori and currys at average prices - Papadoms 35p each, Pullao Rice £1 a portion, Chicken Curry £3.25, and he welcomes Curry Club members to whom discounts are offered, see page 288 for details.

THE PASSAGE TO INDIA
26, Lombard Street, Porthmadog. Tel: 0766 512144
'A small restaurant on the street corner. I enjoyed my onion Bhajia £1.35, Choicken Dhansak £3.10, Pullao Rice £1.20, and Popadoms 30p each.' BR. Reports welcome.

POWYS

The least populated county in Wales has just six curry houses. Reporting is equally minimal and more is welcomed.

BRECON TANDOORI
Glamorgan Street, Brecon. Tel: 0874 4653
Standard curry house.

SHILAM TANDOORI
13, Berriew Street, Welshpool. Tel: 0938 553431
This busy market town boasts Powis castle and its gardens, generous Georgian buildings and the Shilam. Our final UK entry sums up what this Guide is all about. 'a darned good curry in the most unexpected of places.' LJ. 'and a credit to the town for good food and good service.' PM.

Curry Club Members'

DISCOUNT VOUCHER SCHEME

Save Pounds on Curry Dining

To make big savings you must be a Curry Club member (see pages 23 and 50). Each member is issued three vouchers a quarter.

Each voucher is valid at any one of the restaurants who have agreed to participate in this scheme.

To identify them look for **CC DISCOUNT** alongside the restaurant's entry in this guide.

The actual discount each restaurant is willing to give varies from restaurant to restaurant. Some will give a free bottle of wine, or free starters, others 5% off the bill and some are offering as much as 10%.

We have agreed that these discounts are only available at the restaurant's quieter times, and that each Curry Club member will book in advance when using a DISCOUNT VOUCHER.

To find out how much discount you can get and when they give it to you, please PHONE THE MANAGER, then please BOOK.

There is no limit to the number of people Curry Club members may take. One voucher is valid for a discount on one meal and must be handed over when paying the bill.

REMEMBER YOU MUST BE A MEMBER OF THE CURRY CLUB TO GET YOUR VOUCHERS. SO JOIN NOW TO SAVE POUNDS

More information about the scheme and the Club from:

THE CURRY CLUB,
STAFFORDSHIRE STREET,
LONDON,
SE15 5TL.